I0519210

THE CRYPTOZOOLOGY OF CATS

FELINE FOLKTALES FABLES AND FAUNA

C. P. MARSHALL

HANGAR 1 PUBLISHING

A major contribution to the field of cryptozoology! Mystery cats around the world are arguably the most likely scientifically unrecognized species. Carl Marshall is a respected investigator who is both thorough and pragmatic.

— *KEN GERHARD (AUTHOR, TV PRESENTER, AND CRYPTOZOOLOGIST)*

This book is among the most detailed and engaging tomes on the subject of mystery big cats, and it represents a lifelong study of the phenomena, taking into account practically every possible cryptid cat from every single continent. 'The Cryptozoology of Cats' would serve as an excellent guide for field researchers, as well as a wonderful reference source for academics.

— *MATT EVERETT (DIRECTOR, PANTHERA BRITANNIA DECLASSIFIED)*

To my mind, Carl Marshall is the only field researcher who has earnt the accolade of achieving what I like to call the 'Holy Trinity of Mystery Big Cat Discoveries'; being part of the discovery of big cat paw tracks in the Forest of Dean in 2019 - tracks which have essentially been peer-reviewed and verified TWICE; the photographing of a tiger in a region of Sumatra with they have never been recorded previously; and the leading of the discovery of DNA evidence of a leopard living wild in rural Gloucestershire in 2022. This book bears testament to Carl's wisdom, knowledge and passion for the world of wildlife and nature science, and is an astounding contribution to the zoological literature.

— *TIM WHITTARD (JOURNALIST AND DOCUMENTARY PRODUCER/RESEARCHER)*

The Study of Felinology has long been presumed a closed system, a science within which there are no new species to discover. That is, until 'The Cryptozoology of Cats came along!

In this book, Author, Zoologist, and field researcher Carl Marshall expertly lays the foundational evidence to support the existence of a wealth of cryptic cats around the world, covering everything from amphibious Prehistoric Survivors prowling the Amazon Rainforest to Alien Big Cats roaming the British Countryside.

This is a must-have book for all you Feline Fans out there!

— *ANDY MCGRATH – AUTHOR: BEASTS OF BRITAIN.*

For Mum & Dad, whose love and encouragement is limitless, and whose interest in this, as in all my ventures, is never less than my own.

ACKNOWLEDGMENTS

I would like to acknowledge and give my warmest thanks to the following. My parents, John and Frances Marshall, to whom I literally owe everything and whose love and guidance are with me in whatever I pursue. They are the ultimate role models. I would also like to express my sincere gratitude to Dr. Karl Shuker for his friendship, wise counsel, and for agreeing to write the foreword for this book; Andrew 'Geordie' Jackson for accompanying me through numerous sweltering rainforests; Maureen Ashfield for her beautiful artwork, and the late Sid Ashfield (RIP) for never failing to believe in me. Many thanks to the CFZ, especially Jonathan and the late Corinna Downes. I would like to thank Tim 'Mothy' Whittard and Matt Everett from Dragonfly Films; David and Mary for their overwhelming kindness; Doug and Alex Hajicek of Hanger 1 Publishing; Sumatran cryptozoologist and forest guide Dally Sandradiputra for his hard work and hospitality in welcoming us into his home and making us feel like part of the family during our stay in his beautiful country. Finally, I would like to thank Dr. Richard Lamb; Dr. Darren Naish; Rhoda Watkins; Jay Opie; Sarah Hartwell; Jonathan McGowan; Richard Freeman; Neil Arnold; Dr. Isla Fishburn, Kelci 'Saff' Saffery; Dr. Helen McRobie; Prof. Andrew Hemmings; Monty Bell Jr.; Lars Thomas; James Archer; Severinus Majakil (RIP); Robert 'Bobby Dred' Westby; Andrew Remes; Becky Marshall; Artist Danielle Rose; Richard Muirhead; Carl Portman; John Calvert; Emma Bartholomew; Dr. Marta Skowron Volponi; and Alan Friswell.

Carl Marshall and Andrew Geordie Jackson in Sumatra.

CONTENTS

Foreword   xi
Dr. Karl Shuker

Introduction   xv
How This Book Is Arranged   xxiii

The Felidae   1
1. The "Big Cats" of Cryptozoology   15
2. The Lesser Cryptid Cats   179
3. The Lynx Effect   200
4. Anomalous Big Cats, aka Alien Big Cats   212
5. When Folklore and Fable Meet Teratological Reality?   253
6. Fearsome Critters, Lumberjack Tales and Bogeycats   266
7. "I Tawt I Taw a Puddy Tat!"   282
8. Reported Social Behaviour in Otherwise Habitually
   Solitary Species   289
   Conclusions   295

APPENDICES

On the Origins of the 'Dangerous Wild Animals Act'
of 1976   323
Large-Sized Feliform Cryptids by Continent   340
Possible Prehistoric Survivors   342
African "Water Lions", "Water Leopards" or "Jungle
Walrus"   344
Previously of Cryptozoological Significance   348
Solid Evidence: Escapees, Illegal Releases, and
Specimens Captured or Killed in Britain and Northern
Ireland   349
Complete List of Wild Cats Including Sub-Species   351
Selected Texts Cited/Further Reading   366

Resources   389
Afterword   392

FOREWORD

DR. KARL SHUKER

Several years ago, I was idly flicking through various cryptozoologically-themed uploads on Tumblr when I chanced upon a post that was both eye-opening and, indeed, truly life-affirming for me. Its writer revealed how a certain book had played a huge part in his life, and I was amazed to discover that it was one that I'd authored – Dragons: A Natural History (1995). The writer described how it had been a present to him from his mother when he was just a small child and how much he loved it and still does, has read and re-read it countless times, has learnt so much from it, and when still young even carried it about with him wherever he went with his family. He still owns it today (repaired to within an inch of its life in order to save it from falling apart after such extensive use), and he ended his post by saying that in this little book, he had found his life.

To say that I was humbled and yes, almost tearful, was putting it mildly. Down through the four decades of my career as a cryptozoo-logical author of over 30 books and innumerable articles, I've quite often received communications from readers around the world saying how much they've enjoyed and even been inspired by my writings, but until I saw that Tumblr post I had never truly realised just how inordinately influential a writer via their works can be upon other people, even people whom the writer doesn't know personally and whom they will never even meet. Such is the power and the global reach of words.

But why am I saying all of this here? Because one of those persons, someone who has stated directly to me on many occasions how much my writings mean to him and have inspired him in his own cryptozo-ological research, is none other than the author of this present book, C.P. Marshall, or Carl to his many longstanding friends, including me.

Back in 1989, my own first book was published, Mystery Cats of the World, which was also the very first book ever to survey feline cryp-tids on a global basis, and I have since followed it up with two more – Cats of Magic, Mythology, and Mystery (2011) and Mystery Cats of the World Revisited (2020, a massively-expanded, fully-updated second edition of my 1989 book). During those entire 31 years, no other books on this worldwide crypto-subject ever appeared; only now, at last, with Carl's, there is a fourth – The Cryptozoology of Cats.

Consequently, as Carl himself noted to me recently, during his research for it, my own trio of mystery cat books had collectively covered this subject so extensively that it was inevitable, unavoidable, that his book would incorporate and substantially refer to my orig-inal writings and discoveries, but he has painstakingly credited me and them throughout it, for which I am most grateful and which is such a pleasant change from the shameful lack of credit and bare-faced plagiarism that so much of my work has experienced down through the years via various parasitic online coverages of its subjects. But I am not remotely surprised by Carl's diligence and honesty, because this is precisely the kind of man and the kind of totally professional cryptozoological researcher he is.

Also, it is interesting to note how closely our lives have run in parallel with regard to mystery creatures. My first book dealt with mystery cats, and so too does Carl's. As a fully trained zoologist, I have always sought throughout my cryptozoological career to bring to bear a resolutely, unequivocally scientific approach to my investigations and documentation of cryptids, and so too has Carl. In Carl's case, moreover, this is readily seen not only in relation to his bibliographical endeavours but also in regard to his fieldwork.

Whereas chronic health issues have always curtailed my childhood dream of directly seeking cryptids in remote and exotic faraway places, Carl has taken part in several such expeditions, especially in tropical Asia, searching for a variety of different mystery beasts, and he has always demonstrated an admirably conscientious, sophisticated attitude when doing so. As a result, even though my third mystery cat book has been in print barely three years, readers will discover that Carl's contains a number of additional crypto-feline examples that only came to light after mine was published in 2020 and that some of these are ones that he personally learnt about and investigated on-site during his most recent expeditions. Indeed, he actually encountered one such beast in the flesh! I won't say any more about that here, so as not to spoil the surprise for readers, but how many cryptozoologists are able to say that they have directly observed their highly elusive, long-sought-after quarry? Carl can!

No one reading The Cryptozoology of Cats will fail to be impressed by what is so obviously and, in every way, not just an exhaustively-researched book but also a true labour of love. Carl has a profound passion for cryptozoology – this much is instantly evident here – and as he already knows (because I've told him several times!), I fully anticipate that he will increasingly and significantly contribute to cryptozoology in the coming years. He brings scientific sobriety and invaluable expertise to the subject at all times, as opposed to the sloppy silliness presented by some others that have given such potent ammunition to cryptozoology's sceptics, critics, and cynics who strive at every opportunity to demean and debase this emergent zoological discipline.

If cryptozoology is ever to gain mainstream respectability, it needs to be represented by responsible, authoritative researchers, those who have the tenacity to pursue its reclusive subjects both in the library and in the field, and the skill to present their findings in a strictly scientific manner. In my view, this book, together with his expeditionary searches, demonstrates very effectively that Carl is definitely one such researcher – which is why I have such hope, even optimism, that major new animals will indeed be discovered in due course. With the likes of Carl at its fore, as a guiding captain at its helm, the future of cryptozoology is certainly in good hands!

So, enjoy and be educated by The Cryptozoology of Cats – and I strongly suspect (as well as sincerely hope) that following on from this very fine debut book there will be many more full-length works authored by my crypto-friend and near-namesake Carl.

Dr Karl P.N. Shuker, June 2023.

INTRODUCTION

The great French writer, actress, and journalist Sidonie-Gabrielle Colette (b. 1873 – d. 1954) once said there were no ordinary cats. Colette's now renowned and oft-cited statement is found in virtually every reference book on domestic cats, usually accompanied by the comment that all cats – whether big or small, wild or domestic, [known or yet to be discovered] - are in fact "extraordinary animals." From reports of enormous sabre-toothed cats lurking in the rivers and wetlands of tropical Africa, as well as smaller "wildcats" (believed by some to be *Felis silvestris*) existing in rural Southwest England, cats – mysterious, dangerous, and aloof, perfectly embody the spirit of cryptozoology. The fact that cryptozoology relies heavily on oral and material folklore is an uncomfortable pill for many enthusiasts to swallow. In fact, it has been said that "all cryptids are folkloric" (Arment, 2004), and the cryptozoology of cats is no exception.

Often enshrouded in mystery and superstition, cats – particularly black cats – are enigmatic creatures by nature. Mavrogatphobia, or the fear of black cats, seems to have its roots in the medieval belief that animals with dark fur or feathers, such as rats, crows, and ravens, were semi-supernatural omens of death. In 16th century Italy, it was believed that death was foreshadowed if a black cat lay on a sickbed, or if a funeral procession meets a black cat, another family member will soon die. For centuries, the bite from a cat was believed to be poisonous and legends were told that if you directly inhaled a cat's breath, you would succumb to the "wasting disease" now known as pulmonary tuberculosis or TB.

Might there be objective origins for such beliefs? Possibly. Myths, folktales, and legends do not typically come out of nowhere, they are usually initiated by something, an innate effort to comprehend the unusual. In reality, all cats (family Felidae) carry a great number of bacteria that can lead to festering tissue infections when inflicted through a bite wound. One of the more common is the highly pathogenic bacteria *Pasteurella multocida*, which can cross the blood-brain barrier causing potentially lethal meningitis. On June 13th, 1233, Pope Gregory IX issued a decretal called Vox in Rama ("A voice in Ramah") that condemned the heretical belief in Luciferianism thought to be rampant throughout Germany at that time, by authorising a bloody crusade against the worship of Lucifer as a deity. The letter contains detailed descriptions of rites and beliefs, some of which linked cats to witchcraft; even claimed to be in league with the Devil himself. As a consequence, throughout much of the medieval period, cats were cruelly tortured and culled in huge numbers. Annual festivals where cats were killed sprung up, and some continue to this day – although happily, in a more pleasant form (see "Cat Annis", Chapter Five). Many scholars believe it was because of depleted cat numbers that the Plague, carried by rats from the East, was able to gain a deadly foothold in Europe.

When the disease returned in the late 17th century, rumours quickly spread that cats spread the sickness (they didn't) but failing to appreciate the gravity of the situation, the Lord Mayor of London simply ordered that all cats (and dogs) be destroyed, as noted by Daniel Defoe in his Journal of the Plague Years (1722), where he estimated that some 200,000 cats were slaughtered. This was ill-advised, of course, because the real distributor of the Plague was the Oriental flea, which lives on rats, and with dramatically fewer cats to keep their numbers in check, the rat population in Europe soared. As did the death rate, with entire communities being wiped out and corpses littering the streets as there was no one left alive to bury them. But what about traditions associating cats with imminent death, such as the supposed psychic powers of the "funeral cats" already mentioned? Surely this is merely superstition and in direct contradiction to scientific knowledge, right? Well, perhaps there is a grain of truth to these stories after all, or at least something eerily reminiscent.

Enter Oscar the therapy cat. One of six kittens, Oscar was adopted in 2005 by the *Steere House Nursing and Rehabilitation Center* in the city of Providence, USA. Steer House is a 41-bed 'pet-friendly' facility that treats terminally ill patients with Alzheimer's, Parkinson's, and other debilitating conditions. Oscar didn't initially take to his intended role at the facility, where staff described him as aloof and "not a cat that's friendly to people", sometimes, for example, hissing at staff members when he wanted to be left alone. However, after Oscar had been at Steere House for around six months, staff began noticing that he would often choose to nap next to resident patients who died within several hours of his arrival. It seemed as if he was trying to comfort and provide company to resident patients as they departed this life.

Dr. Joan Teno, a physician at the facility, clarified that "it's not that [Oscar] is consistently there first, but the cat always does manage to make an appearance, and it always seems to be in the last two hours." Up to the time of the initial news reports, Oscar had accurately predicted the deaths of 25 resident patients. As far as staff at the Center knew, the only one he missed was when relatives, perhaps aware of his alleged ability and not ready to lose their beloved, requested that he be removed from the room. On that occasion, Oscar reportedly paced outside the room and went into such a frenzy of yowling and scratching at the door that he had to be temporarily removed from the premises. It wasn't long before the staff decided to start contacting the family members of resident patients as soon as they discovered him sleeping next to their loved ones, to notify them, and allow them to say their final goodbyes. Oscar's presence became part of a calming ritual that made the room feel more like a homely setting during a patient's final hours, and according to staff Oscar did not leave the minute they died and would often still be in the room when the undertaker arrived. There was even one occasion when Oscar's prediction was more precise than that of one of the doctors. A resident was showing signs of being close to death, but when the doctor asked the attending nurse whether the cat had been in, she replied that he hadn't. So, to help him maintain his record, Oscar was brought into the room, but after a brief sniff around he promptly left again. It was not until some ten hours later that the resident actually did pass away, and sure enough, Oscar had returned about two hours before and remained in the room.

Dr. Teno, together with Steere House geriatrician Dr. David Dosa, wondered whether Oscar might have been responding to the scent of chemicals released when someone dies, or some other odour emitted during death. *CBS News* consulted several animal experts who suggested various hypotheses, one of which was that he might have been drawn to an as yet unidentified chemical that is released prior to death, and his attendance in rooms with that odour could have been learned behaviour. Regardless of whether Oscar was actually predicting the impending deaths of the terminally ill by catnapping next to them a few hours before is entirely speculative, but we do know that some animals are sensitive to a wide range of cues that we as humans are unaware of, and Oscar's sensitive nose (or rather his Jacobson's organ) may have been detecting minute biochemical changes in a body's metabolism that occur shortly before death, similar to how some dogs can predict epileptic fits before the people themselves can even sense it.

The human imagination is limited, and numerous aspects of nature remain unknown to us; discoveries are yet to be made, and there are concepts we haven't even considered that may be beyond our current comprehension. We may never know if a cat can truly detect impending death, or even if they fully understand what death is, but they certainly know when a fellow housemate is missing or if something familiar has changed. He had probably been present at the deaths of more than a hundred people, but in November 2013, Oscar had his own close brush with death. He was suffering from a severe allergic reaction to something ingested and was rushed into intensive care, where his heart stopped beating and he 'died' for several seconds. Fortunately, quick-thinking vets revived him, and he was taken back to the nursing home where he became a patient himself for a while, before making a full recovery.

Folklore and mystery are not exclusive to black housecats. For the Indigenous peoples of North and South America, the jaguar, particularly the all-black (melanistic) variety, is imbued with great magic and preternatural abilities. The jaguar is remarkable due to its superior physical abilities, such as its climbing, running, and swimming skills, which even surpass those of the Asian tiger. This has earned the jaguar a reputation of superiority, and a beast to be revered. To the Tucano people who live along the Vaupés River and surrounding areas of the northwestern Amazon basin, the roar of a jaguar is associated with thunder and is widely worshipped as a deity in Peru, Mexico, and Guatemala, among other places.

During Chuna's Han Dynasty (202 BC – 9 AD), people believed the tiger (*Panthera tigris*) was the ruler of all wild animals. According to Chinese folklore, a tiger's tail would turn white when it reached five hundred years; the rest of it presumably turning progressively whiter each quincentennial. In this regard, the white tiger became an ancient mythological king of beasts. It was also said that a white tiger would only appear when an emperor is a righteous ruler, or if there is world peace; in which case, they must be very rare beasts indeed! So why are we as humans so fascinated by cats, particularly large species, both real and imagined? One theory is that we have retained a kind of collective "genetic memory", which goes back to when our ancestors were more likely to be preyed upon by big cats than what is presently experienced by most people.

Neuroscientific studies on laboratory mice suggest there is truth to the theorised phenomenon in which certain experiences can influence subsequent generations. In a 2013 study, mice trained to fear a specific smell passed on their aversion to their decedents, which were then extremely sensitive and afraid of the same smell, even though they had never encountered it, nor had they been trained to fear it. The researchers found small changes in brain structure, concluding that "the experiences of a parent, even before conceiving, markedly influence both structure and function in the nervous system of subsequent generations." Could a similar mechanism be involved in some reports of Alien Big Cats? (ABCs).

We are used to our senses providing us with fairly accurate information about the world around us, but our grey matter has a tough job. Information from the world bombards us as a mixed-up series of electrical signals. Our eyes take in light and colour. Our ears pick up sounds. And the brain has to work to make sense of this mishmash of information. This is known as bottom-up processing and the human brain is very good at it. Yet when we see large quadrupeds, particularly when they are darkly coloured and observed under poor conditions, particularly at night, our brains cannot get enough visual information and has to fill in the gaps for us. But the human brain also does top-down processing. It adds information to our perceptions of the world. Most of the time, there is too much information coming in through the senses, and paying attention to all of it would be overwhelming. So, our brains pick out the most important parts and fill in the rest. What you see isn't what's actually out there in the world. It is a picture that the visual cortex of your brain created for you based on electrical signals captured by your eyes. The same goes for the other senses.

Most of the time, this picture is fairly accurate – at least enough to allow us to navigate our daily lives in safety – but sometimes, especially when under heightened duress, the brain adds things that are simply not there. Perhaps we have a genetic predisposition to visualise humanity's primary predator as a basic survival response. Ultimately, it's better to be cautious, than to just hope that what we're seeing doesn't pose a threat. Perhaps this is somehow related to facial pareidolia, the illusion of recognising facial structures in everyday objects, or apophenia, the human tendency to look for patterns in random information. It is quite possible that a similar genetic mechanism is at work which triggers us to see large cats, forcing us into an automatic survival response and increasing our chances of survival even if the perceived threat isn't actually present. I call this theoretical pareidolic phenomenon 'felidolia'. Before the mastery of fire enabled early humans to safely enter caves to avoid dangerous wildlife and unfavourable weather conditions, we were far more vulnerable to predation by big cats.

Today, leopards hunt baboons, monkeys, chimpanzees, and sometimes even small gorillas, and there is now little doubt that their palate for primates included our ancestors over the past three million years. This is directly supported by the fossilised skullcap of an early hominin named *Paranthropus robustus* discovered in a cave at Swartkrans, South Africa in 1949. The cranium section (labelled SK 54), which belonged to a child, has been pierced, leaving two small round holes. These prominent puncture holes match perfectly with the conical lower canines of a prehistoric African leopard. The youngster appears to have been ambushed by a leopard, which then dragged its body into the safety of a tree to eat in peace, just as modern leopards frequently do. The leftovers then either fell from the tree into an entrance to the cave in the ground below, or the big cat could have bypassed the tree by bringing its meal directly into the cave. The leopard's longer upper canines probably pierced the forehead or eyes as it dragged it from points A to B. One moment, this little hominin was carrying on with life as usual in South Africa, circa 1.5 million years ago. The next, a sudden impact, excruciating pain, a crunch, and then nothing, dead in the jaws of one of prehistory's greatest predators.

Early humans were in constant competition with large carnivores for food, and avoiding violent encounters with dangerous predators was part of daily life for our ancestors. As a result, these fierce felines, which tend to be more active after dark when we are most vulnerable, now haunt the dark, boundless landscapes of our subconscious minds. Could this be the solution to the ABC phenomenon? Well, as convenient as it sounds, I highly doubt it. This and other theories are discussed in more detail later in this book. Nevertheless, it is important to recognize that the evidence available does not correlate with the high number of reported sightings of big cats in the British countryside. Now, please do not misunderstand me; there is indeed some evidence of these animals (refer to Chapter 4), it is, however, disproportionate to the sheer volume of annual reports. It is illogical to assume that these animals could exist in such significant quantities and still not be officially confirmed.

For centuries, cats of all sizes have intrigued humans, inspiring stories and legends, all the while eliciting admiration, intrigue, and fear; and while zoomythology can be entertaining to think about, it isn't to be taken literally. Contrary to popular belief, ostriches do not bury their heads in the sand to avoid danger, goldfish have memories that last considerably longer than 3-5 seconds, camels stay hydrated by storing water in their bloodstreams rather than in their humps, and most sharks will not die if they stop swimming. Of course, we recognise these animals and acknowledge their existence, but reports of cryptids should also not be dismissed offhandedly, simply because they are embellished with folklore. Thus, it is understandable – some might even say inevitable – that cats, by walking the fine line between danger and beauty, myth, illusion, and biological reality, have become a firm staple of popular cryptozoology, third only to mystery hominids and lake monsters.

HOW THIS BOOK IS ARRANGED

Despite the very real possibility that some of the "unknown animals" discussed in this work are undiscovered Felidae, a few examples which were once of cryptozoological significance, but are now formally acknowledged (e.g., king cheetahs) have been included to provide a comprehensive overview. Due to the limitations of crypto-zoological data types, and to avoid further confusion, I will hereafter refer to the "true cryptids," i.e., those suspected to be unclassified felid species, yet which might actually belong to different mammalian groups, as a 'Feliform Cryptid.' My usage of this term is entirely for descriptive purposes and does not necessarily imply any specific reference to the Feliformia: a suborder of the order Carnivora consisting of cat-like carnivorans, including cats (large and small), hyenas, mongooses, viverrids (civets, genets, linsangs, and bintur-ongs) and related taxa.

Furthermore, some cryptids such as the Queensland "tiger" may not even be placental mammals (Placentalia), but instead could belong to the infraclass Marsupialia – the marsupials. The distinguishing characteristic of which is that they give birth to very immature, embryo-like offspring that complete their development outside the womb, usually attached to a nipple in a pouch. The remarkable diversity among known marsupials, both structurally and behaviourally, often presents striking examples of convergent evolution – a phenomenon wherein two organisms without a recent common ancestor become increasingly alike as they adapt to a similar ecological niche. As a result, some marsupials exhibit a striking resemblance to moles, shrews, squirrels, mice, dogs, hyenas; and, in prehistoric times, even cats. Others are ecological counterparts, less in structure than in habits, of rabbits and small bears. Even the larger grazing marsupials (such as kangaroos), which resemble no placental mammals, can be thought of as occupying the same ecological niche as the deer and antelope found elsewhere in the world. In fact, kangaroos would probably look more like deer if it weren't for the fact that their ancestors had to be resourceful in order to travel long distances in hot climates with little water and low-energy diets.

Even if some "feliform cryptids" are unknown cats, we cannot hope to accurately identify them without some form of biological material to study and verify. While the cryptids prowling these pages might resemble cats, the information associated with them is open to interpretation and revision until specimens are acquired for classification. Should they exist in the biological sense, and we wish to assign them some sort of label before their official discovery and classification, it can only be that they seem to be hair-covered, air-breathing, warm-blooded vertebrates of unknown species. When a newly discovered animal is classified, it is a requirement for the original describer to designate a holotype specimen (for species or subspecies only) that can be readily accessed by others for verifying the status of other specimens. In the absence of sufficient biological material, cryptozoologists can only offer theories based on personal experience or theoretical knowledge. As a result, the main purpose of this book is simply to try and point readers in the right direction. It serves as a guide to what might exist.

The feliform cryptids herein are organised according to their reputed morphological characteristics and behaviours and listed alphabetically. The Author's Verdict is by no means essential but is found below each cryptozoological entry, indicated in brackets, employing a numerical system of 1 to 5, with 1 representing 'highly unlikely', 2 'implausible', 3 'conceivable', 4 'probable', and 5 'persuasive'. This simple system is developed from my own research and judgment of the available evidence. For the few examples that have been officially documented yet whose precise identities remain uncertain (e.g., the genetic mutation that produces Woolly Cheetahs) this rating system is replaced with additional details regarding the Status of a specified feliform cryptid.

If one is willing to accept my conclusions regarding the potential characteristics and identities of these presumed animals, then great. On the other hand, if this is not the case, I would advise passing over those particulars; carefully examining all of the evidence, and deciding for yourself what is and is not possible.

For each feliform cryptid, details concerning one or more of the following particulars will be discussed.

1. The origin of the name of a specified feliform cryptid, including information regarding the person who first coined it. For those whose common names are not English words, the language of origin is specified. It is important to remember that, as in traditional zoology, the common name for a cryptid is often misleading. The discerning reader will quickly discover that many cryptozoological "cats" do not fit their generally accepted labels. We will come across "tigers" that are clearly not of the species *Panthera tigris*, and "lions" that are so strange, they can't possibly be true lions (*Panthera leo*).

2. Information regarding the geographical area associated with a specified feliform cryptid, such as rivers, mountains, and caves. All placenames reflect those in use as of August 2023, having been updated accordingly.

3. Information regarding the physical appearance of a feliform cryptid. This might include general morphology, approximate size and weight, fur type, head shape, eyes (often described as "glowing"), dentition, shape and length of ears, neck length, shoulder proportions, upper body and lower body regions, as well as the length and thickness of the tail.

4. Not unsurprisingly, many feliform cryptids discussed in this work are described as fast, agile, and aggressive nocturnal predators. When known, I will offer details about their preferred bioregions (e.g., arboreal or terrestrial), vocalisations, prey items, social behaviours, interspecific interactions (including with humans), and hunting behaviours. This could provide insights into how they interact with their environments and with one another.

5. Geographical variants and alternate spellings of names associated with feliform cryptids may be provided.

6. A scientific name. In biology, the formal naming system used for describing species is called binomial nomenclature (that is to say, "naming using two names"). Such a name is known as a binomial name, a binominal name, a binomen, or simply (and imprecisely) a Latin name. The first part of the name (the generic name) identifies the genus to which the species belongs, whereas the second part (the specific name) distinguishes the species within the genus. For example, modern lions belong to the genus *Panthera* and within this genus to the species *Panthera leo*. Both the genus and species names are in Latin grammatical form, though they can be based on words from other languages, particularly Greek. A biological classification that ranks immediately below a species, usually a population of a particular geographic region, genetically distinguishable from other such populations of the same species, is designated by a scientific trinomial (three-part name), e.g., *Panthera leo melanochaita* – a lion subspecies found only in Southern and East Africa. In

certain circumstances, a specimen of significant cryptozoological value has been assigned a scientific name by an investigator who has studied it, such as *Panthera leo maculatus* (Heuvelmans, 1955). Binomial nomenclature is important because it allows people throughout the world to communicate unambiguously about animal species. If and when a cryptozoological animal form is confirmed to be a living biological species, then such a name could be used for its formal scientific description, unless another existing name is more fitting, or it has been previously used for another organism. Many mythical animals have some sort of classification title after them, be it species, genus, etc. And since most can be compared with real animals and their characteristics, they are usually classified based on their traits in common with other animals. For no reason other than entertainment, some of the *"Fearsome Critters"* listed in Chapter Five have also been designated a scientific name, either to make them sound more scientific or to poke fun at such uses, i.e., *binomium ridiculus.*

7. When known, information regarding the characteristics and measurements of paw prints or other impressions reported to have been left by feliform cryptids in a range of substrates, such as sand, clay, or snow.

8. Significant reports are provided, with the majority being testimonial though there may be occasional inclusion of petroglyphs, pictographs, monumental inscriptions, and other significant artefacts. In some cases, a pelt or additional biological sample may be discussed.

9. Extinct or Alive? Should they exist, gaining insight into the current condition of a feliform cryptid 'type' is critical for understanding their chances of long-term survival.

10. Possible biological identities and plausible hypotheses are presented.

Note: It is unavoidable that some examples discussed in this work have been placed into more than one category. This is due to the contentious, debated, and indecisive nature of anecdotal, testimonial, and circumstantial evidence. It is possible that some feliform cryptids might result from amalgamations of different species or legends. However, it is plausible, albeit uncertain, that some feliform cryptids probably do belong to the order Carnivora, suborder Feliformia, family Felidae – the Cats. The only undeniable examples are those that have been confirmed to exist in one form or another (or to have recently existed) and identified using accepted scientific practices. Others that appear to be straightforward may actually be more obscure. Escaped or illegally released big cats could potentially adapt to occupy ecological niches left vacant by species thought to have gone extinct, essentially replacing them, or even actively out-competing them should they survive in small, isolated populations. If they are closely related enough to be able to successfully hybridise, they might even incorporate a species that is declining into their own gene pool.

What Is Cryptozoology?

Cryptozoology is a multidisciplinary field of study that seeks to explore evidence for animals not yet discovered and described by science. The term "cryptozoology" comes from the Greek words "Kryptos," which means "hidden or unknown," "Zóo," meaning "animal," and "Logos," meaning "the study of;" therefore, cryptozoology is the study of the evidence for unknown or hidden animals. Personally, I prefer the term "unexpected animals," as it encapsulates both documented species found in unfamiliar locations as well as potential new species. Displaced species, most notably the infamous "phantom big cats," are sometimes referred to by cryptozoologists as "pseudo-cryptids." Regarding my own research and classification system, I categorise these apparently "out-of-place" felids as *Type 4 unknown animal forms* (see A Question of Classification).

At its most fundamental level, cryptozoology is the study of animals only rumoured to exist. The origin of the word is unclear, as two scientists have both claimed to be its creator. What we do know is that it first appeared in print on January 1st, 1959, in Lucien Blancou's work on the well-known editorial series Que Sais je entitled Geographie Cynegétique du Monde ("Hunting Geography of the World"), where he presented his dedication proclaiming: 'Bernard Heuvelmans, maître de la cryptozoologie' ("Bernard Heuvelmans, master of cryptozoology"). In 1949, Blancou began collecting information regarding the mysterious alleged wildlife of Central Africa, which he continued to do periodically for the next four years. During their private correspondence, Heuvelmans (b. 1911 – d. 1973) seems to have coined the term that is now commonly used and found in most modern dictionaries.

However, in his second book "In the Wake of the Sea Serpents" (first American edition, 1968, p. 508), Heuvelmans also credits Scottish biologist and explorer Ivan T. Sanderson (b. 1911 – d. 1973). While discussing two articles on sea serpents by Sanderson in 1947 and 1948, Heuvelmans wrote: 'When he [Sanderson] was still a student he invented the word 'cryptozoology', or the science of hidden animals, which, I was to coin later, quite unaware that he had already done so.' Presumably, this was at Eton Collage where Sanderson studied the natural sciences between 1924 and 1927. Sanderson was an advocate of Charles Fort (b.1874 – d. 1932), the renowned American author and investigator of anomalous phenomena, and would proudly refer to himself as a "profound Fortean." It was an article written by Sanderson in 1948 titled "There Could Be Dinosaurs" that inspired Heuvelmans to begin collecting information concerning potentially still unknown animals.

In 1955, Bernard Heuvelmans released his seminal work, "On the Track of Unknown Animals" (French title: 'Sur la Piste des Bêtes Ignorées'). In his career, Heuvelmans was critical of conventional zoological methods, stressing that the discovery of new species does not have to be based purely on chance but can be accomplished through targeted efforts if we only acknowledge the possibility that large undiscovered creatures might inhabit the world today. This presented an entirely novel concept at the time and one that continues to inform modern-day approaches to zoological research. There is little doubt that Sanderson played a major role in the early popularisation of cryptozoology. It was, however, Heuvelmans' meticulous amelioration and refinement that transformed what was once a straightforward examination of reports of strange creatures into a methodology worthy of scientific pursuit. It is, in my opinion, only right that Heuvelmans receive the ultimate credit. It appears that Heuvelmans was the first to conceive of the term, followed closely by Blancou's public use of it, and finally, by Sanderson's *post hoc* claim to have coined it first.

Over the years, numerous distinguished investigators have made significant contributions to the study of cryptozoology, both before and after the coining of the term itself. Yet by the early 19th century, scientific opinion had undergone a seismic shift. Suddenly it was unacceptable to express any approval of the idea that large unknown animals might exist, even those reported to reside in the deepest, darkest depths of the oceans. In 1802, Pierre Denys de Montfort (b. 1766 – d. 1820), a French malacologist (an expert in snails), proposed the potential for two undiscovered species of giant octopi in his work *Histoire Naturelle Generale et Particuliere des Mollusques* ("An Encyclopaedic Description of Molluscs"). Following the publication of his book, de Montfort's career, and ultimately his life took a downward turn as he was widely ridiculed and derided by his colleagues and peers. However, in the early years of the second half of the 19th century, de Montfort's theories were vindicated to an extent when it was confirmed that the giant squid exists, classified under the genus *Architeuthis*. Sadly, de Montfort never got to experience this success as he died in poverty in a Paris gutter in 1820.

Constantine Samuel Rafinesque-Schmaltz (b. 1783 – d. 1840) was a self-taught naturalist, archaeologist, linguist, and entrepreneur who made significant contributions to cryptozoology in his lifetime. He described and published over 6,500 new species, came up with a speciation theory of biological evolution 25 years before the publication of Charles Darwin's "descent with modification" theory of evolution, and developed a rigorous classification scheme for sea serpent reports. He is also credited as being the first investigator to acknowledge the Dorsal Jaguar – an occasionally reported cryptid jaguar from Pennsylvania's Alleghany Mountains and the US-Canada border. Despite his troubled career, Rafinesque's brilliance has gone down in history. Although he wasn't wealthy Rafinesque was comfortably settled in Philadelphia at the end of his life, yet, though he received the highest quality medical care available at the time, he would ultimately succumb to stomach cancer on September 18th, 1840.

Heuvelmans was profoundly influenced by the works of Dutch zoologist Antoon Cornelis Oudemans (b. 1858 – d. 1943) who compiled the first comprehensive analysis of sea monster reports in his influential 1882 book "The Great Sea Serpent". Oudemans suggested that many sightings of so-called "sea monsters" could actually be explained by a still undiscovered species of pinniped (seals, sea lions, and their kin), which he called *Megophias megophias*, drawing inspiration from Rafinesque's 1817 classification of the same name. This "seal serpent" was estimated to measure between 20 and 200 feet in length and was globally distributed.

Charles Gould (b. 1834 – d. 1893) was a 19th-century geologist whose notable work "*Mythical Monsters*" (1886, W. H. Allen & Co.) still stands in the field of cryptozoology. As the son of renowned ornithologist, John Gould, and the talented illustrator Elizabeth Gould – both pioneering figures of the natural history movement of the nineteenth century – it is unsurprising that Charles found success in science by pursuing his passion for geological surveying in both Britain and Tasmania. He also collected ornithological specimens, a pursuit that his father would have viewed favourably, as well as material for his book *Mythical Monsters*. His book delves into the cultural significance of dragons in Western, Chinese, and Japanese societies, in addition to unicorns and the phoenix, as well as a series of sea serpents reported off the New England coast in 1817. Charles Gould also published in the *Papers and Proceedings of the Royal Society of Tasmania*, theorising that the Australian 'Bunyip' may have been a pinniped.

Willy Otto Oskar Ley, better known simply as Willy Ley (b. 1906 – d. 1969), was a renowned German American science writer and early space travel advocate who wrote several important books regarding what would come to be known as cryptozoology. In his 1959 classic *Exotic Zoology*, Ley discussed creatures such as unicorns, merfolk, and living non-avian dinosaurs. It is my opinion that Ley's writings are just as important to cryptozoology (usually referred to at the time as "romantic zoology") as anything written by Sanderson, if not more so.

The British zoologist Dr. Karl Shuker is rightly regarded as the world's foremost cryptozoologist. His 1989 "Mystery Cats of the World," revised and updated in 2020 as *"Mystery Cats of the World Revisited: Blue Tigers, King Cheetahs, Black Cougars, Spotted Lions, and More,"* is the definitive source of information regarding enigmatic, unidentified cats, demonstrating a degree of scientific methodological rigour that these days is without parallel in the field of cryptozoology.

A Case for Cryptozoology

The year was 1812, and the famous French naturalist and zoologist, Georges Cuvier (b. 1769 – d. 1832) had just declared that there were no large terrestrial mammal species left to be discovered. If other species were out there, he insisted, scientists would already know about them. Then, in 1819, a mere seven years after Cuvier's "rash dictum", the Malayan tapir was identified as a new species and designated the scientific name *Acrocodia indica* (now known as *Tapirus indicus*). Yet Chinese people living on the edges of rainforests had long spoken of a white-backed tapir-like animal, yet Cuvier, in his bias, flatly stated that, since the reports were not made by trained western scientists, they lacked credibility and therefore the species did not exist. Some have called this racist, while others have pointed out that when animals are steeped in folklore, it can be difficult to determine where to draw the line.

Unexpected discoveries followed in the 19th century, including that of another tapir, Baird's tapir (*T. bairdii*), native to Mexico, Central America, and north-western South America, which wasn't described by science until 1865 even though it is the largest of the three species of tapirs native to the Americas as well as the largest land mammal in both Central and South America. For the past two centuries, it has been shown time and time again that Cuvier's rationale was at best premature, and at worst, flawed. Notwithstanding newly discovered non-mammalian species such as the remarkable discovery of the world's largest lizard, the Komodo dragon a full century later in 1912, the list of newly described "large quadrupeds" continues to grow. The Kamchatka brown bear (*Ursus arctos beringianus*) was first identified in 1898. In 1930, the Chacoan peccary (*Catagonus wagneri*) or 'tagua' was first discovered through fossils and was initially thought to be extinct. Nevertheless, its status as a 'Lazarus taxon' was cemented in 1971 when a living specimen was found deep in the Argentine province of Salta's Chaco region, living blissfully unaware of its apparent extinction. The people of the area had long been familiar with the species; ultimately, however, it took considerable time before western scientists accepted its contemporary existence.

The list goes on – two deer were discovered in the 1800s: *Muntiacus reevesi* in 1839 and *Hydropotes inermis* in 1870, followed by *Chrotogale owstoni* in 1912. *Gorilla beringei beringei*, one of the two subspecies of eastern gorilla, was not officially described until 1902 despite being the world's largest known living primate. For centuries, these mighty "man-beasts" had been hidden in legend and folklore but were finally accepted as a biological reality. The allied rock wallaby (*Petrogale assimilis*), native to northeastern Queensland, Australia, was formally documented by science in 1877, and the largest species of tree kangaroo (*Dendrolagus dorianus*) remained undiscovered until 1883. In 1831, the chinkara from India (*Gazella bennettii*) was discovered, followed by the Saudi gazelle (*G. saudiya*) in Arabia in 1935. Moreover, two new desert warthogs, namely *Phacochoerus africanus massaicus* and the closely related *P. a. sundevallii*, were discovered in Africa in 1908.

That same year marked another huge discovery – the classification of the northern white rhino – the largest land animal by body mass after the elephants, with an impressive length of up to five metres, a height of two metres, and a weight of two and a half tons. Biologist Richard Lydekker formally described the new subspecies and named it *Cera-totherium simum cottoni*. Unfortunately, poaching has caused the near extinction of the northern white rhino – the only surviving members are two females called Najin and Fatu, who live lonely lives at Ol Pejeta Conservancy in Kenya.

In accordance with the subject matter of this book, namely cat-like animals, the fossa of Madagascar (*Cryptoprocta ferox*), actually an impressively agile and giant relative of the mongoose with feline characteristics, was first identified by science in 1833. Growing up to six feet in length from nose to tail tip, and weighing up to 12 kg (26 lbs), the fossa is a slender-bodied animal bearing little resemblance to its mongoose cousins. Interestingly, the fossa combines aspects of three different families of carnivores: the Herpestidae (mongooses), Viverridae (civets and their relatives), and the Felidae. Depending on the local dialect, this extraordinary animal can be correctly pronounced "foosa," "foosh," or "foosha." The fossa bears a strong resemblance to a slender-built mountain lion but boasts a mongoose-like head that is comparatively longer than that of a felid. Its muzzle is wide and short, adding to its cat-like appearance – which is particu-larly striking when observed from a distance.

The fossa has several physical adaptations for climbing that are typical of cats, such as a long tail for balance and semi-retractile claws for gripping trees. Additionally, it also has unique adaptations not found in the Felidae, such as its semi-plantigrade foot morphology, which allows the fossa to walk either flat on the soles of its feet, like a bear, or on its toes, like a cat. When climbing in trees, the fossa walks flat-footed but will quickly switch to toe-tip walking when moving on the ground. Its paws are nearly bare with strong and flexible pads providing added grip. The fossa possesses the amazing ability to descend head-first from trees thanks to its highly flexible ankles, which enable it to clasp tree trunks, allowing for quick movements up or down the tree or a sudden leap to an adjacent one. Previously classified as belonging to the Viverridae family, recent molecular research has placed the fossa in the endemic Eupleridae family, comprising ten known living species in seven genera, commonly known as euplerids or Malagasy carnivorans.

Officially considered extinct, a giant fossa, known to palaeontologists as *Cryptoprocta spelea*, once existed in Madagascar; moreover, based on cryptozoological evidence, it may have survived there undetected to the present day. The giant fossa was initially described in 1902, based on subfossil (green) bones found in caves across Madagascar. Its distinct species status remained uncertain for many years, until 1935 when it was officially recognised as a separate species. It is uncertain when and how the giant fossa became extinct; there is anecdotal evidence, including eyewitness reports of fossa much larger than normal, that the species may not have vanished after all. Madagascar is the fourth largest island by landmass in the world, but sadly much of its varied fauna and flora are now endangered by human activity. Since the arrival of humans on the island, Madagascar has lost more than 90% of its forests, with a devastating 40% of the island's primary forest cover being lost between the 1950s and 2000. According to the U.N. FAO, 21.6% or approximately 12,553,000 ha of Madagascar is still forested; however, of this, only 24.2% (3,036,000 ha) is primary forest – the most carbon-dense and biodiverse form of forest as well as the type best suited for harbouring large new species. Nevertheless, is this sufficient for the giant fossa to have gone unnoticed by science? More on this later.

The Yemeni gazelle (*Gazella bilkis*), commonly referred to as the Queen of Sheba's gazelle, was officially declared extinct in 1951. Sadly, subsequent surveys across their former range yielded no tangible evidence. Nevertheless, in 1985, a photograph depicting a pair of gazelles was taken at a private collection at *Al Wabra Wildlife Preserve* in Qatar, Middle East. Colin Groves (b. 1942 – d. 2017), the late British-Australian biologist, anthropologist, and Professor of Biological Anthropology at the Australian National University in Canberra, speculated that these may have been surviving Queen of Sheba's gazelles. It is deeply regrettable that the majority of cryptozoologists and cryptozoological investigators tend to disregard animals like gazelles, probably viewing them as ordinary, while focusing their efforts on the less plausible cryptids.

Local residents in the current Zimbabwean territory have for many years spoken of a strange feline creature, which they refer to as the leopard-hyena. However, until 1926, European scientists had failed to recognise the reality behind these tales; that the so-called leopard-hyena is actually a striped cheetah. Further information regarding this remarkable discovery will be discussed later. The Bornean yellow muntjac (*Muntiacus atherodes*) was only recognised as a distinct species in 1982. Additionally, a large, very rare, and endangered antelope species called the saola (*Pseudoryx nghetinhensis*), also known as the Spindlehorn, Asian unicorn, and Vu Quang ox, was discovered after remains were found in the *Vu Quang Nature Reserve* in Vietnam by a joint survey by the *Vietnamese Ministry of Forestry* and the *World Wildlife Fund*. The species was initially documented in 1992 by forest ecologist Do Tuoc, with the first living saola being photographed in 1993. The last recording of the species was in 2013 on a trail camera from the *Saola Nature Reserve* in central Vietnam. Since then, locals have reported its presence in and around *Pu Mat National Park* in Vietnam and Bolikhamxay Province in Laos.

The discovery of the Zanzibar servaline genet is an excellent example of the benefits of ethno-knowledge as a potential source of data. Despite being well-known to rural Zanzibaris, European zoologists were unaware of its existence until the late 1990s. In 1995, a wildlife consultant working in Zanzibar named Tony Archer obtained a dried skin and skull from Kitogani in south-central Unguja. It was subsequently described as a new subspecies of servaline genet (*Genetta servalina archeri,* Van Rompaey & Colyn, 1998) and named after Archer. Since 1990, a total of 124 primate species and subspecies have been identified: Madagascar is home to 54 new species, while the Neotropics, Asia, and Africa have 32, 24, and 14 respectively. Sixty-eight are prosimians (lemurs, lorisoids, and tarsiers), along with 52 monkeys and 4 apes. We will focus on the four apes as they are the largest, these are the northern buffed-cheeked gibbon (*Nomascus annamensis*, Thinh, *et.al*, 2010), found in Cambodia, Laos, and Vietnam; the Mishmi Hills hoolock gibbon (*Hoolock hoolock mishmiensis*, Choudhury, 2013) from the northeastern tip of India; the montane dwelling Skywalker hoolock gibbon also known as the Gaoligong hoolock gibbon (*Hoolock tianxing*, Fan, *et.al.*, 2017); and finally, the Tapanuli orangutan – the largest recently described primate. In 1939, only anecdotal evidence was available, and it wasn't until 1997 that the species was officially identified in South Tapanuli on the island of Sumatra, Indonesia, and it took another twenty years for *Pongo tapanuliensis* (Nurcahyo *et.al*, 2017) to be designated official species status.

Cuvier would have classified all these as "large quadrupeds", likely discrediting them as unsubstantiated reports, only to be taken aback later by their eventual discovery. Unfortunately, this attitude persists today, as many biologists maintain an uncompromising stance when it comes to such finds, viewing them merely as isolated incidents, and may, rightfully or not, express resentment when they are associated with the field of cryptozoology. It has been established that the occurrence of previously unknown large animals is not as rare as one might have thought. It is perhaps understandable that we discover new monkeys with some regularity and will sometimes find new herbivores that graze openly and in groups – unlike highly secretive and solitary nocturnal predators like cats. To combat and prevent further impediments, we require new approaches and, in some respects, a new philosophy.

I will end this menagerie of large mammal discoveries since Cuvier's fallacy with two animals that were thought to be extinct, that are in fact much more than just "large quadrupeds". A crash of Sumatran rhinoceros (*Dicerorhinus sumatrensis*) was recorded in 1983 from Sarawak in northwestern Borneo, some 40 years after it was written off as extinct. And in 1988, another remarkable discovery was made in Vietnam: the Javan rhino (*Rhinoceros sondaicus*), a species believed to have gone extinct as early as the 1940s. These mighty mammals are now facing serious risk of extinction; indeed, four specimens, one of them being an adult female, have died from diseases transmitted by wild cattle. As of 2023, their estimated population stands at 76.

The language of scientists is data. Unlike some of my peers and colleagues, I do not consider cryptozoology to be a science, at least not in the way that, say, entomology is a valid branch of zoology concerned with insects, or how palaeontology is the scientific examination of prehistoric life through fossils. Could it be classed as a subdivision of zoology? Zoology is the scientific study of the structure, behaviour, physiology, classification, and distribution of known animals. It is a science, and as such, zoology is about testing hypotheses or offering theories that may explain aspects of the animal kingdom and seeing if they hold up to critical scrutiny. A hypothesis is an assumption made before any research has been completed for the sake of testing; and crucially, hypotheses must be tested against data to become excepted models. A theory, on the other hand, is a principle set to explain phenomena already supported by data. We have data for cryptids. These include tracks, hair samples, vocalisations, photos, and innumerable eyewitness accounts, but unfortunately, data such as these are often rejected by the scientific community in the absence of complete specimens. But be assured, even when data is far less controversial, the scientific consensus is often disunited.

You often hear it said that a single data point teaches us nothing, and I want to be very clear that this is incorrect. To see this, imagine, if you will, we go from one data point (one item in a data table, or one piece of information, about an observation, at a given point in time) to two data points. What happens then? Well, according to this felicitous rule that one data point teaches us nothing, we would suddenly go from knowing nothing to knowing something as we go from one to two data points. But there is nothing inherently special about the second data point. The truly significant change occurs when we go from zero data points, which by definition means we have literally no information, to one data point, which means we have at least some information. If this sounds confusing, think of it like this. One data point is like a single drop in the ocean, but what is an ocean if not a multitude of drops? A rich data set is a collection of single data points and each point provides potentially useful information, it simply needs to be evaluated with a critical and unbiased eye. We shouldn't be astounded to discover data sets like foot morphology and gait inferred from track evidence etc. Although cryptozoology is by no means rich in data, what there is should not be ignored simply out of bias.

As we search for knowledge of the animal kingdom, professional cryptozoologists (those who use scientific methods, not necessarily those who are paid) attempt to fill these information voids by devoting their time to research and by publishing their findings. For me, cryptozoology is best described as a portmanteau of knowledge, typically theoretical, but potentially useful as a systematic and targeted methodology focused on zoological discovery. So far, cryptozoological data has not been able to provide conclusive evidence of a species' existence that would convince the scientific community. It may, however, be used to pinpoint the location of an as-yet-unidentified animal, making it possible to find and document it later.

Cryptozoology has much in common with speculative zoology. Indeed, some might argue that they are fundamentally the same thing. When sound theories rooted in science are given due consideration, the cryptozoological approach could potentially result in some major zoological discoveries. Ultimately, though, only a combination of resources, abilities, and good fortune will tell if these possibilities become realities. Of course, these "unknown animals" are not entirely unknown. If they were, we wouldn't be studying them.

Strictly speaking, they are, for various reasons, largely unaccepted by the zoological community as multicellular, eukaryotic organisms belonging to the biological kingdom Animalia.

These apparently undiscovered animal forms are known primarily from circumstantial evidence, anecdotal/testimonial evidence, or from biological material considered insufficient as evidence by the scientific community. Incidentally, zoologists and wildlife biologists often take advantage of the principles of cryptozoology in their attempts to identify new species for taxonomic classification, however, they rarely, if ever acknowledge it as such. An unknown animal, also known as a "hidden animal", or "cryptid" (a term coined in 1983 by John E. Wall in the now defunct ISC Newsletter) should be unusual, enigmatic, and most importantly, it should be ambiguous, be that in terms of morphology, detectable physiological functions, behavioural traits, or more often than not, its unexpected appearance in either temporal or geographical contexts. It is important to remember that rare and extraordinary animals can be mistaken for fictitious "fabulous creatures" and therefore disregarded by zoologists. But is this really fair or even a responsible scientific approach? Scientists should be very careful indeed not to throw out the last of the zoological "babies" (and by this, I mean the last truly exceptional zoological discoveries – the primary focus of attention in cryptozoology) with the proverbial, cryptozoological "bathwater".

It cannot be overstated that ambiguity is the progenitor of the cryptozoological process. It is the enigmatic nature of cryptids that sets them apart, making them noteworthy; thus befitting of the folkloric process which is fundamental to Heuvelmans' methodology as a potential data source. It is their obscurity that is seen as monstrous in the eyes of those who in some way feel threatened by them. However, ambiguity is a characteristic that cannot be quantified. What might seem unusual to one observer (for example, an outsider unfamiliar with the local wildlife) might be a familiar sight to others. Some cryptids can truly be considered "monsters", i.e. they exist only in the human subconscious. Regardless of what certain YouTube channels would have us believe, not all monsters are cryptids (so please, no more 'Slenderman' cryptid videos!). The term 'monster' is a descriptor we often apply to unconfirmed organisms or "beings" we instinctually fear. Yetis can only be considered monsters while their true identity remains unknown.

However, if undeniable evidence of them were to be discovered tomorrow, the yeti would no longer be seen as a fearsome monster – rather, it would become an exciting new species by joining the ranks of zoology. The legend of the yeti is likely based on three distinct species. Two are almost certainly primates: one appears to be a small ape-like animal, while another seems to be some sort of human or near-human. The final and largest type, purported to be a dangerous hulking carnivore responsible for brutal attacks on yak may, based on my interpretation of the evidence, be an undiscovered species or variety of bear, or even a hybrid of bear subspecies known from the region. Perhaps this last variety, known as *chemo* in Nepal, is the same creature as the Tibetan *dremo*, which is almost always considered to be a sort of strange bear. Going back briefly to the story of the gorilla, these large, but otherwise harmless primates were once subject to the same malevolent behavioural traits now attributed to the Yeti, or "Himalayan snowman". The mighty gorilla was long believed to fight elephants with clubs, as well as the misguided notion that they would kidnap and abuse indigenous women.

These attitudes were the reasoning behind the 1933 classic of the silver screen, King Kong by RKO Pictures. After all, there is a reason for Kong's obsession with Ann Darrow (played by the beautiful Canadian/American actress Fay Wray – b. 1907 – d. 2004) playing out the sexual politics of the era in an apes-are-from-Mars, women-are-from-Venus type scenario. We now understand that gorillas, when unprovoked, are virtually harmless to humans, making them "gentle giants" – which is in sharp contrast to the violent behaviour often exhibited by adult male chimpanzees, which, incidentally, share 98.8% of our DNA and are our closest living relatives. So who is the monster? It is evident that the mighty gorilla is not a monster, and of course, it never was. That being said, whether a new primate, a bear, or something else entirely, I sincerely hope to never see a yeti caged in a zoo!

Officially, cryptozoology is not accepted as a scientific field of study. Biological scientists and folklorists readily denounce cryptozoology as a fringe culture and a "pseudo-science". There is very little in terms of peer review for cryptozoological research, meaning that in spite of its recent surge in popularity, largely made possible by popular social networking websites like Facebook, Twitter, Whats-App, and Instagram, and the online video-sharing platform YouTube, the scientific integrity that cryptozoology requires is significantly lacking. Cryptozoology has slowly regressed from a nascent zoological discipline with genuine potential, into something more akin to paranormal research and new-age mysticism. As a working cryptozoologist with a background in entomology and arachnology (i.e. small things), I believe that the unfortunately popular view of cryptozoology as pseudoscientific monster hunting is largely unjustified if we delve deeper into the inner workings of the methodology. Unlike paranormal research, there are examples that would have once been designated as cryptids, that have been proven to exist. For many years, the platypus was considered an impossible creature and the first specimens were believed to be taxidermy fabrications because of its bizarre attributes. The analytical cryptozoologist isn't searching for monsters, they simply aim to discover and validate the unknown animals behind the myths, behind the monsters, assuming, of course, they do exist.

What Constitutes a Cryptid?

The cryptozoological approach is one that, given time and sufficient resources, might lead to remarkable zoological discoveries. In order for cryptozoology to be successful, it is essential that the habitat requirements necessary for any large undescribed animal to remain unknown are taken into account. Eyewitness reports can offer valuable knowledge, yet it is important to also determine if the region has the potential to not just sustain but hide a viable reproducing population. To be considered a cryptozoological success, a newly described species must have been acknowledged in some way prior to its formal discovery. This could be traditional knowledge of the animal's existence to evidence that does not conclusively demonstrate its presence but can enable cryptozoologists to draw reasonable conclusions.

There are millions of species, mostly invertebrates, that have not yet been scientifically documented. Most of these will be discovered and validated without any prior knowledge of their existence; therefore, by definition, these species cannot be classified as cryptids. Over 1.5 million living animal species have been identified and classified, of which approximately one million are insects (with beetles the most plentiful group). It is estimated that there may be as many as seven million total species, with some sources even suggesting a potential for over thirty million. A cryptid should be distinguished by some atypical characteristic[s]: either morphological, physiological, behavioural, or simply its unexpected presence in a given area or time.

Cryptozoologists conducting fieldwork, regardless of their opinions, are speculative zoologists. The only cryptozoological aspect of fieldwork is amassing fresh testimonial data. A cryptozoologist might have great bibliographic knowledge, but the discovery of a new species in the field depends on their zoological prowess, experience in the field, determination, and luck. Evidence for unknown animals can take various forms, such as archaeological relics, artworks, old manuscripts, stories, oral histories, or direct evidence like material finds or reports from either local people or outsiders such as tourists and explorers. It is better to apply Heuvelmans' methodology in a reasoned and practicable way, thus eliminating any notion that cryptozoology is inherently pseudoscientific. Rather, analytical cryptozoology can be viewed as a form of speculative or theoretical zoology which may lead to discoveries of otherwise undetected animal species before their eminent extinction, or they are discovered randomly at a later time.

Heuvelmans essentially presented a methodology to target possible undiscovered animal forms. As cryptozoologists, it is up to us to decide how we interpret and use data. Some might take up the hunt for mythical beasts like werewolves, spectral black dogs, and the 'Dalby Spook', aka Gef the Talking Mongoose; even those found in creepypasta internet memes. While these strange "animals" might be of interest from a Fortean zoological perspective, they are not essential to cryptozoology and can be viewed as folkloric cultural phenomena or as manifestations of the psyche, depending on one's personal convictions. Regardless of what they may or may not be, entities unrelated to zoology have no place in analytical cryptozoology. For cryptozoology to be accepted as a valid zoological activity, it must first provide zoological results. The best approach is to only focus on biologically and ecologically sound cryptids rather than expending effort and resources searching for cryptids that are improbable, such as the so-called "British Bigfoot". In order to be successful, cryptozoology, the great study of hidden animals, must maintain its zoological foundation and be guided by the basic principles of traditional biology.

Cryptic Diversity Within the Family Felidae

The concept of a species is one of the most fundamental in biology. Charles Darwin even wanted to abolish the concept altogether, deeming it an endeavour in futilely, attempting to define the indefinable. The most widely accepted definition centres around reproduction, stating that a species is defined as a group of organisms in which any two individuals of the appropriate sexes or mating types can produce fertile offspring, even when they are directly related. In general, this definition is both valid and logical, but it can lead to some surprising groupings. For example, due to climate change, polar bears and grizzly bears have been coming into contact and producing fertile offspring.

Should we consider these bears to be one species? In some cases, newly discovered species are entirely novel and have never been researched by scientists before, while in other instances, a species and its subspecies are examined more thoroughly – often through genetic material – and it is agreed upon that they should be distinct species. Scientists had long believed that there were only one species of Brazilian tigrina cat (oncila). However, molecular data now reveals that the tigrina populations in northeastern and southern Brazil are completely distinct, with no evidence of interbreeding between them. These differences mean they are now considered two distinct species, both of which remain largely unknown it terms of their biology.

In 2017, scientists analysed the genetic composition of felid pelts over a century old, revealing that the newly-discovered species of Sunda clouded leopard (*Neofelis diardi*) is, in fact, comprised of two distinct subspecies with different evolutionary histories. Found in the Himalayan foothills throughout Southeast Asia and China, clouded leopards are renowned for their fur patterning which has patches resembling clouds, and for having the largest canine teeth relative to body size compared to any other living cat species. Despite its name, the clouded leopard is not a true leopard. While comparing Asian mainland clouded leopards with those found in the Sunda Islands of Southeast Asia, it became apparent that the Sunda clouded leopard is genetically distinct.

The snow leopard (*Panthera uncia*) is widely considered the world's most elusive big cat. It inhabits remote mountain ranges across Central Asia, occupying an area that spans some 600,000 square miles and encompasses twelve countries. Snow leopards are usually found at high altitudes above 3000 m (1.8 miles) where oxygen levels are low, temperature fluctuations are extreme, and the overall climate is severe. The snow leopard population faces increasing threats, and while it is challenging to calculate their total number, estimates suggest that there are between 3,920 and 6,390 left in the wild.

In a study published in the *Journal of Heredity*, scientists analysed scat (faeces) from known areas where snow leopards inform each other of their presence via scents known as marking sites and identified three genetic subspecies that could be clearly separated by geography. The researchers observed that this species is being heavily affected by poachers and habitat destruction due to human activity, with climate change further contributing to reducing the range and reshaping of their habitats in the near future. In an interview with *Newsweek*, lead author Jan E. Janecka, Associate Professor of Biology at *Duquesne University*, expressed concern about the plight of the snow leopard: "Based on the geographic and ecological differences between some of these areas of Asia – like the Western Mongolia versus the Tibetan Plateau – some researchers had previously thought there may be different subspecies [...] however, to date, these had not been accepted largely due to lack of data and specimens needed to carry out a thorough taxonomic analysis. Compared to other cats, there are much fewer snow leopard museum specimens so to address this question we used genetics."

Most cat species are solitary by nature, with a tendency to be both elusive and enigmatic. In general, wild cats avoid human contact and will generally flee when they sense a human nearby. It is important to remember that even species already known to exist may possess unknown characteristics and this should be taken into account when attempting to differentiate them from other potential unidentified felids. The Amur leopard (*Panthera pardus orientalis*), renowned for its spectacular beauty, is viewed as one of the rarest cats in the world. It's extremely low genetic diversity and drift put its population at risk, making the survival rate for any member of the subspecies completely unpredictable and not dependent on any inherent genetic advantage.

In October 2017, a remarkable event occurred as it marked the first time the vocalisations of Amur leopards had been recorded in their natural habitat. A seven-year-old male, which researchers named Typhoon, was captured on a camera trap in Russia's *Land of the*

Leopard National Park in Primorsky Krai. The park has more than three hundred camera traps scattered across its 2,799 km² (1,081 sq mi) reserve near the Razdolnaya River – which is more than any other protected area in Russia. Despite this progress, much is still unknown about these beautiful but endangered felids. Research published in 2022 suggests that conservation efforts are having a positive effect as wild Amur leopard numbers have now increased to around 120 adults. Sadly, they remain one of the rarest and most critically endangered cat species in the world. Very little is known about the ecology or distribution of the bay cat (*Catopuma badia*), a small wild cat endemic to the island of Borneo.

Historically thought to be a small island form of the Asiatic golden cat (*C. temminckii*), genetic analysis confirmed that it is a unique species and, as such, is likely endangered. The size of a large moggie, the bay cat has dark chestnut red fur faintly speckled with black markings, as well as spots on its lighter golden-brown underside and limbs. A second colour phase of dark bluish-grey has also been reported, as have melanistic specimens. The evidence in historical and modern records suggests that the bay cat is uncommon compared to other wild cats in the same or contiguous geographic locales, and its population density is low, even in preserved habitats. Prior to 2004, only twelve specimens had been recorded, and there were only a few direct sightings. Little is known about their hunting patterns, social organisation, mating habits, or growth cycle; however, findings suggest that the Felidae shows a higher degree of genetic variation than previously suspected.

Considering all the evidence: their elusive and often solitary lives, perfectly-camouflaged fur, opportunistic hunting behaviour, wide array of diets, and ability to survive in a diverse range of habitats – can we honestly say with certainty that there are no new felids to be discovered? I think, based on the available facts, we should at least consider the possibility that some examples may have been overlooked; not merely hidden within the genetic makeup of known species, but potentially animals unknown to science. Indeed, it could be argued that from a purely biological standpoint, they really ought to exist! On March 16th, 2023 a genetic study conducted by the French *Office for Biodiversity* (OFB) and *Claude Bernard University* confirmed, in spectacular fashion, that the mystery wild cat known on the French Mediterranean island of Corsica as "ghjattu volpe" ("fox-cat") is in fact a distinct species. Between 2011 and 2014, camera traps were placed which identified eight individuals exhibiting a homogeneous phenotype known as the Corsican phenotype. Carlu-Antone Cecchini, head of the forest cat mission at the *National Hunting and Wildlife Office* and a representative from OFB stated in 2019 that the fox-cat has been part of the islands' shepherd mythology for generations; these stories claimed that forest cats would attack the udders of ewes and goats. Uncovering this species' genetic lineage was crucial for producing conservation initiatives to protect this highly endangered species.

A Question of Classification

Cryptozoologists frequently devise their own systems for classifying evidence of undiscovered animals. These systems are typically based on the morphological and behavioural characteristics that appear consistently in documented sightings. Over the years, I have developed multiple systems, some of which are fully realised and others which are yet to be completed. As a basic example, I present my five-type system (which includes eight sub-types).

Type 1

Unidentified animal forms similar in appearance to known living species, but exhibiting an unusual or aberrant phenotype (different size, colour, or shape). Examples include Yana puma and Tanuah (Type 1a: unusually large), Warracaba jaguar (Type 1b: unusually small), Spotted lions and Dorsal jaguars (Type 1c: aberrant colour or coat pattern), the Georgia mystery cat, and Long-tailed wildcats, aka Long-tailed bobcats (Type 1d: dysmorphic features).

Type 2

Unidentified animal forms similar in appearance to extinct species. Examples include Tigre dantero and Maipolina (Type 2a: known only from the fossil record), Bali tiger, Caspian tiger, and British lynx (Type 2b: known historically).

Type 3

Unidentified animal forms that appear to be unrelated to any known species, living or extinct. Examples include: Biped panthers and Punchum.

Type 4

Unidentified animal forms similar in appearance to known living species but reported from locations where they shouldn't exist. Both hitherto unknown range extensions/recolonisations (Type 4a) and hypothetical escapees and illegal releases from captivity (Type 4b). Examples include the Alaskan tiger (hypothetical Upper Palaeolithic migration), and Eastern cougar (both 4a), and reports of British Big cats (Type 4b).

Type 5

A catch-all category for data deficient examples, i.e. where there is insufficient information available regarding physical appearance, behaviour, abundance, and distribution for a formal assessment to be made. Example: Seah Malang Poo.

THE FELIDAE

'Cats are a mysterious kind of folk.'

— SIR WALTER SCOTT

Except for Antarctica, Australia, Madagascar, New Zealand, and most oceanic islands, cats are widely distributed throughout the world. Unfortunately, one species of cat – the domestic house cat (*Felis catus*) - has been introduced to many places inhabited by humans and with tragic results for native species. The living Felidae are divided into two distinct subfamilies: Pantherinae (containing the "Big cats," namely five species of *Panthera* and two species of *Neofelis*) and the Felinae (containing the remaining 33 or possibly 34 species in ten genera, which includes the cheetah). Though the mountain lion or cougar (*Puma concolour*) is the second-largest cat in the Americas and fourth-largest cat species globally, it is not a member of the Pantherinae, and therefore, it is not considered a true Big cat – despite being generally larger than leopards but with a considerably leaner build.

Putting measurements aside for a second, the Felidae family can be divided into "roaring cats" and "purring cats". The hyoid bone of purring cats is rigidly attached to their skull via several small bones, whereas large non-purring cats have more flexible, partially ossified hyoid bones which are connected to the skull by elastic ligaments. This prevents the Big cats from truly purring (though they do make a purring-type sound) but gives the larynx enough flexibility to produce a deep, powerful roar. It was long believed that the inadequate ossification of the hyoid bone was the primary anatomical factor for the roaring ability of lions, tigers, jaguars, and true leopards.

However, recent research suggests that this capacity has to do with other physical characteristics – particularly those involving the larynx – and is predetermined by the physical properties of the vocal fold tissue that allow it to stretch and strain. This is a significant distinction between species such as snow leopards, which cannot roar and are therefore not *Panthera*. The 2002 study that defined "purring" more precisely determined that only animals in the "purring cat" subfamily and one or two species of genets (*Genetta tigrina* and likely *Genetta genetta*) can produce such a continuous vibration characterised by alternating between pulmonic egressive and ingressive airstreams, with a frequency ranging from 25 to 150 Hz. As cheetahs and mountain lions belong to this subfamily, they can produce such a sound, although they do not roar.

Another notable distinction is the shape of their pupils. Specifically, big cats typically have round pupils, while most small cats, such as domestic cats, have elliptical pupils. This variance is generally attributed to the type of environment that each species inhabits and their specific needs for light absorption. Most cats are highly adept climbers, except for lions and tigers. Moreover, many species are also proficient swimmers, which may come as a surprise to some. Within the Felidae family, there is a wide range in terms of fur colouration and pattern. Colours range from white to black, while patterns vary from small spots or stripes to distinctive rosettes. Generally speaking, most cat species are born with spotted fur except for the jaguarundi

(*Herpailurus yagouaroundi*), Asian golden cat (*Catopuma temminckii*), and caracal (Caracal caracal). Under normal circumstances, the spotted fur of the lion (*Panthera leo*) and mountain lion cubs (*Puma concolour*) changes to a uniform pelage as they mature into adults. Wild cats inhabit various ecosystems on nearly every continent, including Africa, Asia, Europe, and the Americas. Habitats include forests, deserts, swamps, and high-altitude mountainous terrain. Depending on their preferred prey species, these cats may exhibit nocturnal (nighttime), crepuscular (twilight), or diurnal (daytime) activity patterns.

Prehistoric Species and Common Characteristics to Consider When Examining Evidence for Cryptid "Cats"

Proailurus is thought to be the earliest known cat to have existed after the Eocene–Oligocene extinction event, occurring approximately 33.9 million years ago. Evidence of this species has been found in the Hsanda Gol Formation, situated in the Tsagan Nor Basin of Central Mongolia. The *Pseudaelurus*, which lived in Europe, Asia, and North America during the Miocene between twenty and eight million years ago, was ancestral to two main lineages of felids: the living cats and a group of extinct cats classified under the subfamily Machairodontinae, famously known as "sabre-tooths". The Barbourofelidae and Nimravidae families, often referred to as "false sabre-toothed cats", are not true cats at all. Alongside the Felidae, Viverridae (which includes civets and genets), Hyaenidae (hyaenas), and Herpestidae (mongooses), they belong to the taxonomic suborder Feliformia, which likely diverged between 50.6 – 35 million years ago into separate families.

The Felidae and the Asiatic linsangs are thought to have diverged around 35.2 to 31.9 million years ago, with fossil evidence indicating that the Felidae arrived in North America approximately 18.5 million years ago. During the Early to Middle Miocene period, the

Machairodontinae, with their famous sabre-toothed characteristics, evolved in Africa and then migrated northwards during the Late Miocene. Their extraordinarily large upper canines appear to have been well-suited for preying on large species of megafauna. Results of mitochondrial DNA analyses (DNA inherited maternally) indicate that the living Felidae are monophyletic, meaning they are all descended from a common evolutionary ancestor or closely related ancestral group. Originating in Asia during the Late Miocene epoch, at least ten migrations spread throughout Africa, Europe, and the Americas over the course of around 11 million years. These movements were enabled by alternating sea levels and interglacial and glacial periods.

Acinonyx pardinensis or the "giant cheetah" belonged to the same genus as our present-day cheetahs and would likely have resembled them in appearance; however, it was notably larger, weighing up to 120 – 150 kg (265 – 331 lbs). Its bulkier build allowed the giant cheetah to hunt much larger animals than its modern-day counterpart. Though there is some debate as to whether its weight hindered its running abilities, some argue that its longer legs, bigger heart, and greater lung capacity enabled speeds equal to or perhaps even faster than modern cheetahs. The giant cheetah existed in Europe and Asia in the Pliocene and Pleistocene epochs, ranging from Germany to India and China. It is also believed that due to the colder climate, these cats had thicker fur and were of a lighter colouration than modern cheetahs.

The iconic *Smilodon,* also known as the sabre-toothed tiger, has long been recognised as one of the most formidable prehistoric predators. Its three species ranged across both North and South America: *Smilodon gracilis* was approximately the size of a modern jaguar, and *Smilodon fatalis* was comparable to an African lion in size. The largest species of the genus (*Smilodon populator*) was exceptionally large even for a prehistoric animal, weighing up to 500 kg (1102 lbs), which is almost the same as a fully-grown Kodiak bear! *Smilodon* was not as agile as modern-day big cats, but it was more powerful, with thicker, stronger limbs and necks than modern-day felids, as well as particularly long claws to hold on to powerful large-bodied prey. Its fangs could reach a massive 30 cm (12 inches) in length and were probably perfect for bringing down mammoths, ground sloths, ruminant grazers, as well as large forest-dwelling browsers like tapirs.

The fossil record tells us that *Smilodon* officially went extinct about 10,000 years ago, meaning it encountered humans and probably included us in its diet. But perhaps the most amazing aspect about *Smilodon* is that according to palaeontologists it is the only prehistoric cat believed to have caused the extinction of an entire species. The victim of this competition was *Thylacosmilus*, a sabre-toothed marsupial or marsupial relative that had reigned over South America for millions of years. However, when sea levels dropped and North America became connected to South America, *Smilodon* – a native of North America – moved southward roughly two million years ago and outcompeted *Thylacosmilus*, possibly driving it directly into extinction. In short, *Smilodon* conquered an entire continent and eradicated its less adaptable rivals. Despite being famously known as the "sabretooth tiger," *Smilodon* differed significantly from a real tiger. *Machairodus*, on the other hand, was built more like a tiger; its remains have been discovered in Chad in Central Africa, suggesting that it may have been one of the largest cats to ever live, likely weighing anywhere from 490 kg (1080 lbs) to 500 kg (1102 lbs) – about the weight of a horse. It hunted elephants, rhinos, and other large herbivores.

Xenosmilus is a relative to *Smilodon*, but instead of having long, blade-like fangs, it had shorter and thicker teeth, all of which (not only the canines) had serrated edges to cut through flesh. Believed to be much larger than modern cats, with an estimated weight of 180 – 230 kg (397 – 507 lbs), *Xenosmilus* is thought to have developed an alternate technique of hunting from that of today's cats. Instead of asphyxiating its prey, *Xenosmilus* would bite off a large chunk of flesh and simply wait for the victim to bleed to death. Remains have been found in Florida along with those of giant prehistoric peccaries (pig-like animals) which it likely hunted.

The precise time of *Xenosmilus's* extinction is still unknown, but it lived during the Pleistocene period. In 2021, palaeontologists from *Ohio State University* at Marion and *Gonzaga University* identified a new species of Machairodontine sabre-toothed cat, which lived in what is now North America some 5-9 million years ago during the Miocene epoch. Belonging to the genus *Machairodus*, an ancient relative of the renowned *Smilodon*, it has been given the incredibly difficult to pronounce scientific name *Machairodus lahayishupup* (pronounced Mah-CHI-rho-duss Lah-HIGH-ees-hoop-oop). With a mass reaching up to 410 kg, it is one of the biggest felids that ever existed. Scientists recognised the new species from specimens already in museum collections. Specimens of this species were originally excavated from sites in Texas, Idaho, California, and Oregon. Although only seven specimens are known, scientists were able to diagnose it as a new species based on the dimensions of the leg bones. Skulls and fangs have yet to be found, and all we know about them comes from their humerus and mandibular bones.

One of the specimens was found on the *Umatilla Indian Reservation*, prompting the scientists to honour the Indians by giving it the name "lahayishupup", meaning "ancient cat" in the Cayuse Indian language. Individuals averaged 272 kg (600 lbs) and may have even reached weights of 410 kg (900 lbs). Potential prey species in North America included rhinos, horses, tapirs, camels, and giant ground sloths. It was likely an ambush predator that lived in semi-tropical woodlands. Most of North America was then semi-tropical. At the time, similar species occurred in Eurasia and Africa. *M. lahayishupup* may have been ancestral or related to the ancestor of the well-known *Smilodon fatalis* and the lesser-known *Homotherium latidens*, both from the late Pleistocene. *Homotherium*, commonly referred to as the "scimitar cat," was one of the most successful prehistoric predators. It was found in North and South America, Europe, Asia, and Africa, and adapted well to various habitats, including sub-Arctic tundra. *Homotherium* lasted for five million years until its extinction around 10,000 years ago. Evidence suggests that it was a pack hunter adapted to fast running and active during the day so as not to compete with nocturnal predators. It had long forelegs and shorter hind legs which gave it a hyena-like stance and gait when walking. Although not particularly large by today's standards, some remains discovered in the North Sea suggests they could weigh up to 400 kg (882 lbs), heavier than modern-day Siberian tigers (*Panthera tigris altaica*). Some palaeontologists posit that *Homotherium* were adept mammoth hunters; however, their capacity for high-speed running would have enabled them to pursue swift-footed animals just as effectively.

Compared to fully grown male lions or tigers, modern-day jaguars (*Panthera onca*) are smaller, averaging 60 – 100 kg (132 – 220 lbs); the largest males recorded from South America have weighed up to 150 kg (330 lbs). However, both North and South America were home to much larger jaguars in prehistoric times. These giant jaguars belonged to the same species as those found today but had longer limbs and tails. Biologists theorise that jaguars used to inhabit open plains, but competition with American lions and other big cats necessitated their adaptation to more forested habitats, leading to the development of their current short-legged form.

Giant prehistoric jaguars were comparable in size to modern lions or tigers, but they were several times stronger, with an immensely powerful bite force. Two subspecies of these giant jaguars are known: *Panthera onca augusta* from North America, and the "Patagonian panther" (*Panthera onca messembrina*) from South America. Officially, both subspecies became extinct around 11,000 years ago. Unlike the giant jaguar, the European jaguar (*Panthera gombaszoegensis*) did not belong to the same species as the modern-day jaguar. Nobody knows exactly what the European jaguar looked like. Some scientists have speculated that it may have looked much like a modern-day jaguar, or perhaps, like a cross between a lion and a jaguar. A fossil felid from East Africa is believed to be similar in appearance to the European jaguar and has also been described as having "tiger-like features." This giant jaguar, reaching a formidable weight of at least 210 kg (463 lbs) and likely being at the top of the food chain, was undoubtedly a dangerous and highly efficient predator.

Fossil remains have been discovered in England, France, Spain, Germany, and the Netherlands.

The cave lion (*Panthera spelaea*) was a large species of lion, weighing at least 300 kg (661 lbs), making it on par with the Amur or Siberian tiger – the largest modern-day cat. It was one of the most formidable and intimidating predators during the last glacial period in Europe, and there is evidence that early humans had great respect for it, maybe even god-like veneration. A plethora of cave paintings and statuettes depict cave lions, many of which are maneless or barely even have a ruff around their neck, similar to modern-day tigers. Interestingly, some cave paintings also show faint stripes on its legs and tail, which has led some to suggest that it may have been closely related to tigers.

However, genetic studies conducted on ancient bones have confirmed its original classification as a lion – albeit one with peculiar physical characteristics according to palaeoartists' depictions. Often referred to as the largest cat that ever lived, the American lion (*Panthera atrox*) is likely the most famous of the prehistoric cats, following *Smilodon*. It was distributed in both North and South America, ranging from Alaska to Peru, during the Pleistocene epoch and appears to have gone extinct approximately 11,000 years ago.

Most researchers infer that the American lion was a particularly large relative of modern lions and may even have been a subspecies (*Panthera leo atrox*). Nonetheless, other scientists were not convinced and suggested that the American lion was a distinct species and likely looked different to modern lions. It has also been speculated that the

American lion may have been more closely related to the jaguar. What is certain is that it was the largest felid species in North America during the Ice Age, with a weight of up to 470 kg (1036 lbs) or even 500 kg (1102 lbs), similar to that of a polar bear. There are still debates surrounding its hunting strategies because while modern-day lions hunt in groups, the scarcity of remains of American lions raises questions as to whether they were solitary hunters.

This hypothesis makes sense when considering that *Smilodon fatalis* appear to have been pack predators. By hunting alone and preying on different animals, the American lion could have avoided competition with sabretooths, which may explain their coexistence over such a long period. The fossil of *Simbakubwa kutokaafrika*, which was found to be much larger than a tiger, lion, or polar bear, was discovered by two palaeontologists from Ohio University in 2019 in a museum drawer. Its skull is comparable to that of a rhinoceros. According to a press release from Ohio University, *Simbakubwa kutokaafrika*, which means the "big lion from Africa" in Latinised Swahili, is an enormous lion-like carnivore that ruled Kenya around 22 million years ago. Belonging to the Hyainailourine hyaenodonts group, these solitary predators are considered to be among the largest carnivorous land mammals to walk the Earth. Despite its name, *Simbakubwa* is not a lion or any other kind of cat; rather, it is a member of a group of mammals characterised by their teeth, which resemble those of a hyena despite being unrelated. According to estimates derived from its teeth, *Simbakubwa* weighed roughly 1,308 kilograms (1,888 lbs). To put this into perspective, modern adult lions and tigers weigh around 180 kg (400 lbs), whereas *Simbakubwa* weighed as much as small bison. It also had an equally impressive jaw with blade-like teeth. In addition to the front canines, *Simbakubwa* had three pairs of meat-slicing teeth in the back, whereas felids like modern lions and domestic cats have only a single pair.

All you have to do is look at a big cat and a domestic cat to see their anatomical similarities. Their bodies are built roughly the same, just different sizes. They have powerful legs, flexible backs, sharp claws, and teeth. All of those components work together to make all cats skilled hunters. It is therefore conceivable that any undiscovered cryptozoological forms which belong to this group will probably have comparable qualities. This may include the feliform cryptids' body and limb dimensions, colour, identifiable features such as stripes and spots, and reported habitats.

Below are some common characteristics to consider when examining evidence for cryptid "cats"

Paws: Cats are digitigrade, meaning that they walk on their toes in a manner similar to dogs, with five toes present on their forefeet and four on the hindfeet. All species have retractable claws to varying degrees (in cheetahs, for instance, the claws are blunt and slightly curved, but only semi-retractable). With the exception of the *Acinonyx,* the claws are attached to the terminal bones of the toe by ligaments and tendons and protected by cutaneous sheaths. The plantar pads in both the fore and hindfeet provide stable shock absorbers ideal for running at speed or climbing.

Head: The nose extends only marginally beyond the lower jaw, providing cats with a relatively flat face with large orbits. Additionally, their strong teeth and facial muscles give them an intense and often deadly bite. The dental formula of all adult cats is 2 x (I 3/I 3, C 1/C 1, PM 3/PM 2, M 1/M 1) = 30 permanent teeth. The canine teeth are large, reaching extraordinary lengths in the officially extinct sabretoothed species. The upper third premolar and lower molar are adapted as carnassial teeth. The lower carnassial is smaller than the upper carnassial and has a crown with two sharp, pointed cusps, perfect for slicing through flesh and tough sinew. These are important diagnostic features regarding tooth-pit morphology found on bones collected in the field. A cat's tongue is covered with hundreds of tiny backwards-facing spines called papillae, which rasp flesh from prey and also aid in grooming. Their eyes are large and situated to provide good binocular vision for hunting.

All cats have especially good night vision due to the presence of the tapetum lucidum, a biological reflector system that is a common feature in the eyes of vertebrates. It normally functions to provide the light-sensitive retinal cells with a second opportunity for photon-photoreceptor stimulation, thereby enhancing visual sensitivity at low light levels. This is what gives cats their distinctive eyeshine. As a result, the eyes of felids are about six times more light-sensitive than those of humans, and due to this, many species are at least partially nocturnal. The retina of cats also contains a relatively high propor-tion of rod cells, adapted for tracking movement in low light, which is accompanied by the presence of cone cells for sensing colour during the day. All cats have well-developed and highly sensitive whiskers above the eyes, on the muzzle (but not below the chin), and on the cheeks. Their external ears are large and sensitive to high-frequency vibrations in the smaller species, better enabling them to hunt small prey like rodents. Cats are equipped with a very special piece of equipment known as the vomeronasal organ, commonly called the Jacobson's organ. Located in the roof of the mouth, the Jacobson's organ contains ducts that lead to the mouth and to the nose. This is essentially a scent analyser, enabling cats to 'taste' the air. They cannot, however, detect the sweetness of sugar, as they lack the sweet-taste receptor found in other mammals.

Pelage: Cats living in cold climates have thick, long-haired coats like that of the snow leopard to keep warm. In contrast, those living in tropical and hot environments typically have short fur to stay cool, such as the tiger. Several species display melanism with all-black individuals recorded.

Activity Patterns: All cats are strict carnivores, with the majority of species engaging in solitary, nocturnal predation by stalking or ambushing their prey.

Body: Cats possess lean, muscular physiques and strong forelimbs that help in capturing prey. These attributes, in conjunction with their speed and agility, make cats extremely efficient apex predators.

Tail Length: In most cat species, the tail is typically between one-third and one-half of the length of the body, although exceptions do exist such as the lynx species and margay (*Leopardus wiedii*).

Vocalisations: Felids possess a variety of vocalisations, characterised by slight variations among species, with larger species having deeper sounds and frequencies ranging from 50 to 10,000 Hz. The standard sounds made by cats comprise hissing, spitting, snarling, and growling. Mewing is primarily used for communication between juveniles and adults, while the other sounds tend to be warnings of aggression. Additionally, felids may purr during both inhalation and exhalation phases; whereas pantherine cats are only able to produce a purr-like sound during oestrus/copulation or during suckling as cubs. Although only lions, leopards, tigers, and jaguars can actually roar, snow leopards can produce loud yowls that create a similar resonance.

Anatomical Parameters: Felid species vary in body size, skull size, and weight. The largest living species is the tiger (*Panthera tigris*), which can weigh up to 299 kg (660 lbs) and measure up to ten feet from nose to tail tip. Their skulls range in length from 316 – 413 mm (12.4 – 16.3 in). While lions have a slightly larger maximum skull length of 419 mm (16.5 in) they are generally smaller in body size than tigers. At the other end of the spectrum, the smallest cat species are the rusty-spotted cat (*Prionailurus rubiginosus*) and black-footed cat (*Felis nigripes*). The former species measures 35 – 48 cm (14 – 19 in) and weighs only 0.9 – 1.6 kg (2.0 – 3.5 lb), while the latter has a head-to-body length ranging from 36.7 – 43.3 cm (14.4 – 17 in) with a maximum recorded weight of 2.45 kg (5.4 lb).

Once more, I earnestly urge you, esteemed reader, not to consider this work an exhaustive list of undiscovered felid species; such a representation would be both insincere and unethical, not to mention an affront to the diligent efforts of zoologists and taxonomists around the world. Such a list would be impossible. Rather, it is an assemblage of data related to undescribed cat-like animal forms.

In some cases, there is evidence that they may belong to the Felidae family, but this cannot be confirmed without collecting biological specimens. Cryptozoologists should therefore take an unbiased approach and willingly acknowledge possible inaccuracies in the data.

And with that, I give you, The Cryptozoology of Cats.

1

THE "BIG CATS" OF CRYPTOZOOLOGY

'Familiarity makes the lion more dangerous.'

— JOCELYN MURRAY

PREHISTORIC SURVIVORS?

Aypa

The Brazilian "Water Tiger"

Brazil is the largest country in South America, covering an area of 8.5 million square kilometres (3,300,000 sq mi) with a human population of more than 217 million. It is the fifth-largest country in terms of area and the seventh-most populous nation globally. Home to more than half of the Amazon Rainforest, which accounts for about 10% of all species worldwide, Brazil is renowned for its immense biodiversity, containing over 70% of all animal and plant species. There is perhaps nowhere on the planet more likely to conceal unidentified felids. In Amapá, Brazil's second-least populous state, the *aypa* (Karipúna: French Creole) is described as an amphibious, predatory, cat-like animal with a stout, rounded head and neck resembling a tiger. This provides support for its powerful jaws and large canine teeth, while a mane-like growth of fur around the neck and jaw area may or may not be more defined in males. Some eyewitness accounts suggest that it may have scaly skin on the neck resembling the legendary *dingonek* of Africa; however, these reports may be describing wet matted fur observed poorly and mistaken for scales. The first account of this peculiar feliform cryptid dates back to the 18th century from a French missionary. Dr. Karl Shuker has speculated that the *aypa* could be the same species as the *maipolina* reported in French Guiana. Other so-called "water tigers" include variations such as the *entzaeia-yawá* of Ecuador and the *yaguru* from Argentina and Paraguay.

(Author's Verdict: 2/5)

China's White Sabretooth

A Monstrous Milky-White Cat?

In 2014, Dr. Karl Shuker wrote an intriguing article on his *ShukerNature* blog regarding a big white cat reported from China that supposedly has long sabre teeth. Dr. Shuker was informed of this remarkable feliform cryptid by Canadian cryptozoologist Sebastian Wang, who in turn had learned of it from British cryptozoological researcher Richard Muirhead, one of the foremost authorities in the field and a good friend. Richard's exceptional ability to uncover rare cryptozoological records from library sources is unequalled. In his article, Dr. Shuker examines a Chinese report posted on tieba.baidu.com, which was summarized in English by Wang, discussing a peculiar animal characterised by its dazzling white, sabre-toothed cat-like appearance. According to the author of the original piece, a very large and leucous cat, measuring approximately 4 – 5 meters in length, was observed in May 1994 in the Shennongjia region of China's north-western Hubei Province.

As Dr. Shuker pointed out, there is a unique species of white-furred tiger known as the snow tiger, which exhibits faint yellow stripes. However, this variant would never reach 4-5 m in length and no other subspecies are known to produce white tigers. Furthermore, white tigers with distinct stripes are not recorded among the South China subspecies (*Panthera tigris amoyensis*), the only tiger native to China in modern times. The original article reports that the Shennongjia mystery cat possessed a pair of large curved canines up to 23 cm long, similar to those of the prehistoric sabre-toothed "tiger." The sightings in question were reported from an altitude of 2,800 metres on Mount Shennong Deng, the tallest peak in eastern Shennongjia. (Also see Stripe-less Tigers)

(Author's Verdict: 2/5)

Cigau

A Curious, Maned, Feliform Cryptid Reported to Inhabit Sumatra

Kerinci Seblat National Park is the largest national park in all of Sumatra. It has a total area of 13,791 km² and spans four provinces: Bengkulu, Jambi, South Sumatra, and West Sumatra. The park is renowned among conservationists for its healthy tiger population, estimated to be between 165 and 190 monitored individuals. Providing critical habitat for these animals, Kerinci Seblat is recognised by the

Global Tiger Initiative as one of the twelve most important protected reserves in the world for tiger conservation. Notably, it boasts an impressive occupancy rate of 83%, revealing that a large proportion of the area exhibits signs of tiger activity. There are now more tigers in Kerinci Seblat than in all of Cambodia, China, Laos, Nepal, and Vietnam combined. The tiger is not the only wild felid in Sumatra, which is also home to a number of other kinds of big, medium, and small cats, such as the clouded leopard (*Neofelis nebulosa*), the marbled cat (*Pardofelis marmorata*), leopard cat (*Prionailurus bengalensis* – not to be confused with the true leopard), and the Asian golden cat (*Catopuma temminckii*). If anywhere is perfect for new felid species, the mountain forests of Kerinci and West Sumatra are likely to be it.

Occasional sightings of large unidentified cat-like animals called *cigau* (Indonesian) emerging from rivers have been observed and reported from these areas. Described as a big cat, but smaller than the Sumatran tiger, the *cigau* has more robust forelimbs, creating a sloped-backed stance and an unusual walking gait. The *cigau* is sometimes known as a "golden lion" and is characterised by its golden, yellow, or tan-coloured body with a silvery mane resembling that of a lion. Its tail is short and tufted. Reports indicate that the *cigau* is an aggressive and fast swimmer and that it will attack humans without provocation – eviscerating, or drowning its unfortunate victims.

During an expedition to Sumatra by the *Centre for Fortean Zoology* searching for the elusive orang pendek, cryptozoologist Richard Freeman and Sumatran tiger conservationist Debbie Martyr interviewed a local informant called Sahar Dimus (b. 1969 – d. 2011). According to Sahar, his father had once encountered a *cigau* in the vicinity of Kerinci. Sahar informed them that this would have been sometime during the 1960s. The *cigau* is generally regarded by the local population to be a real animal. However, it is imbued with supernatural abilities and to attack those who violate certain taboos. This concept bears a resemblance to other folkloric beliefs involving tigers.

According to Sahar, one night while working in the forest, a *cigau* had entered his father's camp and grabbed one of the men, evidently due to him helping himself to rice directly from the pot instead of waiting for it to be served. Sahar's father, along with a few other courageous Kubu, pursued the *cigau*. However, by the time they reached their lost companion, he had been fatally mauled and lay lifeless and mutilated on the forest floor. Richard interviewed the forest-dwelling *Orang Rimba* or *Anak Dalam* who live throughout the lowland forests of south-east Sumatra, regarding the existence of the *cigau* and discovered that, although many of his informants knew stories about the creature, or they knew a "friend of a friend" who claimed to have seen one, nobody seemed to have actually observed a *cigau* first-hand. Freeman concluded that the *cigau* is likely to be very rare, if not extinct, in Kerinci due to the destruction of its habitat and hunting pressures. Palaeontologist Darren Naish noted the striking similarity between the *cigau* and Homotherine scimitar cats. According to some studies, these cats possessed long, muscular forelimbs similar to those of hyenas, providing them with a distinctive look.

The youngest Indonesian remains of *Homotherium* and *Hemimachairodus* so far discovered date back to the Middle Pleistocene Era (1.25 – 0.7 million years ago). The widely dispersed *Homotherium* genus is also a possible candidate for the South American *tigre dantero* and *water tigers*, and also for Africa's *tigre de montagne*. Following his first trip to Sumatra in 2003, Richard speculated that the *cigau* could be a larger and more robust relative of the Asian golden cat (*Catopuma temminckii*). If so, *Catopuma leo* would make an appropriate binomen. In Autumn 2022, I put together a research team to travel to Sumatra. Unfortunately, we were unable to find any primary sources, further suggesting the possibility of its extinction. Homophonically, there was some confusion with "bigau" which is an alternate name for the orang pendek used in West Sumatra, making the acquisition of fresh testimonial data all the more difficult.

(Author's Verdict: 3/5)

Coje ya menia

A Larger Than Life "Water Tiger" of Central Africa

Implausibly large for a felid, the *coje ya menia* (Mbundu-Loanda (Bantu): "water lion") from Central Africa, is allegedly a gigantic cat-like creature reported from the Upper Cuango and Cuanza Rivers, Angola, and some other small tributaries. Described as being slightly smaller than a hippopotamus, and possessing large tusks or canine teeth, the *coje ya menia* is a nocturnal ambush predator which migrates to smaller rivers, tributaries, and swamplands during the rainy season. In the 1930s, a Portuguese truck driver heard rumours that something had killed a hippopotamus the previous night in the Congo River. He hired local trackers to search for the spoor of both the hippo and its unidentified killer. Eventually, after several hours, they discovered the remnants of the hippo, which had been severely mutilated yet was uneaten.

Evidence for the existence of this feliform cryptid is limited. The German mammalogist Ingo Krumbiegel (b. 1903 – d. 1990) suggested in 1947 that it could be a surviving sabre-toothed cat but of amphibious habits. Other possible explanations include an undiscovered species of non-avian dinosaur and a huge monitor lizard. Some reports may be misidentifications of hippopotamus activity.

(Author's Verdict: 2/5)

Dilali

Another Maned Mystery Cat?

The *dilali* (Chadian Arabic), or *dilaï*, is a "water lion" reported from parts of Southern Chad and the Central African Republic. In 1912, Lieutenant Nauman of Ulm from the German Imperial Defence Corps discovered that the Kotoko people of Chad's Ouham River were bewildered by his cavalry horse, which they claimed they had never seen before. The natives informed Nauman that they knew of a similar animal with a mane of fur they called "dilai" that occasionally inhabited their rivers and was greatly feared due to its predatory nature. The officer offered a reward of 50 Marks to anyone who could provide concrete evidence of the *dilali* but unfortunately, no one claimed the prize. In 1932, the French naturalist Lucien Blancou received a poorly-described account of the *dilali* from an interpreter and guard in the French colony Ubangi-Shari (now part of the Central African Republic).

Blancou's Baya interpreter described the creature as having a horse-like body and the claws of a lion. Bernard Heuvelmans first suggested that the *dilali* might be a form of the cryptid "water elephant", given its tusks and purported herbivorous tendencies. However, he later hypothesised that many of the Central African "water lions" might be living sabre-toothed cats which had adapted to aquatic habitats. A Zandé guard reported that it also had large tusks similar to those of a walrus, and was a piscivore (fish-eater). An elderly chief mentioned that he had recently seen a dead hippo about two miles from the river which seemed to have been killed by a *dilali*. Based on its original description of having a horse's body with a lion's claws, and its reported herbivorous habits, Heuvelmans also entertained the possibility that the *dilali* might be a living chalicothere, a distant relative of modern horses, tapirs, and rhinoceroses. The chalicotheres had a body and skull which were slim and somewhat similar to those of a horse, with front limbs longer than the hind limbs. This gave them the appearance of a sloped back. Altogether, they resembled an impossible hybrid of horse and gorilla. There is no scientific evidence available to suggest that Chalicotheres were amphibious. If this hypothesis is confirmed, it is logical to conclude that the *dilali* would be recognised as a distinct species.

(Author's Verdict: 2/5)

Dingonek

A Big Cat With Scales?

The *dingonek* is an amphibious cryptid reported from the rivers of Kenya and Tanzania that feed Lake Victoria and the Kikira River, a source of the famous Tana River. Descriptions vary, with some saying it has spots like a leopard or scales like a reptile. Its head has been reported to resemble either that of a lioness with small ears or an otter's head on a short, sturdy neck. The upper jaw has a pair of prominent, straight, tusk-like canines. When viewed on land, its back is broad and similar in shape to that of a hippopotamus. In addition, the *dingonek* possesses short legs with clawed feet, and a long, broad tail. Its total length is estimated to range between 14 and 18 feet (4.2 – 5.4 metres). Variant names include *ndamathia* (Kikuyu/Bantu), and *olmaima* or *ol-umaina* (Nilo-Saharan/Masai). The *dingonek* is typically seen basking on fallen trees or along riverbanks, with only its head being visible when swimming. C. W. Hobley (b. 1867 – d. 1947), a Warwickshire-born colonial administrator in Kenya, observed a large animal of about sixteen feet (4.8 meters) long floating on a log in the Mara River, located on the border between Kenya and Tanzania, during the early 1900s. The spotted creature had features of both leopard and otter, with what seemed to be scales. In 1907, big-game hunter, John Alfred Jordan and his hunting party reported seeing a similar animal with two large upper canine teeth in the Magori River, which feeds into Lake Victoria in Kenya. Additionally, they discovered prints resembling those of a hippopotamus.

Heuvelmans suggested a surviving species of sabre-toothed cat, with the scales only occasionally reported being explained by wet and matted fur. It is important to note that many African "water lions" are described vaguely, and have been given reptilian characteristics. (See *Water Lions*)

(Author's Verdict: 1/5)

Ennidi Tiger

A Long-Fanged, Cat-like Cryptid of the Night

The Ennedi tiger, Ennedi mountain tiger, or Tigre de Montagne (French: "tiger of the mountains" or "mountain tiger") is a large feliform cryptid, bigger than a lion, reported from the Enedi Plateau, the Tibesti Mountains, the Gera Massif in Chad, and the Bongo Massif in the Central African Republic. There are also equivocal reports from the Immatong Mountains of South Sudan and Uganda. They are known by various regional names, including *biscoro*, *coq-djinge*, *gassingram*, *hadjel*, *nisi* or *noso*, and *vassoko*. The Ennedi tiger's fur is reddish in colour with white vertically-oriented stripes and long upper canine teeth that protrude beyond the lips. Reports describe an amphibious animal adapted to hunting large, heavy prey. According to eyewitnesses, the tail is very short or even absent altogether. When French cryptozoologist Christian Le Noël, editor of the journal *Hominologie et Cryptozoologie*, presented his Yulu trackers with colour drawings of tigers, pumas, snow leopards, cheetahs, ocelots, and the prehistoric *Smilodon*, they enthusiastically selected the latter in resemblance to their "mountain tiger". No *Smilodon* fossils have been found in Africa, but *Machairodus* and *Megantereon*, two other sabre-toothed cats, lived in Africa in prehistoric times. Bernard Heuvelmans theorised that *Smilodon* may have descended from one of these species. Given its long canines, he assumed it to be a slow eater. Heuvelmans speculated that a species could have adapted to life in mountains and caves to avoid competition from scavengers and surviving into historical times, possibly taking on the vacant niche of bears in Africa.

(Author's Verdict: 2/5)

Entzaeia-yawá

A Dangerous Bushy-Tailed Beast

The *entzaeia-yawá* of Ecuador is another feliform cryptid said to pose a threat to humans. The Shuar people, located at the headwaters of the Marañón River, describe it as a nocturnal, amphibious predator that triggers fear in even their bravest hunters. Spanish cryptozoologist Angel Morant Forés, wrote "It appears that water tigers show a wide range of colour morphs (black, white, brown, and reddish) [...] bigger than a jaguar and with a bushy tail. *Entzaeia yawá* is regarded as a dangerous creature and attacks on humans are not rare."

The Shuar are said to refrain from entering the river alone for fear of being attacked by the *entzaeia-yawá*. Descriptions of this creature include a tail like that of a cow and webbed paws. When informants were shown images of animal tracks, they identified those belonging to the *entzaeia-yawá* as being similar to bear or otter tracks. Interestingly, the *entzaeia-yawá* is the only "water tiger" that isn't depicted with long sabre teeth.

The story of Carlos Pichama exemplifies the danger posed by this filiform cryptid. His cousin's wife was killed during a fishing trip at the Mangusas River, and it was believed she had been dragged underwater by the creature after he discovered its pawprints tracking hers. To avenge her death, Carlos and his brothers returned to the site where she had been taken and detonated several charges of dynamite, forcing a large unidentified, red-furred animal with long hair to surface in the lake. In 1989, Juan Bautista Rivadeneira reported seeing a water tiger in the Jurumbaino River, near the villages of Rio Blanco and San Ramona. Forés believed that reports could be explained by giant otters; however, he eventually conceded that this was unlikely due to the white throat pattern typical of giant otters not corresponding with descriptions of the *entzaeia-yawá*, not to mention they are not man-eaters.

Rivadeneira later found tracks on a fishing trip to the Mangusas River belonging to a "water tiger" which were following those of his wife – indicating she had been dragged into the water and killed, much like the alleged attack in the Mangusas River. Likewise, Rivadeneira and his brothers returned to the place where his wife was taken and detonated several dynamite charges in the lake. This reportedly brought a large animal with long reddish fur to the surface. Confusingly, the term 'entzaeia-yawá' is also used to refer to caimans and the greater grison (*Galictis vittate*) - a sort of slender-built honey badger with a similarly ferocious temperament. Heuvelmans proposed that the sabre-teeth of machairodonts may not have always been visible. French author Philippe Coudray speculated that the *entzaeia-yawá* could be a living sabre-toothed cat; suggesting that reports describing an animal without sabre-teeth could be attributed to it never having been viewed close enough for its teeth to be seen. According to Forés, a melanistic version is called *wankánin-yawá*.

(Author's Verdict: 2/5)

Guoshanhuang

A Titanic Tiger from China?

Is a prehistoric predator prowling the Chinese provinces of Hubei and Hunan? Known as *guoshanhuang,* this feliform cryptid is said to be similar in appearance to the South China tiger (*Panthera tigris amoyensis*) but considerably larger, with an estimated length of four metres (13 feet), weighing around 500 kg (1,102.31 lbs). Its coat is described as withered or dead grass and patterned with yellowish horizontal stripes. No species of cat has bold, horizontal stripes on its body, so it could be that this patterning is an optical illusion and not the fur of the animal itself. Eyewitnesses of *guoshanhuangs* reported an animal with a longer muzzle than the average tiger, with a pair of long, downward-curving canine teeth. One such animal was reported from Huanggang on Huping Mountain in Hunan Province. It had a yellowish hue and a white patch on its forehead. According to local hunters on Huping Mountain, they had encountered a *guoshanhuang* sometime in the 1960s and its pelt was big enough to cover two oriental dining tables; however, any remains seem to have since been lost. A second specimen was allegedly shot and killed at Liangjiahe Township, Zhushan County in the late 1970s. Wang Junhua, a member of the local scientific commission is said to have viewed its pelt; however, again, no remains have been presented.

In May 1994, Yin Benshun and Wang Benyou, alongside four others, were trekking through the mountainous forest of Laojun Peak when Wang detected a strong animal smell. Soon, Wang caught sight of a large cat-like creature around five meters from his position. He described it as having the appearance of a tiger, measuring 2.94 metres in length and patterned with light brown horizontal stripes. He noted that it was displaying threatening behaviour, baring its teeth while staring at him, leading Wang to cautiously back away for about ten metres before turning tail and running away. Fortunately for Wang, the *guoshanhuang* – if that's what it was – did not seem intent on hunting him but rather on warning him away from its territory, perhaps indicating that it had offspring nearby. The *guoshanhuang* might be a new variety or emerging subspecies of tiger derived from the Siberian tiger, as suggested by Chinese biologist and cryptozoologist, Liu Minzhuang.

To be classed as a subspecies, there must be at least two different categories – otherwise, what is labelled as such would just represent the entirety of the species. This is why our species is known as *Homo sapiens* and not *Homo sapiens sapiens*. David C. Xu suggests in his superb *Mysterious Creatures of China* (2018, Coachwhip Publications) that the *guoshanhuang* might be related to the large fossil tigers from Pleistocene China. According to Xu, *Dinofelis cristata* is a noteworthy specimen regarding the nature of this purported big cat. Additionally, Xu observed that nimravids (false sabretooths) developed long canines and reached considerable sizes, yet it is believed they went extinct during the Oligocene period, much earlier than the true sabre-toothed cats. Xu proposed a second hypothesis: that the *guoshanhuang* could be a creodont, potentially a living descendant of *Sarkastodon* or *Megistotherium*. I agree that the most likely explanation for reports of *guoshanhuangs* is that they are based on an optical illusion caused by seeing ordinary tigers in dappled light. On July 17th, 2016, Hubei Shennongjia was designated a World Heritage Site in recognition of its extraordinary array of flora and fauna and its conservation efforts to safeguard rare, endangered, and endemic species. Is it possible that such untouched habitat could also contain undiscovered felids? Perhaps.

(Author's Verdict: 3/5)

Hadjel

Surviving Sabretooths?

The *hadjel*, also known as *"biscoro,"* is a large feliform cryptid said to inhabit mountainous areas of Chad and the Central African Republic. Described as reddish with white stripes and a thick mane like that of a lion, it may be some kind of surviving sabretooth or an unknown species related to the Pantherinae, that has evolved to occupy the ecological niche previously filled by the extinct sabretooth. It is speculated that the *hadjel* could be similar to the Ennidi tiger.

(Author's Verdict: 2/5)

Iemisch

An Amphibious, Nocturnal, Killer of Horses?

Scientific Name: *Grypotherium Domesticum,* based on the assumption that this unknown animal is a giant ground sloth.

The *Iemisch*, also referred to as *'iemisch listai'* and *'tigre d'acgua'* ("water tiger"), is described as a large, short-faced cat with large canine teeth, no visible external ears, reported from Lake Colhué Huapi in the central Patagonian region of the Argentine Republic. Its feet are short and plantigrade (flat-footed) with a peculiar arrangement of three toes on the front feet and four on the hind feet. The clawed forefeet are equipped with a webbed membrane, allowing both aquatic and land-based activities. Its tail is reported to be long, flat and prehensile. The *Iemisch* was first attested to by the Argentinian zoologist Florentino Ameghino. (b. 1853 – d. 1911) in 1897. From Ameqhino's original letter: 'The animal is of nocturnal habits, and it's said to be so strong that it can seize horses with its claws and drag them to the bottom of the water. According to the description I have been given, it has a short head, big canine teeth, and no external ears: its feet are short and plantigrade, with three toes on the forefeet and four on the hind, three toes are formed by a membrane for swimming, and are also armed with formidable claws. Its tail is long, flat, and prehensile.'

It is widely accepted that the *iemisch* are primarily aquatic, nocturnal hunters that prey on unsuspecting horses by dragging them into rivers. People who claim to have seen the *iemisch* say that they can move as quickly on land as in water. According to the local human population, the *iemisch* is a hybrid of a jaguar and otter, the size of an ox. The German anthropologist Robert Lehmann-Nitsche (b. 1872 – d. 1938) working in Argentina, reported that a local rancher once gave him a piece of skin from an unknown animal. Upon examination, he noticed small plates of bone embedded beneath the skin which, according to folklore, protected them from arrowheads. Additionally, the sample was discovered close to human remains, which prompted Lehmann-Nitsche to believe that the creature may have been hunted by man. Along with Hauthal and Roth, Nitsche later published *The Mysterious Mammal of Patagonia, Grypotherium domesticum* in which he speculated that it was possibly an undescribed species of otter. However, researchers and locals familiar with the region who were consulted, said they had never encountered or heard of such creatures, despite their extensive first-hand knowledge. Furthermore, other prominent scholars have expressed scepticism about Heuvelmans' research, pointing out that the word 'Iemisch' does not correspond with any Patagonian language.

(Author's Verdict: 1/5)

Ikimizi

Yet Another Lion With Spots?

Reports from the Virunga Volcanic region of Rwanda, not far from where the mountain gorilla was discovered in 1902, suggest that the *ikimizi* (Swahili) is a spotted lion looking like a hybrid between a lion and a leopard. It has grey fur with dark spots and a bearded chin. Wild-born lion x leopard hybrids may be responsible for some sightings, as descriptions of both 'leopons' and 'lipards' match those of the *ikimizi*. It may be that natural selection is favouring a mane-less, spotted pelage over the normal type adapted for hunting in open plains. The renowned Swahili scholar Captain William Hitchens concluded that the *ikimizi* was an alternate name for the Nandi Bear or *chemosit*. Hitchens was also the first Westerner to report sightings of a small human-like agogwe while hunting lions in East Africa in the early 20th century. Hitchens theorised that the *Ikimizi* could be evidence of natural selection, an evolutionary adaptation to man's practice of hunting lions with thick manes for sport trophies. (See *Spotted Lions, Bakanga, Bung Bung, Foulempou, Marozi, Ruturargo, Uruturangwe*)

(Author's Verdict: 3/5)

Kimbambangwe

The Livestock Killer

The *kimbambangwe* (Rufumbira: Kinyarwanda) is a leopard-like cryptid known to the Bantu people from Kisoro District in south-western Uganda, where it is said to prowl the Bufumbira depression, particularly in and around the vast tube caves of Bufumbira County. This volcanic field, which covers an area of around 320 km², is surrounded on all sides by high mountains. A prominent feature of the Bufumbira lava field is several long ridges, formed almost entirely of ash and scoria from successive lava flows during the early to mid-Pleistocene era. These sedimentary rocks dip sharply, making them an ideal habitat for a large ambush predator to lie in wait. Despite the area regularly being visited by tourists, reports of the *kimbambangwe* are few and far between. As a result, very little is known about its appearance other than it is supposed to be similar to a melanistic leopard with dark markings and short ears. *Kimbambangwes* are sometimes blamed for mutilating and killing livestock.

(Author's Verdict: 2/5)

Maipolina

Another Dangerous "Water Tiger" From South America?

Reports claim that the Marini, Aprouague, and Oyapock rivers in French Guiana are home to a large man-eating predator measuring up to three metres (9 ft 9 inches) long and one metre (3 ft 3 inches) wide across its back. They have short fawn-coloured fur with white colouration on the chest, and a 15- to 20-cm stripe running down the back from head to tail. The *maipolina* (Wayampi: Tupi-Guarani) is characterised by large sharp claws, brown eyes much like those of a tapir, and a tufted tail like a lion. They have long tusk-like upper canines, often compared to those of a walrus, and they primarily inhabit caves and hollows along riverbanks where they venture out to prey on fishermen in canoes and unsuspecting children swimming nearby. Amaipeti, the son of a Roucouyen chief, notified Lieutenant Colonel René Ricatte (b. 1920 – d. 2007) that one evening he had seen a *maipolina* perched on a rock next to a river. A native Oyampi living on the Oyapock River informed Christian Voillemont that he had once seen a *maipolina* attack a canoe and snatch its occupant away in its powerful jaws. Furthermore, another local told Voillemont that he had once captured a "giant otter with sabre-teeth."

On October 21st, 1962, paramilitary police retrieved a child's body from the Maroni River in Maripasoula. Upon examination, it was found that the seven-year-old boy had been partially consumed and severely mutilated. Examination by Dr. Lamonerie revealed that the boy had been disembowelled, his mouth had been chewed away, and one of his arms had been torn off. Lt. Col. Ricatte witnessed the death certificate for himself. It was suggested that a *maipolina* or *popoke* was responsible for the boy's death and mutilation, as according to the locals, the injuries were not consistent with any of the area's known species. Reports indicate that he had been swimming or bathing in the river when he died; however, it is unclear whether he drowned and was eaten post-mortem, or if he had been killed by the *maipolina*.

The names "mamadilo", "popoke", and "water buba" are synonymous with the *maipolina*. Some have suggested a manatee being responsible but French cryptozoologist Michel Raynal doubts that a manatee is the cause of the fatalities because they are harmless animals and have little to no physical similarities with the *maipolina*. Piranhas have also been blamed. However, these infamously ferocious fish, which are actually omnivorous, and mainly scavengers, have since been dismissed as possible perpetrators of the 1962 mutilation, as even a large shoal of piranhas would be unable to completely sever a human arm. Some have speculated that the *maipolina* and other so-called "water tigers" might be misidentified giant river otters (*Pteronura brasiliensis*). Raynal noted that, while the giant otter typically hunts fish and occasionally caiman, some have been seen eating birds, snakes, and other small mammals. The giant river otter does not bear much resemblance to most portrayals of the *maipolina*; however, one witness did describe it as "a giant otter with sabre-teeth."

Karl Shuker believes that the *maipolina* might be the female counterpart of the *yaguaru* or *aypa*. If so, it is likely that the *maipolina* descended from either the *Smilodon* genus or *Homotherium venezuelensis*, as these are the only machairodonts known to have reached South America.

(Author's Verdict: 2/5)

Malagasy Lion

A Giant Fossa-like Feliform Cryptid

Madagascar's distinctive biodiversity is a direct result of geographic isolation. Geologists believe that 165 million years ago, Madagascar was connected to Africa but began to drift away from the continent sometime over the next 15 million years. Officially, Madagascar has no giraffes, zebras, extant hippos, or felids. However, according to oral traditions, there is something strange with cat-like characteristics living on the island, yet to be identified by science. Paul Cazard was informed by a civil engineer named Belime, that there were large, lion-like animals on the island that lived in deep caves and posed threats to both the local fauna and the island's human inhabitants. Belime described them as dangerous cats that had been ravaging the region. It has been suggested that the Malagasy "lion" may be a surviving species of *Machairodus*, a sabre-toothed cat that was widespread throughout Africa, Eurasia, and North America during the late Miocene period. However, cryptozoologist Dale A. Drinnon has suggested that they could be a surviving population of giant fossa (*Cryptoprocta spelea*). German cryptozoologist Markus Bühler disagrees, believing they are more likely to be alien (out of place) big cats.

(Author's Verdict: 3/5)

Mourou n'gou

The Archetypal "Water-Leopard"

The *mourou n'gou* (Ubangian: Banda, "water leopard") is described as leopard-like in appearance but very large, 2.4 – 3.6 metres in length (7.8 – 11.8 feet); said to inhabit the Central African Republic (rivers Bamingui, Bangoran, Gribingui, Lomba, Kotto, Koukourou, Mbari, and Ouaka) and the Chari River in Chad. They have brownish fur, either striped or dappled with blue and white spots. The head is comparatively small, somewhat resembling that of a huge genet with large canines. Glowing eyes are regularly reported, which is presumably the visible effect of the *tapetum lucidum* reflecting visible light. The tail of the *mourou n'gou* is like that of a leopard but with denser fur. Footprints, much larger than lion's and characterised by a strange circular pattern in the center, have been collected as evidence of the mourou n'gou. According to local folklore, this amphibious beast is primarily nocturnal and capable of easily killing hippopotamuses and elephants which they hunt in pairs. One *mourou n'gou* chases the prey into the water, where the other is lying in wait. They also pose a danger to those navigating canoes and have acquired a certain cultural significance due to their loud vocalisations, said to resemble strong winds. This is reminiscent of the folklore surrounding the jaguar and its association with thunder in South America.

A *mourou n'gou* is said to have attacked a soldier, dragging him underwater and mauling him to death. Blancou visited the Ndele records office to authenticate these events and came across intriguing documents that a rifleman had been reported missing during this period.

"In 1911 (this date has been cross-checked) when he was a porter with a detachment of riflemen going from Fort Crampel to Ndele, Moussa saw one of these soldiers seized by a *mourou-ngou* at the junction of the Bamingui and the Koukourou. The animal was shaped like a panther, a little larger than a lion but with stripes, and about twelve feet long. The background of its coat was likewise the colour of a panther, but its footprint was oddly described as containing a circle in the middle(?). The soldier was in a canoe when the animal came out of the Koukourou 'like a hippo', just where the rivers met, seized the man in the canoe and dragged him into the water capsizing the boat, surfaced once more with the soldier in its mouth and then disappeared. The man paddling the canoe swam safely away, but the soldier's rifle and kit remained on the bottom of the river..."

In May 1930, Blancou killed a hippopotamus on the Mbari River. A loud drawn-out roaring was heard intermittently throughout the night and an animal, which was decided by the natives not to be a Nile crocodile, had begun to feast on the carcass. It appears that this account is based on superstitious fear rather than an actual encounter with a real animal. A *mourou n'gou* was caught in a fishing net on the Bangoran River during the 1950s, and according to reports, it was killed by villagers who may have retained its skull. In an interview with Christian Le Noel, a village chief contested this narrative and suspiciously refused a sizeable sum of money to allow for the viewing of the skull. During either 1962 or 63, reports surfaced that a diamond prospector had seen what appeared to be a *maurou n'gou* swimming in a river. The creature seemed to be moving its head side-to-side as if it were searching for something under the water; this behaviour might also imply that it wasn't a mammal but rather some sort of reptile.

In February 1985, a guide named Marcel reported an encounter with what the local Banda people call *mourou n'gou* near the Shari River. Initially, Bernard Heuvelmans speculated that it could have been a large crocodile of the genus *Osteolaemus*. By 1978, he began proposing the possibility that there might be a surviving sabre-toothed cat adapted to an amphibious lifestyle, however, its behaviour and appearance differ significantly from those associated with what is said to be the true hippo-killing *mourou n'gou*. (See *Water Lions, Coje Ya Memia, Dilali, Mamaime, Nzefu-Loi, Ngoroli, Ntambo Wa Luy*)

(Author's Verdict: 2/5)

The New Guinea "Lion"

What is the Moolah?

It is generally accepted there are no pre-Pleistocene land mammals on the island of New Guinea, with native placental mammals being limited to rodents and bats. However, the palaeo-continent of Sahul –

composed of mainland Australia, Tasmania, New Guinea, and the Aru Islands – was once home to a range of animal species that were distinct from the rest of the world. It has been speculated by some that one of these species may have evolved into a cat-like form; however, there is currently no scientific evidence to confirm this. Nevertheless, there are numerous reports of a large animal resembling a felid on the island. Perhaps there are some unidentified "pseudo-felids", possibly belonging to the mammalian infraclass Marsupialia, still awaiting formal discovery.

The marsupial fauna of New Guinea is highly diverse. It could therefore harbour a convergently evolved "marsupial cat", occupying a vacant ecological niche normally occupied by the Felidae. If the reports of a feliform cryptid in Australia are accepted as credible, then it stands to reason that New Guinea would have comparable accounts. Todd Jurasek of *Jurasek Park Explorations* was informed by locals that a lion-sized, cat-like carnivore existed in New Guinea. The British banker, politician, zoologist, and soldier, Lord Walter Rothschild FRS (b. 1868 – d. 1937) also wrote about a mysterious feline predator similar in appearance to the Queensland tiger of Australia that had gone undetected in New Guinea. According to Malcolm Smith's blog, "Malcolm's Musings," his neighbour Esther Ingram, born to missionary parents in New Guinea, once found a strange cat-like creature that, "was very solidly built, and the head-body length was about five feet.

Both Esther and her father were amazed at how huge it was. So, too, was I, when she stated that it was as high as the table around which we were gathered: about 2½ feet. Yes, Esther agreed, it was probably twice as long as high. Esther, in particular, attempted to study as many details as possible. (Remember, it was very close.) The basic colour was white, with ginger "trimmings" on the tail and ears. Pale gingery, vertical stripes, not well delineated, appeared on the sides, but they did not extend to the back, or dorsal surface, which was completely pale. She specifically noted that the forepaws were cat-like, rather than (say) hoofed like a goat's. She didn't get a glance at the rear paws. The tail was ginger and very long, hanging to the ground. I enquired about bushiness etc., to establish a comparison with a dog's. She said it was a bit coarser or fluffier than the body, but not much.

On the body itself, the fur was smooth. The head was broad, short, flattish, and cat-like. It did not protrude like a dog's. The ears were ginger, mottled with white, and hung down. They were not as long as a spaniel's, but they were long and rounded and gave every indication of being naturally floppy. It was this feature that amazed both of them (and me as well, as it doesn't sound anything like a cat's). Esther also thought she saw whiskers. Explanation? Needless to say, such a creature is not supposed to exist on the island of New Guinea – or anywhere else that I'm aware of. New Guinea belongs to the Australasian faunal zone, which is the domain of marsupials. Cats – especially big ones – are no more supposed to be present than in Australia itself. Nevertheless, alien big cats (ABCs) are being reported in Australia in ever-increasing numbers, but this is the first time I have heard a report from New Guinea. At Esther's insistence, I wrote to Dr Tim Flannery, because he had recently published a book on his mammal collecting expeditions to New Guinea.

His reply was as follows: Regarding the cat-like animal that Ms. Ingram observed, the information provided seems to point to a tree kangaroo. The size would be about right for one of the larger species (well over a metre long) and the ginger-coloured fur on some parts of the dorsum (described as completely pale) may not have been true to life if the headlights were shining on the animal. The tree kangaroo's tail could be mistaken for that of a cat in that it is long and reasonably bushy. Tree kangaroos have short faces and the head is often held low when moving quickly over the ground. I cannot explain the shape of the ears being long and floppy. The short-footed tree kangaroos use a quadrupedal gait and rarely hop. Some species spend much time on the ground. Sightings like the one you made of the 'cat' are always a challenge to identify. Being at night and a fleeting glimpse make it difficult, 'though I am impressed with the detail you have provided. If this is the case, obviously there must have been a serious discrepancy between what was seen and what was perceived.

In response, Esther said that this was impossible. Both she and her father were quite familiar with tree kangaroos. The animal was much larger than a metre – more like five feet, or a metre and a half. (Note that this did not refer to the total length, but merely the head-body length, which is always less than a metre in tree kangaroos.) The tail was quite unlike a tree kangaroo's, although it did reach the ground. It was thin like a cat's, with a bit of a tuft at the end. The hindquarters were not raised, as a tree kangaroo's would have been (because, although a tree kangaroo's hind legs are proportionally shorter than a regular kangaroo's, they are still longer than the fore legs). The forepaws resembled a cat's, not a tree kangaroo's. So there you have it. Secondhand reports. Then Esther recalled an event that took place at Pitanka a week or so before her sighting. The watchman told her he had approached the tea tree plantation when he heard dogs barking, and he saw a big white cat jump from one tree to another. Some of the people at the Pitanka school reported a white animal streaking into the bush. Some of the ex-pupils also spoke of black cats.

Back in Australia, still, in 2000, Esther went to the airport to pick up a missionary's widow, Ruth B-, who lived at Famu, just across the mountain from Pitanka. "You have white ones, and we have black ones," said Ruth. She had seen a photo of a black panther in a magazine and claimed they existed at Famu. So, what is going on? Do alien big cats now exist in Papua New Guinea, and if so, where do they come from? If not, what did Esther, her father, and her foster brother see? The watchman had no doubts about the identity of his white animal. It was a masalai (muss-a-lye): a hobgoblin or evil spirit. I am not in a position to refute it." This purported encounter with the creature, known by the locals as "moolah" occurred either in December 1999 or January 2000 and was one of many remarkable beasties chronicled by Captain J. A. Lawson in his work, "Wanderings in the Interior of New Guinea" (1875). According to Captain Lawson, he had landed on New Guinea in 1871, and among his alleged discoveries was the world's highest mountain (dubbed by him Mount Hercules, and far taller than Everest, yet which could be climbed in only a day!), large ape-men, enormous herds of deer and buffalo numbering in the thousands, the world's tallest tree, huge flightless birds resembling ostriches or enormous rheas, and his hitherto unrecorded *moolah*, a specimen of which he supposedly shot and which was very similar to India's Bengal tiger. This is Captain Lawson's written description of his freshly-killed *moolah*: "This animal was formed exactly like the Indian tiger, nor was it inferior in size, but it was a much more handsome creature. It was marked with black and chestnut stripes, on a white, or nearly white, ground. Its length from the nose to the root of the tail was seven feet three inches."

Based purely on fundamental zoogeographical reasons, Captain Lawson's claims regarding the existence of the *moolah* were arrant nonsense. Astonishingly, however, they were widely accepted as factual for some time before further expeditions to New Guinea revealed that his entire book was nothing but a form of satire on Victorian exploration, rather than having any veracity. The true identity of the enigmatic Captain has never been uncovered. However, the most widespread theory is that he was Robert H. Armit (b. 1844 – d.?), a lieutenant in the Royal Navy with experience as an assistant surveyor in Australian waters and Honorary Secretary of the New Guinea Colonising Association. If Armit's *moolah* was merely a figment of his imagination, then what were the people seeing? Could it be that the cryptozoological Queensland tiger, a possible marsupial that will be discussed shortly, has one or more obscure, closely related species living in remote areas of New Guinea, yet to be discovered by science?

(Author's Verdict: 2/5)

Ngoroli

A Central African "Water Lion"?

Known to the Azande people as *ngoroli,* this feliform cryptid is said to resemble a maned leopard. Eyewitnesses report various descriptions, such as spotted or striped patterns on its pelt that range from yellow to reddish or brown. Its physical characteristics are said to include large paddle-like limbs and two downward-curving canine teeth or tusks. It purportedly hunts hippos, crocodiles, and large fish, and is believed to be primarily nocturnal, often living in caves near riverbanks. Reports indicate they typically range from ten feet long and almost 1.5 metres high at the shoulders. Ingo Krumbiegel speculated that surviving sabre-toothed cats of the genus *Machairodus* might be responsible. Although there is no fossil evidence that sabretooth tigers inhabited aquatic environments, such an evolutionary adaptation cannot be ruled out. Large tusk-like teeth might be beneficial in an aquatic environment, as with the walrus, although they may also be a hindrance when competing for food on land with contemporary big cats.

Could it be that an unknown species of sabre-toothed cat evolved into an aquatic habitat where competition for food is less severe?

Machairodus was a large carnivore, measuring up to the size of a lion (*P. leo*). It possessed large upper canines and carnassial teeth perfectly adapted for slicing through tough flesh and sinew. They first appeared in Eurasia during the Miocene geological epoch about 15 million years ago and held on until about two million years ago in Tunisia. It has also been suggested that an unidentified species of large monitor lizard (family Varanidae) is a potential explanation, as well as the obligatory theory of surviving sauropod dinosaurs such as Apatosaurus, despite the fact that all sauropods were herbivores.

(Author's Verdict: 2/5)

Ntambo wa luy

Destroyer of Canoes

The ntambo wa luy (Luba-Kasai: "water lion") is reported from the Luembé River, Kasai tributary, middle Congo River basin. Belgian big game hunter and author Charles Mahauden once inquired with the Katangan elders if it would be possible to travel upriver from Luembé to Kasanju. The men seemed to avoid his question, but eventually, they shared their hesitation due to their fear of a "water lion" dubbed "ntambo wa luy" that is said to haunt that region of the Luembé where it reportedly attacks canoes before consuming the occupants. The Katangans said they never found its tracks and assumed, based on this, that it rarely leaves the water. According to one elder, during the time of his forefathers, a *ntambo wa luy* had entered their village and killed three men. Since then, none of the tribe would venture downriver in spite of its potential for lucrative hunting; instead, they offered Mahauden a dugout canoe but plainly refused to accompany him. Mahauden asked exactly where the dreaded creature was so he could avoid it and was told it lives between the third and fourth tributaries. So, the next day Mahauden set out alone and found the river beyond the third tributary was rich in wildlife, making him hastily conclude in his memoirs that the *ntambo wa luy* was a purely folkloric creature.

(Author's Verdict: 2/5)

Nzemendim

A Fluvial Feline?

The *nze mendim* (Fang: "river tiger"), also known as *yango* ("water elephant"), *nkweu dzibo, ndamballa, ndzin médzim* or simply *dzin*, is a purported water lion reported from tropical regions of Gabon and Cameroon. It was the first of its kind to be reported by Europeans and was initially thought to be a kind of giant otter.

(Author's Verdict: 2/5)

Onça-tigre

A Tail-less Jaguar?

The *onça-tigre* is an alleged "water tiger" that was reported to Joana Macedo from the Amanã and Mamirauá Sustainable Development Reserves located on the Japurá River in Brazil's Amazon region between 2010 and 2013. This occurred when a Ribeirinho fisherman and his wife witnessed three dead specimens. The *onça-tigre* is said to resemble a large jaguar but without a tail. It supposedly had rear-facing forepaws, and short fur on its back and long fur on its chest. One of the specimens was apparently killed after it attacked a dog. It was about 1.75 metres (5 ft 9 in) in length with a 60 cm (2 foot) tail. It had short, glossy fur that was pale yellow on the throat and chest, white on the underside, and dark black on the back. The third alleged *onça-tigre* specimen met its demise after attacking livestock. It was described as large with a blotched fur pattern and "long fangs sticking out of its mouth". The first specimen was noted to be tail-less and possessed backwards-facing forepaws, leading one to think it probably represents a cultural legend derived from an animal, rare or challenging to locate. The second account described by Joana Macedo alluded to a black cougar, which may be an indication of a rare genetic mutation such as melanism. The third was similar to that of a large spotted, sabre-toothed cat. All three accounts given by Joana Macedo could be unknown variants; however, the third could be an unknown species.

(Author's Verdict: 3/5)

Pamá-yawá

An Amphibious, Tapir-Sized Big Cat?

The Shuar people living in the Ecuadorian Amazon are familiar with a creature they call "pamá-yawá", or "tapir tiger," named for its impressive size that is said to be similar to an Amazonian tapir. This belief stems from their perception that it is the only animal capable of successfully hunting adult tapirs. The Amazonian tapir (*Tapirus terrestris*) and the mountain tapir (*T. pinchaque*) are both found in Ecuador. The mountain tapir, also referred to as the Andean tapir or woolly tapir is the smallest of the four widely recognised species. The thick skin on the nape of its neck helps protect it from predators such as pumas, jaguars, and alligators; however, rare attacks by anacondas and particularly large jaguars can still present a threat to adult tapirs. A Wampula hunter named Pedro Anan Churuwia, who was of notably small stature, reported seeing a large, amphibious feliform cryptid of dark grey colour in the Trans-Cutucu and Sangay volcanic regions of Ecuador. It was described as approximately the size of a tapir, and with paws that were as broad as both of his hands when put together. In 1969, Juan Bautista Rivadeneira, a settler from Macas, claimed to have encountered the mysterious "pamá-yawá" on the Morona River at a distance of about 50 to 60 metres away. He watched it emerge from the river and casually walk along a sandy beach for about ten minutes before disappearing out of sight. The animal was said to be approximately two metres in length and stood around four feet tall at the shoulders. His Shuar guide informed Rivadeneira that he had encountered a *pamá-yawá*. Although remains discovered of predated tapirs could have been killed by large jaguars, the eyewitness accounts of the animals themselves are harder to explain away.

(Author's Verdict: 2/5)

Queensland "Tiger"

A Cat-like Marsupial of Australia?

Queensland covers an expansive 1.8 million km², making it the second largest state in Australia after Western Australia; larger than the U.S. state of Texas by more than twice and seven times larger than the United Kingdom. This enormous region that boasts substantial areas of rainforest and other biodiversity-rich terrain may be well-suited for undiscovered animals. Native Australian species such as kangaroos, koalas, emus, dingoes, platypuses, bandicoots, and echidnas are found in Queensland. The Daintree Rainforest in the northern region has an abundant and diverse array of wildlife, with many endangered species. It is considered one of the most important areas for preserving these species in the world.

The Queensland "tiger", also known as the Queensland marsupial tiger, native tiger, marsupial cat, *yarri, yaddi* (Herbert River Area), and yedna tiger, is generally described as a striped, cat-like animal with pointed ears, about the size of an average dog. Queensland tigers are reported from the wet tropics of Queensland along the northeast coast of Australia. This is an extensive and varied biotope with an array of plants, as well as marsupials and singing birds, along with other rare and endangered species. Reports come from northern Queensland, from Cairns to Cardwell; and in south-eastern Queensland, from Biggenden to Mount Tamborine. The Queensland tiger's tail is described as long and thick, and occasionally a tuft of longer fur is seen at the tip. With an average height of about 45 cm, it is probably much heavier than a domestic cat. According to reports, its limbs are relatively short and its paws possess long dangerous claws. The head is described as cat-like and particularly large in proportion to its body. This feliform cryptid is sometimes described as having brilliant green eyes and large canines or fangs, even on occasion being compared to sabre-teeth. It is arboreal and very aggressive, especially when cornered, where it will make threatening, growling whines, roars and snarls. It appears that wallabies are the preferred prey of the Queensland tiger, but reports suggest that it is also bold enough to attack livestock.

This enigmatic feliform cryptid was first documented in 1871 and is remembered largely due to the significant number of specimens reportedly killed by early explorers and settlers, yet apparently never being preserved for scientific verification. This might suggest the likelihood of undiscovered specimens that could potentially provide new information. For over 150 years European settlers, explorers, hikers, and farmers have come forward to report sightings of the so-called "marsupial tiger"; yet to date no zoologist has received any physical proof of its existence. Descriptions of this feliform cryptid can be found in a number of texts on Australian natural history, such as A. S. le Souef's *The Wild Animals of Australasia* (1926) and Ellis Troughton's *Furred Animals of Australia* (1931). Since the late 20th century, sightings have become less frequent, leading some cryptozoologists to speculate that the marsupial tiger may now be extinct. Reports are remarkably consistent in terms of physical appearance and behaviour and have remained so for over a century. However, reports in recent years describe the animal as considerably larger than a medium size dog, and more like an adult lion. This means that either reports are being exaggerated in recent years, the Queensland tiger is sexually dimorphic, or there is more than one species present.

Queensland tigers are thought to have several colour morphs. The original reports describe its coat as short and rough to the touch, usually with black stripes on its body. Later reports describe its fur as fawn, tan, or grey, but dark brown and all-black examples have also been reported. Therefore, any unidentified cat or cat-like animal, between the size of a springer spaniel and an adult lion, whether it is fawn, tan, grey, dark brown, or black can be labelled a "Queensland tiger".

Scientist and naturalist Carl Sophus Lumholtz (b. 1851 – d. 1922) included the following description of a *yarri,* taken from aboriginal accounts, in his 1989 book *Among Savages.*

"During my association with these savages I learned that on the summit of the Coast Mountains, before mentioned, there lived two varieties of mammals which seemed to me to be unknown to science; but I had much difficulty in acquiring this knowledge. One of the animals they called yarri. From their description, I conceived it to be a marsupial tiger. It was said to be about the size of a dingo, though its legs were shorter and its tail long, and it was described by the blacks as being very savage. If pursued it climbed up the trees, where the natives did not dare follow it, and by gestures, they explained to me how at such times it would growl and bite their hands. Rocky retreats were its favourite habitat, and its principal food was said to be a little brown variety of wallaby common in Northern Queensland scrubs. Its flesh was not particularly appreciated by the blacks, and if they accidentally killed a yarri they gave it to their old women. In Western Queensland, I heard much about an animal which seemed to me to be identical with the *yarri* here described, and a specimen was once nearly shot by an officer of the black police in the regions I was now visiting."

Ion Llewellyn Idriess OBE (b. 1889 – d. 1979), an Australian author who spent much of his life in rural Queensland, claimed two separate encounters with a Queensland tiger near the Alice River. Idriess claimed: "Up here in York Peninsula we have a tiger-cat that stands as high as a hefty, medium-sized dog. His body is lithe and sleek and beautifully striped in black and grey. His pads are armed with lance-like claws of great tearing strength. His ears are sharp and pricked, and his head is shaped like that of a tiger. My introduction to this beauty was one day when I heard a series of snarls from the long buffalo grass skirting a swamp. On peering through the grass, I saw a full-grown kangaroo, backed up against a tree, the flesh of one leg torn clean from the bone. A streak of black and grey shot towards the 'roo's' throat, then seemed to twist in the air, and the kangaroo slid to earth with the entrails were literally torn out. In my surprise, I incautiously rustled the grass, and the great cat ceased the warm feast that he had promptly started upon, stood perfectly still over his victim, and for ten seconds returned my gaze for gaze. Then the skin wrinkled back from the nostrils, white fangs gleamed, and a low growl issued from his throat. I went backwards and lost no time in getting out of the entangling grass. The next brute I saw was dead, and beside him was my much-prized staghound, also dead. This dog had been trained from puppyhood in tackling wild boars, and his strength and courage were known by all the prospectors over the country. The cat had come fossicking round my camp on the Alice River."

It seems Idriess' account is taken verbatim from a story provided by D. H Lawrence (b. 1885 – d. 1930) in his 1923 novel *Kangaroo*, prompting cryptozoologist Michel Raynal to conclude that his two sightings were deliberate hoaxes. However, Malcolm Smith showed this wasn't the case and that it was actually Lawrence who took the story from Idriess, who originally published it in the periodical *Bulletin* on June 8th 1922, under a pseudonym. A Bullocky near Cardwell reported observing a "tiger" in 1864, and a large striped cat was apparently chased up a tree by the 13-year-old son of Cardwell police magistrate Brinsley G. Sheridan shortly before 1871. "One evening strolling along a path close to the shore of Rockingham Bay, a small terrier, my son's companion, took a scent up from a piece of scrub near the beach, and followed, barking furiously, towards the coast range westwards.

My boy (thirteen years of age, but an old bushman, who would put half those described in novels to the blush) followed and found in the long grass, about half a mile from the spot the scent was first taken up, an animal described by himself as follows: — 'It was lying camped in the long grass and was as big as a native Dog; its face was round like that of a Cat, it had a long tail, and its body was stripped from the ribs under the belly with yellow and black. My Dog flew at it, but it could throw him. When they were together, I fired my pistol at its head; the blood came. The animal then ran up a leaning tree, and the Dog barked at it. It then got savage and rushed down the tree at the Dog and then at me. I got frightened and came home. It was just dark when the boy came home in a high state of excitement and told me the story. From inquiry, I find that this is not the first time a similar animal has been seen in this neighbourhood. Tracks of a sort of tiger have been seen in Dalrymple's Gap by people camping there, and Mr. Reginald Uhr, now Police Magistrate at St. George, whilst one of the native mounted police officers in this district, saw the same animal my son describes.

The country is so sparsely populated, and the jungles (or, as we call them here, 'scrubs') so dense and so little known, that I have no doubt that animals of this kind exist in considerable numbers, the abundance of food and their timidity preventing our more intimate knowledge of their habits. I shall be most happy to send you, should it be my good fortune to drop across one of them, its skin and skeleton. I only regretted, as my poor boy did, that he had not my revolver, as he says he stood when it was fighting with the Dog, at less than a yard from the animal."

In 1926, another "tiger" was killed by dogs, and in 1930, G. de Tournoeur and P. B Scougall observed a Queensland tiger while riding horseback between the Fraser Coast Region and the Gympie Region. They "dismounted and were startled to find the cause to be a large animal of the cat tribe, standing about twenty yards away, astride of a very dead calf, glaring defiance at us, and emitting what I can only describe as a growling whine. As far as the gathering darkness and torrential rain allowed us to judge, he was nearly the size of a mastiff, of a dirty fawn colour, with a whitish belly, and broad blackish tiger stripes. The head was round, with rather prominent lynx-like ears, but unlike that feline, there was a tail reaching to the ground and large pads. We threw a couple of stones at him, which only made him crouch low, with ears laid flat, and emit a raspy snarl, vividly reminiscent of the African leopard's nocturnal 'wood-sawing' cry. Beasting an angry tattoo on the grass with his tail, he looked so ugly and ready for a spring that we felt a bit 'windy '; but on our making a rush and cracking our stockwhips he bounded away to the bend of the creek, where he turned back and growled at us."

A man by the name of Gamer reportedly encountered a large grey cat with dark-orange stripes while travelling through the bushlands close to Bidwell, Queensland in 1954. In 1969, Australian zoologist Gary Opit witnessed a large quoll-like creature with a marsupial-like walking gait along Brisbane's Gold Coast Highway. He was alone and had a good view of the animal. Furthermore, he claimed to have had multiple sightings north of Mount Tamborine. Gary's brother, John Opit, also reported an encounter with the elusive creature. John detailed his experience:

"At about 11 pm, as I travelled south through long stretches of darkened forest with very little other traffic, I observed a large carnivorous mammal suddenly cross the road directly in front of my vehicle. It emerged about 30 metres in front of the car on my side of the road (the left-hand or eastern side) and I saw its head, shaped something like a mastiff dog, protrude from the vegetation and watched it walk across the grassy road verge and onto the bitumen. I applied the brake not wanting to hit what at first, I thought must be a dog. Then I accelerated up to it when I realised that it was not a dog. It stood approximately 60 cm at the shoulders, had a body length of about 75 cm, and a tail of the same length.

The snout protruded from a round head with small, pricked ears. It had a powerfully built body covered in brindled somewhat thick fur with indistinct stripes appearing beneath the thinner black outer coat The fore and hind legs were about the same size, the rump and hind legs appeared reasonably powerful and what was distinctly noticeable was a marsupial-like waddling gait that particularly caught my attention. It reminded me of the gait of a brush-tailed possum only this animal was very much larger. Its robust form, muscled legs, and large feet indicated to me that it was adapted to terrestrial locomotion with a strong tree-climbing ability. It had a long straight thickly furred tail with six bands or stripes across it and the tail did not wag from side to side as it walked across the road. When my car closely approached the strange animal, it raised all the hairs on the tail, as a dog may raise its hackles when disturbed, as if it was attempting to make itself look larger. This very distinctive banded tail was the last I saw of the animal as it disappeared into thick vegetation on the western side of the road. At no time did it look at my closely approaching vehicle or increase its speed as it crossed the road."

In the 1970s, John questioned whether the animal he observed, which he said resembled a civet, was the same species as Ellis Troughton's "marsupial cat". Naturalist Janice Plunkett then collected over 100 eyewitness accounts of similar animals from Queensland during the period of 1970 to 1973. As previously noted, reports of Queensland tigers describe an increase in size beginning in the 1980s. Mike Jones observed a black-striped panther-sized animal consuming a dead calf in the mountains near Mareeba, Queensland, in 1983. Subsequently, Gary Opit received an account of a marsupial lion purportedly inhabiting the Billunudgel Nature Reserve circa 1985. Opit's informant "was driving along the coastal sandy four-wheel drive track (now closed to all but walkers, cyclists & national park vehicles) that runs just behind the beach at 2 P.M. returning home from a late night out when a black panther-like animal crossed the track right in front of his car. He described it as being very heavily built, like a bear crossed with a panther, and positive from its appearance that it could only be a marsupial lion which he had read about in a book on Australian prehistoric fauna, but which he didn't have much interest in. It scared him with its powerful, unconcerned attitude. It had a thickly furred curved tail. He drove on and seconds later an emu, perhaps being hunted by the animal, ran up from behind past the car, unusual for a diurnal bird, which further shocked him as he thought it was a big cat-like beast attacking his car."

According to Australian cryptozoologist Rex Gilroy, two fishermen, Jim Spriggs and Tony Banks, were camping near the Wenlock River on the Cape York Peninsula in November 1990 when, just before sunrise, they heard a nearby sound. Upon further investigation, they observed a grey creature with black stripes running away from them.

"Before the creature ran off into the trees, we both noticed it was a female with a reversed pouch, which was carrying a pup, said Jim to me later. Tony was walking down the track from their four-wheel drive vehicle later that morning when he found a number of strange, large paw impressions in the dirt, which he took to be those of the mystery animal. The creature we saw was rather thickset and would have been about 5ft [in] length from nose to tail tip. I think she stood about 1 ½ ft on all fours, and I think the tail looked a little bushy."

In 1995, a Goldsborough Valley resident named Mark "Wharfie" Camplon was relaxing on his veranda when his dog became alarmed by something moving about in the nearby brush. Hearing a deep guttural growl, he later stated: "...once you are here, away from civilisation and all the noise and lights, it's easy to believe that a creature could live for years away from the eyes of man. You could lose an army up here, let alone a family of cats or something similar. Especially if they were well adapted to the area."

In late September, the corpse of a female Queensland tiger was allegedly discovered beside the Bruce Highway roughly 12.5 miles south of Cardwell in the Cassowary Coast Region. It was described as the size of a small cattle dog (a "Queensland Heeler"), with a cat-like face, short pointed ears, robust hindquarters, and stripes on its torso from the spine down to its undersides. It had regularly spaced stripes on a dark tan background, with a small white tip on its tail. The dark brown hairs below the chest had black tips, forming four black stripes. Unfortunately, the remains were too damaged and decomposed for a conclusive identification and it is thought that no testing other than basic morphology was ever performed on the specimen.

On June 21ˢᵗ, 2002, a family driving through Gilderoy, Victoria reported seeing a large animal resembling a wombat near an abandoned logging camp. They were:

"Driving slowly with the Rangie's lights and spots on, one child commented that something was coming down the hill towards the road as he could see the undergrowth moving around. Thinking it might be a kangaroo or wombat I slowed down. The thing came off the hillside and got onto the road. My first thought was it looked like a quoll on steroids it was so big. It was uniformly dark in colour, about 80 cm at the shoulder and about 1.5m from nose to tail. The head had the same sort of stub nose, like a Tasmanian Devil (with the same sort of heavy jaws), and a long tail like a kangaroo which it seemed to use for balance or steering - (it didn't move about like a cat, it looked fairly rigid and slightly curved). The thing looked large and powerfully built, but it had a quite graceful (almost arrogant) stride to it. I stopped; it walked into the middle of the road (and our lights); turned and looked at us for perhaps 30 seconds and sauntered across to the other side where it went down into the gully. I drove to the spot, got out and took a mobile spot to the edge of the gully. The animal followed the creek for about 10-20m, crossed it and disappeared into the bush on the other side. My family and I looked for tracks but the road was pretty much covered with gravel and small rocks and so not much could be seen. However, the smell in the air where the thing had been pretty unspeakable – rotting flesh."

In March 2008, a resident of Singleton, New South Wales claimed to have observed an animal like a "giant quoll", which may have been the Queensland tiger. To further encourage eyewitnesses to come forward, an anonymous man known only as "Mike" offered a $1,000 reward for any person who could obtain a clear photo of the animal.

It is highly likely that, like most of Australia's terrestrial mammals except for a small number of bats and rodents, the Queensland "tiger", if it exists, is a marsupial. There are numerous reports depicting typical marsupial traits such as a stiff kangaroo-like tail, a wombat-like head and at times even having a pouch. Aboriginal knowledge of the *yarri* also supports the theory that the "tiger" is a marsupial. Some cryptozoologists hastily refer to this feliform cryptid as *Thylacoleo*, claiming it is a descendant of the Pleistocene marsupial lion (*Thylacoleo carnifex*) or a smaller unknown relative. Some Australian naturalists have suggested that the Queensland tiger could be a Dasyurid marsupial (the family containing quolls and the Tasmanian devil). In his book *Furred Animals of Australia* published in 1931, Ellis Troughton suggested that the "striped native cat" was a novel Dasyurid. Despite being sceptical, Darren Naish believes that Gary Opit's report and others like it were likely referring to an unknown flesh-eating marsupial. Due to its more recent extinction date, some cryptozoologists have suggested that the Queensland tiger is related to the mainland Thylacine (*Thylacinus cynocephalus*).

However, George Eberhart has noted that the distinctive tusk-like teeth, curved claws, and leopard-like vocalisations are not indicative of Thylacine biology. Additionally, many reports since 1980 are likely referring to big cats that have been illegally released or escaped from captivity. Reports of similar animals from southern Queensland's Gold Coast are commonly referred to as *Punchum*.

(Author's Verdict: 3/5)

Rungwe tiger

Tim Davenport, a British scientist affiliated with the *Wildlife Conservation Society*, was searching for the Kibunji or Highland Mangabey when he stumbled upon reports of an unidentified big cat referred to as the Rungwe tiger. While the existence of this animal is yet to be confirmed, it has sparked significant interest among wildlife experts. Davenport noted "It's some sort of striped animal, and we haven't come across anything more than the description. Whether it's a striped hyena or aardwolf way out of its range, or whether it's a spirit animal or a new species, we can't be sure. But finding these things is often the thing that gets us out of the tent in the morning". Further research is needed.

(Author's Verdict: 4/5)

Shanbiao

A Small Unidentified Tiger Species?

The *shanbiao* (Mandarin: "mountain biao") is said to be a big cat but is smaller and less robust than the South China tiger (*P. t. Tigris*); thought to have either a white or pale yellow coat reported from western Hubei Province and eastern Chongqing. On April 20th, 1996, farmers Qin Wanfu and Qin Wanjun from Xiliuxi Village in Changyang Tujia Autonomous County, allegedly killed a big cat with a yellowish-brown coat patterned with black oval spots. The animal was measured as having an overall body length of 1.48 meters (4.9 feet) and a tail length of 0.93 meters (3 feet). The shanbiao is some-times associated with the guoshanhuang, in which case, it is assumed to be the subadult form. Other theories suggest the existence of the fabled Biao; a possible subspecies of tiger; reports of tigers or leop-ards with unusual colouration, or hearsay.

(Author's Verdict: 3/5)

Tennessee Red Cheetah

A Large Muscular American Cheetah?

"Red Cheetahs" are sometimes reported from the forests and agricul-tural lands of Tennessee. They are described as having similar features to the common cheetah (*Acinonyx jubatus*) found in Africa and Asia. They are more powerful and built less for high-speed running than typical cheetahs, which prefer open grasslands. Once found across Asia, today cheetahs only survive in small isolated populations in Iran. The Tennessee Red Cheetah has a distinctive appearance, evident not only in its muscular build and bulldog-like facial features but also in its dark-spotted, golden pelage with vivid crimson fur running down its back. Traits such as these may give the "red cheetahs" an advantage over competitors such as grey wolves and coyotes. Tennessee Red Cheetahs are around five feet in length, comparatively tall, and around four feet at its broadest point at the shoulders reminding observers of a large and muscular cheetah. Cheetahs are quite adaptable and can inhabit multiple ecological systems, such as shrublands, grasslands, savannahs, and hot desert areas.

Tennessee has a temperate climate with average temperatures ranging from 40°F in winter to 83°F during summer months. The coldest month of the year is January, with an average low of 32°F and a high of 48°F. Therefore, the climate in Tennessee is suitable for cheetahs to survive. Habitat wouldn't be much of a problem either, as Tennessee is the most diverse inland state in the US. Its forests are populated by various mammalian species, such as porcupines, deer, rabbits, and black bears. Additionally, both the Hatchie and Wolf Rivers are crucial sources of drinking water and provide ideal habitats for fish, terrestrial animals, and plants. Thus, it can be concluded that Tennessee's robust ecology might facilitate the presence of cheetahs.

Despite its promising conditions, it is unlikely that Tennessee's habitats are capable of concealing the presence of such a sociable species whose intricate social systems, hunting habits, and nomadic or territorial ways of life would be easily recognisable. Cheetahs produce a range of vocalisations, such as chirping (or "stutter-barking") when they are feeling excited, such as when they have gathered around a fresh kill; yelping by mothers to locate lost cubs or by cubs to find their mothers and siblings, which can be heard up to two kilometres away; churring (or chortling); purring (like the purring of domestic cats but much louder), and threatening sounds such as coughing, growling, hissing, and yowling. To my knowledge, there are no reports from Tennessee that detail the diagnostic vocalisations and behaviours of cheetahs.

Karl Shuker reported on this feliform cryptid in his "Menagerie of Mystery" column in the Spring 98 issue of *Strange Magazine*. Bryan Long had also posted a note on AOL's Periscope website, *The Cryptozoology Zone*, where he mentioned that a small hunting party from Tennessee's Jackson County had shot a large and strange-looking cat in 1996. But fearing the possible consequences, they hid its remains in an undisclosed basement. According to Long, who had seen a photograph of the carcass, it resembled a cheetah but with a red stripe running from the back of its head to the tail. Furthermore, its head and paws were also red and its golden-brown body featured both black spots and stripes. The photograph once belonged to one of Long's colleagues who sold it to an unidentified biology student. Both the jaguar and jaguarundi have been considered as potential candidates, however, as Karl Shuker highlights, neither species truly fits with descriptions of the animal. One witness remembers a mother with two cubs emerging from a nearby thicket.

Consequently, they dashed across a field seemingly sensing danger, but sadly not fast enough. The farmer took aim at the adult and killed her on the spot. Without their mother to provide protection and nourishment, it is presumed that the cubs perished soon after. The farmer then skinned the dead female and used the remains to feed his pigs. Afterwards, he presented its pelt to his neighbours before displaying it publicly only to discover that it had been stolen a few days later. Some have speculated that reports of "red cheetahs" may actually be exaggerated accounts of peculiar-looking pumas; perhaps comparable to the *onza*. It is unlikely that the red colouration was simply dried blood. Could it be this cheetah-like feliform cryptid is an unrecognised living species of *Miracinonyx*, a subdivision of the sabretooth tiger believed to have gone extinct around 12,000 years ago? There may be undiscovered specimens that could be useful in determining the true identity of this feliform cryptid.

(Author's Verdict: 2/5)

Tigre dantero

A Small Surviving Sabre-Toothed Tiger?

The *tigre dantero* (Spanish: "tapir eating tiger"), also known as "*el wairarima,*" and Acavar Specimen is a striped cat-like predator with long tusk-like teeth reported from the high-altitude rainforests of Peru, Venezuela, Columbia, and Ecuador. In 2017, Bill Gibbons was informed by a resident of the Madre de Dios region of Peru named David Angel, that a large sabre-toothed cat with brown fur stalks the northern cloud forests. They are described as roughly the size and build of a jaguar and highly elusive and wary of human activity. A reported encounter with the creature in 1991 describes it as being about the size of a jaguar, with tawny fur, powerful forelimbs, and a short tail. Venezuelans say it hunts tapirs, leading to some confusion with the much larger *pamá-yawá* of Ecuador. Sometime before 1961, a French traveller named Picquet told naturalist and wilderness writer Peter Matthiessen (b. 1927 – d. 2014) of his encounter with a big cat in either Columbia or Ecuador. Despite not being able to specify the country, Matthiessen believed Picquet to be truthful but suspected he might have been mistaken about what he saw. In 1991, a Pemon hunter named Tirson Sosa reported a jaguar-sized cat with a short tail drinking from a pool of water near Venezuela's Carrao River. Sosa identified the animal as a *wairarima*, although this term can also refer to a different feliform cryptid and also a small but busy Venezuelan town in Aragua state.

Officially identified as a "mutant jaguar". Some theorise that the *tigre dantero* is a small variant of the sabre-toothed "tiger". If they are sabre-tooths, it is likely they descended from either *Smilodon* which ranged throughout much of South America, and *Homotherium venezuelensis*, which was found as far south as Venezuela and Uruguay. Bernard Heuvelmans speculated that the *tigre dantero* could potentially be a surviving descendant of the sabre-toothed *Thylacosmilus*, a metatherian mammal closely related to marsupials that lived in South America during the Late Miocene to Pliocene epochs before

Felidae arrived in South America. It is plausible that some reports may actually refer to another cryptozoological "cat" known as the Striped Jaguar, found in Peru; thus it could be a colour variation of the jaguar.

(Author's Verdict: 2/5)

Tigre de montagne

"Tiger of the Mountains"

With powerful jaws and prominent canine teeth, this mysterious feliform cryptid is known for its strength. Also called the "African tiger," the *tigre de montagne* (French: "mountain tiger") is said to be considerably larger than the standard lion (*Panthera leo*); estimated to be 1.5 meters tall at the shoulders with a red or reddish-brown coat and stripes sometimes reported. The regional names for some of the best-known examples reported from North-Central Africa are unknown, leading to the generic term *'tigre de montagne'* being used as a catch-all term for some of these feliform cryptids. African "tigers" are characterised by the long fur on their legs and paws, as well as either a short, hyena-like tail or no tail at all. According to the Yulu people, there is also a melanistic form. Reports suggest they are primarily nocturnal and inhabit caves in arid mountainous regions. They are formidable predators reported to take down large game species like antelope. A loud bellowing roar is sometimes heard and likened to that of an elephant.

A second category of amphibious, long-fanged feliform cryptids called "water lions", are reported from certain regions of Chad and the Central African Republic. However, since they occupy different habitats, it is plausible they constitute distinct species with their own unique ecologies and behaviours. Some labourers in the Acholi Hills, in the western ranges of the Immatong Mountains in what is now South Sudan, reported a large unknown cat-like creature:

"Some labourers [...] clearing firelines came to me with a tale of having seen a large animal, bigger than a lion and very broad. Its head was large, with a pointed muzzle, and a black mouth with long canine teeth. The general colour was brownish, with vertical yellowish-white stripes on its flanks. It left an elongated footprint, the size, and shape of that of a small boy, but with claws. The beast was quite unknown to them, and they were very scared about it."

Many cryptozoologists believe these "mountain tigers" belong to the subfamily Machairodontinae, commonly known as sabre-toothed cats. Furthermore, eyewitnesses have officially identified the animals they observed as "sabre-toothed cats" or "sabre-toothed tigers". Machairodonts were once common in Africa and the fossilised remains of several genera have been discovered in Chad. Heuvelmans speculated that a species of sabre-toothed cat could have evolved to become nocturnal and inhabit mountainous regions in order to avoid competition with lions, thus potentially occupying the ecological niche in Africa left vacant by bears. Some reports may be aberrant spotted hyenas as suggested by Major Anderson. A list of alleged 'tigres de montagne' includes coq-djinge: Massif des Bongos, Central African Republic; gassingram: Central African Republic; hadjel: Guera Massif, Chad; nisi: Tibesti Mountains, Chad; tigre de montagne: Ennedi Plateau, Chad; vassoko: Central African Republic; yassou: Ouaddai Highlands, Chad; "Imatong tiger": Imatong Mountains, South Sudan; and "cave lion": Mali.

(Author's Verdict: 3/5)

Yaguarú

A Giant Otter-like Cat?

The yaguarú, also known as 'yaguaro', is a feliform cryptid reported from Argentina and Paraguay, described as a "water lion" that kills cattle and horses by pulling them beneath the surface of lakes and rivers. Another giant otter-like cryptid with menacingly large canines, known as the *Iemisch*, has been reported from Patagonia; however, the relationship between the two is uncertain. The *yaguarú* (Guaraní: "water tiger", or alternatively "father of the dog") are described as donkey-sized carnivores with strong, stout legs with otter-like features, dark brown woolly fur, an elongated head, long canine teeth, erect ears, sharp claws, and a long, tapering tail. They are reported to inhabit deep waters at river confluences, where they live in hollows inside riverbanks.

According to Guaraní folklore, the *yaguarú* lives in deep caves. Strangely, they are sometimes described with five eyes. A Guaraní sculpture of the *yaguarú* depicts it with long fangs, a pointed nose, and erect ears, but without the long tail mentioned in other accounts. According to legend, a brave warrior named Guarán killed a *yaguarú*. Reports suggest they prey on human females and emit an unpleasant fishy odour. Thomas Falkner, an English Jesuit missionary and explorer, encountered a *yaguarú* during his travels along the Río Paraná in 1752.

He described his encounter in detail: "I shall here give an account of a strange amphibious animal, which is an inhabitant of the river Parana, a description of which has never reached Europe; nor is there even any mention made of it by those who have described this country. What I relate here is from the concurrent asseverations of the Indians, and of many Spaniards, who have been in various employments on this river: besides, I myself, during my residence on the banks of it, which was near four years, had once a transient view of one; so that there can be no doubt about the existence of such an animal. In my first voyage to cut timber, in the year 1752, up the Parana, being near the bank, the Indians shouted, "Yaquaru!" and looking, I saw a great animal, at the time it plunged into the water from the bank; but the time was too short to examine it with any degree of precision." And "It is called yaquaru, or yaquaruigh, which (in the language of that country) signifies the water tiger. It is described by the Indians to be as big as an ass, of the figure of a large overgrown river wolf or otter, with sharp talons and strong tusks, thick and short legs, long shaggy hair, with a long tapering tail." Adding that: "The Spaniards describe it somewhat differently: as having a long head, a sharp nose like that of a wolf, and stiff erect ears. This difference of description may come from its being rarely seen, and, when it is, disappearing suddenly. I look upon this last account as the most authentic, having received it from persons of credit, who assured me that they had seen this water tiger several times. It is always found near the river, lying on a bank, from whence, on hearing the least noise, it immediately plunges into the water [...] It is very destructive to the cattle which pass the Parana, for great herds of them pass every year; and it generally happens that this beast seizes some of them. When it has once laid hold of its prey, it is seen no more, and the lungs and entrails soon appear floating upon the water [...] It lives in the greatest depths, especially in the whirlpools made by the concurrence of two streams, and sleeps in the deep caverns that are in the banks."

George Chaworth Musters (b. 1841 – d. 1879), a British Royal Navy commander and explorer renowned as the "King of Patagonia", acquired reports from the nomadic Mapuche ("People of the Earth") regarding the mysterious "water tiger". Musters observed two ostrich carcasses floating in shallow water on the Senguer River in Argentina's Chubut province. Suggestions of cougar, jaguar, and maned wolf were dismissed; instead, Musters considered the possibility of the legendary yaguarú. Subsequent authors have linked this incident to the *iemisch*. Certain characteristics of the *yaguarú*, such as its large size, claws, and semi-aquatic lifestyle are similar to those of a jaguar. However, the presence of tusks and a woolly coat suggest otherwise. It is noteworthy that the Neotropical otter (*Lontra longicaudis*), also known as the "water tiger", possesses short powerful legs and a tapered tail. Karl Shuker offers an alternative theory, that the *yaguarú* might be living sabre-toothed cats adapted to aquatic habits, which he suggests is the only identity that accounts for all the features ascribed to it. Charles Bruce Chatwin (b. 1940 – d. 1989), who is renowned for his book *In Patagonia* (1977), suggested that the *yaguarú* might be a caiman. Other so-called "water tigers" include the *aypa*, *maipolina* and *entzaeia-yawá*.

(Author's Verdict: 2/5)

Yassou

A Surviving Homotherium?

In 1932, Lieutenant-Colonel André J. V. de Burth d'Annelet released a travelogue titled *A Travers l'Afrique Française...* ("Through French Africa"), in which he highlights a mysterious leopard-like big cat that had been reported from Chad's Ouaddaï district, referred to as *yassou*. The *yassou* (Nilo-Saharan) is a "tigre de montagne" reported to possess both feline and bear-like characteristics. Notably, its feet share a similarity to that of a bear – that is, they typically walk on the soles of their feet (plantigrade). On the other hand, cats are digitigrade, meaning they walk on their toes. There was, however, a species from Pliocene and Pleistocene Africa known to palaeontologists as *Homotherium*, or the scimitar cat, that officially went extinct around 1.5 million years ago. This species was at least partially plantigrade, leading to speculation that the *yassou* may be a surviving member of this species or a closely related species.

(Author's Verdict: 2/5)

Vassoko

A Horse-Sized Cat with Glowing Eyes?

Another "*tigre de montagne*," the *vassoko* (Fertit language) is reported from Birao in the Central African Republic's Vakaga Prefecture. According to M. H. R Maudry, Governor of the Birao Autonomous District, it is a large, horse-sized cat-like creature usually described with its head held at a low position, and small ears similar to those of a canine, and long sabre-teeth. The colour of its fur is uncertain, but similar to the *gassingrâm*, it is said to have phosphorescent eyes which "illuminate like lighthouses." Some sources claim that it has hairy legs which erase its footprints, while others connect this intriguing ability to its bushy tail. It remains unknown whether this supposed behaviour is a sign of intelligence and intent, or simply a byproduct of its singular physiology. This powerful predator is said to inhabit caves in the mountains, where it emits noises that resemble those of an elephant. Reports also suggest that it carries its prey on its back. According to most reports, it is accompanied by large swarms of butterflies. Maudry's informants included two Africans, one of whom was a poacher, who claimed to have observed the *vassoko* first-hand.

(Author's Verdict: 2/5)

Wanjilanko

A Sabre-Toothed Killer of Lions

The *wanjilanko* (Jola: Diola) reported from the Casamance Forest in South-West Senegal is generally described by eyewitnesses as a big, long-fanged "cat", sometimes associated with the *tigre de montagne*. Information regarding this feliform cryptid was initially communicated to Karl Shuker by naturalist Owen Burnham, who spent his childhood in Senegal. Owen recalled it was a nocturnal predator and was bigger than a lion. Its fur was adorned with green spots and stripes, and it had exceptionally long canine teeth. The *wanjilanko* is said to be aggressive and prey on lions. It inhabits the most isolated and wild parts of the forest, only appearing at night to hunt, while retreating into the dark depths of caves during daylight hours. The fauna of the forests of Senegal, particularly the Casamance region, has significantly decreased during the 21st century as a result of unsustainable deforestation, illegal hunting, and political instability. Owen Burnham discovered that while hunters in the area still recalled the *wanjilanko*, it seems to have disappeared along with its purported prey, the lion. If this animal truly existed, it is now probably extinct.

(Author's Verdict: 2/5)

Warrigal

A Blue Mountains Marsupial Lion?

Frequently associated with the marsupial lion (*Thylacoleo carnifex*), the *warrigal* (Gandangara) is a large, feliform cryptid reported from Australia's Blue Mountains, where it is also known as the Blue Mountain lion, Erskine Gap monster, Lithgow panther, Megalong monster, and Rock lion. L. A. Adams described three photographs of what he termed "warrigals", noting that the Blue Mountains "lion" spotted near Erskine Gap is a surviving *warrigal,* causing considerable debate among bush-walking circles. "It was widely accepted at the time that there existed a small group of large and shaggy wolf-like animals whose home was located between Breakfast Creek, Mouin Creek, and Cox's River. Since 1934, this area has been known as the Wild Dog Mountains on maps, and there have been many reports of sightings of "warrigals" in the area. In October 1937 a party reported having seen on White Dog Ridge "the decaying body of a huge animal like a dingo, but about 5 feet long." which had apparently fallen over a cliff known as Kelpie Rocks. In April 1945 a party descending the Korrowal Buttress of Mount Solitary watched through binoculars four "warrigals" loping across Cedar Valley. Cattle run half wild along central Cox's River and on two occasions in 1949, three months apart, I have come across the freshly killed and badly mutilated bodies of calves on the Cox's River near Konangaroo clearing. I have seen three photographs of "warrigals," but all were taken at so great a distance as to make them practically worthless for identification purposes."

Warrigals are characterised by their muscular, lion-like bodies, which typically measure between six and seven feet in length and three feet high at the shoulders. Its coat is composed of varying shades of brown fur, complemented by a long shaggy mane or ruff around its neck. Its most notable feature is its large protruding canine teeth, similar to those found on sabretooths. The *warrigal* left a series of tracks that were approximately five to six inches long and five inches wide, with an interval of 9.5 inches between them. In 1889, there was an abundance of reports of livestock being killed and eaten in Megalong Valley by an animal that had large, cat-like pawprints. In October 1937, a party reported having seen on White Dog Ridge "the decaying body of a huge animal like a dingo, but about 5 feet long" that had apparently fallen from a cliff known as Kelpie Rocks. In April 1945, a bush walking party travelling down Mount Solitary's Korrowal Buttress claimed to have seen four *warrigals* travelling across Cedar Valley. In 1955, Blue Mountains residents and police carried out an extensive search of bushland between Wentworth Falls and the Blaxland-Glenbrook area due to reports of a large creature with shaggy hair resembling a lion. A *warrigal* was reported again in 1972 from the Mulgoa district south of Penrith near Blue Mountain's eastern cliffs after it allegedly attacked and killed multiple sheep. In 1977, three hunters in the same region reported that they saw a *warrigal* that ran away after they shot at it. Rex Gilroy declared that he found fresh cat tracks in a nearby cave in Medlow Bath a year later. Campers near Hampton, located west of Katoomba stated seeing a *warrigal* in 1988. And in February 2001, two bushwalkers claimed to have seen a five-foot-long black creature perched on a tree limb eating a wallaby in Wollangambie.

It has been suggested that the *warrigal* are escaped lions or other big cats, but Karl Shuker is sceptical of this hypothesis because of the animal's long-standing history. Gilroy speculated that warrigals were living marsupials (*Thylacoleo carnifex*) with large upper canine teeth that are also thought to be the identity of the Queensland tiger. Karl Shuker noted that, if the *warrigal* is a marsupial lion, there must be two species, as the *warrigal* is decidedly different from the better-known Queensland tiger. A picture of a *warragal* sketched by Gilroy for a *Psychic Australian* article shows the animal with long sabre teeth.

(Author's Verdict: 2/5)

NEW LIONS, LEOPARDS AND/OR LION X LEOPARD HYBRIDS

Abasambo

A Spotted Lion?

Abyssinia presents the appearance of an elevated mountain plateau towering like an ancient citadel above the surrounding landscape. Here we find many distinctive species of wildlife, like the rare rusty red Abyssinian wolf, more commonly known as the Simien jackal or Simien fox, Menelik's bushbuck or *dukula*, and the mountain nyala. Yet based on traditions among the Habesha people, something more mysterious also inhabits the Abyssinian mountains – a big cat classified as a lion (*Panthera Leo*) but with rosettes and spots on its sandy coat. The *abasambo* (Afroasiatic) is said to be aggressive and to hunt in pairs. It was first recorded by Italian naturalist and explorer Orazio Antinori (b. 1811 – d. 1882) in a letter sent to fellow explorer Georg Schweinfurth shortly before his death in Ethiopia. In his letter, Antinori described the *abasambo* as: "An extremely ferocious carnivore, which, according to the information given by the natives, is a beast with light, short, erect hair, which is halfway between the lion and the leopard. If the information is correct, it will come, when it is well-known, to extend the list of felines in North Africa. When Captain Cecchi stayed at the camp of Degiac Imer, military governor of Gudru [south of the Blue Nile], he was on the spot when an abasambo, after digging a hole through the wall of a hut during the night, seized a young boy who slept by the door and sank his fangs into his flesh. Because of the shouting by the people, the animal fled, but the boy, who had had his chest torn, died a few hours later. The natives know and distinguish by particular names, the leopard, the cheetah, and the black leopard, which they call Ghissila. What, then, maybe this great species that, by its colour, size, and power, is set between the Lion and the Leopard?"

Possible explanations include lion x leopard hybrids, atypical specimens of lion and leopard, a distinct species or subspecies of lion
adapted to life in forested and mountainous habitats, or misidentifications of inadequately observed standard lions or leopards.

(Author's Verdict: 4/5)

American Maned Lions

North America

For many years, people in the United States, especially the eastern
states, are reporting sightings of maned lions. North America is home
to six native wild cat species, including two "big cats" the jaguar (the
only living American *Panthera*) and mountain lion, as well as smaller
cats like the ocelot, jaguarundi, bobcat, and Canada lynx, which are
all too small to be realistically mistaken for African lions. Jaguars
once roamed as far north as the Grand Canyon, but the northernmost
breeding population now resides in Sonora, Mexico, just south of the
Arizona border. In any case, the jaguar is famous for its rosettes,
which are not reported in sightings of American maned lions (AML
hereafter). The cougar does resemble a small African lioness, hence
its other name "mountain lion," although they lack the manes of true
African lions and do not otherwise match descriptions. They are also
known as California lions and *Lunkasoose* (in Maine) and have been
reported sporadically for over two centuries.

AML appear to have a vast geographic range from Arkansas (Dierks
& Dover); California (El Toro, Fremont, Lake County); Florida (Loxa-
hatchee); Georgia (Alapaha, Berrien County); Illinois (Centralia,
Decatur, Joliet, Peoria County, Piatt County, Rockford, Roscoe, Will
County, Winnebago County), Indiana (Abington, Elkhorn Falls,
Warrick County); Iowa (Muscatine, Wapello); Maine (Penobscot
County); Missouri (Cross Timbers); Nebraska (Ceresco, Surprise,
Waterloo); Canada (New Brunswick: Gagetown, McAdam. Ontario;
New Jersey (North Brunswick), North Carolina (Rutherfordton), Ohio

(Clinton County, Dodson Township, Geauga County, Groesbeck, Hillsboro, Lorain County, Mentor, Miami Township, Morning Sun, North Avondale, North Olmsted, Springboro); Oklahoma (Craig County, Rogers County, Vinta), Pennsylvania (Bald Eagle Mountain, Clinton County, Jackson, Lackawanna County, Newton Township, Nicholson, Pike County, Susquehanna County, Wyoming County), Texas (Fort Worth); Washington (Spokane, Tacoma); and West Virginia (Marlinton). They are typically characterised as mature male lions, measuring five to eight feet in length and three feet tall at the shoulders. They have shaggy fur that has been described as tan or brown, with powerful acromiotrapezius and triceps muscles, and a long tail with a tufted tip. Although spots are rarely reported, some have described striped or partially striped specimens.

It is not uncommon for AML to be seen travelling in pairs; oddly enough sometimes alongside large black animals believed by some to be melanistic eastern cougars. They are said to roar loudly which would be a physiological impossibility for a cougar. Lacking a flexible hyoid bone, cougars are unable to truly roar. AMLs are said to prey on domestic animals like pigs, chickens, colts, lambs, dogs, and cats. In 1797, pioneer Peter Pentz killed an unknown cat-like animal with a shaggy, brownish-yellow mane while delivering an urgent message to the settlers in Center County, Pennsylvania. Allegedly, Pentz shot the animal in a cave on Bald Eagle Mountain, though there is no evidence that its remains were presented for scientific examination. In 1868 a similar lion-like animal was killed by hunter Archie McMath near Lake County, California after it had terrorised the region. Its forequarters were stockier than its rump and it had black stripes running along its shoulders and back as well as down its front. Its fur was denser and darker around the neck, giving it an effect resembling a mane. The animal's length was estimated at around 11 feet, and it had black stripes along its shoulders.

AMLs were sighted from various parts of North Carolina in the late 19th century. Reports described its overall length to be around 11 feet and to weigh over 140 kilograms (300 lbs). Whatever it was reports ceased after the 1890s. In August 1948, an AML was seen alongside an animal resembling a big black cat near Elkhorn Falls, Indiana. They seemed to migrate eastward into Ohio, as sightings ceased in Indiana around that time. Nebraska has its own noteworthy reports regarding this alleged animal. In November 1951, locals recalled an unsuccessful lion hunt around the village of Ceresco, and on August 1st, 1954, farmer Arnold Neujahr observed what seemed to be an African lion with a densely furred mane two miles west of the hamlet of Surprise in southwestern Butler County.

In June 1960, Leo Paul Dallaire observed what appeared to be an African lion on his farm near Kapuskasing, Ontario. He described it as a big maned cat with light tan colouring and a four-foot tail with a tufted tip. This event might be related to other incidents that have taken place in Butler County in the vicinity of Rising City involving animals of a similar description. On November 10th, 1979, several residents of Fremont, California reported a large lion-like animal in the Coyote Hills Regional Park. Officer William Fontes observed a similar animal in the Alameda County flood channel and estimated it to weigh between 136 and 181 kg (300 – 400 lbs). On July 30th, 1986, Cindy Belmont and her brother observed a beige tiger-like animal with a long tail near Jackson, Pennsylvania, which was accompanied by an animal resembling a large Border Collie. In June 1992, Ohio police received multiple reports of a seven-foot-long, cat-like animal with a mane. Witnesses claimed it was an African lion, but police believed it was a large Golden Retriever.

On June 5th, 1996, Helen Grabb witnessed a similar creature while driving on Canyon Drive near Spokane, Washington. She stopped her car just feet away from the creature and noticed its dark tan fur and long brown mane. The report prompted a two-day search that did not result in success. A record number of AML sightings were reported in 2002. In Niles, Michigan, the Young family observed an unusually large cream-coloured cat with a long tail roaming their property. Reports of similar sightings began to proliferate; but no lion was ever found. In September, four maned lions were allegedly shot dead near Quitman, Arkansas. However, again, no DNA analysis was performed. Speculation arose linking them to animals that had escaped from a local safari park; nevertheless, this was officially denied by park representatives who confirmed that none of their animals were missing. During the same month, Troy Guy and Ashley Clawson reported an AML while driving down Poga Road in Carter County, Tennessee. Additionally, Evelyn Cable claimed to have seen an animal resembling a lion with a thick mane on Highway 321.

In July 2008, multiple observers in El Paso County, Colorado, near Colourado Springs witnessed an animal with a red mane and long tail; one of them even managed to capture it on camera chasing a dog. Sharon Harding Shaw provided two additional mobile-phone pictures as well as tracks as evidence, which established that the animal was not a cougar. The nearby *Serenity Springs and Cheyenne Mountain Zoo* declared that none of their big cats had escaped. A formal investigation was conducted; however, no big cats were found. In 2015, an AML was reported across the city. It began on July 20th when various people reported that they had seen it roaming in their area. Over the subsequent weeks, other citizens, as well as police personnel, encountered the animal. Herbert Ball recounted his own sighting, stating that, "she was walking down the hill sideways, putting her feet crossways. She was snooping down with her head like she was fixing to attack somebody. The people over there were having a cookout ... and I ran over there to tell them there was a cat coming their way. But what the cat did is change her mind — she went under the bridge and relaxed."

This report prompted a substantial police response, with officers initiating an ambush at a bridge overlooking a ravine and deploying snipers to neutralize the potentially dangerous predator. Two of the officers reported seeing a big cat, however, it abruptly fled into dense vegetation.

The primary explanation for AML reports is escaped African lions (*Panthera leo*) from nearby zoos. Such occurrences have been noted, and some could have been unreported by private proprietors, despite the fact that this likely wouldn't explain 200+ years of reports over such a vast geographic region. AMLs are sometimes described with stripes. A theory is mass misidentifications of a domestic dog breed. Karl Shuker has highlighted that both the Chow Chow and the Brittany Spaniel have been put forward as potential explanations by experts. In addition to size, the bear-like Newfoundland dogs, initially bred and employed as working dogs by fishermen, may also provide a comparable match. Loren Coleman and Mark A. Hall suggested an intriguing possibility – that some American lions (*Panthera atrox*) may still survive. Pleistocene fossils of this species have been unearthed from Alaska to Peru. Male specimens were larger than African lions, boasting longer limbs and shorter muzzles with greater jaw strength. Coleman and Hall theorised that female *P. atrox* might be responsible for sightings of eastern cougars with melanistic fur.

(Author's Verdict: 2/5)

Peruvian Jungle Lions

South America

Reports of a lion-sized, reddish-brown animal with a short mane or ruff around the neck have been documented from Peru's Yanachaga Mountains and National Park. Cryptozoologist Peter Hocking initially found these accounts to be interesting but largely dismissed them until he received a detailed report from a professional ranger at *Yanachaga National Park* and heard of an account involving a dead specimen. 'This cryptid is reported to be large, the size of an African Lion, With long hair around its neck, but shorter than that of the African lion. Its colour is said to be entirely reddish-brown. Rangers have reported seeing this felid in the park, and one of my native helpers claimed to have once examined a dead specimen killed outside the Park, near Shiringamazu'.

In his writings, Karl Shuker has suggested that South American "jungle lions" may be a large species of brown-furred, maned felid that has yet to be identified and described by science.

(Author's Verdict: 3/5)

Black Lion

Melanistic Lions?

As the name implies, "black lions" are said to be members of the species Panthera leo that are either completely or partially black in colour. Several sightings of dark-hued lions have been reported over the years, mainly from South Africa's *Kruger National Park* and the Iranian Zagros Mountains of West Asia; however, none has ever been confirmed as truly melanistic. In *The Travels of Marco Polo*, Book 3, Chapter 22, written by Rustichello da Pisa recounting the Italian explorer Marco Polo's travels through Asia between 1271 and 1295, it is claimed there were black lions with "no mixture of any other colour". During the late 1800s, the renowned English archaeologist Sir Henry Layard excavated Nimrud and Nineveh and while doing so discovered a majority of the known Assyrian palace reliefs. It was in Nineveh where he learned that a very dark lion had been killed by soldiers of the Luristan regiment. In 1940, W. L. Speight claimed that an experienced game warden he knew had seen an entire pride of black lions in *Kruger National Park*. In 1963, June Kay (June Vendall Clark) published her book *Okavango* wherein she reported observing a black lioness at close range. C. A. W. Guggisberg, the then-authority on African lions and author of *Wild Cats of the World* (1975), corresponded with Loren Coleman regarding claims of black lion cubs sighted in western Tanzania in 1980. Their existence was never confirmed.

The late George Adamson, famously known as the "Father of Lions" and depicted in the 1966 film Born Free and its accompanying best-selling book of the same name, mentioned an almost black lion in his

1986 autobiography *My Pride and Joy*. This lion was reported in Tanzania, a nation that Adamson, a Kenyan wildlife conservationist, devoted much of his life to protecting. Sadly, George Adamson died tragically in 1989 at the age of 83 while attempting to rescue his assistant and a young European tourist from Somali bandits in *Kora National Park*.

Reports of black lions may be sightings of standard lions that have rolled in thick, dark mud as a way of cooling themselves; however, there may be genuine cases of melanistic lions. Melanism is a mutation found in several wild cats, including leopards, jaguars (both known as "black panthers"), servals, clouded leopards, bobcats (but surprisingly not the other lynxes), and Temminck's golden cat. Hence, a melanistic lion would be surprising but entirely possible. Lions with unusually thick, almost black manes have also been observed and documented.

(Author's Verdict: 3/5)

Buffalo Lions and the Notorious Tsavo Maneaters

Large, Mane-less, Man-Eating Lions

'*The camps of the workmen had also been surrounded by thorn fences; nevertheless, the lions managed to jump over or to break through someone or other of these, and regularly every few nights a man was carried off, the reports of the disappearance of this or that workman coming into me with painful frequency.*' John Henry Patterson.

They are perhaps the world's most notorious wild lions. In March 1898, the construction of a railway bridge over the Tsavo River in Kenya was delayed by two maneless male lions that had inexplicably developed a taste for human flesh, resulting in a nine-month reign of terror. The unnerved labourers tried in vain to frighten the maneaters away, forcing people to flee the area and halting the construction of the bridge. Lt. Col. John Henry Patterson, the civil engineer responsible for the costly project, eventually stepped in and shot the Tsavo lions in December 1898, subsequently allowing the railroad to be finished a few months later. Patterson turned the lions into trophy rugs from his hunt, and they remained demeaned floor ornaments until 1925 when he sold them for $5,000 to the *Field Museum* in Chicago.

The museum's taxidermist-in-residence then restored the lions to their former glory by mounting them as taxidermy specimens and displaying them in a diorama. Colonel Patterson later told the story of the killer lions of Tsavo and the hunt that eventually ended their bloody reign of terror, in his 1907 book *The Man-Eaters of Tsavo and Other East African Adventures*. Colonel Patterson initially stated that the pair had killed 135 railway workers and indigenous Africans, however, later research determined the number to be closer to 35, which is still a terrifying amount of bloodshed. The Tsavo lions had an overall length of 9 feet and 8 inches, with an estimated weight of 181 kg (400 lbs). In 1991, a man-eating lion of extraordinary size – thought to be one of the largest ever recorded – was killed in the Luangwa River Valley in Zambia.

This lion was over three metres (10 feet) in length and weighed around 230 km (500 lbs). Reports indicate that it had killed and eaten six people near Mfuwe, the most populated settlement within the valley. Since 1998, the specimen has been on display at the *Field Museum* in Chicago, along with the infamous Tsavo lions. In Zambia's *South Luangwa National Park*, lions with these characteristics and behaviours are commonly referred to as "river lions" or "buffalo lions". Apart from the notorious Tsavo attacks by a pair of male lions, buffalo lions tend to be solitary animals and very aggressive, often including humans in their diet. They are known to prey on large animals, particularly buffaloes, thus giving them their name. In 1998, a pair of mane-less lions were photographed in *Tsavo National Park* after successfully bringing down an adult buffalo.

Possible explanations include hormonal imbalances or genetic defects, the possibility of a new subspecies of African lion, or even

C. P. MARSHALL

that they may represent a new species altogether. A more plausible suggestion is that these lions are the result of "unnatural selection" wherein big-game hunters target lions with thickly furred manes leaving the maneless individuals to proliferate. Some have speculated that these maneless lions may be descendants of the Middle Pleistocene cave lions (*Panthera leo spelaea*), albeit smaller in size. Ultimately, 13,000 years is not a long time from an evolutionary standpoint. The biggest mystery is why the Tsavo lions developed such an insatiable appetite for humans in the first place. Was it food scarcity resulting in desperation? A learned behaviour made after feasting on the remains of conveniently, already-dead railway workers? Or was it the painful effects of dental injury? Researchers Bruce Patterson and Larisa DeSantis of *Vanderbilt University* used advanced techniques and discovered that the wear patterns on their teeth mirrored those of zoo lions which consume soft foods and do not crack open bones for marrow. Previous X-ray imaging of the lion's remains revealed that they had substantial dental problems, including a root-tip abscess in one of the canines. Researchers now suspect that the lions of Tsavo, as well as the Mfuwe lion, switched to hunting humans for practical reasons: to put it bluntly, they were easier to catch and chew.

(Status: Identified)

Bung-bung

Another Lion x Leopard Hybrid?

Described as a large spotted lion-like carnivore from Africa's Cameroon, the *bung-bung* (Nilo-Saharan) is thought by some to be a lion-leopard hybrid, with grey fur patterned with dark spots as well as a beard or ruff on the lower jaw. Other possibilities include misidentifications of other species and hearsay. Other forest lions found in Africa include the *bakanga, ikimizi, foulempou, marozi, ruturargo, uruturangwe,* and *ruturango.*

(Author's Verdict: 3/5)

Chakpuar

A Long-Necked Lion?

The *chakpuar* (French Senegalese) reported from Senegal in West Africa, is described as a red, long-necked lion similar to the Sudanese *abu sotan*. The concept of long-necked cats is not new in Africa; ancient Egyptian and Mesopotamian artwork featured serpents with cat-like bodies – thought to be either lions or leopards. No ancient texts contain a name for this creature, but modern references to it use the term "serpopard" as a portmanteau. But whether there is any link between the *chakpuar*, and the long-necked cats depicted in ancient Egyptian and Mesopotamian artworks remains to be seen.

(Author's Verdict: 2/5)

Damasia

A Unique Unknown Colour Variant of the Leopard?

Scientific Name: *Panthera pardus var. melanostica*, based on the Grahamstown specimen.

The *damasia* (Gikuyu: Bantu) reportedly inhabits the Aberdare High-lands of central Kenya where it is typically described as a dark patterned leopard, believed by the Gikuyu people in the northern highlands to be distinct from the usual black variety. It was originally alluded to in a letter sent to *The Field* by hunter G. Hamilton-Snow-ball, published on October 9th, 1948. In his letter, he primarily discusses spotted lions, but he also mentioned that during the 1920s, he had shot a big cat that he initially thought was a leopard, albeit a large, darkly coloured specimen. Yet, when he showed his Agikuyu porters, they were emphatic that the animal he killed was not a '*chui*' (their name for the leopard) but a '*damasia*'. They believed, that just as the *marozi* is distinct from the lion (*simba*), the *damasia* is different from the leopard.

The *damasia* has long been known to the Agikuyu people of the Aberdare's, but according to tradition, when seen by outsiders, they are typically mistaken for leopards. The Aberdare mountains are already home to one cryptozoological cat, the spotted "*marozi*", it is, therefore, conceivable that this region with an average elevation of 3,500 metres (11,480 ft) may have a few zoological revelations left in store to upend the applecart of scientific orthodoxy. It should be noted that many native tribes in tropical Africa will classify animals as distinct if they exhibit different sizes or colours from the usual specimens of the same species, or if they are seen as more dangerous to humans. As such, the *damasia* may be a unique, unknown colour variant of the leopard.

(See *Dark Leopards, Grahamstown Mystery Cat, Ndalawo,* and *Kibambangwe*)

(Author's Verdict: 4/5)

Dark leopards (Unidentified)

"Shadow Leopards"

Scientific Name: *Panthera pardus* var. *melanotica*, based on the Grahamstown specimen.

As the name suggests, like the *damasia* these are generally regarded to be dark leopards but with distinct coat patterns from the normal solid black variety. Dark leopards are said to inhabit the eastern Cape Province, South Africa; Aberdare Highlands, Kenya; Bufumbira County, south-west Uganda, and the Virunga Mountains region of Rwanda (similar animals are also reported from Hong Kong, China; Kerala State, India; and Bali, Indonesia).

Pseudo-melanism is extremely rare in leopards but a few specimens with this mutation are known. Specimens have excessive markings that have merged into an unbroken expanse of black pigment. In some specimens, the area extends down the flanks and limbs; only a few lateral wisps of golden brown indicate the normal background colour. Any spots on the flanks and limbs that have not merged into the mass of swirls and stripes are unusually small. As pseudo-melanism is not well understood and local folklore often classifies unusual individuals as belonging to different species, it can be challenging to make determinations regarding these animals. It is possible they represent an unidentified colour variant of the leopard. (See *Damasia, Kibambangwe,* and *Ndalawo*)

(Author's Verdict: 4/5)

Grahamstown Mystery Cats

Only Known from Two Specimens Killed Near Grahamstown, South Africa

Scientific Name: *Felis leopardus [Panthera pardus]* var. *melanotica.*

In the early 1880s, Mr. F. Bowker killed the first Grahamstown mystery cat approximately forty miles northeast of Makhanda (formerly known as Grahamstown) in South Africa's Eastern Cape Province. Intrigued by its singular appearance, Bowker sent its tanned skin to Dr. Albert Günther (b. 1830 – d. 1914), keeper of Zoology at the *Natural History Museum* in London, England. The specimen's distinctive features included an absence of rosettes and a mass of small individual spots that merged into a solid black expanse from the back of the head to the base of the tail. A chromolithograph based on the specimen depicted a dark area running down the dorsal surface of the tail. The base colour is tawny, which brightened to a deep orange on its shoulders. Initially, Günther believed that the Bowker specimen was a wild-born leopard-lioness hybrid; however, on March 3rd, 1885, in the *Proceedings of the Zoological Society of London*, he concluded that due to certain noteworthy characteristics and its already noted leopard-like features that it was actually a pseudo-melanistic leopard. In 1886, Günther obtained a second pseudo-melanistic skin from a specimen killed in Collingham, which was around 25 miles from the previous specimen. The accompanying note provided information about this particular skin and Günther documented it in the *PZSL* on April 6th that year. Seven other less pronounced pseudo-melanistic specimens have been recorded, including two pelts and sightings of two living specimens found only in South Africa's Eastern Cape Province. Since the opening decade of the 20th century, there have been no further reports regarding these colour morphs. Günther named this variety *Felis leopardus* var. *melanotica* and they have since become known as 'melanotic leopards'. Both specimens have white underparts with large black spots, and heads patterned similar to a leopard. They measured 6 feet 7 inches in length and had a 2.5-foot tail. Despite being widely considered hybrids, the Grahamstown mystery cats appear to be pseudo-melanistic leopards. (See *Damasia*)

(Author's Verdict: 3/5)

Green Leopards

Green Around the Whiskers

In 1986, Bernard Heuvelmans published his "Annotated Checklist of Cryptozoological Animals" in the ISC journal *Cryptozoology* which briefly mentioned reports of green leopards in Africa. Heuvelmans' reference was one of his own books. Following Heuvelman's passing in 2007, this important and much-delayed work was finally released with no reference to any green leopards. Upon discovering this, Karl Shuker contacted French cryptozoologist Michel Raynal, a longstanding correspondent of Heuvelmans, to solicit his opinion on Heuvelmans' error. Raynal confirmed in his June 22nd, 2011, reply that Heuvelmans had indeed been mistaken and verified there was no mention of green leopards in his book. Subsequently, the origin of this remarkable claim remains obscure. Dr. Shuker suspects that the answer to the mystery of the green leopards may actually be a simple one; Heuvelmans had simply misremembered a short note from Guggisberg's 1961 book *Simba: The Life of the Lion*, confusing lion with leopard and unintentionally creating a cryptid that never actually existed. This type of mistake is not uncommon and has served as the source for other lesser-known cryptozoological animal forms.

(Author's Verdict: 1/5)

Green Lion

Lions of Green Should Never be Seen

As previously documented, C. A. W Guggisberg's book *Simba: The Life of the Lion,* and Dr. Karl Shuker's *Mystery Cats of the World...* both make reference to a purported "green lion" seen only once by a prospector in western Uganda. Mammal hair has only two kinds of pigment: one that produces black or brown hair and one that produces yellow or reddish-orange hair. Mixing those two pigments is never going to yield a bright green. Thus, Karl Shuker theorises that it may have been a standard lion coated in green slime from a stagnant, algae-choked pond.

(Author's Verdict: 2/5)

Marozi

The Archetypal Spotted Lion of Africa

Scientific Name: *Panthera leo maculatus* (Heuvelmans, 1955).

Commonly referred to in the cryptozoological literature as a "spotted lion," the *marozi* is reported primarily from Eastern Africa's mountainous regions, particularly the Aberdare Range in Kenya. The Bantu word "marozi" translates to "solitary lion" and denotes an animal roughly 1.7 meters (5.58 feet) in length. It is worth noting that some of the largest recorded leopards are equal to or even larger than this size. In 1913, an Algerian leopard was reported to have measured 2.69 meters (8.83 feet) before being skinned. The *marozi* is known for its tawny fur with greyish-brown spots or rosettes on its back, sides, and limbs; a pair of *marozi* skins kept at London's *Natural History Museum* provide evidence of this characteristic feature, with each rosette measuring between 5.08 cm and 7.62 cm in diameter.

The *marozi* is commonly believed to be a subspecies of lion (*Panthera leo*) that has adapted to the shaded forest habitat. As is typical of most felids, they have fully retractable claws and a tail length of 84 cm, with an overall height between 90 and 105 cm and weighing between 100 to 180 kg. Footprints attributed to *marozis* have been observed as having cat-like qualities, being smaller than those of full-grown lions, but larger than those of leopards. Other names by which they are known include *ntararago* (Kenya), *ikimizi* (Rwanda), and *abasambo* (Ethiopia). *Marozis* usually travel together in pairs or small prides rather than alone. The *marozi* is claimed by zoologists and cryptozo-ologists to be either a unique race of lion adapted for montane rather than savanna-dwelling habitat, a rare wild hybrid between leopard and lion, or an adult lion that has retained its juvenile spots. Natural-ist, A. Blayney Percival (b. 1875 – d. 1941) killed a spotted lioness and her cubs in Kenya in 1924.

While Africans have known these animals since time immemorial, the first documented encounter by a European occurred in 1931, when a farmer named Michael Trent shot and killed two specimens, a male and a female, at an elevation of 3,000 metres that had been raiding his farm in the Aberdare Mountains. He preserved their skins but not the infinitely more important skulls or skeletons. In 1931, R. E. Dent, a game warden in Kenya, observed four large spotted lions at an alti-tude of 10,000 – 11,000 feet on Mount Kenya. Shortly after, his trap-pers reported what appeared to be a hybrid between a lion and a leopard in the Aberdare's which they then released. G. Hamilton-Snowball also encountered two more spotted lions on the Kinangop Plateau at an elevation of 3,500 m (11,500 ft). However, when they were shot at, the marozis quickly fled the area, apparently unharmed.

In 1935, Kenneth Gandar Dower led an expedition to the Kenyan highlands hoping to discover this unique variety of lion but he only found tracks near 12,500 feet. Although some sources claim that *marozis* are a hybrid of a lion and hyena, this is highly improbable given that these two species have vastly different DNA and are natural rivals. It is more likely that *marozis* constitute an unrecognized subspecies or an emergent species adapted to mountainous rather than savannah habitats, evidenced by their spotted coat, smaller body size, and lack of thick manes in adult males, which could be beneficial traits for forested areas. It has also been speculated they are natural wild-born hybrids between lions and leopards, which would likely render them infertile if true. The most likely explanation is that *marozis* are specimens of *P. leo* with an unusual genetic anomaly that allows them to maintain their juvenile spots into adulthood.

(Author's Verdict: 4/5)

Mayanja Monster

A Spotted Lion, Giant Cheetah, or Something Else Entirely?

In early 1974, the people of the Mayanja-Kibuke district of Kenya were living in fear of a strange tiger-headed, rosetted, cat-like creature described by some as a giant cheetah. Reports indicate that it had been devouring local animals and evading hunting parties attempting to kill it. Leopards are very rare in the region and there had not been a confirmed lion sighting for more than 25 years. However, given its reported behaviour, a surviving leopard population is the most probable explanation.

(Author's Verdict: 2/5)

Mint Leaf Leopard

A New Clouded Leopard?

Reported from China, the "mint leaf leopard" is a large feliform cryptid described with lanceolate markings resembling mint leaves. Reports may be mistaken observations of clouded leopards (*Neofelis nebulosa)* roaming south of the Yangtze River, or an unknown, closely related variety. The mint leaf leopard's present status is unknown.

(Author's Verdict: 3/5)

Mngwa

What was the "Strange One"?

Sometimes said to purr instead of roaring, the *mngwa* (Swahili "strange one") also known as *"nunda"* (a Swahili word with several meanings, such as *"fierce animal," "cruel man,"* or *"something heavy"*) is described as a large grey, man-eating carnivore reported from Tanzania's coastal forests, part of the ecologically significant Eastern African Coastal Forests Ecoregion. *Mngwas* are as big as the biggest lions and possess grey fur with brindled tabby-like markings.

According to reports, it poses a considerable risk to humans and domestic animals. Pawprints, believed to be from a *mngwa*, have been discovered that were similar in size to those of a lion but resembled those of a leopard. Patrick Bowden and another game hunter visited a village where it was rumoured that a *mngwa* had grabbed a small child; they proceeded to pursue the tracks into a nearby forest but discovered no other sign of its presence. Upon further examination of the tracks, Bowden concluded that they were not from a lion but rather what seemed to be an immense leopard. Fur collected from stakes on which the *mngwa* allegedly broke into a kraal, showed morphological differences when compared with leopard hair.

In 1922, a series of suspected *mngwa* attacks were reported in Lindi, south-eastern Tanzania (then called Tanganyika). At the time, Captain William Hichens (died October 2nd, 1944) was serving as Native Magistrate in the coastal village. Hichens recalled: "It was the custom for native traders to leave their belongings in the village market every night, ready for the morning's trade; and to prevent theft and [...] to stop stray natives sleeping in the marketplace, an askari or native constable took it in turns with two others to guard the market on a four-hour watch. Going to relieve the midnight watch, an oncoming native constable one night found his comrade missing.

After a search, he discovered him, terribly mutilated, underneath a stall. The man ran to his European officer, who went with me at once to the market. We found it obvious that the askari had been attacked and killed by some animal – a lion, it seemed. In the victim's hand was clenched a matted mass of greyish hair, such as would come out of a lion's mane was it grasped and torn in a violent fight. But in many years no lion had been known to come into the town."

Captain Hichens was met the following morning by an Arab governor of the district along with two frightened-looking native men. The men had been "out late the previous night, they said, they had slunk by the marketplace lest the askari should see them and think them evildoers; and as they crept by, they were horrified to see a gigantic brindled cat, the great mysterious *nunda*, which is feared in every village on the coast, leap from the shadows of the market and bear the policeman to the ground."

The Arab governor described the animal to Hichens, recounting that this wasn't the first time that the village of Lindi had been gripped in fear by the *mngwa*. That night Hichens kept watch with two armed police officers, but alas, nothing happened. Hichens expressed his dissatisfaction and embarrassment during the following day's parade by delivering a discourse to the native constables about the foolish-ness of superstitions. He bitterly regretted his words when another constable was viciously attacked and killed that very night, with the presumed perpetrator being the *mngwa*. In the victim's hands were clasped tufts of grey tangled fur. Hichens sent a sample for testing but received the disappointing response: "Probably cat". Over the following month, more attacks occurred at other small coastal villages and several people arrived at Lindi to inform Hichens that "a huge grey-striped animal like a cat, but as big as a donkey, was seizing men by night."

Armed police officers were stationed in the area and traps and poison were laid, but the animal always seemed to be one step ahead of them. As quickly as the attacks started, they suddenly stopped. However, in the 1930s, another series of predations occurred in Hichens' district. To try and get a better understanding of what had happened, Hichens invited an old native hunter to Mchinga (a small Tanganyika coastal village) who was thought to have survived an attack by the *mngwa*. "Not long ago a man was brought to me at Mchinga, on a litter and terribly mauled by some great beast. He said it was a *mngwa*, and as he himself was a brave and skilful native hunter, who had often tracked down lions, leopards, and other "killers" with me and other white men, why should we suppose that in this case, he mistook a lion or a leopard for some other beast? He had nothing to gain by telling me lies; on the contrary, as a hunter, he depended for his livelihood on being absolutely truthful and trustworthy."

The *mngwa's* tracks, fur, and size, being different from those of lions and leopards make it a likely case of mistaken identity. Karl Shuker has speculated that it could have been an abnormally large leopard, while Heuvelmans suggested an undiscovered species of African golden cat. This species is known to exhibit a wide variety of coat patterns and colours, with some displaying spots ranging from tan to black and others having spots visible exclusively on their bellies or inner legs. Although small in size, the African golden cat inspires fear throughout its range for its rumoured ferocity.

Additionally, some reports state that the *mngwa* never roars, but instead purrs like a moggie. As we have seen, big cats don't purr as the small cats do, and purring and roaring are mutually exclusive, so lions, tigers, true leopards, and jaguars are all incapable of truly purring, while every other cat can purr, but not roar. The throat structure of the African golden cat means that, like the cougar, it purrs instead of roaring. It has been suggested that the *mngwa* attacks during this time may have been perpetrated by human assailants; Mel and Fiona Sunquist wondered whether groups of Tanganyikan witch doctors, known as mjobo or "lion men," were responsible for these events. Karl Shuker rightly pointed out that a mjobo could have faked the tracks by placing clumps of fur from any grey-coloured animal into the hands of the victims. Conversely, Edward Steere's work *The Nunda, Eater of People* attributes these violent acts to an abridged version of a Zanzibari fairy tale called "Mkaaah Jeechonee, the Boy Hunter" collected in 1870 in *Swahili Tales*. The story goes that: 'One day, Sultan Maaj'noon's cat (which he'd been feeding to the extent that it grew enormous) caught a calf and the sultan refused compensation on the grounds that technically he owned both animals.

The next day it killed a cow, then a donkey, a horse, a child, and then a man. Finally, it took to hiding in a thicket ambushing whatever went by, but the sultan would still not address the complaints being made. One day, the sultan went out to see the harvest with his six sons and the cat sprang out and killed three. Devastated, the sultan now demanded its death. Soon after, seeking revenge, Maaj'noon's youngest son set out after the cat, which was called "Noondah" (the eater of people) but could not track it down for many days. Finally, he and his slaves found its tracks and followed them over a mountain and through a large forest where they engaged the ferocious beast. The prince and his slaves threw spears into it killing the maneater. The next day they carried it back to the town where the people and Sultan rejoiced because they had been delivered from their nocturnal tormentor.'

Investigators at the time of the killings rejected lions and leopards as suspects on account of the *mngwa's* spoor, hair and size. However, Karl Shuker speculated that the *mngwa* could conceivably have been a very large aberrantly patterned leopard, explaining why its pawprints resembled those of a gigantic leopard. Bernard Heuvelmans argued against this possibility, writing that it was difficult to imagine how even a genetic abnormality could turn the plain coat of a lion or the spotted coat of a leopard into the brindled grey coat of the *mngwa* and instead theorised that it could have been a giant undiscovered relative of the African golden cat (*Caracal aurata*). Some accounts of the *mngwa* appear to allude to a modern-day version of Sultan Maaj'noon's cat. However, descriptions of its physical characteristics, including its greyish fur with brindled tabby-like markings, as well as its purported inability to roar and preference for purring, indicate that it might be more closely related to the house cat or an unknown species originating from the ancestral Felinae.

(Author's Verdict: 3/5)

Nellimpatti Leopard

A Surviving Bali Leopard?

The Nellimpatti leopard (Balinese) is described as a small leopard with a dark coat, reported from the Southeast Asian island of Bali. In 1975, two officers from Indonesia's *Nature Protection and Wildlife Conservation Service* reported what they thought was a melanistic leopard in the Prapat Agung region of northwest Bali. In 1979, leopard-like nocturnal vocalisations were heard in northern Bali, and zoologists discovered fresh pugmarks in a nearby dried-up riverbed. The Nellimpatti leopard may be a small unknown subspecies of leopard native to Bali, or possibly, reports are of subadult leopards exhibiting melanism and descended from leopards allegedly introduced from Java at some point in the past. If this purported "big cat" is not a leopard, it is conceivable, albeit unlikely, that the reports could refer to juvenile specimens of the extinct Bali tiger exhibiting melanism. The Nellimpatti leopard, regardless of its identity, is now likely to be extinct.

(Author's Verdict: 3/5)

Ndalawo

An Unidentified Leopard-like Beast of East Africa

The *ndalawo* (Central Sudanic) is reported from north-western Uganda. Its pelage is described as almost black on its back, and "hyena grey" on its sides and underparts. Besides the extremities and the lower jaw, the *ndalawo* has practically no patterning. In 1928, Charles Pitman (b. 1890 – d. 1975), a naturalist and conservationist who worked as a game warden of the Uganda Protectorate, first mentioned the *ndalawo*. He provided a more detailed description in his 1931 book *A Game Warden Among His Charges*, using the alternate spelling "ondurlarwo". Based on local native accounts, the *ndalawo* are man-eaters hunting in packs of three or four individuals that make eerie laughing vocalisations at night. A skin was supposedly procured but sent out of the country before it could be examined. Consequently, Pitman concluded that the *ndalawo* was one and the same as the *mngwa* or *nunda* of Tanzania's coastal forests.

Some cryptozoologists classify the *ndalawo* as a Dark Leopard. Other examples include the *damasia* from Kenya, the *uruturangwe* from Rwanda, and the *kibambangwe* from Uganda. Pitman concluded that the *ndalawo* was a "partly melanistic leopard", an identity also suggested by Karl Shuker who believes it is the most likely of its kind to represent a truly unknown species. An unknown leopard-like hyena has also been suggested and descriptions of its laughing vocalisations hint it may be related to the spotted hyena (*Crocuta crocuta*), otherwise known as the laughing hyena. (See *Damasia, Dark Leopards, Kibambangwe,* and *Uruturangwe*)

(Author's Verdict: 4/5)

Ntarargo

A Spotted, Lion-like Beast of East Africa

Scientific Name: *Panthera leo maculatus* (Heuvelmans, 1955).

The *ntarargo* (Lukonzo: Bantu) is another feliform cryptid described as a cross between a leopard and a lion. Also known as *kitalargo* and "wonder leopard", these large cat-like carnivores are described by eyewitnesses as having long tails and a lightly spotted fur pattern. *Ntarargos* are said to have sharp retractable claws, a characteristic commonly found in felids. Possible explanations include naturally occurring lion x leopard hybrids, pseudo-melanistic leopards, an unrecognised subspecies, or an emergent lion species adapted to remote mountainous forested habitats. The most likely explanations are aberrant specimens of the normal lion (*P. leo*) with a rare genetic mutation that causes them to retain their juvenile spots or old and/or exceptionally large leopards. Since Uganda's independence from the British Empire, the alleged *ntarargo* habitat in the Rwenzori Mountains has repeatedly become a sanctuary for rebel groups, making it highly unlikely that any practical field research regarding this feliform cryptid will be carried out there in the foreseeable future.

Pogeyan

Smokey, Ghost-like Cats of India?

The *pogeyan* (Tamil) is reported from India's Western Ghats, primarily from the high-altitude grasslands of Anamudi Peak, in the Nilgiri mountain range, and *Eravikulam National Park* forest. It is darkish grey in colour and reportedly has a long tail and small rounded ears. Similar in size to a leopard, the *pogeyan* (also known as *Pogeyan Puli*, "smoky cat", or "the smoky cat that comes and goes like mist") are very elusive and seldom seen, and if they are observed, they appear only briefly before disappearing like ghosts into the forest.

Kadur Sandesh, a renowned Indian wildlife filmmaker and conservationist renowned for his contributions to BBC *Planet Earth II* with David Attenborough, might have observed a *pogeyan* in 1999. His sighting took place during daylight hours in the high-altitude grasslands surrounding Anamudi, the tallest peak of the Western Ghats. Familiar with the local wildlife, Kadur quickly realised that this animal was very different from anything he had seen or heard of before. Due to their proximity, Kadur felt hesitant to frighten it by moving closer and thus did not get the opportunity to snap a photograph, and camera traps equipped with heat-sensitive technology and baited with singing replicas of the Black-capped Chickadee were found to be ineffective.

Following Kedur Sandesh's observation, which was made public in the 2008 BBC documentary *The Mountains of the Monsoon*, more sightings would soon be reported. In an article for *The Hindu*, journalist Jananaki Lenin uncovered other reports of the mysterious "smokey cat". Among these was Santosh Mani, a tea estate manager in Munnar, who reported seeing a *pogeyan* twice over a period of five years. According to Mani, during both observations, the cat-like creature had been crossing from one tea field to another. Mani described the *pogeyan* as "a cat almost as big as a leopard with a long tail, but it had no spots." James Zacharia, an official from the *Kerala Forest Department*, noticed a creature of similar appearance watching him from a rocky outcrop while ascending a slope in Eravikulam forest, Kerala.

The *pogeyan* may be Indian leopards (*Panthera pardus fusca*), possibly melanistic. Out-of-place Asian lions have also been suggested as have aberrant-coloured leopards and tigers, misidentified caracals, wild cats, civets, and potentially an unknown felid species. The 'cobweb' leopard (a leopard with the condition piebaldism) can also appear solid grey from a distance due to its sparse white guard hairs dispersed throughout its coat. The *pogeyan*, whatever they are, may still be present.

(Author's Verdict: 3/5)

Sai Kung Mystery Cat

Another Mystery Felid from Hong Kong?

The Sai Kung Mystery Cat was a blackish-grey, cat-like creature reported from the Hang Hau region of Sai Kung (Hong Kong's New Territories) during the mid to late 1970s. The animal was highly elusive and posed a danger to local domestic dogs, with more than 20 canine fatalities occurring in Pik Uk and Junk Bay in October 1976. As is commonly the case, a police search yielded no results. On October 30th, people from the village reported seeing a large animal with a leopard-like appearance. Moreover, at the end of November/start of December, one villager claimed to have seen what he thought looked like a dark tiger on two separate occasions within the span of two weeks; estimated to be approximately 90 cm tall and 1.2 meters long. A previous account of a "dark tiger" was shown to be a German Shepherd/Chow crossbreed. Another police search was conducted and this time, they were successful in finding tracks and the *Agriculture and Fish Department* later referred to the subject.

Twelve years later, another mysterious cat was reported to have been killed in Hong Kong. Additionally, similar creatures have since been observed and reported in the area. In March 2019, the *HONG KONG BUZZ* reported that in 2018, twenty-five cats had gone missing without a trace in Ta Ku Ling village, located in the Sai Kung District. Several of these cats were strays that local villagers had taken into their homes as pets. Despite notices being circulated and social media being used to spread awareness, the cats remained unaccounted for. While it is possible this was the result of human interference, the isolated location of the village – with no pedestrian or vehicle traffic – leads one to believe that an animal could have been responsible for their disappearance. In the first half of 2018, multiple cats began to disappear, culminating in 20 being unaccounted for by the end of the year. The following 12 months saw a continuation of this mystery, with an additional five cats disappearing without a trace. While some online commentators suggested that the felines were being harvested as edible food sources during winter, other Internet users proposed alternative theories such as stray dogs or wild animals like boars, snakes and big cats. Possible explanations include misidentifications and exaggerations of large dog breeds and their nocturnal hunting activities, as well as escaped melanistic leopards or mountain lions.

(Author's Verdict: 3/5)

Sahara Lions

Are Saharan Lions Really Extinct?

Scientific Names: *Felis leo* (Linnaeus, 1758), *Felis leo barbaricus* (Meyer, 1826), *Felis leo nubicus* (Ducrotay de Blainville, 1843), and the current taxonomy *Panthera leo leo* (Pocock, 1930).

Officially extinct in the wild for 60 to 70 years, Saharan lions or Barbary lions, as they are often known, are still occasionally reported from Africa's Sahara Desert. The lion has disappeared from 94% of its historic range and is now only found in parts of sub-Saharan Africa. Historically, Barbary lions mainly inhabited the grasslands, scrub or open woodlands, where they hunted their prey more efficiently, but they could live in most habitats aside from tropical rainforests and therefore, contrary to popular belief, the lion is not the true "King of the Jungle", that position rightfully belongs to the tiger! The last known African lions in the Sahara survived in small populations until they went extinct sometime in the mid-1900s. It is not impossible they may still exist in the wild and it should be noted that there is a highly endangered subspecies Asiatic lion (*Panthera leo persica*), with only one very small population surviving in India's Gir Forest – which incidentally is the only place in nature where wild lions and tigers can potentially meet.

Officially the last Barbary lion was shot by a French colonial hunter near Tizi n'Tichka, Morocco in 1942, and today, it seems the only Barbary lions left in the world are found in zoos and are now part of a global and collaborative breeding programme to help ensure their future survival. Barbary lions have been recorded throughout history. The Romans are known to have used them in the Colosseum as a cruel spectacle, in which they were forced, generally through mistreatment and starvation, to enter into gladiatorial battles, and thousands of these imported big cats were cruelly slaughtered during the reign of Julius Caesar (49 – 44 BC). They were also kept in the menagerie at the Tower of London to be offered as gifts to royal families of Morocco and Ethiopia, and it is believed that the lions we call "Barbary lions" today are hybrids directly descended from these "royal lions" and other subspecies. Barbary lions, also known as *Atlas lions, Berber lions, Egyptian lions,* and *North African lions* were large, darkly maned lions, known from the mountains and deserts of the Barbary Coast of North Africa from Morocco to Egypt. They are now considered officially extinct in the wild with fewer than a hundred individuals left in captivity. Specimens of Barbary lions kept in museums are coloured light to tawny brown and pelts from males have manes of varying colour and thickness, but they are generally impressive and attract notice. Unfortunately, they also attracted the attention of big game hunters. Head-to-tail length varies from 2.35 to 2.8 m (7 ft 8 in – 9 ft 2 in), and of lionesses around 2.5 m (8 ft 2 in), and the skulls of Barbary lions vary in size from 30.85 to 37.23 cm (1 ft 0.15 to 1 ft 2.66 in).

In the wild Barbary lions were often seen in pairs or in small prides comprising a male and female with one or two cubs. Between 1839 and 1942, when Barbary lion populations had already been decimated, reports still involved solitary animals, pairs, and small family groups. Analysis of these records shows that these lions retained pride behaviour, even under prolonged persecution and a high mortality rate, particularly in the eastern Maghreb region. The size of prides was likely similar to prides living in south and sub-Saharan habitats, whereas the density of the Barbary lion population is considered to have been lower in wetter habitats. When the Barbary stag and gazelles became rarer in the Atlas Mountains, lions, in order to survive, naturally began preying on domestic pets and livestock herds, triggering a deadly effective killing campaign against them.

Until 2017, the Barbary lion was considered a distinct lion subspecies. Results of genetic and morphological analysis of lion samples from North Africa published in 2008 showed that the Barbary lion does not differ significantly from lion specimens collected in the west and northern regions of Central Africa. It now falls into the same phylo-geographic group as the Asiatic lion (*Panthera e oleo*, formerly *P. l. persica*) and is closely related to West African lion populations.

The Barbary lion was purged from its kingdom following the increase of firearms and valuable bounties for shooting lions, especially those with thick, prominent manes, popular with big game hunters. A complete review of hunting and sighting records revealed that small groups of lions may have survived in Algeria until the early 1960s, and in Morocco until the mid-1960s.

It was reported by 19th-century hunters that the Barbary lion was the largest lion in the world, with wild males weighing up to 270 to 300 kg (600 to 660 lbs). However, it is difficult to verify the precision of data collected during field studies. Captive specimens were considerably smaller but were kept under such poor conditions that they possibly never attained their full potential size and weight. These days for the safety of their keepers, captive lions in zoos, safari parks, and circuses are generally overfed. It was once believed that the thickness and colour of a lion's mane could be used to categorise it as its own subspecies. However, mane development has been found to vary widely among lions of different ages and geographic regions, making this trait insufficient for specific identification. The size of the manes is not regarded as evidence of Barbary lion ancestry. Instead, results of mitochondrial DNA analysis (DNA passed down maternally) support the genetic distinctness of Barbary lions as a unique haplotype. The presence of this haplotype is considered a reliable genetic marker used to identify captive Barbary lions. It is possible that Barbary lions may have developed long-haired manes due to the lower temperatures in the Atlas Mountains than in other regions of Africa. At the beginning of the 21st century, the *Addis Ababa Zoo* had 16 adult lions on display with dark brown manes extending through the front legs, closely resembling Barbary lions. Their ancestors were captured in southwestern Ethiopia as part of a zoological collection for Emperor Haile Selassie of Ethiopia (b. 1892 – d. 1975). More research is needed, and new searches organised, if only to ascertain whether a few small isolated populations haven't survived somewhere in the Sahara unnoticed by humans.

(Author's Verdict: 3/5)

Tubao

Is the Tubao an Unknown Pattern-less Leopard Morph?

Reports from northern and northwestern China suggest that the *tubao*, also known as "earthly leopard" or "*tubaozi*", is a nocturnal feliform cryptid said to be smaller than the North China leopard (*Panthera pardus japonensis*). Colouration ranges from shades of sandy yellow, earthy yellow, to greyish, and always without spots. The *tubao* is aggressive and reported to frequent residential areas where they hunt domestic animals, often dogs, when their natural food sources are limited. Much like leopards, they store leftovers in trees or underground caches, probably marking them with urine as prevention against scavengers. Similarly to foxes, if fresh prey is easily accessible, *tubaos* may not be inclined to revisit previous hoarded meals; hence them appearing gluttonous and wasteful.

The earliest record dates back to the 14th century. The fifth poem from *Yuangongci Baishou* (Hundred Poems of Yuan Dynasty Royal Court Life) mentions the imperial concubine wearing a sleeveless garment made out of *tubao* skins. Contemporary reports have been documented across Shanxi, Shaanxi, Qinghai, and Gansu Provinces as well as the Ningxia Hui Autonomous Region; even in the suburbs of Beijing. In 1950, a Chinese military officer dispatched to Qingyang County in easternmost Gansu Province was informed by locals of a leopard living in a cave in Xigou Valley to the west of the country that had been attacking people after dark. Accompanied by five soldiers armed with automatic machine guns and rifles, the officer proceeded to the location and eventually succeeded in killing the animal. Upon examination, its body was observed to be sandy yellow without any discernible spots or stripes; it also had robust limbs and a tiger-like head accompanied by small, normal-shaped ears.

In April 1951 or 52, three leopards were seen travelling together through the village of Dongliang, Gujiao County in central Shanxi Province. Two local hunters, brothers called Li, and other people who had seen the animals identified them as a North China leopard alongside two greyish-furred *tubaos*. In 1973, an animal researcher allegedly observed a *tubao* exhibited at the *Zhangjiakou Zoo* in northern Hubei Province. It had a plain yellowish coat and a conspicuously large head, somewhat reminiscent of a lioness. Professor Zhao Yuping of the *Beijing University of Posts and Telecommunications* claimed to have observed a *tubao* attacking prey near his hometown in Hubei Province sometime during his childhood. This would have been during the late 1970s or early 80s.

It is possible that the *tubao* might be an unrecognised species belonging to the Felidae family or a genetic variation of the North China leopard, potentially a patternless morph. The Asian golden cat (*Catopuma temminckii*) is comparatively small but matches the colouration sometimes reported in *tubao* encounters, as does a caracal (*Caracal caracal*). Thus, it could be argued that the *tubao* represents an expansion in range for the Central Asian caracals. Nevertheless, Zhou Shiqi and Yoshio Abe from *Hiroshima University of Arts and Science* have suggested that the lynx (*Lynx sp.*) are possible candidates.

(Author's Verdict: 4/5)

Uruturangwe

A Hyena-like Leopard or a Leopard-like Hyena?

Reported from Rwanda's Mount Muhavura and Mount Sabinio in Central Africa, the *uruturangwe* (Swahili) is described as a big cat roughly the size of a leopard with a coat resembling that of a hyena and possessing long, retractable claws. It is reported that the *uruturangwe* is a dangerous animal that kills its prey through asphyxiation, similar to leopards. Reports also tell us they have a strange vocalisation resembling laughter and that they hunt in packs of three or four. It has been speculated that the *uruturangwe* could be pseudo-melanistic leopards, although some of its reported behaviours, such as cooperative hunting, are unknown in leopards. It might be an imaginary hybrid between a leopard and a hyena, or alternatively, a large hyena so distinct from other species in terms of its physical characteristics that it was mistaken for and feared as a leopard. (Also see *Kibambangwe*)

(Author's Verdict: 3/5)

Wobo

A Hybrid of Lion and Leopard or a Distinct Species Unknown to Science?

Larger than a lion (*P. leo*), the wobo (Ethio-Semitic) or "mendelit" (also spelt 'mantillit') is characterised by its yellowish-brown fur with black stripes; observed in the rocky mountainous regions of Ethiopia in East Africa. The German explorer and ornithologist (b. 1824 – d. 1876) Martin Theodor von Heuglin, was the first to mention this creature, along with the *abu sotan* of Sudan:

'Is the Wobo a variety of leopard, an [hybrid] of lion and leopard, or a particular species not yet well known? I could not decide in a formal way. The animal is depicted as the wildest, boldest, and most powerful predator, and in some reports is yellowish in colour and has dark longitudinal stripes. It seems to exist throughout Abyssinia, but none of the Europeans who live there has been able to give us a more precise description, and the information that the natives themselves have reported does not agree at all between them.'

Heuglin explained that wobos are larger than leopards and lions, they are grey with black stripes and come from the hottest lowland forests. He reported that a pelt from a *wobo* was kept in the main church of Ifag, having been observed by numerous individuals including Emperor Theodore (Tewodros). The *wobo* is also mentioned in Henryk Sienkiewicz's 1912 Sudanese adventure novel *In Desert and Wilderness.*

The following passage appears in an 1853 book entitled "Life in Abyssinia v.i," written by English traveller Mansfield Harry Isham Parkyns (b. 1823 – d. 1894). In it, Parkyns describes his experiences and observations during the three years he spent in the modern territories of Eritrea and Ethiopia between 1843 and 1846. "There is an animal, which I know not where to class, as no European has hitherto succeeded in obtaining a specimen of it; it is supposed by the natives to be far more active, powerful, and dangerous than even the Hon, and consequently held by them in the greatest possible dread. They call it 'wobbo' or 'mantillit,' and some hold it in superstitious awe, looking upon it more in the light of an evil spirit with an animal's form than as a wild beast. Their descriptions of this animal are vague in the extreme: some say that its skin is partly that of a lion but intermixed with that of the leopard and hyena; others, again, assert that its face is human, or very like it. It appears in the valleys, happily, only rarely; for they say that when it takes its abode near a village, it pays nightly visits, entering the very houses, and carrying off the children, and even occasionally grown-up persons. One had been killed some years ago on the river Werrey, and its skin presented to Oubi, but I could never discover what became of it. I heard of a village which had suffered considerably from its depredations, and for several days watched every night in the neighbourhood, but without success."

Several of Parkyns' contemporaries questioned whether he was referring to a lamia: a mythical creature with human-like qualities that,
according to classical Greek mythology, preys on children.

(Author's Verdict: 3/5)

Yamamaya

A Small, Unknown, Insular Variety of Clouded Leopard?

Is there an unknown clouded leopard subspecies inhabiting Japan's
Iriomote Island? In the local Yaeyama language '*yamapikaryaa*' means
something like "the creature of the mountains with flashing eyes."
Cats are referred to as 'maya' by the islanders, who can easily distinguish between domestic cats and a larger unknown species they call
yamamaya. Inhabitants of Sonai and Komi on the island's northwest
coast know it as *kunzumayaa* and *toutouyaa* respectively. Currently,
there is no definitive proof of the *yamamaya's* existence, but there are
many believable accounts from people who live both on and off the
island. The *yamamaya* is described by observers as being roughly
twice as big as a domestic cat; with a tail that is long in proportion to
its body, and a coat pattern that is significantly different from that of
the Iriomote cat (*Prionailurus bengalensis iriomotensis*). There are at
least 47 documented eyewitness reports, however, reports have
decreased since the 1960s which may be attributed to the animals'
migrating towards the centre of the island that is uninhabited, or it
could be a result of their dwindling population – perhaps both.

In 1965, Japanese novelist and children's writer Yukio Togawa questioned a local hunter who claimed to have killed a large cat with a
pelage like that of a tiger. He apparently disposed of its body on the
southern part of the island. The hunter stated that, up until ten days
prior to the interview, the cat's skeleton was still situated where he
had concealed it; however, recent rainfall had caused it to be washed
away or scavenged. In the summer of 1978, a hunter reported seeing a
big cat in a tree. The animal was described as having a shoulder

height that reached an adult human's knee, twice the size of a house cat, with a tail that was estimated to be at least 60 cm long, and greenish-striped fur. Moreover, it had oddly shaped spots and a long, low-hanging tail. The hunter watched it for several minutes until it seemed to detect his presence; swiftly yet silently it descended from the tree and darted away into the woods with remarkable agility and speed.

On June 2nd, 1982, the Japanese newspaper *Yomiuri Shimbun* reported on an experienced boar hunter who had seen the *yamapikaryaa* near Mount Dedou on ten separate occasions. He also mentioned that he had once caught and eaten one and claimed to have observed an adult female with a cub. For many years, American investigative journalist Brent Swancer, living in Japan, has been gathering accounts of this and other unidentified creatures. In 2003, Mr Shimabukuro, who operates a fishing boat on the island, allegedly spotted a *yamamaya* in the mountains while hunting wild pigs. Whilst in a clearing he observed a large spotted, cat-like creature estimated to be slightly over a metre long. It suddenly leaped down from the top of a large boulder, landing directly in front of Shimabukuro before retreating into the forest. As the animal ran away, Shimabukuro noticed that it was spotted, and it had an incredibly long tail. On September 14th, 2007, Professor Eiyuu Akiyoshi of *Shimane University* was carrying out ichthyological research on Iriomote Island when he spotted a dark shadow at the edge of the forest approximately 2.5 meters from his position. Professor Akiyoshi observed the creature at Sakiyama Peninsula, an area that is rarely visited in the western region of the island. He said it was considerably larger than the Iriomote cat; around one meter long, with a very long tail and black spots like those of a leopard. The professor noted how it fixed its gaze on him before walking away into the forest. Based on these reports, the *yamamaya* seems to be reticent towards humans, opting to flee rather than engage in conflict. This prudent behaviour is similar to that of a clouded leopard.

It is plausible that the *yamamaya* is an unclassified, isolated subspecies of the clouded leopard (*Neofelis nebulosa*). A subspecies of this cat identified as *Neofelis nebulosa brachyura* once existed in Taiwan 200 km west of Iriomote, however, no verifiable observations of this species have been reported since the 1980s. Is it feasible that all these reports are false? As recently as 2006, a new species of clouded leopard (*Neofelis diardi*), was identified in Borneo. Approximately 90% of Iriomote is comprised of remote mountains blanketed in a subtropical forest, providing an ideal habitat for a species that thrives on secrecy. With the interior of the island still largely unexplored, there is a reasonable chance that the *yamamaya* could be an entirely unknown species or subspecies.

(Author's Verdict: 3/5)

Zanzibar Leopard

Is the Zanzibar Leopard Still Alive?

Scientific Name: *Panthera pardus adersi,* Pocock 1932.

The native fauna of Zanzibar includes the recently identified Zanzibar servaline genet (*Genetta servalina archeri*; Van Rompaey & Colyn, 1998), primates, bush pigs, small antelopes, the African palm civet, and, as evidenced by trail-cam in June 2018, the supposedly extinct Zanzibar leopard. Due to relentless human development and encroachment, the leopard is probably restricted geographically to the *Jozani Chwaka Bay National Park* in the south of the island. The Zanzibar leopard has a pale-yellow coat covered with brown spots. It is officially extinct but is still reported occasionally from Unguja Island, in the Zanzibar Archipelago. The Zanzibar leopard is slightly smaller than its mainland relative due to the phenomenon of insular dwarfism – the evolutionary process and condition whereby large animals develop or display reduced body size when their population range is limited to a confined environment, particularly on islands.

They also have noticeably longer tails and a lower walking gait than other leopards.

Due to the lack of genetic analysis, the exact classification of the Zanzibar leopard remains uncertain, and it has also been classified as a population of the larger African leopard subspecies *(Panthera pardus pardus)*. Some believe that the Zanzibar leopard is a subspecies endemic to Ungula (Zanzibar) Island. There is limited knowledge of the behaviour and ecology of this species, although it is likely to have similar characteristics to its African counterpart and perhaps a comparable diet. The conflict between the islanders and leopards intensified during the 20th century, resulting in the demonisation and persecution of the Zanzibar leopard. According to native accounts, they were viewed as pets maintained by witches who use them for mischievous and malicious purposes – a concept very similar to that of a witch's 'familiar' found in Western demonology. It was thought to disrupt villages and held them accountable for the loss of livestock. Following the Zanzibar Revolution of 1964, rigorous extermination campaigns quickly ensued. Under the command of a "witchfinder," an anti-witchcraft and leopard-killing campaign spread rapidly, and by the 1990s the majority of scientists concluded that the Zanzibar leopard was lost forever.

Despite unconfirmed sightings continuing, the Zanzibar leopard population was officially declared extinct by the mid-1990s; however, the islanders maintain that the leopard is still alive. In 1997 and 2001, reports of leopard scat discoveries made their way around the island, however, both samples were unfortunately lost before scientists had a chance to study them. Compared to mainland populations, the morphological differences of these leopards indicate less genetic diversity; therefore, all African populations of leopards are now considered to fall under one subspecies. Six pelts were deposited at museums, including the type specimen at the *Natural History Museum* in London and a sun-faded taxidermy specimen in the *Zanzibar Museum*. Martin T. Walsh and Helle V. Goldman's 37-page pamphlet published in 2016 stated that the survival of the Zanzibar leopard was highly unlikely, even referring to them as "imaginary beings."

Multiple reports have been made since the Zanzibar leopard was officially declared extinct, and deaths of livestock are still being attributed to it. The *Jozani-Chwaka Bay Conservation Project* planned a leopard conservation program in 1997; however, when wildlife experts visited the island, they were unable to find any evidence of the species and thus the program was abandoned. Local wildlife officials, on the other hand, remained hopeful. Some Zanzibaris have proposed the idea of approaching alleged witch doctors to ask them to show their leopards for money. Some people who live in Zanzibar claim to have seen a Zanzibar Leopard. Others say that leopards have killed their livestock in recent years.

In 2018, two years after Walsh and Goldman had mocked the apparent survival of the Zanzibar Leopard, American adventurer, and wildlife biologist Forrest Galante captured footage of a leopard in Zanzibar on a trail camera. The video was later shown on the television program *Extinct or Alive* for the channel Animal Planet. In a somewhat typical fashion, some authorities have refused to accept this video as reliable evidence due to the fact that its exact location has not been revealed. However, Gilante has defended its authenticity, citing the necessity of keeping the exact location undisclosed in order to protect the animal. We chose to employ the same approach when we documented the *harimau tingkiah*, as it is not always imperative to disclose the exact location right away, particularly if it is not in a national park or other safeguarded area. Possible explanations for the Zanzibar Leopard's apparent survival include specimens of other leopard subspecies that have either escaped or been illegally released from captivity, and some have even speculated that an African lion may have been introduced to Zanzibar. DNA evidence may be the only way to verify the Galante video, providing corroborative biological material can be collected in the near future. Ideally, another trail camera video will record a specimen visiting an area where hair, skin or scat samples can be gathered, analysed and identified – either confirming or denying the presence of leopards formerly known as *Panthera pardus adersi.*

(Status: Species Identified, Subspecific Confirmation Required)

NEW CHEETAHS AND/OR CHEETAH X LEOPARD HYBRIDS

Black Cheetah

Melanistic Cheetahs?

A melanistic variant of the cheetah has yet to be confirmed, however, black cheetahs have been reported from the Trans-Nzoia District in Kenya and Zambia in southern Africa. They are described as having a black coat with faint, shadowy spots referred to as "ghost markings," that are hidden by excess melanin. This tells us that there are different molecular mechanisms that code for melanism vs. coat patterns in cats. For a cat to have a solid black coat a homozygous recessive (a/a) genotype is present called a non-agouti. The non-agouti suppresses the gene responsible for tabby markings in domestic cats, and similarly, it inhibits the spotted pattern in big cats, though not entirely.

At least 14 of the 35+ species of wild cats – including jaguars, leopards, and bobcats – carry the gene that causes melanism, or a surplus of melanin, or pigment, in a cat's fur. In a letter to *Nature in East Africa,* Captain H. F. Stoneham of the British Army's East Surrey Regiment reported seeing an all-black cheetah in the Trans-Nzoia District of Kenya in 1925. The Irish naturalist and author Brian Vesey-Fitzgerald (b. 1905 – d. 1981) also observed a black cheetah walking beside a typical spotted cheetah in what is today Zambia. These events were first mentioned (unreferenced) on page 269 of C. A. W Guggisberg's *Wild Cats of the World* (1975). The primary explanation for reports of black cheetahs is observations of melanistic cheetahs (*Acinonyx jubatus*, suggested Latin trinomial: *Acinonyx jubatus* var. *furvus*). Their black coat can be attributed to natural and hereditary melanin or pigment, comparable to that of leopards and jaguars, which probably points to a deficiency of genetic diversity.

(Author's Verdict: 3/5)

Indian White Cheetahs

Although exceptionally rare, white or cream cheetahs, commonly referred to as Isabelline, are no longer of cryptozoological significance since they have been recorded in Africa. A probable partial albino specimen with blue spots was presented to the Mogul Emperor of India, Jahangir (b 1569 – d 1627) at Agra. The description of the white cheetah is in Vol. I, pp. 139-40.

"In the third year of his reign (1608 AD.), the emperor recorded the following event: 'On this day Raja Bir Singh Deo brought a white cheeta [sic] to show me. Although other sorts of creatures, both birds and beasts, have white varieties, which they call tuyghan, I had never seen a white cheeta. Its spots which are (usually) black, were of a blue colour, and the whiteness of the body was also inclined to bluishness." "Of the albino animals that I have seen there are falcons, sparrowhawks, hawks {Shikara) that they call bigu in the Persian language, sparrows, crows, partridges, florican, podna {Sylvia olivacea) [sic.], and peacocks. Many hawks in aviaries are albinos. I have also seen white flying mice (flying squirrels) and some albinos among the black antelope, which is a species found only in Hindustan. Among the chikara (gazelle), which they call safida in Persia, I have frequently seen albinos."

Jahangir's description appears to be that of a partial albino, also known as a chinchilla mutation, with spots appearing silvery-blue on a light blue background. There is no further evidence of this presumed animal though it has been suggested that Raja Bir Singh Deo obtained it from the forests in his homeland of Bundelkhand. The bluish colour, and the whiteness of the body, which is also slightly blue, indicates the chinchilla mutation which limits the amount of pigment on the hair shaft. Despite the spots being composed of black pigment, the less dense pigmentation which did not reach all the way to the follicle would have created a hazy, bluish effect. It is plausible that historical reports of Indian white cheetahs resulted from normal cheetahs displaying partial albinism, caused by homozygosity for the full-colour gene's recessive "chinchilla" mutant allele. Regrettably, in 1951 the cheetah was officially declared extinct in India; though there were sporadic sightings until 1970.

(Status: African Counterpart Recorded)

King Cheetah

Long Live the King!

Scientific Name: *Acinonyx rex*, proposed by Reginald Pocock in 1927; modified to *Acinonyx jubatus* var. *rex* in 1939.

King cheetahs are renowned for their beautiful thick, golden-yellow coats with blotchy patterns instead of defined spots, and were once considered a distinct species from the standard form. The exact number that exists in the world is unknown, yet it is estimated that there could be as few as ten left in the wild, with a further fifty or so in captivity. It was originally known in the West as Cooper's cheetah following its discovery by Major A. Cooper in 1926 but is also known as Mazoe leopard, royal cheetah, *nsui-fisi* and *chui-fisi* (both meaning "leopard-hyena") and Rhodesian cheetah. King cheetahs have been reported from Zimbabwe, Botswana, Mozambique, and the Northern Province of South Africa.

There is also an account of a poorly preserved skin recovered in 1992, from Burkina Faso in West Africa. They have slim athletic bodies, albeit slightly larger than usual, built for high-speed running, with blunt slightly curved and only semi-retractable claws that act like running spikes, used to increase traction while chasing down fast-running prey. Ridges running along the footpads act like car tyre treads, providing additional traction on uneven terrain. Instead of the usual spots, the king cheetah has also developed dorsal stripes, thick and bold, running the entire length of the back. Specimens consistently show three primaries, with two shorter stripes flanking them in adults, with blotches like irregularly shaped ink blots covering the base fur over the flanks and chest. For reasons unclear, king cheetahs often have a more pronounced mane than the standard spotted variety. Its tail is also unique, being both striped and ringed. There are two dorsal stripes not ending at the rump, but instead running on along it before thick bands continue toward the tip. King cheetahs seem to be primarily nocturnal, as opposed to the traditional cheetah's preference for diurnal hunting in the early morning and late afternoon.

From the early 1800s, stories began reaching European hunters and adventurers of a legend from the Manicaland Province of a beast known as *nsui-fisi* or "leopard-hyena". In 1926, Major Alan Cooper – who was in charge of the *Queen Victoria Memorial Library and Museum* in Southern Rhodesia (now the Republic of Zimbabwe) – sent photographs of an unusual striped pelt to both *The Field Magazine* and the *British Museum of Natural History*. Cooper theorised that it may have been a hybrid exhibiting characteristics of both leopard and cheetah. Reginald Innes Pocock, the renowned British zoologist at the *British Museum of Natural History*, disagreed with Cooper's analysis and proposed based off of the photo that it was an aberrant leopard. Cooper contested Pocock's theory and the following year sent him the pelt. Belatedly, the *nsui-fisi* was confirmed as a genuine striped cheetah from southern Africa. This is a perfect example of the potential viability of a practical cryptozoological methodology.

In 1927, Pocock described the king cheetah as a new species assigning it the name *Acinonyx rex* or "king cheetah". However, in the absence of proof to support his claim, he later withdrew his proposal. In 1929, taxonomist and Professor of Zoology Miklos Kretzoi went a step further, by giving the king cheetah full generic status as the sole member of a completely new genus, which he named *Paracinonyx,* thus giving it the specific epithet *Paracinonyx rex*. In 1974, after a 30+ year hiatus of alleged and recorded sightings, a plausible report was made describing a coalition of striped cheetahs, said to be upwards of 20 individuals in the very heartland of *nsui-fisi* territory, Manicaland Province. They were observed by a mining engineer and his wife but unfortunately were not photographed. Sometime later a skin was retained from a king cheetah that had been killed by villagers but this invaluable zoological specimen was lost after being handed to the local District Commissioner and has not been seen since. In 1974, a remarkable series of photographs were taken at *Kruger National Park* featuring a live, wild, king cheetah. The pictures showed the majestic cat rising from tall grass and slowly walking away toward scrubland, eventually merging into a thicket of vegetation and disappearing once more.

A hardback publication entitled *Our South African National Parks*, published in 1940 features an illustration of the Kruger cheetahs on page 70. Rather than the typical spotted variety, it appears to represent striped king cheetahs. Despite the 1974 photograph and the incontrovertible evidence of existing pelts, belief in the king cheetah as a "myth" was still prevalent at this time, with numerous respected academics still of the view that it was somehow a hoax. In 1978, Lena and Paul Bottriell's now famous *King Cheetah Expedition* began with the couple spending 18 months in southern Africa, collecting any information they could find regarding the king cheetah. The Bottriells significantly increased the number of known king cheetah specimens, even identifying some historically 'lost' specimens, including the only acknowledged king cheetah skull known at that time. Furthermore, they sent hair samples from both king cheetahs and those of normal cheetahs and leopards to South Africa's *Institute of Medical Research* for scientific investigation. In an interesting twist, the results implied that the cuticular scale pattern on king cheetah hair shafts doesn't correspond to those of the spotted cheetah, but closer resembles the "petal" pattern of the leopard. To my knowledge, this detail has never been resolved.

In May 1981, two king cheetah cubs were born in South Africa – one male and one female – at the *De Wildt Research Centre* and Netal's *Pretoria and Seaview Game Park* respectively. The female cub's mother, named Jumper due to her habit of jumping fences, had to be moved from De Wildt to Seaview during her pregnancy. Both cubs were sired by a male caught in the Messina district of the Transvaal, now known as Northern Province. This is the same region that the Bottriells had determined would be part of the king cheetah's wider range. A pair of adolescent king cheetahs were observed in *Kruger National Park* in 1986, where the Bottriells had centred their investigations; meanwhile, a scientific paper was published on De Wildt's king cheetahs bred over the four to five years since the above-mentioned cubs in 1981. This study, derived from De Wildt's records of captive-bred king cheetahs, suggested that the complex variation observed is consistent with that which produces the tabby pattern in domestic cats.

By 1987, Lena Bottriell's acclaimed work, *King Cheetah: The Story of The Quest* was released by the esteemed academic publishing house Brill of Leiden. This book has since been regarded as the definitive source on the history of the king cheetah and a must-read for those interested in feliform cryptozoology. Unprecedented, a king cheetah was discovered in 1992 outside the Bottriell's and historical record's official target area. A very poorly preserved skin had been seized from a local villager in Burkina Faso in West Africa, a region curiously similar to the king cheetah's preferred habitat of large forests, dense scrub, and thicket scattered with open savanna. This means the king cheetah is either developing in areas where spotted cheetahs are rare, or the skin has been illegally imported. The poorly tanned quality of the specimen suggests that the former is more likely. In 1992 the Bottriells acquired clear photographs of a coalition of four adult cheetahs: two king cheetahs with two normal spotted cheetahs, from *MalaMala Reserve* in Sabi Sands, only about 20 km south from the adolescent king cheetahs reported at *Kruger* in 1986. In 1993, Margaret Thatcher, the two-time British Prime Minister, encountered an extraordinary sight while on safari – two rare king cheetahs making a successful kill alongside two spotted cheetahs. This remarkable sighting was captured in a series of photographs.

In 1992, Paul and Lena were invited by the *University of Veterinary Medicine Vienna* to participate in a historic phylogeographical study of the cheetah's evolutionary history in relation to geography. The study encompassed nearly 400 biological samples across the cheetah's range from South Africa up through all regions of Africa where cheetahs have been found historically, including Western Asia and the Russian steppes, as well as India. The Bottriells eventually gathered an additional twelve samples of the king cheetah, with nine of them being from the wild and four sourced from Japan's *Tama Zoo* and *Singapore Zoo*, along with fossil material from *Acinonyx pardinensis*, a two million-year-old giant European cheetah potentially possessing fur comparable to the heavy forest-style markings of the king cheetah. In September, a team of researchers revisited the tabby theory by conducting a study to identify the gene responsible for tabby variations in domestic cats.

By using more than 70 samples each from blotched and mackerel cats, they were able to determine the gene responsible. Included was a single captive-bred king cheetah from a North American facility of De Wildt origin, where they were able to identify the Transmembrane aminopeptidase Q (Taqpep) gene as the cause of the rare phenotype. This discovery poses an intriguing question – was this the original phenotype before they began retreating from forested or woodland environments due to human encroachment? Thus, the pattern of king cheetahs is not random, but rather consistent and uniform; as opposed to it being a new development in a biogeographical race that has evolved in response to niche differentiation. The original markings resurrected in the modern spotted cheetah are driven by the geographic imperative of the loss of habitat, where cheetahs are forced back into scrubland country not suited to grazing or other human activity in the last 150 years or so. The Bottriells concluded that the king cheetah's markings probably represent the species' original coat pattern.

All recorded king cheetahs show the same consistency and uniformity of markings. But just as no Bengal tiger's markings are exactly the same, each king cheetah has unique markings individual to it, much like a zebra's stripes or a human's fingerprints. One last detail that should not be overlooked is that there are no documented instances of king cheetahs with significantly reduced stripes, or without blotches, nor tails without both stripes and bands. Furthermore, a king cheetah with a spotted tail has never been recorded.

It is clear that there are still unresolved questions. At present, the king cheetah is generally regarded as a single-locus variation of the standard spotted cheetah and is no longer thought of as a separate species or subspecies. This mutation can, however, be considered beneficial, offering genetic variability from which natural selection can occur. It is also possible that the king cheetah might represent a hereditary regression to a period when Africa was colder and more forested.

(Status: Identified)

King Cheetah (Asian)

Is the Elvis of Cheetahs Also in Asia?

Despite the cheetah's once broad distribution, there is no documented record of a king cheetah found outside Africa. However, this does not mean that no evidence exists. As discussed in the introduction, clues to the possibility of feliform cryptids can be inferred from archaeological artefacts, artworks, historic manuscripts, tales, and oral traditions. In particular, it is historical artwork that suggests the king cheetah phenotype was once present in Asia. On February 21st, 2011, *Fortean Times*, a British magazine that pays homage to the anomalous phenomena popularised by Charles Fort, received an email from Laura Beaton with an image for Dr. Karl Shuker to examine. The following day, Dr. Shuker received an email directly from Laura containing additional information. It became evident that the 16th-century watercolour and gold painting entitled *"Akbar hunts near Lahore and Hamid Bakari is punished by having his head shaved and being mounted on an Ass"* originally appeared in the 'Akbarnama' (Book of Akbar): the official chronicle of the reign of Akbar the Great, the third emperor of the Mughal dynasty which lasted from 1556 to 1605. The official website for the *Victoria and Albert Museum* in London, which purchased a partial copy of this manuscript in 1896, describes the painting as follows.

"This illustration of the Akbarnama is the right side of a double-page composition. The entire composition depicts a ceremonial hunt. The Mughal emperor Akbar (r.1556–1605) is depicted in the centre of the painting mounted on horseback with his sword raised. At the top right, Hamid Bakkari is shown being punished for firing an arrow at one of the servants of the court by having his head shaved and being forced to ride backward on an ass."

The painting depicts a hunting scene with several wild animals and among them is a single dead specimen of an unusual cheetah covered with short, faint stripes, not spots. As incredible as it may seem, cheetahs were once used as hunting animals to catch prey, particularly deer, but they were also habitually killed and skinned for their fur. The cat in the image, apparently killed during the hunt, has a gracile build with long slender limbs, a long banded tail, and fur patterned with short stripes. A characteristic 'teardrop' streak can be seen clearly running down from the cheetah's eyes to its mouth. Its morphology is distinctly cheetah-like, as evidenced by comparing its form with those of the normally spotted cheetahs also depicted in the painting. Moreover, using the nearby chital deer carcasses depicted as a reference of scale, the cat is clearly comparable in size and therefore is far too large to belong to any of the smaller Asian felids. Dr. Shuker noted that: "Although the dead cat's striped pelage is less ornate than that of most of the African examples on record, taking its striping together with its overall morphology the felid that it most closely resembles is the king cheetah. Bearing in mind that all other mammals in this painting are depicted in a painstakingly accurate, naturalistic manner, there is no reason to assume any different for the portrayal of the dead striped cat."

I couldn't agree more. The dead striped cat depicted in the painting almost certainly represents an Asian equivalent of the African king cheetah or a similar mutation.

(Author's Verdict: 4/5)

Kitanga

A Lion-like Cheetah?

The Kitanga (Embu: Bantu), often referred to as the "forest cheetah," is described as having a large cheetah-like build, but with shorter, more robust limbs and other lion-like characteristics. It is reported from the Embu highland forests of Kenya in East Africa and Senegal in West Africa – where cheetahs (*Acinonyx jubatus hecki*) are critically endangered. Possible explanations include a genetic mutation of the cheetah adapted to this type of habitat or spotted lions recorded in low-visibility conditions.

(Author's Verdict: 3/5)

Mpisimbi

A Big Cat With a Sweet Tooth?

The *mpisimbi* (Bantu) is said to inhabit east and central Africa, where it is known only from a brief description by Captain William Hichens, who wrote that it was a "leopard-hyæna, which eats sugar-cane." Karl Shuker speculates that it could have been an East African king cheetah, since its South African name '*nsui-fisi*' also translates as 'leopard hyena', and Hichens himself recorded that the *nsui-fisi* "was reputed to be a raider of grain and sugar-cane." Hichens wrote that he had unsuccessfully hunted the *mpisimbi* several times. *Mpisimbi*, which are strongly associated with grain and sugarcane plantations, are more likely to prey on smaller animals that are attracted to these potential food sources rather than exclusively eating these food sources themselves. All cats, being obligate carnivores and not having the sweet taste receptors found in other mammals, would not be aware that sugar cane is sweet.

(Author's Verdict: 4/5)

Qattara Cheetah (Unidentified)

Another Unresolved Cheetah Morph?

The Qattara Depression (also spelt Qaṭṭārah) is a substantial low-lying region located in the desert of northwestern Egypt. It serves as an important natural habitat for the cheetah, with the majority of recent sightings reported from areas in the north, west, and north-west part of the depression, including Ain El Qattara and Ein El Ghazzalat's isolated wild oases and neighbouring Acacia groves. At least five cheetahs have been recorded around the Sitra water source in the Qattara Depression in the western and northwest parts of the country. There is, however, another more peculiar unconfirmed cheetah reported from the Qattara Depression, specifically in the

Matruh Governorate. Referred to simply as the Qattara cheetah, reports describe a pale-furred cheetah with thicker fur than normal. Reports date back to at least the 1960s when in 67, a Bedouin shepherd captured a specimen.

During the 1990s, cheetah-like tracks were found and photographed on two separate occasions in the same region. These light-furred cheetahs might represent an isolated population, like the speckled Saharan cheetahs living in Niger's Ténéré Desert, in West Africa. Like the Qattara cheetah, the Saharan cheetah (*Acinonyx jubatus hecki*) is quite different from the other African cheetahs. Its coat is shorter and almost white in colour, with black spots over the spine that fade into light brown on the legs. The face has few, or sometimes, no spots at all, and they often lack the famous tear stripes that usually run from the medial canthus of each eye down the side of the muzzle to the corners of the mouth. Their anatomy is basically the same as that of the sub-Saharan cheetah, except that it is moderately smaller. Until quite recently this desert-adapted cheetah roamed the sparsely vegetated patches of the Sahara, preying on what was then an abundance of gazelles and other natural prey species.

During the latter half of the 20th century, as gazelle numbers plummeted due to extensive hunting pressures and habitat destruction, and with cheetahs themselves classified as semi-game animals, the once distinguished Saharan predator became drastically reduced to a small, highly fragmented population that is now on the precipice of extinction. The *Zoological Society of London* estimates that just 250 remain in countries like Niger and Algeria. The decline of the cheetah, however, is not limited to its Northern African population. During the last century, the cheetah has become extinct in India, Iraq, Syria, Jordan, the Arabian Peninsula, and Sinai, and is rapidly declining in numbers and geographical range in sub-Saharan Africa. Scientists now estimate that fewer than 8,000 African cheetahs are living in the wild today. In 2001, the cheetah was added to the *Red List of Threatened Species,* and as of 2021, *Acinonyx jubatus* is listed as vulnerable under criteria A4b; C1. of the code. In Egypt, it has been concluded that the cheetah, which formerly ranged over much of the northern part of the Western Desert, is now limited to a meagre part of its former range at the north-western part of the Qattara Depression, and it is among these small isolated populations that the pale coloured and thickly furred "Qattara cheetah" emerged. Cheetah tracks have been found in a number of localities from the Qattara Depression. The Bedouins and other people frequenting this area also confirmed the presence of a very small population of cheetahs. The few individuals documented from the region survived by roaming over a vast area of the desert in search of resources. The Qattara cheetah probably represents a genetic mutation triggered by limited genetic diversity.

(Author's Verdict: 4/5)

Shuker's Cheetaline

A Beautiful Pale Colour Morph

African white cheetahs, also referred to as "cheetalines" by Dr. Karl Shuker in his 2012 book, *"Cats of Magic, Mythology and Mystery"*, show fine markings resembling those of the servaline cat morph, which gives them their name. In 1921, Reginald Pocock described the first cheetaline from a skin obtained in present-day Tanzania from a cheetah shot by Lt Col. W. T. Gregg. On September 5th, 2011 Dr. Shuker received an email from wildlife artist Guy Combes containing information about a second cheetaline exhibiting a finely speckled pattern observed in Kenya. Additionally, Combes provided colour photographs that affirmed the specimen was genuine. Based on the photographic evidence, Dr. Shuker speculates in his updated *Mystery Cats of the World Revisited*, that the Kenyan cheetaline may be a leucistic specimen because its eyes, nose, and even the characteristic tear-drop markings are pigmented as normal, proving the specimen wasn't albino. Guy Combes has been petitioning for the protection of the Kenyan cheetaline since 2010. White cheetahs are extremely rare but they do exist. Specimens may be displaying partial albinism, specifically, they possess two copies of the recessive chinchilla mutation for the full-colour gene.

(Status: Identified)

Woolly Cheetah

Another Densely Furred Cheetah

The last African 'crypto cheetah' for us to consider is the woolly cheetah, an enigmatic *Acinonyx* species reported from Nel's Point in the Beaufort District of South Africa's Cape Colony. They have longer, denser fur; thicker bodies, and stouter limbs than normal cheetahs, although it is possible that some reports may have been optical illusions of the long fur. These cheetahs have dense "woolly" fur, particularly on the tail and neck where it forms a sort of ruff or mane. Cheetahs with longer, thicker fur have been documented on multiple occasions. Unfortunately, they were killed rather than taken alive, which means that the mutation that causes the woolly cheetah may no longer be present in the gene pool. A painting of a woolly cheetah implies not only a long-haired cheetah but a red, possibly erythristic, specimen.

On June 16th, 1877, Philip Sclater, Secretary of the Proceedings of the Zoological Society recorded:

"An animal sold to us on the 29 May by Mr. Arthur Mosenthal of as a Cheetah, but which appears to belong to a new species of the genus Felis, distinct from, although closely allied to that animal. It is a male, probably not quite fully grown. It presents generally the appearance of a Cheetah (Felis Jubata) but is thicker in the body, has shorter and stouter limbs, and a much thicker tail. When adult it will probably be considerably larger than the Cheetah and is larger even now than our three specimens of that animal. The fur is much woollier and denser than in the Cheetah, as is particularly noticeable on the ears, mane, and tail. The whole of the body is of a pale isabelline colour (yellowish fawn), rather paler on the belly and lower parts, but covered all over, including the belly, with roundish dark fulvous blotches. There are no traces of the black spots which are so conspicuous in all the varieties of the Cheetah which I have seen, nor of the characteristic black line between the mouth and eye."

From the Secretary's Report, *Proceedings of the Zoological Society*, June 18th, 1878:

"Mr. Sclater called the attention of the members present to the unique specimen of his Felis lanea (P.Z.S. 1877, p. 532), still living in the Society's menagerie, and read the subjoined extract from a letter of Mr. E. L. Layard, relating to this animal: It will you to know that there is a second specimen of your Felis lanea in the South-African Museum, sent from the same place (the Beaufort-West Karras) by the late Arthur V. Jackson, who killed it himself. Unfortunately, I received the skin in very bad condition. The ground colour is much paler than on your plate, almost white. Jackson and I thought it an albino (or rather erythrism) of F. jubata (see Catalogue of S. A. Museum, p. 38, No 82, Gueparda jubata, specimen b). On p. 39 of the same Catalogue, I remark that we have had notices of a second species of Maned Leopard [cheetah], with solid spots and with retractile claws, from Natal. The claws of your animal are not shown on Smit's plate. What is their structure?"

Proceedings of the Zoological Society, May 3rd, 1887:

"The case [...] seems much to resemble those of the singular form of Cheetah (Felis lanea of Sclater), of which only five specimens are known, all from the very limited area of Nel's Point, in the Beaufort District of the Cape Colony, and the equally aberrant Leopard (F. pardus., Var. melas; see Trimen, P. Z. S. 1883, 535, and Gunter, P.Z.S. 1885, pi. xvi. P. 243), of which only three examples are known, from the neighbourhood of the Koonap River, in the Fort-Beaufort District on the eastern side of the Cape Colony. It is very noticeable that, in all three cases, the abnormal form does not replace the normal one to which it is so nearly related, but occurs in the midst of the latter, quite isolated, yet appearing to maintain and perpetuate (albeit in but very few individuals) its particularities of colouring or of pattern."

In *Harmsworth Natural History* (1910), R. Lydekker describes the "hunting leopard" or "*chita*", as the cheetah was then known:

"The hunting leopard of South Africa has been stated to differ from the Indian animal in its stouter build, thicker tail, and denser and more woolly fur, the longest hairs occurring on the neck, ears, and tail. This woolly hunting leopard was regarded by its describer as a distinct species (*Cynaelurus lanius*), but it is, at most, only a local race, of which the proper name is *C. jubatus guttatus*."

Erythristic cheetahs have dark, orange-brown, or yellowish-brown spots against a golden background colour. Cream (or Isabelline) cheetahs have red spots on a pale background, known as ghost markings. In 1921, Pocock shot a cheetah with very little patterning in Tanganyika (now Tanzania). This may be the same genetic mutation that produces an Abyssinian-type pattern in domestic cats. Any patterns are restricted to the face, legs, and tail; with possibly a few thin stripes around the neck and barring on the legs. The background is the typical colour, only the pattern is missing. A spotless cheetah, known as a "golden cheetah", was photographed in Kenya in 2011. It had the well-known black facial markings typical of *Acinonyx*, but instead of being spotted, it had a pale sandy coat, much like a mountain lion, with "freckles" only on its back.

This colour morph is either triggered by an unknown mutation or by an existing recessive gene hidden within the local cheetah population. The presence of black facial markings and small pale spots rules out both albinism and leucism. Its physical characteristics closely match descriptions of the 1921 specimen shot in Tanzania. The appearance of unusual cheetah morphs suggests improved variability in the species through genetic mutation. Cheetahs show considerably less variability than many other wild cat species due to a genetic bottleneck more than 12,000 years ago, that led to inbreeding and subsequent loss of genetic diversity. Cheetahs experienced their first bottleneck event roughly 100,000 years ago when they began to expand their range into Asia, Europe, and Africa. This expansion is believed to have occurred rapidly, dispersing the cheetah over a very large area, thus restricting gene flow. All modern African cheetahs share such similar DNA that it is believed they are all descendants of a single mother and her cubs. This results in the limitation of genetic variation, infertility, and an increased vulnerability to disease. The woolly cheetah appears to be a normal cheetah but has longer, thicker fur. (Suggested trinomial: *Acinonyx jubatus* var. *lanatus*).

(Status: Identified, Mutation Unknown)

ATYPICAL TIGERS

Abu sotan

A "Wobo" by Any Other Name?

The *abu sotan* in Sudanese Arabic is allegedly a regional name given to the *wobo* reported from Ethiopia. It is believed to be a large, light-furred, big cat with dark blotches or stripes that resemble a tiger. Rumoured to inhabit the Rahad River and Blue Nile districts of Sudan, it was described by 19th-century German explorer and ornithologist Theodor von Heuglin as having a strangely long neck and pale fur marked with large black spots or longitudinal stripes. The notion of long-necked cats is nothing new in Africa. The ancient Egyptians and Mesopotamians depicted "serpent-necked lions" in their artwork, portraying an animal with the body of a felid (lion or leopard) and the head and neck of a serpent.

There is no name for this creature recorded in any of the known ancient texts; however, today, the term "serpopard" is commonly used to refer to ancient artefacts depicting these mythical serpent-necked big cats. Nelson Mandela (b. 1918 – d. 2013), the South African anti-apartheid activist who served as South Africa's president from 1994 to 1999, discussed the potential existence of an endemic African tiger species with fellow prisoners on Robben Island in his 1994 autobiography, *Long Walk to Freedom*. "One subject we hearkened back to again and again was the question of whether there were tigers in Africa. Some argued that although it was popularly assumed that tigers lived in Africa, this was a myth, and they were native to Asia and the Indian subcontinent. Africa had leopards in abundance, but no tigers. The other side argued that tigers were native to Africa, and some still lived there. Some claimed to have seen with their own eyes the most powerful and beautiful of cats in the jungles of Africa. I maintained that while there were no tigers to be found in contemporary Africa, there was a Xhosa word for tiger, a word different from the one for leopard and that if the word existed in our language, the creature must once have existed in Africa. Otherwise, why would there be a name for it?"

It is fascinating to find that there is a word for "tiger" in South Africa's Xhosa language. It has been established that the Xhosa word for tiger is "ingwe" and leopard is "ihlosi." However, the latter term can also be used to refer to tigers, making things somewhat complicated. This reminds me of how jaguars are often referred to as *"tigre"* in Latin countries. Nonetheless, according to a knowledgeable source conversant in Xhosa, while "ihlosi" may be used interchangeably, the term "ingwe" specifically refers to an actual tiger. It is conceivable that the *abu sotan* could be aberrant lions whose juvenile spots have merged into stripes that were kept to adulthood, or leopards whose spots have merged into stripes. Additionally, they may have been imported tigers from India or a hitherto unknown species of African tiger.

(Author's Verdict: 3/5)

Alaskan Tiger

Tigers of the Last Frontier?

A potentially new felid species has been reported from the wild US state of Alaska, where wintertime temperatures dip to 0°F/-18°C to

-30°F/-35°C from November to March; a harsh environment not conducive to a high human population (733,583 in 2022), making Alaska the least densely populated American state. Well-known North American mammals have crossed the Bering land bridge (Beringia) from Asia during multiple migration events. Fossil evidence shows that the Eurasian lynx arrived in North America approximately 2.5 million years ago, while the grey wolf is believed to have arrived during the Pleistocene epoch—roughly 700,000 years ago. Additionally, brown bears are believed to have ventured into Alaska around 100,000 years ago; however, they did not move south until 13,000 years ago following mass migrations of large mammals such as mammoths.

The first lions to cross into North America were a lineage of cave lions around 165,000 years ago. Due to climate change which caused Beringia to flood, these lions became isolated from other Asian populations and subsequently adapted, eventually evolving into the American lion (*Panthera atrox*). Approximately 63,000 years ago, a second wave of cave lions migrated into eastern Beringia – the area currently encompassing Alaska and Yukon. For reasons that are yet to be determined, these cave lions remained separated from American lions that had already populated southern regions. The most recent fossils, two specimens from Consolidated Pit 48 in Edmonton, Canada, date to about 11,400 years ago.

The bones of American lions have been found in Palaeolithic waste sites, suggesting that human predation contributed to its extinction. It is possible that at some point in the last 10,000 years, following the eradication of the cave lion in northwestern North America, the so-called Alaskan tiger, also known as the "White Death", may have descended from the Siberian tiger (*Panthera tigris tigris*), which could have potentially made a similar migration, giving rise to an unknown American linage. It is said that the Alaskan tiger is quite large, ferocious, and dangerous to humans. Local folklore states that it gains a new stripe for every human it kills. Although observations are scarce and contemporary reports are even rarer, people have been sporadically reporting sightings of a large tiger-like animal roaming the swamplands outside of Paxton for many years. If it exists, this is likely due to it inhabiting a remote and inhospitable subarctic habitat, featuring long, intense winters and short mild summers. Destination America's popular TV show *Alaskan Monsters* has an episode in Season I searching for the rumoured tiger.

In the episode 'The Alaskan Tiger', the team planned to capture and sedate the beast, however, it managed to evade them by changing directions. The swampy terrain then made it even more difficult to continue the search, leading them to give up without providing definitive proof of the tiger's existence. Throughout their range, tigers prefer to hunt deer. The red deer, one of the largest deer species, is no longer found in Alaska and there are no deer that live north of the Gastineau Channel. Where tigers do exist – the Indian subcontinent, the Indo-Chinese Peninsula, Sumatra, China, and the Russian Far East – wolf populations decrease because of direct competition and other ecological factors.

Perhaps utilising wolf statistical data to pinpoint potential target areas might be a productive approach for finding and identifying the alleged Alaskan tiger. Across Alaska, there are an estimated 7,000 to 11,000 wolves. However, wolf packs vary significantly in size and range within Alaska's parks; for example, they disperse between *Denali National Park and Preserve* and *Yukon-Charley Rivers National Preserve*. Other large Alaskan animals that could serve as prey for tigers include beavers, brown bear cubs, caribou, foxes, moose, river otters, and wolverines. While it is conceivable that an Alaskan tiger is an unknown variety descended from the Siberian tiger which migrated over Beringia, there is no concrete evidence to support its existence and thus may be a cautionary tale.

(Authors Verdict: 2/5)

Bái hǔ

An Unidentified White Tiger?

The *Bái hǔ* is said to be a white tiger or tiger-like animal reported from China, with evidence of its presence dating back at least 2,500 years. During the latter part of the 10th century, however, sightings of *bái hǔ* were rare, leading some to speculate that it may be extinct, if indeed it ever existed. Nevertheless, available documents indicate that it once had an expansive range across multiple regions, from Nan County (in present-day Southern Henan or Northern Hubei Provinces); Donghai region (in present-day Southern Shandong or Northern Jiangsu Provinces); Dayyao Mountain area, central Guangxi Zhuang Autonomous Region; and as recently as the early 1950s, from the Wanyang Mountain area in Southern Hunan. Reports of *bái hǔ* were also occasionally documented from areas that correspond to present-day Anhui, Jiangxi, Shanxi, and Yunnan provinces. The *bái hǔ* may indicate a hitherto undocumented, historical expansion of the Bengal tiger subspecies (*Panthera tigris tigris*) into the interior regions of China. A stunning colour morph of this subspecies is known as the White or Bleached Tiger; its white fur is due to a genetic mutation that blocks dark pigmentation. Another possibility that should be taken into account is that the *bái hǔ* could be an unrecognised felid species or subspecies, which has likely gone extinct due to human interference and environmental degradation. It could also be a *zouyu*, or simply an exaggerated myth or folktale. Bái hǔ is also one of the Four Symbols of the Chinese constellations (See *Zouyu*)

(Author's Verdict: 4/5)

Bali Tiger

Is the Bali Tiger Still Alive?

The Bali tiger, now known as *Panthera tigris sondaica* (formerly *P. t. balica*), is an apparently extinct tiger population that was endemic to the Indonesian island of Bali in the Lesser Sunda archipelago. Other names include *harimau bali* and *samong*. It is recognised as the smallest tiger in the Sunda Islands, though no official record of it has been made since the late 1930s; however, there are reports indicating that it may have survived in small numbers until at least the 1940s or even the 1950s. It was originally regarded as a distinct subspecies of the tiger which had been assessed as extinct on the *IUCN* Red List in 2008. However, in 2017, felid taxonomy was revised and updated, and the subspecies *P. t. balica* was subordinated to *P. t. sonaica*. This effectively replaced the Bali tiger's status from an extinct subspecies to a geographically-extinct population of *P. t. sondaica*.

The Dutch colonisation of the island in the mid-19th century sparked the onset of large-scale tiger hunting. Hunters typically employed a heavy steel foot trap as a means to capture tigers, with bait placed strategically to lure them in. Once trapped, hunters then shot the tigers using high-powered hunting rifles from close range. In 1941, *West Bali National Park* was established as the first game reserve in the country; however, it came too late to stave off the extinction of Bali's tigers. In 1972, two tourists reported that officers of the *Balinese Forestry Department* mentioned evidence suggesting that a population of Bali tigers may still exist on the island. Though it is likely that Bali's tigers are now extinct, there remains a slim possibility of a very small population existing in the interior of the island. However, this is probably wishful thinking.

(Author's Verdict: 2/5)

Black Tiger

Are There Black Tigers?

At least thirteen wild cat species are known to display melanism, these include the Asian golden cat (*Catopuma temminckii*), Geoffroy's cat (*Leopardus geoffroyi*), pampas cat (*L. colocola*), oncilla (*L. tigrinus*), jaguar (*Panthera onca*), leopard (*P. pardus*), and serval (*Leptailurus serval*). It is important to remember that not all species can be black, for instance, there are no fully documented black pumas, no black snow leopards, and no truly black tigers. Despite the confirmation of extremely dark tigers from skins found in zoos, there has yet to be a specimen that is entirely black. Additionally, numerous eyewitness reports of big cats thought to have been misidentified as black tigers have been reported from India, Java, and Myanmar (formerly Burma). Nevertheless, these sightings have yet to be verified. Those who have seen the animals up close have reported that they have black stripes on a solid black background, similar to the spots of melanistic leopards and the shade of black is only slightly different than that of the actual stripes. This implies that the genetic mechanisms for melanism vs. coat patterns are mutually exclusive.

One of the most widely held misconceptions by those who are critical of cryptozoology is that an unknown animal must be identified as a dramatic new species for it to be viewed as a success. Analytical cryptozoologists should focus only on biological realities. Nothing more. After all, hypotheticals aside, there can only be one truth and numerous falsehoods. A hitherto unconfirmed colour phase due to a mutant gene should be of great interest to a serious cryptozoologist. If this colouration is attributed to a recessive gene that might still be present in existing tigers, then new specimens could re-emerge from the gene pool if a considerable amount of parental lineages are heterozygous for their designated mutant allele. Some reports of "black tigers" have been confirmed as being very large melanistic leopards, commonly referred to as black panthers (see Giant Black Panther).

It is also conceivable that the animals reported were ordinary tigers covered in dark soil or some other dark material, seen from a long distance away and/or under imperfect lighting conditions. In addition, optical illusions may have further contributed to these perceptions. The differences in lighting and shadows can create the illusion of animals being much darker than they really are. Nevertheless, given there is no genetic reason why black tigers should not exist, true melanistic tigers cannot be ruled out as a possibility. After all, as the saying goes, absence of evidence does not mean evidence of absence. Until melanistic specimens are confirmed in the species *Panthera tigris*, the black tiger will retain its rightful place in cryptozoology.

(Author's Verdict: 4/5)

Bornean Tigers

An Undiscovered Tiger Population Hidden in Borneo?

Despite its geographic proximity of 1,350 km to the nearby island of Sumatra, no confirmed observations of tigers have been recorded in Borneo. Unconfirmed reports of tiger-like animals from the north, east, and interior regions of Borneo have been reported; however, they have yet to be confirmed. In the late 1990s, author and conservationist Erik Meijaard gathered evidence that suggests the existence of tigers on the island in recent times. Intriguingly, local indigenous groups like the animistic Dayak people have biological materials from tigers such as skulls, teeth, and skins.

The Bornean "tiger" is believed by some to be a true tiger species endemic to the Island of Borneo. It has been speculated that this potential species could be relatively small, similar to its Sumatran counterpart. According to locals, it is larger than a Bornean clouded leopard and is mainly brown with pale stripes. According to the traditions of the Dayaks, the Bornean tiger, unlike the Sunda clouded leopard, does not climb trees and instead favours the shaded forest floor. Tigers can easily climb trees but they seldom do so, except when the cubs are young. Their sharp and protractile claws provide a powerful grip to hold the tree trunk and climb up comfortably. But as they grow larger their body weight becomes a hindrance and they tend to live terrestrially. It is also worth noting that Borneo is home to ungulate species that the tiger would typically prey upon, like the Bornean bearded pig (*Sus barbatus*), the sambar deer (*Rusa unicolour*), and the Bornean yellow muntjac (*Muntiacus atherodes*).

The Bornean tiger's present status is unknown. Possible explanations include a small remnant population of tigers (*P. tigris*) thought to have been extinct in Borneo since the late Pleistocene/early Holocene, or perhaps the tiger was reintroduced in the not-so-distant past by the sultans of Sabah, Sarawak or Brunei. Of all the big cat species, tigers are probably nearest to extinction, with fewer than 3,900 remaining in the wild. They exist now in only 4% of their historic range and much of this decline has occurred in the past twenty years. Thus, further research is needed before we can confidently dismiss the circumstantial evidence of Bornean tigers.

(Author's Verdict: 3/5)

Brown Tigers

Reports have surfaced suggesting the existence of unconfirmed brown tigers, also known as "red tigers." These tigers vary in colour, usually appearing with light brown markings on an orange-red background. Complicating matters further is the fact that Indian zoos use the term "brown tiger" to separate regular tigers from the more costly white tigers. According to F. G. Alexander in the 1910 *Harmsworth Natural History*: "Concerning the tiger's colouration, my field of observation has been limited to Rajputana, Central India, and Bundelkhand, the jungles in which may be called "open jungles."

The colour of all the tigers killed by myself and my brother's sportsmen has, with two exceptions, been of a light red ochre. I once lured a cave tiger from its lair before sundown by tethering a bleating goat to a post in front, and within twenty yards of the underground cave. The incident occurred in the Asseerghur jungles. The colour of that beast was dark red ochre, far darker than that of any other tiger I ever killed. I have seen Siberian and Chinese skins, and have killed tigers during the hot weather, monsoon, and cold weather; and as regards the length of their hair, I have found very little difference between a cold-weather tiger and a hot-weather tiger. There was, however, one exception.

In Pertabgurgh territory – which is within twenty miles of Neeinuch – on one eventful Sunday I killed an adult male tiger. Judging by the teeth, he was very old. In length, he was only 8 feet 1 inch, but his fur was quite an inch long all over the body; his colour was ruddy ochre, the ruff round the neck was particularly full, and his whole appearance led me to regard him as a dwarf-like specimen. If the skin had been exposed for sale in a furrier's shop, it would have been accepted as a Chinese or Siberian specimen. This uncommon beast was killed in the autumn of 1888. There is no doubt that in dark jungles, such as those of the Siwaliks or the Dun forests, animals' skins assimilate themselves to the localities wherein the beasts live. That is Nature's general rule, but in open jungles, the pigment of the tiger's skin is invariably light. The Beemashunkur, Canara, and Belgaum jungles contain darker-coloured specimens, and I have seen skins from them all which were, on average, far ruddier than the thirty-one I have obtained and a dozen more which I have seen killed. Black-and-white tigers are but freaks of nature, and can no more be accounted for than can albino blackbuck or black panthers. In the markings of tigers and tigresses, I have noted that the black markings on the body and belly are broader on the male and that the double black band often surrounds an island of white or ochre, whereas in the tigresses such "surroundings" are by no means so common."

There are also records from India from the early 20th century that describe stripe-less, golden Bengal tigers. In 1929, Reginald Pocock documented a dark orange-brown tiger with stripes that were visible against its background colour. He wrote: "Possibly the red tiger, illustrated in our coloured plate and recorded below under the heading *Panthera tigris septentrionalis*, should come into this category of aberrations. It is a unique type with all the black pigment abstracted from the stripes, leaving them reddish-brown and only a little darker than the ground colour. A mounted male specimen labelled Persia and presented by Messrs. Rowland Ward.

This also is a rich-tinted specimen with numerous narrow stripes. On the top of the head and down the back the stripes are black, but they fade to brown on the flanks, and on the outside of the thighs they are only a little darker than the ground colour; they are also brown on the base of the tail and even on the belly and chest. The tendency toward the longitudinal fusion of the stripes on the croup is also noticeable. The white spot over the eye is smaller than in Indian tigers, and this appears to be a general feature in this race, but this specimen exhibits the peculiarity of having the spot on the back of the ear tan instead of white. This tiger resembles the specimens mentioned by Satunin in the brown tint of the stripes, but the brown is more extensive.

The dressed skin of a tigress ticketed 'Northern slopes of Mount Elburz' was presented by Col. R. L. Kennion who told me it was presented to him by a native chief. This tiger, represented in the coloured plate, is of extreme interest. The ground colour and the pattern are as in the Afghan specimen, but there is not a trace of black on the skin, all the stripes being brown and indistinctly defined owing to their approximation to the general hue of the coat, It is possible, of course, that this skin may represent a red variety, comparable to a red cat and coming into the same class as the black and white aberrations of the tiger above described. On the other hand, it must be noted that the complete suppression of the black pigment in the stripes is merely an extension of the process observable to a lesser degree in the mounted male specimen described above. The available material, indeed, of this race seen by me and recorded by Satunin seems to show a nearly complete gradation between the black stripes typical of tigers in general and the reddish-brown stripes of the Mount Elburz example. (Pl. I coloured.)"

In *The Journal of the Bombay Natural History Society* (v39: 1937-8), S. H. Prater recounted that: "Mr. W H Carter (Times, Oct 16th, 1936) writes "In one of the official district Gazetteers of Bengal there is mentioned a local variety of tiger which had lost its stripes as camouflage in the open sandy tracts of Sunderbans. The uniform colour scheme adopted was, however, brown." Note how this account differs from the original report in *The Provincial Geography of India – Bengal, Bihar and Orissa, Sikkim*, by L. S. S. O'Malley in 1917, which stated: "...those frequenting the sand dunes along the sea face of the Sundarbans have almost lost their stripes in adaptation to their environment so that their coats are of a tawny orange with only a few dark lines." Dr. Kota Ullas Karanth, a conservation zoologist and one-time director of the *Wildlife Conservation Society's* India Program, recalled in his book *"The Way of the Tiger"* (2001), that sometime during 1993, an orange-brown tiger with only the slightest patterning had been photographed at *Nagarahole National Park* located in Karnataka, India.

In April 1989, the *Indian Forester* published a paper titled "Tiger Without Stripes", authored by S. A. Sagar and L. A. K. Singh from *Similipal Tiger Reserve* in Orissa. The report mentioned several instances of Bengal tigers that had less to no stripes but were mostly orange-brown in colour. A stripe-less tiger was reported in 1961 by a senior state officer in Chitrakonda close to the Orissa-Andhra Pradesh border and in 1977 by an experienced tracker 800 km away in North-West Similipal; in 1979 by the same tracker in North-East Similipal; and in 1988 by a forest guard at North Similipal. Also, brown tigers with regular black stripes on a pale brown background have been reported from Thailand. Some historical reports of brown tigers may refer to the colour morph known as the "golden" or "strawberry" tiger. Notably, sightings of both stripe-less brown tigers and alleged black tigers appear to be limited to a single geographical region (Odsiha) leading to speculation that these unusual coat patterns may result from inbreeding and the expression of recessive or aberrant genes. Like observations of alleged black tigers, stripe-less brown tigers are located in a single geographical region, suggesting inbreeding is allowing the expression of recessive or aberrant genes to be reproduced in subsequent generations.

(Author's Verdict: 4/5)

Caspian Tiger

Is the Caspian Tiger Truly Extinct?

Traditionally thought to be extinct since the 1970s, the Caspian tiger (*Panthera tigris virgata*), also known as Balkhash tiger, Hyrcanian tiger, Turanian tiger, and Mazandaran tiger was a large tiger of West and Central Asia. Despite its supposed extinction, hunters in remote parts of Azerbaijan, Tajikistan, and Turkey continue to assert its existence. The Caspian tiger is mostly reported from Talysh, Azerbaijan, and the Cudi Mountains of Iran and Turkey. Its skull morphology significantly overlaps with and is almost indistinguishable from other tiger specimens from mainland Asia. Some Caspian tigers were intermediate in size between Siberian and Bengal tigers. Bengal tigers weigh slightly less than Siberian tigers, yet both of these big cats regularly weigh 270 kg (600 lbs), if not more.

In 1922, the last confirmed tiger was killed near Tbilisi, Georgia, after it had killed domestic livestock in the area. A pair of tigers were allegedly killed in Selcuk, Turkey, in 1943. Several tiger pelts found in the early 1970s near Uludere, Şırnak Province indicate the contemporary presence of an eastern tiger population. Surveys conducted in Şırnak revealed that between one and eight tigers were killed each year until the mid-1980s and that tigers had likely survived until the early 1990s. Sadly, due mainly to academic indifference, in addition to significant security issues, no further field research has been carried out in the region.

In Azerbaijan, the last known tiger was killed in 1932, however, there have been reports from the Talysh Mountains in later years. In Iran, one of the last confirmed tigers was shot in *Golestan National Park* in 1953, and another specimen was observed in the Golestan area five years later. The last known tiger killed in Turkmenistan occurred in January 1954, in the Sumbar River valley in the Kopet-Dag Range. The last record from the lower Amu Darya River was an unconfirmed report in 1968, near Nukus in the Aral Sea area.

By the 1970s, tigers had been eradicated from the Amu Darya River and the Pyzandh Valley located in the Turkman-Uzbek-Afghan border region, while the Piandi River between Afghanistan and Tajikistan acted as their "last stand" until the late 1960s. In 1948, the last Caspian tiger was recorded in the vicinity of the Ili River in Kazakhstan, which was the final known stronghold near Lake Balkhash. The last confirmed specimen in Afghanistan occurred in 1967. In 1998, an unsubstantiated sighting of a tiger in the vicinity of the Afghan-Tajik border in the Babatag mountain range in Denizli Province was reported. Then, in May 2006, a Kazakh hunter claimed to have seen a Caspian tigress accompanied by cubs near the same area. In the 1970s, a pharmacist in Eastern Turkey procured what may have been an illegally obtained Bengal pelt. Phylogeographic data revealed that the Caspian and Siberian tiger populations once shared a continuous geographic range until the early 19th century. It is possible that small isolated groups of Caspian tigers still survive in remote parts of Azerbaijan, Tajikistan, and Turkey, existing on the brink of extinction. Nevertheless, it should be noted that illegally introduced tigers of other subspecies might also inhabit these areas.

(Author's Verdict: 3/5)

Doglas

Is the Doglas an Unexpected Hybrid?

Possibly derived from the Hindi (Indo-Aryan) language, meaning "double-faced" or "two necked", the earliest known recorded use of the word 'doglas' is found in the Trinidadian newspaper *Penny Cuts*.

The *doglas* is reported to be a leopard-like big cat, with an estimated body length of eight feet, reported from India. It is usually described as having a greyish coat, striped shoulders, and a body that sometimes has rosettes. Its head has been compared to that of a leopard, featuring a ruff similar to that of a tiger, and its tail is long and curved – again likened to that of a leopard. In 1910, Frederick Codrington Hicks reported that the local people were very familiar with the large and peculiar cats he had encountered, which may have been a leopard x tiger hybrid.

According to Hicks' records, the animal's weight varied from approximately 22.6 kg (50 lbs) up to the size of a fully grown tigress (168 kg or 370 lbs), "There is a persistent idea among the natives all over India that the largest males of this species frequently mate with tigresses, who point as proof to the excessively prominent stripes with which some of these largest panthers are marked in the lower portions of the body. But this I think is a mistake, for I once, and once only, had the fortune to shoot a true hybrid, between a panther and a tigress I think, which was a vastly different looking animal to that referred to by the natives as a 'doglas'.

It happened shortly before I was mauled that I beat for what I thought was a tigress, the footmarks of the animal being like that of a female feline. During the beat the spotted head of a panther of extraordinary size pushed its way through the grass, followed by the unmistakable striped shoulders and body of a tiger, though looking a bit dirty as if it had been rolling in ashes. I succeeded in dropping this extraordinary creature dead with a shot in the neck, and, on examining it, I found it to be a very old male hybrid, with both its teeth and claws much worn and broken; its head and tail were purely that of a panther, but with a body, shoulders, and neck-ruff unmistakably that of a tiger, the black stripes being broad and long though somewhat blurred and breaking off here and there into a few blurred rosettes, the stripes of the tiger being the most predominant on the body. One of the peculiarities of this creature which I particularly noticed was, that though it was male, it had the feet of a female and measured a little over 8 feet in length.

This unique trophy, I am sorry to say, disappeared during the general confusion that followed my being mauled; it may have been sold off with others of my things while I lay unconscious, or it may have been stolen; I never succeeded in tracing it again. Having thus once seen a true hybrid, I am inclined to doubt whether there is really anything in the native idea of connecting some of the larger species of panthers, which they call 'doglas', with tigers; on the other hand, it has yet to be proved whether such a hybrid as I shot is capable of breeding again, or whether it is sterile. If they are capable of breeding again in their turn with other panthers, then there may be a great deal in this idea of the natives; in which case it may well be that it is originally owing to such crossings with tigers that we have the large species of panthers in India."

The *doglas* may be wild-born leogars (interspecific hybrids of a leopard and a tiger). Additionally, in September 1965, a purported leoger pelt was reportedly put up for sale. Several other cases of purported leogers have been reported, but these are often just unusual pelts that could be attributed to genetic mutations instead. As most of these reports are likely hoaxes or misinterpretations, it is difficult for scientists to conduct research into the biology of leogers. There is no concrete evidence that leogers exist in the wild; however, if they do occur infrequently, they would probably be infertile.

(Author's Verdict: 3/5)

Green Tiger

An Emerald Green Tiger... Cringer, is that you?

In June 2017, Karl Shuker received a thought-provoking email from James Nicholls in Perth, Australia. The email included a link to an account on *Reddit*, posted on Christmas Day 2016 by someone with the username AnathemaMaranatha. From their style of grammar and spelling, Karl deduced that they were probably of American nationality. The *Reddit* post recounted observations in 1969 with a "green tiger" near the Cambodian border by an entire light infantry company comprised of about 100 American soldiers. James Nicholls wrote: "Okay. I saw a green tiger. I wasn't alone. We were out towards the Cambodian border in the summer of 1969, an American light infantry company of about 100 or so guys. We were operating in flat-lands, thick jungle, along a river. (Saigon River? Not sure.) Bright, sunny day. We were proceeding single file when point platoon came to a stop, there was some yelling (we were stealthy – yelling is bad) from the point, then the platoon radioed for the Command Post (CP – the company commander and his people) to come up to point. When we got there, we found the point team glaring at each other – some kind of tussle. Point and drag were standing in the machine gunner's line of fire glaring at him. The machine gunner had wanted to shoot. Point and drag stopped him. He didn't like that.

"The object of discussion was across a jungle opening maybe 15 meters away, just peeking at us over the elephant grass. It was a big tiger – the biggest I've ever seen, Frank Frazetta-style big, but without the lady. Here's the insane part. The tiger was white where a tiger is white and black where a tiger is black, but all the orange parts were a pale green. We all saw it, maybe twenty grunts and me. The machine gunner was arguing that we have to shoot it, because otherwise no one would believe it. He had a point. But the rest of us were just awestruck. I mean, it might as well have been an archangel, wings halo and all. I felt an impulse to kneel. I don't think I was alone. The tiger stood there checking us out for maybe 15 minutes, not worried, not angry, just a curious cat. Then he turned and disappeared. Don't believe me? That's okay. I don't believe it myself. I mean WTF was that? Hallucinogenic elephant grass? Some trick of the light? The tiger walked through some kind of green pollen just before we saw it. No freakin' idea. There it is, OP. I don't believe it, and I saw it. Or hallucinated it. Me and all my blues. Make of it what you will. I'm done."

AnathemaMaranatha then added: "I apologize for not making clear that the tiger was scaring the shit out of all of us. He did NOT look sick or malnourished. He looked like he could be right in the middle of all of us in no time flat. He thought so, too. Didn't seem the least bit scared of us [...] I guess he wasn't hungry."

Dr. Shuker assessed the validity of the source of the story, taking into account that it could have been written by someone with direct experience in Vietnam. The post was well-received by Vietnam veterans. But what did the company actually see? Perhaps the distinctive fur colouration described could have been the result of the tiger having rolled in alga-choked water or in wet grass, as Karl mentions in his article. However, if that were the case, one would expect to see the entire tiger to have a greenish hue. Conversely, eyewitness accounts have reported seeing distinctive black stripes and pallid underparts, thus suggesting that rolling around in algae-filled water or grass is not a viable explanation. An optical illusion due to reflected light is possible; however, considering the duration of the observation (roughly 15 minutes) and that multiple witnesses reported it instead of one solitary onlooker, this seems improbable. The "green tiger", which was seen by multiple individuals yet only described once, remains an enigma.

(Author's Verdict: 3/5)

Harimau tingkiah

The "Creeping Tiger", aka "Tall Tiger" of West Sumatra

I first heard of this feliform cryptid through online communication with Dally Sandradeputra, Indonesia's only active cryptozoological investigator and guide for our 2022 expedition to Sumatra. According to Dally and several others, *harimau tingkiah* (Indonesian for "creeping tiger") is seen in the Indonesian regency of Tanah Datar in the West Sumatra province; usually around the Minangkabau village of Pariangan. Eyewitnesses describe a strange tiger with an odd walking gait, seen in the vicinity of "the garden" - a semi-cultivated area on a mountainside near Pariangan. The *harimau tingkiah* is sometimes considered a quasi-paranormal being by locals, who give it the same level of intelligence and cunning as humans.

Searching for Harimau Tingkiah.

We directly experienced this folklore when a plantation owner solemnly suggested that a *harimau tingkiah* had stolen one of our trail cameras. We had found one to be missing, and supposedly, the *harimau tingkiah* was aware that we were searching for it and had removed the device from its secure position with an uncanny human-like capability, taking it away into the night without leaving any trace of broken plastic or damaged straps. According to this gentleman, the *harimau tingkiah* was actively hindering our efforts to find it.

During our second week of research in "the garden" with Dally, we were able to identify its likely species. The *harimau tingkiah* (Indonesian: pronounced 'ha-ri-mow ting-keh') is a genuine flesh and blood tiger. It appears to represent either natural range expansion in the island's growing tiger population or a hitherto unknown remnant population. Our expedition would eventually discover irrefutable evidence in the form of clear paw prints and trail camera video recordings showing a wandering tiger at a location in Sumatra where, according to Dally, the porters, the owner of the plantation, and the *World Wide Fund for Nature* (WWF), tigers have not been officially recorded before. We also found tracks nearby from what appears to be a different, much smaller individual.

So by arduously searching for this strange feliform cryptid, we eventually realised, and then subsequently demonstrated beyond a reasonable doubt, that *harimau tingkiah* is, in fact, a real flesh and blood tiger, hitherto unknown from the region. While unlikely to be distinct in terms of its taxonomy, our data demonstrates incontrovertibly that there is a small undocumented, yet potentially viable tiger population living around Pariangan, West Sumatra. It seems these magnificent big cats are so rarely seen as they [re]populate the region they have become almost ghost-like in the minds of the local people. Detractors will likely reject the cryptozoological significance of our discovery by claiming that since the data didn't lead to a strange new species, it's not a cryptozoological success.

This attitude completely misses the point, as by lending credence to anecdotal evidence ingrained in folklore, we provided invaluable ecological and conversational data; undeniable proof that tigers do in fact inhabit the area. Perhaps they have been there all along. It should be obvious to anyone with even the most basic understanding of tiger behaviour and physiology, that there is absolutely no way that a tiger could have carefully untied and carried away our missing camera. If a tiger had decided to rip the camera from the tree out of some sort of territoriality, there should have been pieces of the plastic casing, broken straps, mechanism, etc. scattered nearby, yet there was nothing to be seen. No evidence of the camera was found, and after a detailed search of the surrounding jungle, the only tracks we discovered belonged to a tiger. Our porters and the plantation owner were convinced that this was definitive proof of the *harimau tingkiah's* involvement. In terms of cryptozoology, our discovery lies somewhere between a true cryptid and what is sometimes referred to in cryptozoological circles as a "pseudo-cryptid", i.e. a known species found outside its expected range. Regardless, our success in Sumatra clearly illustrates the advantages of utilising cryptozoological techniques as a potential data source – namely, a doorway to zoological exploration through cryptozoology.

Sandradeputra, Dally. pers comm, Sept, 17th 2022.

(Status: Species Identified, Hitherto Unknown Population, Folkloristic Embellishments)

Javan Tiger

Do Tigers Still Inhabit Java?

For decades, the Javan tiger has been considered extinct, as there have been no confirmed sightings since the mid-1970s of the big cat that roamed the jungles of Indonesia's fifth largest island. To the locals, the Javan tiger was a brutal beast, powerful enough to break the legs of water buffalo and was much persecuted by the islanders. It ranged over much of Central and Eastern Java, from Lawu Mountain, Mount Ariuno, *Meru Betiri National Park*, Mount Merapi, and *Mount Merbabu National Park*. The tigers of Java were small in comparison to the Asian mainland subspecies and similar in size to the Sumatran tiger. The males were approximately 2.5 metres (8.2 feet) in length and weighed between 100 and 141 kg (220 – 311 lbs). The tigresses were considerably smaller weighing between 75 and 115 kg (165 and 254 lbs). Its smaller body mass is attributed to the size of the available prey species in Java, and to Bergmann's ecogeographical rule that within a broadly distributed taxonomic clade, populations and species of larger size are found in colder environments, while populations and species of smaller size are found in warmer regions, correlating external temperature and the ratio of body surface to weight in homeothermic (warm-blooded) species.

Their stripes are unique among tigers In that they are long and thin, and slightly more numerous than those of the Sumatran tigers that once shared its scientific name *Panthera tigris sondaica*. The Javan tiger also exhibits some intriguing characteristics. Other than the carnassials being comparatively long compared with those of other tigers, and therefore perfect for slicing through large chunks of meat, the external surface of the occipital bone above the superior nuchal line is surprisingly thin, and its nose is long and narrow. Based on these subtle differences, the Javan tiger was assigned to the level of species in 1929 and given the scientific name *Panthera sondaica*. The last confirmed sightings occurred in 1976 and although officially declared extinct in 2003, tigers are still occasionally reported in Java, most notably from the island's *Meru Betiri National Park*.

In November 2008, the mauled body of a female hiker was found in *Mount Merbabu National Park*, Central Java, allegedly savaged by a tiger. The local villagers who discovered the remains also reported tiger sightings in the area, firmly establishing the contemporary cryptozoological status of the Javan tiger. In January 2009, villagers claimed to have seen a tigress with two small cubs close to a village near a massive volcano called Gunung Lawu straddling the border between East and Central Java. Several fresh tracks were found, but by that time, the animals that made them had made good their escape. Following the October 2010 eruption of Gunung Merapi ("fire mountain"), two villagers reported finding large feline paw prints in the ashes, sparking fears that a tiger was roaming abandoned farms in the area. However, officials of the nearby national park doubted whether the paw print belonged to a tiger. A big cat alleged to be a Javan tiger was photographed in Mount Arjuno, Eastern Java in 2016.

In the photo, we see a tiger walking on a small path in a forested area. The photo was taken from above, making it unclear where it was taken. Therefore, many have doubted its authenticity. Iwan Kurniawan, the project manager of *Javan Langur Center* in Batu, said that the forests around Mount Mujur and Mount Indrokilo are too unhealthy to sustain a breeding tiger population. "In general, the forest of Mt. Arjuno is in a bad condition. Many habitats have been destructed and converted into farms. It is quite impossible for a tiger to live there," said Iwan on June 25th, 2016. Meanwhile, agreeing with the *Javan Langur Center*, another organisation working for wildlife and forest conservation, *PROFAUNA*, also doubted the authenticity of the photo. PROFAUNA's chairman, Rosek Nursahid, said: "There were reported sightings of a Javan tiger, but we have never seen one. Only the Javan leopard has been confirmed to occur there." Although doubting the photo, Rosek added that *PROFAUNA* will carry out a field investigation to confirm or deny the verity of the claim. If it's later proven true, the authorities will have to implement stricter vigilance in this area because it is also a favourite site for hunters. Bambang Darmadja, the chairman of *Meru Batiri National Park*, is clearly not convinced the tiger is extinct; or that all the evidence consists of mistaken observations of Javanese leopards, stating "I am optimistic that the Javanese tigers still exist at Meru Betiri, although no TNMP officer has seen the animal personally and the [five] trap cameras that we installed several years ago didn't produce any pictures of the nearly extinct wild animal."

In August 2017, a wildlife ranger working at *Ujung Kulon National Park* captured a photograph of what appeared to be a Javan tiger while it was feeding. A research team was enlisted to verify the presence of this alleged tiger, but an expert identified the creature in the picture as a Javan leopard instead. Although there were many signs which suggested otherwise, it is still vaguely possible that there may be a small surviving population of Javan tigers that are on the very brink of extinction, making them almost impossible to detect.

(Author's Verdict: 3/5)

Maltese Tiger

Between Cryptozoology and the Blue Colour Morph

The Maltese tiger, or *lanhu* (literally "blue tiger") seems to be an unconfirmed colour morph of the tiger, reported mostly in the Fujian Province of China, but similar animals have also been reported from Korea. They are characterised as having a blue-grey base colour, with a deep blue on the ribcage and clearly defined black or dark grey stripes. Maltese tigers are predominantly reported in the South Chinese subspecies (*Panthera tigris tigris*), which today is critically endangered, due to the illegal and continued use in traditional Chinese medicine and the alleles that make it "blue" perhaps being extinct.

Harry R. Caldwell (b. 1876 – d. 1970), a Methodist missionary, ornithologist, and big game hunter, who shot and killed tigers throughout much of Fujian Province, noted that in the September of 1910, he had observed a strange tiger near Rongcheng (Fuzhou). According to Caldwell, he had the blue tiger in his rifle sights, but apparently also in the line of fire were two young children, forcing the experienced hunter to lower his rifle, thus abandoning the shot and losing the opportunity to prove the existence of the blue tiger. In 1922 another hunter claimed to have killed a blueish-grey South China tiger, and in 1924, another blue tiger was reported from the same region. Caldwell claimed he had another sighting in 1925, but again without acquiring the essential biological specimen.

The *lanhu* may be a Maltese colour morph triggered by a genetic mutation. Karl Shuker suggests that the stripes described in the original reports may simply have been lighter than the witnesses noticed during the observation, or there is possibly a separate genetic mutation for the darker stripes reported.

(Author's Verdict: 4/5)

Seah Malang Poo

A Data Deficient Feliform Cryptid Reported From Thailand

The *seah malang poo*, reported from *Khao Sok National Park* in Thailand, is said to inhabit the karst limestone mountains of the area, characterised by barren terrain, caves, sinkholes, and subterranean rivers. Eyewitnesses described a robust, brown-coloured, cat-like creature with black stripes. A seah malong poo (sometimes incorrectly spelt "seah malang paa") was allegedly shot and killed during the 1930s, and its skin was sent to the *Bangkok National Museum*, the oldest museum in Thailand. To date, however, no authentication of this specimen has been issued by the museum and there is insufficient data to form hypotheses for accurately identifying the *seah malang poo*. Possibly extinct.

(Author's Verdict: 2/5)

Shing Mun Tiger

A Barking Big Cat?

The alleged Shing Mun tiger from the Shing Mun Valley area of Hong Kong, is thought to have a leopard-like or tiger-like appearance, measuring around four feet long. Additionally, it is purported to have luminous eyes and a long tail, as well as the strange ability to bark like a dog. In July 1965, a senior student of the Diocesan Girl's School reported seeing a tiger while picnicking with classmates on the lower slopes of Tai Mo Shan, the highest mountain in Hong Kong. A search was conducted but only revealed flattened grass that could have been left by a tiger. Subsequent sightings were reported and hunts were organised but ultimately no concrete proof of its existence was found.

In late October at the village of Shatin near the Chinese border, Chan Pui, a local builder, proposed that the animal in question was not a tiger, but rather a wolf or domesticated dog that had become wild. Given that there are no known tigers, leopards, or wolves living in Hong Kong, it is much more likely that an escaped or illegally released exotic felid is the cause.

(Author's Verdict: 2/5)

Stripe-less Tigers

The stripe-less tigers of the Indian subcontinent are either uniformly brown or whitish-cream in colour. They are reported from open sandy areas, which is an unusual habitat for tigers. One potential explanation for this phenomenon could be a yet undescribed colour polymorphism in the tiger. Morph shifts are compatible with the idea that polymorphism is advantageous for populations and species. Experimental and comparative data indicate that colour polymorphism is associated with reduced extinction risk. Stripe-less leucistic (white) tigers, which are a result of a genetic condition resulting in the near-absence of stripes, have been documented. In 1820, Georges Cuvier described such a specimen exhibited at the Royal Menagerie at Exeter Change in London, England, as "a white variety of tiger [...] with the stripes very opaque, and not to be observed except in certain angles of light."

If leucism in tigers can result in the production of rare, stripe-less variants, is it possible that darker specimens exhibiting the chemical pheomelanin or individuals with true genetic mutations may be able to do so as well due to an unforeseen genetic factor?

(Author's Verdict: 4/5)

Tanuak

A Giant Patternless Tiger?

The massive *tanuak* (Indonesian, pronounced 'tan-oo-ah') of West Sumatra is said to be tiger-like in appearance, often monochromatic and usually in shades of yellow. It is reported to be much larger than usual for big cats, boasting a wide back similar to that of the Sumatran rhinoceros. It is said the *tanuak* has a short face, more so than the typical tiger, and is sometimes described as having both feline and anthropomorphic features. Enormous tracks have been discovered and attributed to the *tanuak*. It has a long tail, large muscular limbs, and enormous paws with long dangerous claws. While its size is probably exaggerated, the *tanuak* may represent a population of larger than normal Sumatran tigers or an extremely large, unknown species, possibly related to the *cigau*.

(Author's Verdict: 2/5)

Xinjiang Tiger

A Surviving Caspian Tiger?

The Xinjiang tiger (Uyghur: Turkic), also referred to as the Tarim tiger, Lop Nur, or Lop Nor tiger is typically encountered in wooded and wetland areas or by large oxbow lakes, ranging from Lop Nur (Lop Nor) and the Konqi (Kongque) River basin to western China's Xinjiang Uygur Autonomous Region. Reports also originate from Hotan in the south-west; Karashar in the north; Kuche in the north-west, Korla centrally; Aksu and Bachu to the west; as well as remote regions of Altyn-Tagh and Tian Shan, together with Urumchi. It is believed that Xinjiang tigers are more vividly coloured than other tigers and primarily subsist on wild boar, Mongolian gazelles, and the kiang, the largest of the wild asses. The tiger was once abundant throughout China, boasting large populations at the close of the 19th century. Unfortunately, this majestic big cat became critically endangered during the 20th century.

In 1768, while exiled in Xinjiang, Ji Yun composed a poem about reported tiger hunting paths. He also noted an account of a woodcutter who had allegedly encountered tigers in the mountains west of Urumchi (formerly Dihua). It was the renowned Russian geographer and explorer Nikolai Przewalski (b. 1839 – d. 1888) who first introduced the outside world to this alleged big cat in late 1876. He attempted to capture or kill a specimen for classification, but his attempts were unsuccessful. In February 1885, Przewalski explored Xin'abudan in Lop Nur and witnessed a tiger hunting wild boars there. During his explorations, he described several species until then unknown to science, such as the takhi (aka Przewalski's horse), Przewalski's gazelle (*Procapra pryzewalskii*), and the Bactrian camel (*Camelus ferus*). Unfortunately, all of these are now endangered species!

In 1934, a Swedish doctor named Hemel was given a photograph of a tiger pelt during a field research investigation, and tiger tracks were discovered in Ala'er, western Xinjiang in 1950.

In 1953, a group of herdsmen from Tierege Leke Kulecun, a locality in Xinjiang with an elevation of 1247 metres (4091 ft), allegedly killed a tiger and preserved its skin. If this is true then its whereabouts are unknown. In the 1980s, an officer from the Tacheng Military Subarea of northern Xinjiang reported witnessing a tiger that had been caught and killed by local herders. As is often the case, no trace of the tiger remains. In August or September 2001, retired cadre Yang Shulin apparently had a frightening encounter with an approaching tiger on his way to Altyn-Tagh in north-western China. They came to within forty metres of each other, close enough for Shulin to see its brightly coloured fur was made up of black, brown, yellow, and white. In October 2001, an employee named Wu Shiguang of the *Tourist Administration Prefecture of Bayingolin Mongol Autonomous Prefecture* apparently found several tracks belonging to tigers along the Lower Tarim

River flowing into Lop Nur along the northern edge of the Takli-makan Desert.

The Xinjiang tiger might be a surviving variety closely related to the Caspian tiger; however, the Caspian tiger was much larger. Therefore, it is possible that the Xinjiang tiger is a small endemic subspecies that has undergone genetic isolation and developed in its own unique way. It could also represent an unrecognised subspecies of the tiger native to the landlocked Xinjiang Uygur Autonomous Region.

(Author's Verdict: 3/5)

Zouyu

Is the Zouyu a Cheetah, a Snow Leopard, or Something Else Entirely?

Commonly referred to as *zouwu*, *zouya*, and *zouyu*, this feliform cryptid is believed to be a white tiger with black spots or stripes inhabiting northern and north-western China. Reports suggest it is incredibly swift on its feet and has an intimidating appearance, yet by all accounts is surprisingly gentle in nature. Interestingly, if the *zouyu* (Chinese) is a felid, it is unique in its dietary habits as, unlike other felids, it seems to be primarily herbivorous, but may also eat carrion. This is noted in the *Huainanzi* – a collection of scholarly works from before 139 BC where it is described as a "benevolent" creature that feeds only on already dead animals. The earliest known literary reference to a *zouyu* occurs in the *Shan Hai Jing* ("Classic of Mountains and Seas"), which may have been composed as early as the 4th century BC. According to the text, a *zouyu* lived in the protagonist Lin's home-land, likely in present-day northern or north-western China.

Additionally, the *Classic of Poetry* written between the 11th and 7th centuries BC contains a poem called 'Zouyu' which describes it as a "righteous" animal, white-furred, with black stripes." Captive *zouyus* are depicted in the imperial gardens in Zhang Heng's emotional commentary *Dongdufu* ("Eastern Metropolis Rhapsody") from the Great Ming dynasty (1368 – 1644). According to the *Book of Qi*, an official record of the Southern Qi dynasty, in 478 AD, a '*zouyu*' came down from Wujie Mountain in Andong County, which is the present-day city of Huia'an, northern Jiangsu Province.

The Zhōu Shū (Book of Zhou) is an official record of the short-lived Northern Zhou dynasty, which spanned from 557 to 581 AD. According to the work, there was an encounter with a *zouyu* in Lizhou, located in present-day Guangyuan County in northeastern Sichuan Province, believed to have taken place either in 574 or 575 AD. The original Zhōu Shū contained fifty chapters, though some of them have been lost over time and replaced using other sources. According to the *Minghuang Zalu* – a collection of stories surrounding Emperor Tang written during the reign of Emperor Xuanzong of the Tang Dynasty (618 to 906 AD) – a fur coat made from a *zouyu* pelt was sent to the Xingqing Palace in Xi'an. In October 1404, Zhu Su, Prince of Wu, presented the emperor of Beijing with a *zouyu* that was described as "cloud," "snow," or "hoarfrost" coloured and adorned with black spots, which had been captured near Junzhou in north-western Hubei Province. After being presented with the zoological curiosity, the emperor was greatly impressed by its unusual appearance and commanded for it to be shown in the capital.

Li Long, commander of Nanjing's garrison in Jiangsu Province, delivered a pair of *zouyus* to the emperor in Beijing in April 1429. These were taken from Shigu Mountains located in modern-day eastern Anhui Province's Lai'an region where they were described as stealthy, light-furred animals patterned with black stripes. A misrepresentation of the *zouyu* appears in the highly overrated 2018 fantasy film *Fantastic Beasts: The Crimes of Grindelwald*, as an elephant-sized cat composed of a hybrid mix of lion and tiger features including large eyes, four upper tusks, and a ruffled tail.

Possible explanations for the *zouyu* include a snow leopard (*Panthera uncia*) or a closely related, undescribed species. Characteristics, such as its lightly coloured pelage, and long, densely furred tail are reported. The snow leopard's inability to roar, its habit of caching food, and its great patience as an opportunistic hunter, may have made it appear benevolent to early observers. Perhaps the *zouyu* is a white tiger or an albino king cheetah as suggested by scholar Wang Ting. The cheetah hypothesis is less likely simply because the Asiatic cheetah (*Acinonyx jubatus venaticus*) is not native to China and unless the species has been introduced at some unknown point in the past, the cheetah is an unlikely explanation. In 2012, a fossil claimed to be a "Chinese cheetah" and given the scientific name *Acinonyx kurteni* was demonstrated to be a forgery. Some cryptozoologists, such as Jan Willem Duyvendak, have suggested that the *zouyu* may be exaggerated accounts of the giant panda (*Ailuropoda melanoleuca*). The panda's dietary habits might explain why the *zouyu* is considered benevolent. Another theory is that *Sivapanthera* may not be extinct. Fossils of this Pleistocene big cat, which probably looked much like a larger and sturdier cheetah; adapted for high-speed running, have been discovered in northwestern China. *Sivapanthera* differed from modern cheetahs by having relatively longer brain cases, flatter foreheads, narrower nostrils and larger teeth.

(Author's Verdict: 2/5)

ONZAS AND OTHER CURIOUS COUGAR-LIKE CRYPTIDS

Beast of Bladenboro

A Hoax or a Variety of Eastern Cougar?

In 1953, North Carolina experienced a period of unrest following a series of vicious attacks on domestic animals, mainly dogs. The Beast of Bladenboro was described as a black cat-like creature measuring approximately three to four feet in length, with a 14-inch tail and standing about 50 cm high. Reports suggest it was aggressive and potentially sanguivorous (a creature that feeds primarily on blood); responsible for the deaths of nine dogs and one pet rabbit, either through decapitation or by crushing their skulls and lapping up the blood. In addition, large pawprints resembling those of a cat were also found, believed to belong to the mysterious creature.

On December 29th, the "beast" struck for the first time in Clarkton, close to Bladenboro. In an effort to track down the creature, almost 1000 people took part in a search on January 6-7; however, nothing was found. Descriptions varied greatly, with it being reported as having a cat-like appearance but as to what species was never ascertained. Other reports noted that it resembled a bear, coyote, wolf, wolverine, and even an escaped police dog. One resident described it as "about four and a half feet [1.4 m] long, bushy, and resembling either a bear or a panther", while another said it was "small", remarking there was "a little one just like it [...] running beside it". A local newspaper reported an encounter with the creature: "It was bout [sic] 20 inches [50 cm] high. It had a long tail, about 14 inches [35 cm]. The colour of it was dark. It had a face exactly like a cat. Only I ain't ever seen a cat that big."

A hunting party from Wilmington, 96 km (60 miles) southeast of Bladenboro, tracked the creature for three miles (4.8 km) through swampland. According to them, the tracks showed 2.5 cm (1 inch) claw marks, and they estimated the animal to weigh somewhere in the region of 35 to 40 kg (80 – 90 lbs). It would make occasional circling movements, indicating that it might have had offspring or a mate nearby. On January 4th a "half-dozen brave youths" spent the better part of a day searching for the "beast" with their dogs, while that night, Police Chief Fores and eight to ten other officers began their own search. The next day witnesses reported an attack on a dog that ran away injured. A subsequent search of the area revealed two sets of tracks near one of the attack sites, indicating that one animal was significantly larger than the other. Later that night, another witness reported seeing, "a big 'mountain lion' near some dogs three houses down."

According to Fores, the witness found tracks on a dirt road near her home that were "bigger than a silver dollar", i.e., noticeably more than 38.10 mm (1.50 inches) in diameter. That same day, more than 500 people and their dogs searched for the "beast" through the woods and swamps around Bladenboro and on January 6th, hundreds more joined the hunt. According to one source, Fores planned to use dogs as live bait in a bid to lure the creature; however, this callous strategy was quickly abandoned. Later, a boy named Dalton Norton reported encountering a large cat which he claimed made a noise like a baby crying. The next day, around 800 to 1000 people had gathered; however, by the next evening, only four students from the *University of North Carolina* were still looking for the creature. As is often the case when large numbers of armed individuals act without central guidance, things quickly got out of hand, enough for Mayor Woodrow Fussell to declare that he would terminate the hunt due to safety concerns unless either another obvious kill was made or if a more reliable witness came forward.

On January 11th, two vehicles came to an abrupt stop to avoid hitting a creature claimed to be the Bladenboro beast. It was described by one of the drivers as having "runty-looking ears" and a "brownish and tabby" colouration and was roughly four feet (1.2 m) in length. Two days later a local farmer, called Luther Davis discovered a bobcat trapped in Big Swamp near Boardman and Orrum villages which he killed with a rifle shot to the head. This incident reminds me of Steven Spielberg's Jaws where the mayor of Amity Island is presented with evidence regarding the presence of a giant great white shark yet still maintains that the beaches should remain open. The mayor of Bladenboro also introduced a possible false narrative that the creature had been found and destroyed (and photographed by Fussell). Later the same day, Bruce Soles, from Tabor City was driving away from Bladenboro when he struck a large cat-like creature with his vehicle. According to Soles, the animal had spotted fur similar to a leopard and was 60 centimetres (24 inches) high, and weighed between 35 and 40 kg (75 to 90 lbs). Soles took the deceased animal back home with him to Tabor City. A third man by the name of Berry Lewis is sometimes credited as having killed the creature, which has caused confusion as to whether it was this or Davis's cat that Mayor Fussell had photographed. Mr. Lewis was apparently hunting in a completely different area of Bladen County when he shot his "beast".

A. R. Stanton, of Lumberton, North Carolina speculated that the Beast of Bladenboro may have been a crossbreed German Shepherd known as 'Big Boy' which he had gifted to a First Nations boy living close to Big Swamp. Stanton said that Big Boy was dark in colour and sported a long, bushy tail. He further stated that Big Boy could easily leap over six-foot fences with ease to hunt chickens. It is conceivable that the Beast of Bladenboro may have been exaggerated reports of a hitherto unknown variety of eastern cougar living undetected in North Carolina.

(Author's Verdict: 2/5)

Black Cougar

Black "Panthers" Sure, but Black Cougars!?

Melanism is a common mutation observed in many cat species and has been linked to processes such as camouflage, thermoregulation, and parasite resistance. To date, however, there have been no confirmed sightings or carcasses of truly black cougars discovered in the wild and furthermore, none have been bred in captivity. In spite of the lack of physical evidence, there have been reports of solid black cougars or black cougars with pale undersides. In 1959, a particularly dark specimen was killed by Miguel Ruiz in Costa Rica, estimated to weigh between 45.3 and 54.4 kg (100 – 120 lbs). This is thought to be one of the darkest specimens ever recorded. Accounts of melanistic cougars have also been reported from Kentucky; one of such speaks of a black cougar with a yellow-coloured underside that escaped during the deer season. The cougar, scientifically named *Puma concolour* ("concolour" meaning one colour) displays an impressive range from light to dark.

All cougars have lighter undersides, particularly on the throat and chest; however, melanistic specimens – those with a mutation that cancels out the white colouring on these areas – add an extra layer of complexity to this creature's alleged appearance. Reports of melanistic cougars with paler undersides are therefore puzzling. Perhaps a recessive mutation known as the black and tan allele is responsible. Mammals homozygous for this mutation have black fur, but the underparts are pale or cream in colour. The question is, does this apply to the cougar? A Colourado hunting guide claimed that during the late 1950s, or possibly the early 60s, he had shot and killed two cougars that were almost black, yet they were white in all the places where cougars usually are, i.e. the chest and undersides.

Furthermore, many of the cougars taken from that area had noses that were dark, whereas they are usually a light pink colour. Melanism, which is a congenital excess of melanin, has been observed in various felid species. Although there are no known specimens, nor are there any historical records of black cougars, there is no genetic reason why they can't exist. Black cougar sightings have been reported near lowland marshes, where dark silt is common, and this may explain some cases. It is plausible that some sightings might be attributed to cougars whose fur has become darkened by silt or another dark-coloured material. Scientists remain sceptical that melanistic cougars exist. Despite reports of extremely dark cougars from Central America, physical evidence, such as a dead specimen or a detailed photograph, has yet to be obtained. Observations could be visual illusions. Subtle differences in lighting conditions and shadow can create illusions where animals appear darker than they really are.

(Author's Verdict: 3/5)

Cuitlamiztli

A Vague Puma-like Predator of Mexico

Cuitamiztli is thought to mean "glutton cat" in the Nahuatl language (Uto-Aztecan). Sightings have been reported from Mexico, particularly from the highlands where it is said to pose a danger to both humans and animals, particularly the deer it typically hunts. Bernal Diaz del Castillo (b. 1492 – d. 1584), a Spanish conquistador who participated in the bloody campaigns against the Aztec Empire, recounted witnessing a wolf-like animal in the menagerie of Montezuma II at Teotihuacan in 1520 – a sighting which some have connected with the *cuitlamiztli*. Karl Shuker has suggested that it could be explained by surviving *Chasmaporthetes ossifragus*, also known as the hunting or running hyena. *C. ossifragus* is the only Hyaenid fossil discovered in North America. Alternatively, some believe it may be an *onza*.

(Author's Verdict: 2/5)

Mexican Ruffed Cat

Unidentified Catlike Creatures Reported From Mexico's Sierra Mountains

Also referred to as the Nayarit ruffed cat, biologist Ivan Sanderson purchased two pelts of this animal from a mountain village in 1940 in the Mexican state of Nayarit. Unfortunately, these specimens were later accidentally destroyed by the Belize government before other scientists had a chance to examine them. Furthermore, Sanderson reported that he located another pelt for sale in Colima that same year, yet he failed to acquire it. Mexican ruffed cats (MRC hereafter) typically measure between 1m 37cm (4ft 6in) and 2m 13cm (6ft 12in) from nose to tail tip. Their fur is brown with dark stripes on the upper legs and flanks, and the lower legs exhibit hues ranging from dark brown to black and the tail can grow up to 45 cm (1.5 m). Moreover, MRCs are thought to not possess any facial markings, except for

a long neck ruff which hides the ears. Additionally, they are characterised as having long legs and large paws with yellowish claws.
Locals from the Sierra Mountains in the Mexican state of Nayarit
have noted that MRCs do not resemble the jaguar, cougar, or
jaguarundi. Some cryptozoologists theorise that they may be a population of small-sized sabre-toothed cats; however, due to their dark
and light brown stripes resembling those found on tabbies, others
suggest they are nothing more than unusually large house cats
(approximately 1 m – 2 m!). It has also been postulated that MRC may
be abnormal specimens of the Mexican bobcat (*Lynx rufus escuinapar*,
syn. *L. r. oaxacensis*), which is found in the region.

(Author's Verdict: 3/5)

Onça

A Puma-like Predator of Brazil

Reported from São Paulo, Brazil, the *onça* is a large and mysterious
carnivore resembling descriptions of the *onza* reported from Mexico.
On February 28th, 2006, John Kirk, a cryptozoologist and the President of the *British Columbia Scientific Cryptozoology Club* shared a
report published on Loren Coleman's *Cryptomundo* website.

'Tony and his family lived on a huge farm outside of the bustling
metropolis of Sao Paulo, Brazil. The Xavier family busied themselves
with raising cattle, and crops and enjoying the good life that a
successful enterprise can bring [...] One night while driving home to
the farm Tony caught site [sic] of something on the side of the road,
as he drew closer to the object, it moved out into the middle of the
road. He could see, in the beam of his headlights, a very large cat, like
none he had seen before. This mystery felid was so different from the
jaguars that haunt the Amazon forests and was certainly no cougar.
After a moment or two the mystery cat bounded into the bush leaving
Tony shaking his head at what he had seen.

Upon returning to his farm, he asked the farmhands about any strange cats thought to lurk around the farm and described what he had seen to them. They looked at him in amazement and could not believe Tony's good fortune. You see Tony was born in Hong Kong to a respected Portuguese/Spanish family and had only moved to Brazil in the early 1950s, for a foreigner to have seen an animal that few Brazilians ever had was indeed an astonishing stroke of luck. The farm workers told Tony that this species of cat was unknown to most people and was only seen deep in the depths of the jungle. Most of them had never seen it for themselves and had only heard from others about their brief sightings. They said the creature had a light-covered coat and part of the animal was spotted, I know not where, but it was not a leopard or a jaguar. The farmhands told him that the cat was known as an Onca, but not the jaguar that is known by that (*Panthera onca*) and that it was very rarely ever seen. For it to have been out on a road near a farm within earshot of Brazil's largest city was even more remarkable.'

(Author's Verdict: 3/5)

Onza

Large but Gracile, Puma-like Cats of Mexico

In the mid-1930s, two seasoned American hunters, brothers Dale and Clell Lee, launched a venture providing guided hunting trips in the Sierra Madre of the Mexican state of Sonora – a region celebrated for its wilderness. In 1938 Joseph Shirk, a wealthy Indiana banker, hired the brothers to relocate their operation to the southern mountains of Sinaloa, with the aim of hunting jaguars on La Silla Mountain in northeastern Mexico. After a week-long expedition, they eventually cornered and killed a felid that was neither a jaguar nor a typical cougar; its body was larger than usual for its species and it had longer legs and ears than any indigenous Mexican wild cat. The Lees were aware of rumours about a feline predator known as "onza" (from the Spanish word "onsa," which translates to English as "ounce") and became convinced that the animal they killed was the same creature described in historical accounts.

To document their discovery, they measured and photographed their "onza" before skinning and butchering it. Joseph Shirk then took its skin and skull back to Indiana with him as a trophy. The Lee brothers shared their story with zoologists and the American press, yet they were met with disinterest and ridicule. Consequently, they all but abandoned the entire episode until twenty years later when Arizona author Robert Marshall interviewed them. Marshall then travelled to Sinaloa to research the alleged cat, about which he wrote a compelling book, *The Onza* (Exposition Press, New York) in 1961. Onzas are considered more aggressive than regular mountain lions and are reported to attack and kill even the most ferocious hunting dogs. The Spanish conquistadores noted what could have been onzas dating as far back as 1519, though descriptions may also refer to jaguarundis (known as "onza" in some Mexican states). 'Onça' is the Brazilian-Portuguese word for the jaguar (and the source of its scientific name *P. onca*), where the spotted jaguar is known as "onça-pintada" and its melanistic variety as "onça-preta." It is also referred to in some areas of Brazil as "onça-parda."

Cats that resemble onzas were kept in the royal zoo of Emperor Montezuma II, referred to under the Aztec name "cutlamiztli." Some cryptozoologists have proposed that *onzas* are descendants of the American cheetah (*Miracinonyx*), which is more closely related to pumas than to modern cheetahs. *Miracinonyx* is thought to have gone extinct before the last Ice Age, around 10,000 years ago. In January 1986, a rancher by the name of Andres Murillo shot what he believed was a jaguar and brought its body to someone referred to as "Vega". Upon examination, it was found to be female and weighed 27 kg (60 lbs). It measured 1.1 metres in length, excluding its 58 cm long tail. Descriptions state that the animal resembled a large puma but had more slender striped limbs, longer ears, and tail. It also had "the appearance of a cougar with a long thin body and lanky dog-like legs." Vega informed Rodriguez and Ricardo Zamora, two deer hunters who had stumbled upon a large cat at about 10:30 p.m., that was similar to an animal his father had shot during the 1970s, the skull of which he still owned. Fearing they would be mauled by a jaguar, Rodriguez promptly shot the animal before realising that it wasn't a jaguar or a normal cougar. They took the body back to Rodriguez's ranch and contacted "Mr. Vega" who declared it was an "onza".

Subsequently, Ricardo Urquijo, Jr. suggested taking the body to Mazatlán for closer examination, where a deep wound on one of its hind legs was discovered but other than that it was in good health. In yet another version of the same legend, it was Andres Murillo, the farmer who owned a ranch in the San Ignacio District of Sinaloa, who had killed an animal believed to have been similar to that shot by the Lee brothers. Through DNA analysis, it was concluded that the Sinaloan specimen was a known subspecies of cougar and not an American cheetah or any other unknown species. Researchers from *Texas Tech University* conducted an examination of the frozen remains of an *onza* during the 1990s and determined that it was likely a genetic variety of *Puma concolour* and not a distinct species. In Mexico, there is further confusion as the word "onza" can refer to multiple species. According to local folklore, there are two different species of jaguarundi and one of which is the *onza*. Contemporary reports point towards a regional variant of the common mountain lion, perhaps adapted to its particular environment. Locals have theorised that *onzas* might be jaguar x mountain lion hybrids. Some have even suggested that they could be classified as a new species closely related to mountain lions. However, it is more likely they are under-nourished specimens of the typical large-bodied pumas.

(Status: Identified)

Pennsylvanian Mountain Lion

Surviving Pennsylvanian Pumas?

The last known mountain lion in Pennsylvania was killed by Thomas Anson in Berks County in 1871. However, many believe that a small population still exists in some of the remote areas of the state. Eyewitnesses describe seeing large, tan or light brown-coloured big cats with long tails, oftentimes comparing them to an African lioness due to their muscular build. Mountain lions, also known as cougars, pumas, panthers, catamount, mountain screamers, Mexican lions, painters, red lions, and American lions (+ at least another thirty or so English names alone) are quiet, typically solitary and secretive with a tendency to hide from people. As a species, mountain lions have the widest range of any wild terrestrial carnivore living in the Americas, extending all the way from Canada's northernmost Yukon Territory to South America's Southern Andes – spanning nearly 48,000 km or 30,000 miles. This impressive geographic range is due to their unparalleled ability to thrive in virtually any habitat; though they were eradicated across most of their eastern range in the first two centuries following European Colonisation. But despite being declared officially extinct in Pennsylvania, reports continue to surface of what appear to be mountain lions. In 1966, Peggy Ann Bradnick experienced a harrowing incident when she was kidnapped at gunpoint and forced to travel through the backwoods of south-central Pennsylvania. This event quickly became one of the largest manhunts in American history. In her book, *The Voice in the Mountains*, Peggy Ann claimed to have seen a mountain lion during her ordeal. Furthermore, Senator Roger Madigan (b. 1930 – d. 2018), who attended an outdoor party during this time, corroborated her sighting as he too reported seeing a mountain lion.

Pennsylvania is currently home to just one wild felid: the bobcat. Bobcats are rarely seen is in the wild, resulting in them sometimes being confused with mountain lions. Coyotes, which are much smaller and have shorter thickly furred tails, sharp faces, and large triangular ears have also been mistaken for mountain lions. Even orange and tan house cats have been mistaken for mountain lions. House cats typically weigh eleven pounds and are only one foot tall, in comparison to a mountain lion's size; they also usually carry their tails erect with a noticeable bow, while mountain lions have a long, heavy tail. This is perhaps their most defining identifying characteristic. The tail of a mountain lion can be 1/3 its body length. Used for balance and rudder-like direction changes when chasing prey, it's thick and muscular with a dark tip. Bobcats have distinctive stub tails and even large domestic cats have smaller tails that don't compare with the powerful tail of mountain lions. Pennsylvania would be incredibly difficult for the western subspecies to reach. Any mountain lions attempting to reach Pennsylvania would face significant challenges traversing the Great Plains, navigating highways, and circumventing cities in order to survive. It is unlikely that individuals attempting such a journey would survive. Furthermore, a juvenile female has not been recorded in the Midwest, much less in Pennsylvania for over a century. Without a shift in this pattern, it is not possible to have breeding populations. Several images purported to depict real Pennsylvania mountain lions have been confirmed to be forgeries.

(Author's Verdict: 2/5)

Yana puma

An Enormous, Solid Black Feliform Cryptid From Peru.

The *yana puma* (Quecha: "black puma") is typically described as a large cat-like animal, solid black in colour with large greenish eyes. It is considered to be nocturnal and is dangerous to humans during these hours. The *yana puma* is often said to make loud roars during the night. George Eberhart speculated in his *Mysterious Creatures: A Guide to Cryptozoology* (ABC-CLIO) that the *yana puma* might be a black jaguar or even a black puma. However, not only are melanistic pumas unproven, but due to the absence of an elastic ligament in the epihyal bone which forms part of the larynx, pumas cannot roar. Furthermore, a melanistic jaguar's spots may be faint but they can still be seen in its coat. Taking reports at face value, it is clear that neither species fits the description of the *yana puma* due to their smaller size.

(Author's Verdict: 2/5)

LONG-TAILED BOBCATS

A Greater Tailed Bobcat?

Bobcats, also known as American wildcats, are elusive and nocturnal animals that are rarely seen by humans. Despite this, they roam throughout much of North America and can adapt to a variety of habitats such as forests, swamps, deserts, and even suburban areas. They are roughly twice the size of an average house cat, with long legs and large paws and a brown or brownish-red body with a white underbelly. In addition, their tufted ears resemble those of the large Canadian lynx belonging to the same genus. The bobcat is probably best known for its short, black-tipped tail. This gives these beautiful cats their common name, as the tail appears cut or "bobbed". Still, there are reports suggesting the existence of another lynx-like cat with much longer tails in certain regions of North America. Witnesses often describe them with various colours ranging from solid brown to tiger-striped on the body, legs, and tail. But generally speaking, they are sandy grey with yellow or buff colouration on the underbody between the hind legs. Long-tailed bobcats, also known as "long-tailed wildcats" are reported to be slightly larger than a medium-sized dog, with a large, broad head in proportion to their body size, and sharp claws and teeth. Witnesses describe seeing a ringed tail, measuring about one foot in length, along with a single dark stripe or series of dark patches extending from the shoulders along the spine to the tip of the tail. Generally, their chin and throat area is a lighter grey than the rest of their body, sometimes appearing white. Known for being nocturnal hunters occupying large ranges, long-tailed wildcats are typically reported in rocky and wooded areas and are most commonly sighted in Pennsylvania's Allegheny Mountains, Bucks County, Blue Ridge Mountains, Clinton County, Fayette County; Nockamixon State Park; Snyder County; Tioga County; and Reading Prong Mountain range (southern end), as well as Arkansas and Virginia's Shawnee Nat'l. Forest area.

Bobcats with Long Tails September 1951.

"Strange animals appear at times, and no one can say for sure what they are. Such an animal was caught in a fox trap south of Wharton by Lynn Wycoff. Since it was an unusual specimen, Wykoff [name is rendered both ways in the article] decided to keep it alive. With the help of his father, he managed to free it from the trap and get it into a steel bear cage. He was scratched on the face and severely bitten on a thumb. Hundreds of persons saw the captured animal, but nobody seemed to know what it was. All agreed that it was a nasty tempered snarling beast."

The Wykoffs named her Bertha after a particularly mean woman their father once knew.

"Sure, I'd call it a wildcat and let it go at that," said Lynn, "But who ever saw a wildcat with a tail like that!" The caudal appendage was about a foot long. Prior to 1840, Burrell Lyman of Roulet could have answered Lynn. One year he claimed to have killed two bobcats with long tails. One aspect of the cat's behaviour intrigued many who saw it. Regardless of the number facing it, the cat followed everyone moving around the cage. "Guess Bertha just doesn't trust people," said Lynn.

Three months after the animal was captured, Lynn said, "It is a big cat now. Nobody can tell me that it is a bobcat. Their colour lightens as they grow older, but this animal's colour has not changed". Is it any better tempered? "Not a bit, if anything it's worse." *(Amazing Indeed: Strange Events in the Black Forest Vol. 2, Robert R. Lyman, Sr., 1973, The Potter Enterprise, Coudersport, PA, page 70)*

One might wonder whether certain accounts refer to real long-tailed bobcats and what the advantages of shorter tails might offer. The common bobcat (*Lynx rufus*) has a relatively short tail typically ranging between ten and twenty centimetres (4 – 8 inches) long. One theory is that since bobcats and lynx, both belonging to the *Lynx* genus, typically hunt on the ground for rodents and hares (Lago-morphs), they have not evolved a long twitching tail that might alert prey, in addition to larger predators of the bobcat's presence. So, short tails, large paws, and very long hind legs might be the result of an evolutionary arms race between the *Lynx* genus and their primary prey: rodents and lagomorphs. A short "bobbed tail" can also be advantageous in colder climates as it significantly reduces the body surface area and subsequent heat loss. In general, lynx weigh very little compared to their body size.

Therefore, the absence of a long tail might also reduce their body weight, which in turn prevents sinking in snow. Yet, southern bobcats seem to rule out a thermoregulatory reason. Hunting on the ground and thermoregulation theory does not explain all the short-tailed cats (lynx, bobcat, caracal, and servals). Moreover, the Issoire lynx (*Lynx issiodorensis),* the probable predecessor of the *Lynx* genus seems to have originated in Africa; therefore a cold environment was not involved in its early development. Lynx, caracal, and serval often jump straight up to catch birds, but lagomorphs will also jump up to confuse a predator. Perhaps the long tail is therefore inhibiting these vertical jumps. In the Iberian lynx, these vertical leaps are often observed. Could this be a remnant of the hunting habits of *L. issiodorensis?*

A short tail may be an adaptation for ambush hunting and pursuing prey over short distances in closed forested terrain. Movement and hunting in a forested habitat with rocks, fallen trees, and bushy thickets could be a reason for not having a long tail which would probably be a disadvantage. Yet I know of no explanation that provides all the answers for selective advantage. Perhaps a mutation arose in the common ancestor of the *Lynx* genus that produced a reduced tail; it was evolutionarily neutral, i.e. it provided no selective advantage or disadvantage and was maintained in the lineage. As with the *Caracal* genus and most of the extinct sabre-toothed cat lineage that includes *Megantereon* and *Smilodon*, they all have somewhat reduced tails. Until a compelling argument is presented, it seems that natural bobtails have no clear selective advantage or disadvantage.

Juvenile bobcats have been observed moving in single file between hiding places, each with their tail raised to a vertical position. The white underside of each tail is conspicuously visible to the individual immediately behind, enabling them to avoid danger by staying together. A similar behaviour occurs in cheetahs when the mother is leading the young through tall grass. Whether the tail is short or long may be less important than the visibility of its signal value. As ecologically marginal populations are likely to encompass important components of genetic diversity, the loss of such populations is likely to result in the loss of rare and potentially beneficial adaptive genotypes. If unique adaptations are present, outbreeding depression may result from the introduction of maladapted individuals; the influx of their genes into the population may swamp the well-adapted gene pool and break down co-adapted gene complexes. Therefore, if the absence of a genetic mutation is yielding longer tails in *Lynx sp.*, and if multiple specimens are collected within one or more sufficiently large biotopes, with tails that are about half as long as their rear legs, despite the specimen's known taxonomy, it could rightfully be considered a biological example of this feliform cryptid.

It doesn't matter that a new taxonomy might not be required; the potential discovery, should it come to fruition, would be both real and unexpected, and a success for all life sciences. Hybrids of bobcats and domestic cats (*Felis catus*) have been suggested although there is no tangible evidence that such hybridisation occurs. Other hypotheses are surviving eastern cougars (*Puma concolour cougar*), large feral house cats, or the possibility of unconfirmed European wildcats (*Felis silvestris*) being introduced by early colonists in North America. It is also possible that some reported sightings are misidentified known species such as the red fox. (See *Celofay* and *Tinicum Cat*)

(Author's Verdict: 3/5)

Georgia Mystery Cat

Another Long-Tailed Bobcat?

Located approximately a half mile from the confluence of the Hudson and Broad Rivers in Screven County, north-east Georgia, reports of the "Georgia mystery cat" quickly began to spread. Described as resembling a large domestic cat with facial features and tufted ears typical of a bobcat and was said to stand between 2.5 – 3 ft tall at the shoulders, measuring up to 4 – 5.5 ft long including its unusually long tail. Nocturnal vocalisations associated with this feliform cryptid are said to invoke fear among those who hear them echoing through the night. A felid purported to be the Georgia mystery cat was recorded on a hunter's trial camera (posted by Loren Coleman on Cryptomundo on September 30th, 2010).

Coleman noted that the V-shaped pattern on its face differed from the lines found on mountain lions and jaguarundis. The animal in the photo is a felid; however, its exact dimensions cannot be determined based on the photograph alone. The cat's size relative to the swamp grass in the background does not provide enough evidence to deduce whether it was unusual and perhaps quite large. Swamp grass can reach heights that make it difficult to confirm or deny that this animal is a member of the big cat subfamily. The cat in the photo does resemble a mountain lion, however, its ears are more elongated and pointier than one might expect. Additionally, they appear to be too small compared to the head to be just an oversized domestic cat.

Its impressive jaws are evident due to its prominent facial muscles. The only felid species presently inhabiting Georgia is the bobcat (*Lynx rufus*), but this particular animal lacks the facial ruff or ear tufts that characterise the species. Perhaps Georgia has its own unique variety of long-tailed bobcats, or maybe greatly outsized house cats. Surprisingly, a domestic cat and a bobcat cannot produce viable offspring despite their similar appearances. While some rumours suggest that there are hybrid bobcat x domestic cats, these claims are in fact false. No scientific evidence exists to support this theory due to the distinctive reproductive systems of these organisms. A previous proposal posited that colonists from Europe could have brought European wildcats (*Felis silvestris*) with them when they colonised North America; however, the cat captured on camera is definitely not a 'wildcat' at least not in the European sense of the name. (See *Long-Tailed Wildcats*)

(Author's Verdict: 3/5)

ANOMALOUS JAGUARS?

Arizona Jaguar

Is the Arizona Jaguar Still Alive?

The Arizona jaguar is considered to be an extinct population distin-guishable by its smaller size compared with the more robust jaguars of South America. Initially named *Panthera onca arizonensis* (Gold-man, 1932), it ranged from Senora in Mexico to the southwestern United States until 1939.

In 1996, Warner Glenn, a cattle rancher and hunting guide, reported seeing a jaguar in the Peloncillo Mountains of Arizona. His subse-quent efforts as a researcher of jaguars culminated in the successful use of webcams which recorded four more of these majestic animals. On February 20th, 2009, the *Arizona Game and Fish Department* recorded a male jaguar, later named Macho B, caught in a snare in

Southern Arizona just ten days prior. Macho B was released but had to be recaptured ten days later due to injuries sustained during his initial capture. In September 2012, the *U.S. Fish and Wildlife Service* recorded a male jaguar in the Santa Rita Mountains of Arizona using trail cameras, naming him El Jefe, which literally translates to "the chief" or "the boss" in Spanish.

This was the only known jaguar living in the United States since the death of Macho B.

El Jefe disappeared in 2015, thought to have migrated back into Mexico. This was confirmed almost seven years later, when a collective of conservation groups reported that he had been photographed using a motion-detecting camera on November 27, 2021, in the central part of the state of Sonora. On November 16th, 2016 a seventh confirmed jaguar was documented in the southwest. This was the farthest north a jaguar had been recorded in decades. On December 1st, 2016, another previously unrecorded jaguar (presumably male) was recorded by trail cameras at Fort Huachuca in Cochise County, located approximately 15 miles north of the Mexico-Arizona border. In February 2017, the same animal was observed again, and on July 22nd, 2018 a photograph sadly revealed that this specimen had died. In April 2021, Ganesh Marin, a PhD student at the University of Arizona, captured a young jaguar on his video feed while studying ecosystems along the US-Mexico border. Perhaps people are seeing remnants of the original Arizona population that were officially extinct in 1905; alternatively, it could also be a southern jaguar migration northward from Mexico, or a leopard or jaguar that has escaped or been set free from captivity.

(Author's Verdict: 4/5)

Carraguar

Say Hello to the Night Jaguar! "Lost in the Shadows"

According to an intriguing article from Chad Arment's informative BioFortean Review series, Colima, a small state in western Mexico, was home to a mysterious and dangerous feliform cryptid known variously as carraguar, renegrón or "night jaguar." It is said to resemble an abnormally large melanistic jaguar with a noticeably coarser fur type and extreme ferocity. However, due to the scarcity of reports available which are all over a century old, there is not much known about the *carraguar*. There do not appear to be any recent accounts that could shed light on what this creature might be if it exists at all.

(Author's Verdict: 2/5)

Dorsal Jaguar

A "King Jaguar"?

Scientific Name: *Felis dorsalis* (Rafinesque-Schmaltz, 1883)

There has been speculation of an unknown jaguar (*Panthera onca*) seen in the Alleghany Mountains of Pennsylvania and along the 49th parallel from the Rocky Mountains to the Strait of Georgia. The dorsal jaguar is greyish in colour, with a pale brown neck with a prominent black stripe running down its back. Additionally, two rows of ringed spots can be seen on each side, black above and brown below. According to some accounts, Dorsal Jaguars are approximately 3.04 m (10 ft) long, including the tail. This contrasts with the largest recorded jaguars which reach around 2.5 m (8.2 ft) give or take a few centimetres. The Dorsal Jaguar was first described in 1833, in *The Atlantic Journal and Friend of Knowledge, a Cyclopaedic Journal and Review*, by Constantine Samuel Rafinesque-Schmaltz, who wrote: 'The Jaguars are the spotted Tygers [sic] of America, found from

Mexico to Paraguay [...] another Jaguar still larger and of a different species has lately been seen as far as Lake Erie, and in lat. 42. One was shot by the Seneca Indians, to whom it was totally unknown, and another was killed in the Alleghany mountains of Pennsylvania. These animals were totally distinct from the common jaguar; they must have been wanderers from New Mexico or the Oregon mountains and probably belong to a new species that I propose to call *Felis dorsalis*, owing to the black band on the back. There are several other species of jaguars in South America, little known or not well distinguished. Dorsal jaguars are grey-coloured with a black line or band running along the middle of the back and two rows of ringed spots on each side, black above, and brown below. Total length is 10 ft including the tail, body 6 ½, tail 3 1/3. Very different from *Felis pardalis* [the ocelot] by size four times larger, neck and back, &, etc.'

It is possible that the animal described by Rafinesque was an eastern cougar (*Puma concolour cougar*). This was theorised in 1946 by Stanley P. Young and Edward A. Goldman, and a photo of a New Brunswick cougar shot in 1953 had a stripe similar to the "*Felis dorsalis*" description. However, reports of "ringed spots" suggests they could be the jaguar's rosettes rather than anomalous spotted cougars. An alternative theory is they could have been hybrids from crossing a cougar and jaguar, such as the one reportedly shot by Sacha Siemel in Mato Grosso during the early 20th century. They may be related to an enormous cougar that has retained its juvenile spots into maturity or some sort of genetic mutation like the king cheetah, which is related to both cougars and jaguarundis. The grey colouration reported also supports the 'concolour' pelage associated with cougars, making it instead a "dorsal cougar." Finally, it could have more in common with the much larger Pleistocene North American jaguar: *Panthera onca augusta*.

(Author's Verdict: 4/5)

Onça-canguçú

A New Jaguar Species?

The Portuguese word "onça" translates to jaguar, and the Tupi term "canguçú," derived from "akangusu," means "big head." As such, the *onça-canguçú* can be interpreted as the "big-headed jaguar." According to palaeontologist Darren Naish, it could also mean 'the jaguar that is larger than other cats and hunts in pairs.' The *onça-canguçú*, also known as the "white-throated black jaguar", is reported from the states of Matto Grosso, Rio Madeira, Rio Aripuanã, and Amazonas in the Brazilian Amazon. It is described as a big cat resembling a jaguar, having black fur with a white ruffed collar or bib-like marking on its throat, and a tufted tail. In comparison to the jaguar, it is larger but at the same time smaller than the African lion (*Panthera leo*). Unlike a jaguar, there are no rosettes present on its coat. Cryptozoologist John Kirk published a report on Loren Coleman's *Cryptomundo* on February 28th, 2006. 'The extraordinary Marc van Roosmalen, discoverer of several new monkey species in Brazil, heard from locals in the Aripuana that a mystery cat called the Onca-cangucu lived in the area. It had black fur with a white ruff and a tail that was tufted. The locals offered van Roosmalen a skin and skull of the animal in 2001, but so far have not lived up to their promises. This has left van Roosmalen pondering if the animal isn't really a black species of the Jaguar (Panthera onca).'

Dr. van Roosmalen has gathered numerous accounts of the *onça-canguçú*, yet so far has been unsuccessful in finding and observing a living specimen. He did learn from a Caboclo community near the Uira-Curupa River, that a nine-year-old girl had tragically been killed by a pair of *onça-canguçú*. The skull of an adult *onça-canguçú* said to have been shot years ago by a man who has since passed away, is the possession of the tribe. According to Roosmalen, although yet unconfirmed, the *onça-canguçú* could potentially be an as-of-yet unidentified species of the *Panthera* genus, distinct from *P. onca*. Another story told of two people capturing a cub whilst its parents were swimming in the nearby river. According to the account, the cub died but they retained its skull. Marc van Roosmalen has obtained another skull from local hunters, saying in an interview, that this and the arboreal giant anteater are the only animals of which he lacked genetic samples.

(Author's Verdict: 3/5)

Peruvian Striped Tiger

A Striped Jaguar?

The dense rainforests located in the Rio Abujao, Pozuzo, and Rio Palcazu regions of Peru, as well as Ecuador and Columbia, are reportedly the stomping grounds of a mysterious big cat described as being similar to a jaguar in size but with tan-coloured fur with white tiger-like stripes. Reports suggest that it stalks and kills hunters in these areas. The brilliant naturalist and wildlife writer Peter Matthiessen (b. 1927 – d. 2014) recalled in his book *The Cloud Forest: A Chronicle of the South American Wilderness* (Viking Press, NY, 1961) of meeting a seaman called Picquet while travelling through Paraguay, who had described to him "a rare striped cat not quite so large as a jaguar and very timid, which possesses two very large protruding teeth," that apparently inhabits the high altitude rainforests of Columbia and Ecuador. It has been claimed that the skulls of the "striped tiger" do not match any known species. Possible explanations include pseudomelanism, also called abundism, wherein a jaguar's rosettes have turned into a mosaic of stripes and swirls resembling the striped pelage of a tiger.

The leopard-spotted jaguar from Peru is an established colour morph of the jaguar. Similar colour polymorphism has been witnessed in other big cats and would not be totally unexpected in *P. onca*. In 1994, Peter Hocking obtained a skull that has been claimed to be that of a female "South American striped tiger." His published photographs show the skulls face-on, and it was noticed that the alleged striped tiger's skull was notably narrower than a normal female jaguar, but its canine teeth were no larger than those of the normal jaguar. As both specimens had been boiled in the de-fleshing process, no DNA was found. To identify the skulls, Darren Naish *et al.* undertook morphometrics: thirty cranial and thirteen mandibular measurements were taken and added to a database comprising nearly three hundred specimens of more than thirty felid species. Fisher's linear discriminant method was used by Naish to determine the skulls as *Panthera onca* with strong probabilities for both cranial and mandibular datasets. Hocking's specimens and the reported "striped jaguar" seem to be distinct.

(Author's Verdict: 4/5)

Rainbow Jaguar

Over the Rainbow

The "rainbow jaguar" or "rainbow tiger," also known as the howler monkey tiger in the native Shuar language, and also by other names such as *tshenkutshen*, *tsenkutsenku*, and *tsenku-tsenku* with the suffix 'yawá' meaning 'seven ribbons tiger' (or rainbow tiger), is an enigmatic feliform cryptid that, should it exist as a unique species, could either be a felid or an arboreal marsupial. Rainbow jaguars are reported from the cloud forests of *Sangay National Park*, Cordillera de Cutucu, Ecuador; *Cuyabeno Wildlife Reserve* located in the Putumayo Canton in the Sucumbíos Province and in the Aguarico Canton, Orellana Province.

Generally, they are described like a jaguar, but perhaps slightly smaller. Their chest and the front and torso exhibit stripes of red, yellow, black, and white. The primary colour is described as either black or white and is said to have "flat-palmed paws," signifying that it walks with the entire surface area of its feet touching the ground and is equipped with sharp claws and powerful limbs. The rainbow jaguar is noticeably "humped" in the sagittal plane. One report describes its canine teeth as longer than those of a jaguar. They are said to be predominantly arboreal, leaping from tree to tree with incredible speed and agility, but is also a capable hunter on the ground. They are sometimes seen hunting in pairs and are considered by the Shuar to be the most dangerous animal in the forest as depicted in their traditional poetry.

In 1959, Policarpio Rivadeneiram, a Mecas settler, allegedly shot an animal in the forest of Cerro Kilamo or Cerro el Quilamo, near the Abanico River that closely resembled local descriptions of the rainbow jaguar. According to Rivadeneiram, the animal darted through the trees directly at him and just before the would be attack, he promptly shot it in the head. Once the commotion had died down and the dust had settled, Rivadeneira carefully ventured closer and inspected the deceased creature, which was discovered to be a white spotted cat-like animal with a humped back. Its chest possessed "rainbow-coloured" hues, and its strong muscled limbs ended in peculiar feet that resembled those of a monkey, featuring flat palms. The travel writer Joe Kane wrote in 1998 that, deep within Ecuador's Cuyabeno Wildlife Reserve on the border of Columbia and Peru, home of the much oppressed Cofan indigenous people, this animal is commonly referred to as the "howler monkey tiger" due to its peculiar characteristics.

It is conceivable that the rainbow jaguar is an as-yet-undiscovered relative of the margay (*Leopardus wiedii*), the only felid with articulated ankles that allow for it to descend vertical tree trunks head-first. As *L. wiedii* is too small to be responsible for accounts of the rainbow jaguar and does not possess many of the characteristics described by those who have seen the creatures first-hand, it stands to reason that there may exist a larger, closely related, morphologically distinct species responsible for some reported sightings. If the rainbow jaguar is eventually discovered and shown to be congeneric with the margay and is simply a larger relative, *Leopardus gigas* might make a suitable, if elementary binomen. Angel Morant Forés collected reports of a mysterious creature from the Macas region in central Ecuador. He consulted Rosa Garcia Perea, a mammal expert from the *National Museum of Natural Sciences* in Madrid, about the description of this creature. She was intrigued and promptly refrained from ruling out the possibility of a new, previously unrecorded species of felid. Perhaps the descriptions of monkey-like "hands" are not to be taken literally and are actually a behavioural metaphor, relating instead to its arboreal abilities. On the other hand (pun intended), they are also suggestive of a marsupial such as the officially extinct Australian marsupial lion (*Thylacoleo carnifex*). It is possible that the rainbow jaguar could be an unidentified colour variant of the jaguar that has recently made a kill and has blood and viscera from its prey drying on its chest.

(Author's Verdict: 3/5)

Shaishai yawá

Feliform Unknown

The Shuar people of Ecuador report the existence of a white-coated, cat-like creature with solid black spots referred to as *shaishai yawá*.

These creatures are believed to be smaller than a jaguar but larger than an ocelot. Angel Morant Forés speculates that the *shaishai yawá* may, in fact, be an albinistic jaguar; however, this does not explain the presence of peculiar dark black spots on its fur, as there should be a significantly reduced or non-existent amount of melanin present.

(Author's Verdict: 1/5)

Siemel's Mystery Cat

A Large, Spotted, Cat-like Creature of Brazil

TWO FRIENDS (LEOPARD AND DOG) IN CARL HAGENBECK's ZOO.
This is the Hagenbeck's puma-leopard cub (now preserved at the Natural History Museum in Tring) Most photo reproductions show only the "pumapard" and not the terrier dog. This is the full photo from "From Jungle To Zoo" by Ellen Velvin, F.Z.S., published 1914

Only known verified photograph of a live pumapard (public domain).

As if Brazil hasn't already been productive enough, the biodiverse Mato Grosso state presents us with 'Siemel's mystery cat', a large yet unidentified feliform cryptid. This alleged felid is characterised by a light tan base, dotted with dark brown spots, and a dark dorsal stripe.

The Latvian-born adventurer Sacha Siemel (b. 1890 – d. 1970) claimed to have killed a cat during his travels in the Mato Grosso state of Brazil in the early 20th century, believing it to be a hybrid between the two species that inhabit the region – the puma and jaguar. While there is no verifiable evidence – photographic or otherwise – to support the existence of such hybrids, it remains a genetic possibility as "pumapards" (puma x leopard hybrids) were successfully bred in Germany during the 1890s. These animals had grey coats with brown rosettes. It is likely that intergeneric puma x jaguar hybrids would bear a resemblance to pumapards, though their markings would be more reminiscent of jaguars than leopards. Furthermore, these hybrids might have a more powerful build. An alternative hypothesis is that the mystery cat observed by Siemel was in fact an adult puma that had retained its juvenile markings.

(Author's Verdict: 2/5)

Speckled Tiger

Another Abnormal Jaguar?

Occasionally reported from the rainforests of Peru, "speckled tigers" or "speckled jaguars" are said to be roughly the size of jaguars but with a larger head. They are typically grey in colour and adorned with solid black specks. It is likely that the speckled "tiger" is an unidentified colour morph of the jaguar, where the spots have broken down into smaller specks.

(Author's Verdict: 4/5)

Warracaba Jaguar

Aggressive, Pack Hunting, Jaguar-like Cryptids of Guyana

The warracaba jaguar, also known as the "warracaba tiger" or simply "*warracabra,*" is generally thought to be a diminutive variety of jaguars reported from Guyana. They are believed to be highly efficient pack hunters, sometimes with dozens, allegedly even up to a hundred fiercely dominating a territory. The warracaba jaguar seems to be unafraid of campfires and has even been reported to be inquisitive of human activity, some suggest that they may even be drawn to it. They make a high-pitched vocalisation similar to the sound of a grey-winged trumpeter (*Psophia crepitans*), also known as the warracabra bird, which inspired its name. Henry Kirke (b. 1842 – d. 1925) related in his 1898 book *Twenty-Five Years in British Guiana*:

'There is a mysterious beast in the forest called by the native Indians the "warracabra". All travellers in the forests of Guiana speak of this dreaded animal, but strange to say, none of them appear to have seen it. The Indians profess the greatest terror of it. It is said to hunt in packs (which tigers never do), and when it howls awake the echoes of the forest, the Indians at one take their canoes and wood skins as the only safe refuge from its ravages.'

The *warracaba* may be folklore based on the observed social behaviour of pumas travelling in family groups. Similarly, its namesake, the 'warracabra', a guinea fowl-like bird with a long neck and legs, and a short chicken-like beak, is highly gregarious and may form flocks of up to one hundred individuals. Warracabras feed on insects, small vertebrates, and fallen fruit from the forest floor. Grey-winged Trumpeters are also known for their elaborate and noisy courtship displays that could be mistaken as something more mysterious. The warracaba legend may be based on rare social behaviour exhibited by jaguars, albeit somewhat exaggerated.

(Author's Verdict: 3/5)

2

THE LESSER CRYPTID CATS

'The smallest feline is a masterpiece.'

— LEONARDO DA VINCI

Not all feliform cryptids are menacing "man-eaters"; many are quite small. The lesser cryptid "cats" range in size from that of a house cat to a lynx, but despite their smaller size, they often retain many of the behaviours of their larger cousins and are nonetheless top predators in their environments.

Alabama Mystery Cat

Known From a Single Photograph

On April 13th, 2021, a journalist with the American newspaper, the *Bangor Daily News*, published a photograph which they had received from a reader named Rusty Fondren. The photo showed an unusual cat that is still officially unidentified, prompting speculation among readers as to whether it was a boldly marked European shorthair cat or a striped Bengal cat with a silvery ground coat. The Bengal cat is a domesticated cat breed created from hybrids of domestic cats. Although extremely unlikely, a hybrid cat descended from the uncon- firmed European wildcats *(Felis silvestris)* reported in North America, supposedly introduced by early Colonists from Europe has also been suggested. Perhaps it was a domestic cat with significant wildcat DNA in its gene pool.

Savannah cats and ocicats were also mooted as possible identities in the *BDN* article, however, as shown in the photograph, the cat's mark- ings might suggest otherwise. The cat is certainly muscular, and healthy, and appears to be taking a leisurely stroll. Going by its body language something in the wooded area has caught its attention and the dipped tail may indicate caution. Its tabby stripes are well-defined but broken, a trait not uncommon in domestic cats. Finally, although the article says there isn't much to help judge the cats' overall size, it's almost certainly smaller than it initially looks judging from the barrel in the background. In fact, if you expand the image and look closely at the barrel, you can see there is an arched entrance hole cut out of it, and it is fixed to some kind of structure. It appears that someone with a kind heart has fashioned it into a shelter for this and other homeless cats. The size, tail, and gait of the cat in the photo are all consistent with those of a regular house cat. Additionally, its coat pattern is also characteristic of domestic cats.

(Status: Unidentified Breed)

British Jungle Cats

Out of Place Jungle Cats

It is thought there exists a small, yet viable population of jungle cats *(Felis chaus,* also known as the "swamp cat" or "reed cat") living in the wilds of Great Britain. According to some accounts, they were taken on board ships from India in the 1800s to be used as ratters and when the ships returned to England they escaped and somehow managed to survive in small populations. It is well-established that jungle cats and domestic cats can hybridise successfully. In 1988, a jungle cat was struck by a vehicle in West Lane, Hayling Island. Subsequently, news of similar cats, counting potential hybrid progeny, has spread throughout the region. The original Hayling Island jungle cat is now kept at the Hampshire County Museum's storage facility located at Chilcomb House in Winchester. Eyewitness accounts and photographic evidence point to the possibility that a substantial number of jungle cats are living in the wild in Britain and that they even account for a small portion of reported sightings of "big cats".

The Hayling Island specimen is believed to have escaped from a private collection, but it should be noted that other sightings on Hayling Island both pre-date and post-date this incident. One year later, a dead jungle cat was found near the market town of Ludlow in Shropshire and was subsequently delivered to *Ludlow Museum* for examination. Some contend that it may have bred with domestic cats, potentially leading to abnormally large offspring still inhabiting the region today. Karl Shuker noted a local domestic cat named Jasper that was significantly larger than average, with markings similar to those of a jungle cat. Mr. Evans of Richards Castle discovered the Ludlow jungle cat, which was preserved in a defensive position by a taxidermist and is now in Karl Shuker's private collection.

(Author's Verdict: 5/5)

Fitoaty

What is the Black-Furred Fitoaty?

The *fitoaty*, also known as *pisukary*, is said to be larger than a domestic cat, with slick black fur and a lean, muscular body reported from the lowland rainforests of the Masoala peninsula in the northeast of Madagascar. Prior to the first European contact, numerous Malagasy folktales featured references to the "fitoaty". In October 1939, Paul Cazard provided one of the earliest mentions in a report published in the *Chasseur Français* newsletter. It has been suggested that the large melanistic cats found on Madagascar may have resulted from breeding between "forest cats", which were likely introduced to the island over a millennium ago, and the "village cats" which arrived at a later date. In 2013, Dr. Cortni Borgerson, an anthropologist from Massachusetts University, published a paper that showed evidence of the presence of *fitoaty* cats among the people living in the Masoala Peninsula. Dr. Borgerson had seen one of these cats in person while walking along a village path just outside *Masoala National Park's* limits in 2011. In 2015, a team of seven scientists published a peer-reviewed paper containing two photographs of *fitoaties* that might indicate the presence of an unknown species. They appear to be approximately the same height and weight as a fossa; which would make the *fitoaty* nearly twice the size of domestic cats. Additionally, their distinctive long legs, slender frames, and gracile heads were noted as being different from those of regular feral cats. It's possible that the *fitoaty* is a genetically unique phenotype adapted to life in Madagascar. Conversely, in his 2013 paper, Dr. Borgerson's speculated that it could be a separate species altogether.

(Author's Verdict: 4/5)

Kellas Cats

Cryptozoology in Action

The Kellas cats are small black felines, lightly flecked with white guard hairs, initially documented from Kellas in Scotland. Before 1984 when a specimen was provided by local gamekeeper Ronnie Douglas, these distinctive black cats – now known to be interspecific hybrids – were widely regarded to be imaginary and the few reported sightings were treated as hoaxes or misidentified standard black house cats. In Highland folklore, the legendary *Cait Sith* or 'Fairy Cat', which has a similar appearance to the Kellas cat, suggests that intro-gressive hybridisation has been occurring for a very long time. After the 1984 specimen, there was considerable media coverage and more captures took place, including an unsuccessful attempt by British researcher Di Francis (b. 1943 – d. 2021) to raise Kellas kittens.

Unfortunately, Francis made the unfortunate decision to feed the kittens only muscle meat, which can contain only 10% - 20% protein and 2% - 22% fat – ultimately leading to fatal malnutrition. Based on their DNA the Kellas cats were eventually determined to be interspecific hybrids between domestic cats and the remaining Scottish wildcats. After several generations of hybridisation and backcrossing with pure-bred wildcats, the Kellas cat has established a stable form characterised by its gracile build and small head, giving it the appearance of longer ears and canine teeth. A typical specimen also has a comparatively short tail. Notably, one specific example identified as the Dufftown cat or "rabbit-headed cat" exhibited Siamese/Oriental traits, perhaps suggesting which domestic breed was involved in its hybridisation. According to Dr. Andrew Kitchener, Curator of Mammals and Birds at the *Royal Museum of Scotland*, out of eight

Kellas cats, he studied: "One animal is clearly a melanistic wildcat, the others are hybrids; some of which are very close to the wildcat while one is much closer to the domestic cat." More on Kellas cats later.

(Status: Identified)

Muirhead's "Burrowing Cat"

A Secretive Subterranean Feline?

British cryptozoologist and researcher Richard Muirhead, in an online correspondence with Karl Shuker, drew attention to a curious feliform cryptid known as a "burrowing cat." On January 26th, 1925, the *Leeds Mercury* published the following report.

"Captain Buchanan was engaged in scientific work, for Lord Rothschild and the British Museum, brought back some remarkable relics of his journey through the heart of the Sahara. His Collection was the first brought from here. One of his most valuable specimens was the skin of a "burrowing cat," the only specimen in any collection in the world. This animal greatly resembles a cat but is able to borrow like a rabbit. It is beautifully marked, has a fine coat, and lynx-like ears. Captain Buchanan started from Lagos, Nigeria, travelled up country about 700 miles to Cano, and then across the vast deserts to Algiers."

The sand cat (*Felis margarita*) naturally comes to mind, but as noted by Karl Shuker, its existence has long been established making Muirhead's "burrowing cat" something of a mystery. The "burrowing cat" evokes the traditional Icelandic legend of Urðarköttur, otherwise known as the "Ghoul Cat" or "Wasteland Cat". As a youngling, the Urðarköttur will bury itself in the ground, usually in a cemetery. If left undisturbed, it will remain there for three years and is referred to as a "corpse cat" during this period. Upon emerging from the ground, its gaze is said to be so malevolent and severe that it brings about immediate death to all living creatures. Once it departs the cemetery, according to some reports, it will reside on rocky inclines, preying upon sheep, birds, and humans. Muirhead's Burrowing cat may be some sort of Mustelid or Viverrid.

(Author's Verdict: 2/5)

Mitla

A Strange Cat-like Creature First Reported by Percy Fawcett in 1914

The *mitla*, also known as Fawcett's Cat-Dog, is "a black doglike cat about the size of a foxhound" reported from the Madidi Forest in the Cuzco region of the Bolivian Amazon. It is described as either a cat-like dog or a dog-like cat and is typically dark brown or black in colour. In 1914, Colonel Percy Fawcett (b. 1867 – d. 1925 or later), a British geographer, artillery officer, archaeologist, and explorer who spent much time in Brazil, was the first to report the *mitla*. In his writings, Fawcett states that:

'In the forests were various beasts still unfamiliar to zoologists, such as the mitla, which I have seen twice, a black doglike cat about the size of a foxhound.'

There is no denying that Percy Fawcett was a man of great resilience and practicality. He was, after all, a soldier and a surveyor; a fearless explorer, whose explorations were an inspiration for both Indiana Jones and Sir Arthur Conan Doyle's "The Lost World". Yet he also possessed a fantastical side, was idiosyncratic, with an inclination towards the spiritual, dabbling in matters of the occult. He was also convinced that an ancient city, which he and others believed existed, lay undiscovered in the heart of the Mato Grosso region of Brazil. Fawcett named this lost city 'Z' (Zed), and he and his son would go missing while searching for it in 1925, probably in tragic circumstances. What should we make of the Colonel's assertions regarding zoological matters?

In 1907, during an expedition, Fawcett reported encountering a 62-foot (19 metres) long snake, an observation which was met with incredulity by scientists. He also spoke of discovering other creatures unknown to zoology, such as the Apazauca spider believed to be responsible for the deaths of several native people, and a canine called the "tiger hound". No one believed him, they laughed at his stories, and while there's little hope in the validity of his giant snake, Fawcett's double-nosed dog remained a cryptid until the mid-2000s, when Colonel John Blashford-Snell returned from South America with photographic evidence of its existence. Considering that it took nearly a century for someone bold enough to discover his double-nosed dog, there is still a possibility that Fawcett's "cat-dog" will one day be discovered. Ivan Sanderson, the man who may or may not have originally coined the term "cryptozoology", also claimed to have seen a *mitla* during an animal collecting trip where he unsuccessfully shot at one of the animals. He later acquired part of a pelt which he likened to "that of a huge black serval with pricked ears and tiny lynx-like tail." However, regrettably, Sanderson failed to mention what happened to this priceless zoological specimen after. We are starting to see a pattern here.

The esteemed English conservationist, author, and director of Jersey Zoo Jeremy Mallinson (b. 1937 – d. 2021) searched for the *mitla* in Bolivia in 1965. Mallinson wrote: 'By the time we paddled our way across the confluence of the Abuna with the Madeira... I recognised that I had not thrown any further light on the question of whether Colonel Fawcett's legendary animal had ever existed or not. Perhaps the *mitla* had been nothing more than a melanistic form of one of the several species of South American tiger cats or, as has been suggested, the black form of the jaguarundi which can grow to about the size of a foxhound and could, to a non-zoologist, appear to be half-dog, half-cat. Both Senor Carlos and Professor Gaston Bejarano confirmed that the black form of the jaguarundi occasionally occurred in the northeastern regions of Bolivia. However, I learned one important fact from my travels in this great integrated region of rivers and forests: that while these remoter areas of the Amazon basin still remain in existence, the forests could well harbour such animals as the mitla that are still strange to science, but it would only be by chance if their presence ever came to light'.

Mallinson speculated that the *mitla* could be a melanistic variant of the jaguarundi (*Herpailurus yagouroundi*). Other explanations include an obscure species or subspecies related to the jaguarundi. Karl Shuker prefers the short-eared dog found in Bolivia. The late *University of Chicago* biologist and cryptozoologist, Dr. Roy P. Mackal (b. 1925 – d. 2013) suggested that the Bush Dog (*Speothos venaticus*) could be responsible for *mitla* reports; Dr. Shuker noted, however, that adult Bush Dogs have reddish fur and considerably shorter limbs than the creature described in accounts of the *mitla*.

(Author's Verdict: 3.5)

Ngo ngoe

Another Cryptozoological Mystery From Flores

Flores is one of the Lesser Sunda Islands situated to the east of Sumbawa and Komodo Island, and to the west of the Solor Islands and Alor Archipelago. Trigonoceps vultures are present on the island, suggesting that it once supported mammalian carnivores; and thus, the vague potential for a cat species to remain undetected by science. The Nage people, who descended from the indigenous population of Flores, describe the *ngo ngoe* (Nage: Austronesian) as a strange cat-like animal around the size of a standard domestic cat breed, though there are some that suggest it may be larger. They are reported to be aggressive and to hunt both birds and small rodents on the island, but occasionally also larger animals such as immature deer, wild piglets, and the Flores giant rat. While this behaviour has not been verified first-hand by the Nage people, it is described in their folklore. There is much variability in the information available regarding this feliform cryptid.

When asked, some of the Nage said that the *ngo ngoe* had ears that are longer in proportion than those of other cats, while others disagreed.

Whereas the coat pattern of domestic and feral cats is recognised to vary, most of the Nage describe the *ngo ngoe* as having stripes similar to those of a small tiger. Another less frequent comparison is to the striped hide of an immature wild hog. One particular specimen was described with thick fur around its jaw. Two dead specimens were described as black in colour, with white or pale coloured spots on its tail. The fur of the *ngo ngoe* is rougher than a domestic or feral cat, but smoother than a dog. Reports indicate they are active during both daylight and darkness hours (cathemeral) and have been heard making deep vocalisations at night resembling "noh noh", giving rise to its onomatopoeic name. When it is treed, which is typical during the day, the *ngo ngoe* are said to be silent, even when brought down and attacked by the Nage's hunting dogs, of which they say several are needed to dispatch just one nimble and aggressive *ngo ngoe*. The Nage assert that while feral kittens can be tamed, the immature *ngo ngoe* can't, they are just too wild and aggressive to accept a life of domestication. Furthermore, due to its larger size and formidable reputation, most Nage questioned the possibility of interbreeding between the ngo ngoe and domestic cats. It has been speculated that male *ngo ngoe*, typically known for their fearlessness, are hesitant to enter the territories of female domestic cats. On the other hand, there are reports they can hybridise with feral cats; but this has yet to be confirmed. Two experienced hunters suggested that the *ngo ngoe* is a unique variety of wildcat "original" to Flores, and not directly related to feral cats. However, they did not eliminate the possibility of them breeding with feral cats. According to one report, *ngo ngoes* have smaller litters than other cats, typically consisting of two or three kittens.

Taken at face value, the descriptions of the Nage people suggest there is an unidentified wild felid inhabiting the island, yet to be uncovered and classified by international zoologists.

(Author's Verdict: 3/5)

Super Siamese Cats

Outsized "Siamese" Type Cats?

Reports of oversized Siamese cats, typically seen in the Newton Abbot and Teignbridge areas of South Devon, England, but occasionally spotted further afield in Powderham and Dartington, are consistent in their characteristics. They are generally small to medium-size with long limbs and a slumped walking gait. A black mask resembling a pedigree Siamese cat has been seen. They appear to be primarily active during crepuscular hours, usually observed hunting in pairs at dawn or dusk. A witness interviewed by Jonathan Downes recounted their experience with one of these cats while driving between Ipplepen and Newton Abbot.

It is interesting to note that pure-bred Siamese cats interbreeding with other types of *F. catus* typically produce offspring that lack the distinctive colouration and are usually black or tabby. However, some inherited traits such as the pointed facial structure and the kink in the tail can persist. Furthermore, there have been no reports of wild cats with tail kinks living in Devonshire. Jon writes in his criminally underrated *Mystery Carnivores of the Westcountry*:

'The reports of sizeable creatures with 'Siamese' markings and features continue and I feel that it is unlikely that all the animals reported could be stray 'purebred' Siamese cats. It is even more unlikely that hypothetical colonies of 'stray' Siamese would breed true, and so these animals, whatever they are, are a real mystery.'

(Author's Verdict: 2/5)

Transcaucasian Black Cat

The "Demon Cat" of the Caucasus

The Transcaucasian Black Cat was first documented in 1903 from the Transcaucasia region of the former USSR, which today comprises

Armenia, Azerbaijan, and Georgia, collectively known as the Caucasian States. Initially classified as *Felis daemon*, it has since been reclassified to the level of either a feral domestic cat or a melanistic Caucasian wildcat. The colouration of the "Demon Cat" varied from black with a reddish tint to reddish-brown, and slightly paler on the underparts, inside of the legs, and underneath the tail. A reddish tinge is common in outdoor living black cats and is caused by sun bleaching.

Transcaucasian Black Cats may have white guard hairs dispersed throughout their fur; a trait that is found in mixed-breed black cats as well as in Scottish Kellas cats. It is probable that the so-called "demon cat" is an introgressive hybrid of wildcat and domestic cat. In 1904, an entry titled "The Black Wild Cat of Transcaucasia" by C. Satunin of Tiflis was published in the research journal *Proceedings of the Royal Society of London*. Satunin's work referred to a cat with characteristics similar to that of a large male house cat, with a coat of black or rusty brown, and a light sprinkling of long white guard hairs. Additionally, it had a significantly longer tail than its domestic counterparts, along with white claws with "a mother-of-pearl lustre" and "habits unknown." It is uncertain what Satunin observed, however, *Mysterious Creatures: A Guide to Cryptozoology* (2002) offers three possible explanations. *(1) "Felis daemon" – a black variant of the Caucasian wildcat Felis sylvestris caucasica. (2) The black wild cat was simply a melanistic feral domestic. (3) Satunin's cats were hybrids of feral domestic cats and Caucasian wildcats, much like the Kellas cats of Scotland.*

The species designation *Felis daemon* was shown to be unfounded, as it was eventually determined to be a feral cat, possibly a hybrid of wildcat and domestic cat. As for Satunin's other discovery, the Caucasian wildcat, this subspecies is now recognised (*Felis silvestris caucasica*). Domestic cats can easily interbreed with European wildcats as they are closely related. Satunin's description of *Felis daemon* closely matches the Kellas cat.

(Status: Identified)

Wildcats (Anomalous)

The Corsican wildcat has long been part of the folklore of Corsica's nomadic shepherds, with stories being passed down from generation to generation detailing how these unusual felines would attack the udders of their ewes and goats. The people living in the region refer to them as ghjattu volpe ("fox-cat") due to their size – approximately 90 cm (35 inches) from head to tail – and their signature ringed tail with a black tip. Other distinguishing features include boldly striped front legs, dark hind legs, and a reddish-brown stomach. The whole of the coat is dense and silky. They have "wider ears, short whiskers, and highly developed canine teeth" compared to standard domestic cats. The colloquial fox-cat was first recognised as a real animal at the end of the 19th and early 20th centuries; since which time the population has been the subject of more or less accurate descriptions. In 1929, Louis Lavauden proposed the scientific name *Felis reyi* after describing a skin and skull from a female specimen at Biguglia in the Haute-Corse department, which he believed to be a new species. In 1951, Reginald Pocock reviewed *Felis* skins kept at the London *Natural History Museum* and reclassified the specimen as a subspecies of the African wildcat. However, in 2017, the taxonomy of the Corsican fox-cat was revised and it was determined that its DNA is almost identical to both the ancestral African wildcats and their domestic descendants, leading to the conclusion that it was simply a large domestic cat. Zooarchaeological research in Corsica suggests that the fox-cat was likely introduced to the island during the Roman Empire and most likely originated from domestic stock.

After decades of speculation and debate, this animal became part of a focused research effort when a specimen was unexpectedly found in a chicken coop in 2008. Scientists swiftly began analysing the cat's genetic makeup and made an important breakthrough in 2012. Mr. Benedetti, a scientist working on the project, stated, "By looking at its DNA, we could tell it apart from the European wildcat, *Felis silvestris silvestris*. It's close to the African forest cat, *Felis silvestris lybica* [note, this species is considered the ancestor of all modern domestic cats, hence their genetic similarity] but its exact identity is still to be determined."

In 2016, researchers set up cameras and traps and successfully captured another specimen. Three years later, Pierre Bendetti, the Chief Environmental Technician of France's *National Hunting and Wildlife Office* offered a comment: "We believe that it's a wild natural species which was known but not scientifically identified because it's an extremely inconspicuous animal with nocturnal habits", adding "It's their size and their tail that earned them the name fox-cat across the island." On March 16th, 2023 the French *Office for Biodiversity* (OFB) revealed the results of a genetic study conducted in partnership with the *Office of the Environment of Corsica* and supported by the *Laboratory of Biometry and Evolutionary Biology*; this research proved that the fox-cat or ghjattu volpe is an endemic species, distinct from domestic cats. The findings of the study published in the journal *Molecular Ecology*, titled *"Population genomics of Corsican wildcats: Paving the way toward a new subspecies within the Felis silvestris spp. complex?"* show for the first time the Corsican wildcat's unique genetic identity. Regardless of whether it was introduced during the Roman Empire, scientists now believe the species evolved from a little-known ancestor that originated in Africa and the Middle East thousands of years ago.

These discoveries, together with the tagging and surveillance of the endangered population, will hopefully guide future conservation efforts. This discovery of a unique genetic lineage is not only essential for the proper protection and conservation of the endangered species but also has cryptozoological significance, as evidenced by Charles-Antone Cecchini's remarks when he confirmed, according to Mr. Benedetti's colleague: "The cat-fox is part of our shepherd mythology." The *ghjattu volpe* was deemed so unusual that it warranted a blended name, also demonstrating its cryptozoological significance.

(Status: Distinct Species Confirmed)

Perhaps, then, if the Corsican fox-cat is a distinct species, scientists should probably not be so hasty when disregarding other potential wildcats. Reports of cats resembling *Felis silvestris* have long been reported from the southwest of England, located more than six hundred miles away from the nearest wild population in northern Scotland. Wildcats are typically larger, stronger, and more aggressive than domestic cats. Whereas the average domestic cat is not longer than 80 cm (tail included), wildcats can reach up to 1.2 metres.

In March 2018, a particularly large specimen, estimated to be around four feet long, was captured on camera in Aberdeenshire's Clashindarroch Forest and nicknamed "the Clashindarroch Beast". The wildcat typically has a longer and bushier tail than its domestic counterpart, with a rounded tip in contrast to the latter's tapered tail. A stripped tabby pelage and bushy tails with distinct bands are frequently found in both domestic and feral cats. Domestic cats have smaller skulls and shorter bones compared to European wildcats, but such subtle anatomical differences would be difficult to recognise during a brief observation. While recent DNA research has identified five wildcat species as the closest group of ancestors to domestic cats, it is generally believed that the African wildcat (*Felis lybica*) is the wild ancestor that was first domesticated in the Fertile Crescent around 10,000 years ago.

There have been reports of cats remarkably like wildcats from Cornwall for some time. A correspondent of the *Centre for Fortean Zoology* once had a cat that was given to him when his family lived in Cornwall. He was told, by the cat's original owner, that it was descended from a *"Cornish wildcat"*. This may signify that the cat's ancestors were feral farm cats. In any case, cats resembling wildcats have also been spotted in Haldon Hills and at Holcombe near Dawlish, South Devon. The late Devon writer and wildlife artist Trevor Beer (b. 1937 – d. 2017) observed some cats that he concluded to be wildcats on Exmoor in 1984. Hope Bourne (b. 1920 – d. 2010) in her 1963 book *Living on Exmoor* described aggressive cats the size of foxes apparently living in the area of Room Hill immediately before World War One.

Karl Shuker wrote: 'Their ferocity was renowned throughout the area – apparently, not even the farm dogs would dare to attack them, and the cats would unhesitatingly kill any farm cats they encountered.'

Fred Milton, past president of the Exmoor Pony Society, recalled to Bourne one of his own sightings when he observed one of these cats slinking down a nearby lane.' Similar cats have also been seen in the Exeter area of Devon. According to local witnesses, there was once a large and healthy population of "wildcats", at least twice as large as the normal domestic cat, living wild in the St. Leonard's area of Exeter in the late 1970s. They were often observed frequenting an area of wasteland; at that time, one of the last remaining signs of the destruction of the Second World War. "Wildcats" were no longer reported after the area was redeveloped during the 1980s.

At least once, kittens said to be from this colony were adopted by local residents, and they seemed to readily settle into the comfortable life of a domestic cat. One particularly large male, which was described as being the alpha of the colony, reportedly measured more than a metre from nose to tail. Such cats have typically been dismissed by commentators as being feral domestic cats, albeit very large, stunningly patterned specimens. There is the possibility of wildcats being smuggled into mainland Britain from Ireland where laws on keeping exotic animals are less stringent. Illegally held wildcats may explain why owners often do not come forward when cats resembling wildcats are captured, shot, or found dead. The notion of an "Irish wildcat" is controversial because the Scottish form of the European wildcat does not officially exist in Ireland, where historically, the name "wildcat" was instead used in reference to pine martens. However, in western Kerry, the marten was known as the "tree cat" whereas the term "hunting cat" was supposedly used for a true wildcat. Some of the material offered in support of Irish wildcats is found in ancient Celtic mythology.

A 9th-century poem, translated by Eugene O'Curry and published by Sir William Wilde (Oscar Wilde's father), tells of the ancient Irish hero, Fionn mac Cumhaill being held captive by Cormac mac Art, the King of Erinn. The King vowed to set him free only if a male and female of every species of wild animal in Ireland are delivered to him at Tara. The poem goes on to list many different wild animals, including a pair of cats found in a cave in Cruachain, County Roscommon. The usage of "hunting cat" in Ireland in connection to supposed wildcats was also noted in the mammalian chapter of Reverend J. G. Wood's (b. 1827 – d. 1889) three-volume *Illustrated Natural History* (1859 – 63), as well as an anecdotal account taken from *Notes on the Irish Mammalia* by Irish naturalist William Thompson (b. 1805 – d. 1852). After having remarked on grouse feathers found strewn about near a breakwater, as well as several grouse corpses found beheaded nearby but otherwise untouched, the local game-keeper set a trap and caught two specimens of what have been claimed to be genuine wildcats, one adult and one juvenile. Other alleged wildcats and wildcat hybrids have been killed and their morphometric descriptions were said to have corresponded to the African wildcat rather than the European form.

Jimmy Greene, a wildlife ranger now patrolling Laois and Offaly, believes that wildcats exist in Ireland. Greene claimed to have seen a wildcat and its kitten in the *Slieve Bloom Mountain range* in Offaly. "I knew straight away it was not an ordinary cat. It was a pure wildcat. You have to be up early in the morning or at night to see them. I didn't think we had them in Ireland before that, but there are also reports of them in County Wicklow."

Subfossil remains of what were once thought to be wildcats were discovered in 1904, in Edenvale, Newhall, and Barntick Caves, County Clare, which at the time seemed to confirm the theory that a small wildcat species once existed. These, however, were eventually shown to be domestic cats from the Irish Bronze Age, 2000 – 500 BC.

The *Mediterranean wildcats* on the Balearic Isles, Corsica, Crete, Sardinia, and Sicily, though part of the *Felis sylvestris* species complex, are said to belong to the African subspecies. The *Majorcan wildcat* is thought to be extinct, yet numerous sightings of "wildcats" on the island have been reported, which appear more like true wildcats than domestic cats. The taxonomic status of the *Cretan wildcat* remains unclear, as some biologists consider it to be introduced stock, a European wildcat (*Felis silvestris silvestris*), or a hybrid between European wildcats and domestic cats. The *Sicilian* and *Sardinian wildcats* were once thought to be closest to the African wildcat but are now known to be isolated populations of feral cats (*Felis catus*) introduced during the Roman Empire.

Known only from a handful of specimens and once thought to be a subspecies of the African wildcat, the *Île du Levant Wildcat* or *Lynx de la paille* on the island of Le Levant (one of the Mediterranean Iles d'Hyères off the coast of the Var in France) has been reported and even allegedly killed in traps, but as usual, specimens collected have not been presented for examination and formal identification. It is described much like the other Mediterranean examples, though somewhat larger, perhaps weighing ten kilograms or more. In 1958, Bernard Heuvelmans witnessed one of these "wildcats" attacking feral domestic cats. Thus, in 1986, he designated the Mediterranean cats' subspecific status as *Felis silvestris levantina*.

Yameneko

Another Unknown Felid From Iriomote Island?

The Iriomote wildcat, also known as *yameneko*, is a small and mysterious felid, approximately the size of an average house cat, with fur ranging from grey to reddish brown in colour, reported from Iriomotejima Island at the southern end of Japan's Ryukyu Islands. They are often described as having dark spots in dense longitudinal rows, that more or less merge into complete rings. In Japanese, they are called Iriomote-yamaneko "*Iriomote mountain cat*". In local Yaeyama dialects, they are known as *yamapikaryaa* ("that which shines on the mountain"), and *meepisukaryaa* ("that with glowing eyes"). Tetsuo Koura from the *University of the Ryukyus* allegedly captured a kitten in 1962.

In 1964, Tokio Takano of *Waseda University* informed Japanese zoologist Yoshinori Imaizumi (b. 1914 – d. 2007) of rumours of a "yameneko" living in the mountains of Iriomote. In February 1965, Togawa visited Yaeyama after hearing stories of wild cats living on Iriomote from a newspaper columnist. Initially assuming that people were mistaking escaped and feral house pets for wild animals, Togawa corroborated with Koura who believed there was truth behind the stories. Koura assigned Togawa with collecting tangible evidence which required him to travel back to Iriomote and collect information on the Iriomote cat as well as an actual specimen. Upon arriving on the island, Togawa discovered that due to food shortages, people had resorted to cooking Iriomote cats and using their meat for soup. Traps that had been set resulted in cats being killed for the pot, which made it difficult to collect biological samples.

In May 1965, prior to Togawa's return to the island, a group of school children on a field trip encountered a weak and injured male Iriomote cat at the base of Maaree Waterfall on Haemita Beach. The children's teacher took the cat in but it later died. Another teacher preserved its skin in formalin and buried the skeleton in a wooden box behind the school. Togawa subsequently exhumed the remains, which became the type specimen. Additionally, scientists acquired the crushed skull of a kitten from nearby Yubu Island, which was then reconstructed by Imaizumi. Togawa and Koura returned to Iriomote the following month to obtain a complete set of remains, a live specimen, and any ecological data they could get. According to hunters only one or two cats were caught each year, and the number of remaining cats is low. A small number of Iriomote cats have been kept in captivity.

A five-week-old male was discovered on June 14th, 1979 after being separated from his mother. The kitten was named Keita and was kept at the

Okinawa Zoo until it died aged thirteen years and two months. A female specimen was also kept at the *National Museum of Nature and Science.* This specimen is believed to have been nine years and seven months old when it died. On August 6th, 1996 "Yon", an Iriomote cat was hit by a vehicle and subsequently rehabilitated at the *Iriomote Wildlife Conservation Center*, where Yon stayed until his death on April 9th, 2011, at the estimated age of fifteen years and one month. Yon was then preserved by a taxidermist. Initially classified as its own genus *Mayailurus*, today the *yameneko* is generally thought to be either a subspecies of the leopard cat (*Prionailurus bengalensis iriomotensis*) or a species in its own right (*Prionailurus iriomotensis* or *Felis iriomotensis*). (Also see *Iriomote Mountain Cat*)

(Status: Identified)

Yeli

Killer of Domestic Cats

The *yeli* is rumoured to inhabit northern China, where it preys on domestic cats. Described as a large wildcat with a prominent head and large teeth, this formidable creature is thought to be both ferocious and cunning. An alleged incident involving the trapping of a *yeli* in a snare took place in the late 1960s or early 70s; the animal reportedly escaped after a brief struggle with its captor. Later, a *yeli* was apparently injured by a shop owner but managed to escape. Li Fangjian apparently witnessed a strange cat-like creature while hunting wild boar near Laoshan during the 1960s, which he believed was the mysterious *yeli*. It was sitting on its haunches about ten feet (three metres) from him, staring threateningly in his direction. According to Li, he fired at the beast as it was getting ready to attack and brought its carcass back home with him. In the early 1990s, a young boy reported an encounter with a large, black cat in a residential area of Hedong District, Tianjin. Described as having large eyes and proportionately longer and thicker limbs, it was able to effortlessly jump over a 2.3 metre (7.5 ft) wall before disappearing. In July 2002, a 70-year-old man from Xinzhuang Village in Baodi District was shocked to discover a cat resembling a wildcat preying on his rabbits. As he approached it, the animal hissed, demonstrating no apprehension toward him whatsoever.

Possible explanations for the *yeli* include a melanistic wildcat, introgressive hybrids between wildcats and domestic cats, a distinct regional phenotype of an isolated feral cat population, an isolated population of fishing cats or a hybrid of fishing cats and domestic cats, a Chinese mountain cat, a variety of jungle cat, a leopard cat, and even a mustelid.

(Author's Verdict: 3/5)

3

THE LYNX EFFECT

'Lawk! What a monstrous tail our cat has got!'

— HENRY CAREY

The British Lynx

Scientific Name: *Lynx lynx* (Linnaeus, 1758)

Approximately 5% of big cat sightings reported in Great Britain are described as resembling lynxes. Critics often attribute these accounts to misinterpretations of large domestic cat breeds (presumably tail-less or bobtailed), and while some of the reports may have been domesticated varieties, others were genuine cases of Lynx species. The Eurasian lynx (*Lynx lynx*) is larger than you might think, which can lead to mistakes wherein large domestic cats or hybrids between domestic breeds and related species are misidentified as lynx. The Siberian lynx (*Lynx lynx wrangeli*), a subspecies of the Eurasian lynx, is the largest, with some males weighing up to 38 kilograms (84 lbs). For comparison, the average male domestic cat usually weighs between 3.6 and 4.5 kg (7.9 – 9.9 lbs). There are many credible reports of lynx sightings, and it must be noted that on multiple occasions, a lynx has been spotted in a certain region and eventually captured, re-captured, or regretfully killed, but fully documented and verified. In 2001, Carol Montague reported a sighting of a lynx in Cricklewood, perched on a fence between two gardens. This was not the first time that such an occurrence has been recorded; sightings were reported back as far as 1991 on the outskirts of North London and South Hertfordshire. For the record, it is my prediction that the first 'exotic' felid species to be unequivocally proven to be breeding and reproducing in Britain will be the lynx.

Cobbett's Spaniel-Sized Mystery Cat

William Cobbett (b. 1763 – d. 1835), an author, soldier, and political reformer, wrote about his childhood experience in 1770 in his renowned book *Rural Rides* (1830), which is still in print today. He described being close to the ruins of Waverley Abbey when he noticed a peculiar cat, "as big as a middle-sized Spaniel dog" climbing into the hollow of a dead elm tree. Several years later, while in self-imposed political exile in New Brunswick, Canada, Cobbett observed a North American lynx, which he referred to as a "lucifee," stating that "it seemed to be just such a cat as I had seen in Waverley."

Forest of Dean Mystery Cat

In December 2019, nine-year-old Monty Bell Jr. (known to his family and friends simply as Mj) was searching the Forest of Dean in Gloucestershire for signs of boar activity like rooting behaviour, scrapes, and spoor, when he came across a peculiar paw print. At first, Mj was not certain what it was he had discovered but soon realised that there were no visible claw marks present on the track. While the absence of claw marks is not necessarily proof that the print belongs to a felid, Mj – who is a brilliant young naturalist – alerted me to the specimen so I could see it. Despite the lack of claw marks, there were several obvious indicators that this was not made by a dog, but rather

by a medium-sized felid species. This area of Gloucestershire is notorious for its large and often destructive population of feral boar, but it
also has a long history of reports involving big cats. The Forest of
Dean potentially serves as part of a migratory route used by these
animals when travelling from Wales into southwestern England.
Numerous sightings of large black cats, suspected to be black leopards, have been reported in this area. As jaguars are not well-suited to
the British climate, they are less likely. Additionally, there have been
accounts of faun and grey-coloured animals which may have been
cougars. Furthermore, there is evidence that a smaller yet no less
exceptional species of mystery cat may also inhabit this ancient
forest.

*Monty Bell Jr - Carl's apprentice who found the suspected Lynx tracks in the Forest
of Dean in 2019.*

Forest of Dean big cat tracks from 2019 - 1 of 2.

Forest of Dean big cat tracks from 2019 - 2 of 2.

Forest of Dean big cat tracks from 2019 - the X text.

Approximately eight years before, Andrew Remes, a forestry worker at the time, captured an image of a very similar paw print on his mobile phone about a mile from where Mj made his discovery. Interestingly, these two sites are located on opposite sides of the River Wye, suggesting that they may belong to different animals.

Unfortunately, as our intention was merely to observe any wild boar from a safe distance, I did not bring plaster for making casts. So, I took photographs of the track from various perspectives and utilised an object of scale to calculate its size prior to performing the "X test" by crossing two thin, straight twigs in an "X" pattern. In general, this practical, yet simple technique, is applicable only to symmetrical prints such as those belonging to the Canidae family (including dogs and their relatives). If a track shows no sign of distortion due to slipping on wet or steep terrain, and the sticks don't go through any of the other toes or the plantar pad, it is probably not a dog spoor. The asymmetry of Mj's discovery, combined with the absence of claw marks and a faint three-lobed plantar pad at the rear of the foot, suggests that an average-sized felid species may be responsible. We can see evidence of the animal's foot structure which is consistent with that of a felid. Additionally, there is an easily identifiable dog track located slightly to the right of the mystery track, further illustrating clear discrepancies.

I quickly sought out the professional opinions of zoologists and wildlife biologists to assess the photographs. To date, only one of these has speculated that the print belongs to a canid – even then, they initially believed it was feline until I revealed the location where the print was found. The purported expert then recanted and instead stated it belonged to a dog. Generally, healthy canine tracks are symmetrical. If Mj's track had been made by a dog, the two sticks would have fit neatly between the first and second toes, as well as the third and fourth toes, without making contact with either side of the plantar pad or any nearby toes. I always believed that the primary purpose of science was to determine what is true rather than to ensure one's own theories are validated; however, it appears that some academics believe differently. Mj's find is unlikely to be from a dog and is possibly a lynx. It is almost certainly feline. Dr. Darren Naish commented: "From what I can see, they certainly look like large cat tracks to me. Breadth, disposition of the digital pads, space between the toe pads and plantar pad, all suggest a felid." Dr. Richard Lamb, an entomologist and one-time colleague from the *Stratford upon Avon Butterfly Farm* in Warwickshire, England who often takes the time to investigate reports of big cats, was more cautious, concluding: "I've had a good look at these and all I can say is inconclusive. They could be a domestic dog, but a medium-sized felid cannot be ruled out." Dr. Karl Shuker agreed they were probably feline: "Thanks for showing me these, and yes, I too think they are most likely to be feline – the general proportions and layout certainly seem to indicate this, especially the squatness and asymmetry, plus, as you yourself note, the X test. Size-wise, lynx seems reasonable, also the particular shape is reminiscent of lynx."

This track has been further confirmed since the initial publication of my paper for *Animals & Men*. I am grateful to author and documentary filmmaker Timothy Whittard for granting me permission to reproduce it here. "Dr. Isla Fishburn, a zoologist and animal behaviour expert who specialises in canines and has worked with wolves was asked to comment on the tracks. As to be expected, Dr. Fishburn was cautious but said: "The prints indeed could be from that of a big cat, but they may also be from a canine where their true pad pattern has been distorted given the conditions of the substrate the track was created in. It excites me to think of big cats continuing to exist in parts of the UK as wild populations. The tracks are certainly not typical of a true canine print, but the photos alone don't tell us much of the story about what made them." Helen Motteram, a dog training expert, and owner of the Cheltenham-based family-run business, 'Social Paws', agrees, suggesting "the track does not appear to be from a dog … "I have heard there may be pumas breeding in Britain – I am no cat expert, but I think it's definitely possible."

Gloucestershire-based big cat field researcher, Frank Tunbridge was recently called out to investigate the discovery of similar tracks found in February 2022 at *Rudge Hill Nature Reserve*, Stroud. Commenting on the evidence of MJs discovery, Frank said: "The track exhibits features of a felid paw print, such as a coronet shape arch of toe impressions, a leading front toe, a large hind pad, and of course the classic absence of claw impressions, or if any, very sharp and needle–like." Kelci 'Saff' Saffery, who stars alongside Joe Exotic and Carole Baskin in Netflix's smash-hit documentary series *'Tiger King: Murder, Mayhem & Madness'* said: "The paw print is definitely a cat, what with the lack of claws." And Kate Saunders, with *'Pawprints to Freedom'* added: "We asked several of our volunteers and specialists for their opinions, and none of them thinks the track came from a dog." Prof. Andrew Hemmings of the *Royal Agricultural University* in Cirencester also noted the "lack of claw marks". Other characteristics of the track observed by Prof. Hemmings include: "The compressed (rather than elongate) arrangement of the metatarsal/carpal pad and toes. Also, there would appear to be a bi-lobed element to the anterior portion of the metatarsal/carpal pad – although this is quite ambiguous in the photo... *As ever, it's difficult to say, but my conclusion is erring on the side of the cat."*

So clearly a number of significantly interested parties feel this print is more likely feline than canine in origin, even though the different enthusiasts, experts, academics, and professionals questioned had some contrasting observations. Jon McGowan, a naturalist, illustrator, lecturer, and taxidermist based in the south of England has been investigating the big cat phenomenon of Britain for decades. Commenting on the prints found in the Forest of Dean, Jon said: "The tracks are likely from a lynx, as the shaping of the rear plantar pad shows that the middle lobe is noticeably lower than the two side lobes. This is what I would expect from a lynx."

It appears that an individual or perhaps members of an unauthorised "rewilding" operation have been releasing lynxes (or at least a lynx-like felid of unknown species) into the Forest of Dean for at least the last eleven years, possibly even longer. This may be a measure to control deer populations or reduce fox numbers, or it could be an individual who is well-connected and has a strong affinity for lynx and is unwilling to wait for the bureaucratic process.

At the Royal Agricultural University (left to right, Carl Marshall, Professor Andy Hemmings, Jon McGowan).

The presence of lynx fossils in Scotland tells us they went extinct in the UK during the medieval period, approximately 1,300 years ago. But could they have survived undetected in the British Isles? Well, perhaps, but the truth is, it's not very likely. It is more plausible they are either escaped or illegally released animals and/or their descendants. A feral population of lynx, with their minimal range requirements, smaller size, elusive nature, and crepuscular hunting habits, would be one of the more suitable felid species, or even groups of closely related species, likely to not only survive but thrive, largely undetected in the Forest of Dean.

(Author's Verdict: 4/5)

Bulgarian Lynx

Extinct or Alive?

The Eurasian lynx is believed to have been extirpated from Bulgaria in the 1940s; however, unconfirmed reports of animals resembling lynx have prompted speculation that the species may still exist in some areas. In addition, higher numbers of deer and reintroduced Eurasian lynxes in other parts of Europe may have a positive effect on its return. A representative for the *WWF* revealed that lynxes have been photographed in Bulgaria in recent years. According to Elena Gancheva, who coordinates the WWF's "Adopt a Lynx" campaign, three individuals – two males and one female – have been captured on trail cameras in the western Osogovo Mountain range, located at the Bulgarian-Macedonian border. "For long, the lynx was believed to be extinct from Bulgarian lands but now we have certain evidence that it is coming back."

The overhunting of the Bulgarian lynx was responsible for its eventual extinction, with the last wild specimen being killed in 1947. According to the *World Wildlife Fund Bulgaria*, it is likely that the species had migrated to Bulgaria from its neighbouring countries such as Macedonia and Serbia. Small, isolated populations may exist in Bulgarian forests that have yet to be discovered and may have been genetically replenished by recent migrations and releases. Gancheva noted that the Eurasian lynx can only flourish in environments where there is minimal human activity. As part of *Rewilding Europe's* efforts, this species has been introduced to five of their operational areas: Italy's Central Apennines, Croatia's Velebit Mountains, the Oder Delta, Swedish Lapland, the Southern Carpathians, and most notably Bulgaria... Watch this space!

(Author's Verdict: 3/5)

Tinicum Cat

A Small but Mighty Cryptid "Cat"

The Tinicum cat is a small, fierce, feliform cryptid reported from the rocky and wooded hills of Bucks and Fayette Counties Pennsylvania, as well as potentially southern Illinois. It derives its name from the town of Tinicum, where a specimen was allegedly killed in 1922; however, other regional names include Indian Devil, Nockamixon cat, timber cat, or wood cat. According to eyewitnesses, these bobcat-like animals measure approximately 0.76 meters in length and 0.32 meters high at the shoulders. Tinicum cats have coats that are sandy-grey in colour, with yellow and buff-coloured patterns. Their backs have a dark dorsal stripe that stretches from the shoulders to the tip of the tail and may also feature tiger-like striping on the body, legs, and tail. Unlike feral domestic cats, Tinicum cats have a notably thicker winter coat. Moreover, they possess round heads with flat ears and wide grey faces with regular black stripes measuring 17.7 cm across their ears. Finally, their powerful jaws hold strong teeth; they have white whiskers and a conspicuous white spot on the throat. The forelimbs measure approximately 0.43 meters in length and the hind legs are 0.33 meters, with a thick banded tail measuring 25.4-27.9 cm, ending in a black tip.

During the early 19th century, hunters reported that these cats were abundant when the first settlers arrived; however, their numbers had significantly declined over time. In 1857 and 1858, C. H. Shearer captured three specimens in Irish Gap, Pennsylvania. For three years there had been reports of two mysterious cats making terrifying screams at night in the area around Tinicum Township, Bucks County. On January 16th, 1922, following several days of tracking, Tunis Brady was finally able to capture a male specimen using a trap near its rocky den. The animal put up quite a struggle; thus requiring Brady to shoot it before delivering its body to state game warden Warren Fretz from Doylestown who took photos before having it preserved by a taxidermist.

Unfortunately, the current whereabouts of the specimens are unknown. At the time, locals did not consider it to be a bobcat or a domestic feral cat; most believed that it was either an indigenous wildcat (*Felis sp.*) or one brought by European settlers long ago. It has been speculated that the Tinicum cat could have been a hybrid between a bobcat and a feral cat, although no such hybrids have ever been officially documented. Other potential explanations include an established phenotype of regional feral cats or an introduced jaguarundi, though these do not typically have stripes.

(Author's Verdict: 3/5)

4

ANOMALOUS BIG CATS, AKA ALIEN BIG CATS

'Beware of the night, child. All cats are black in the dark.'

— JEAN GENET

AUSTRALIA

Reports of anomalous big cats and the savage deaths of livestock attributed to them are not a new phenomenon in Australia. Notwithstanding the fact that no physical remains other than from unusually large domestic and feral cats have ever been discovered, rumours of pantherine predators slinking through Australia's coastal forests and bushlands have been whispered about for almost two hundred years. There are three primary theories to explain the existence of Australian big cats. The most popular of these suggests that mountain lions kept as mascots by US military personnel during World War II were secretly released into the wild before their regiments departed. Another often-cited idea is that large cats escaped from zoos or circuses in the past. The third and potentially most plausible explanation is connected to the exotic animal trade.

Big Cat by Night by Danielle Rose.

By the 1850s, news of Australia's gold rush spurred an influx of Chinese migrants, who brought with them exotic animals for food and purported medicinal purposes. This might explain why sightings tend to occur along Eastern Australia's Great Dividing Range, as well as in Southwestern Western Australia, both locations where early gold mining occurred. Reports of big cats in mainland Australia first emerged shortly after the establishment of Europe's first permanent settlements in the 1830s. The earliest recorded sighting was reported in 1836 near Adelaide when a sailor asserted that he encountered, "a catlike animal with orange fur, black stripes down its back and white tufted ears, hunting for marsupial rats near a body of water." This seems to be a report of the *Queensland Tiger*. A public auction of the menagerie at Melbourne's *Cremorne Gardens*, on November 23rd, 1863 recorded the sales of "two black-mane lions worth £500 in England purchased by Mr. Coppin for £400 on account of the Zoological Society; tiger, lion cub, panther, monkeys, eagles, and a peafowl".

Small private menageries were a popular form of entertainment and highly valued local attractions in the mid-19th century. The legal restrictions imposed when it came to purchasing and providing adequate housing for large, potentially dangerous animals, along with an increase in advertisements offering big cats for sale in classified ads of the time, fuelled an underground market for exotic animals between the 1850s and 1870s.

In the 1890s, panic surged throughout Tantanoola, South Australia after reports of a large, predatory cat had been menacing local dogs and slaughtering farm animals, particularly sheep. It was said that a Bengal tiger had escaped from a travelling circus in the 1880s and roamed the Australian bush, with accounts claiming over 4,000 sheep missing as far away as Robe and Bendigo. On August 25th, 1895, Tom Donovan shot and killed an animal that was believed to be the Tantanoola Tiger on Mount Salt Station after it had killed a lamb. The "tiger" was preserved by a taxidermist and is now proudly displayed at the Tantanoola Tiger Hotel. After examination, however, it turned out that it was not a felid at all, but an Arabian wolf.

The presence of this wolf in Australian bushland is believed to have been due to its survival from a shipwreck offshore several years before. The exotic animal trade was prevalent during the late 19th century and classified ads often featured both standard and melanistic leopard cubs for sale. South Australian ethnobotanist Neville Bonney, who wrote two books on the Tantanoola tiger, asserted that in 1883, two circus caravans collided on the road between Robe and Mount Gambier allowing a pair of tigers to escape. An unsuccessful search was conducted by circus personnel before they departed without success, leaving a notice at the Overland Inn informing the licensee of the incident. This story has all the hall-marks of being a local legend. For many years, sightings of big cats have been reported from the Gippsland region of southeastern Victoria. In 2005, a hunter named Kurt Engel shot and killed an animal he believed to be a black panther near Sale in eastern Gippsland. Engel estimated it to measure approximately 1.5 meters in length and kept its tail as a trophy, which was 60 cm long – significantly larger than those of standard domestic cats.

Subsequent DNA analysis confirmed that the animal was *Felis catus* – an abnormally large feral cat. Before the 2010 election, the Victorian Coalition made a commitment to thoroughly examine the alleged existence of Australia's big cats and make a definitive determination as to whether there was any truth to it. Understandably, this proposal was met with scepticism. When asked jokingly if the government would be investigating other fantastical tales, Peter Walsh, who was at that time the Minister of Agriculture, pointed out that for the farmers whose livestock had been killed by the mystery predator, it wasn't a joke but rather an alarming reality. A 2012 study by the *Arthur Rylah Institute for Environmental Research* concluded that there is no wild population of big cats due to a lack of tangible evidence.

The analysis used the case of the Lithgow Panther, where video footage of a large black felid in the Central Tablelands of New South Wales was examined by zoo, museum, and national parks staff who determined it was a "very large feral cat, two to three times normal size." The study suggested the "most parsimonious explanation" for many of the reported sightings in Victoria is that they are also large feral cats. However, it went on to note some peculiar anomalies.

"Some evidence cannot be dismissed entirely, including preliminary DNA evidence, footprints, and some behaviours that seem to be outside the known behavioural repertoire of known predators in Victoria." The study revealed details of partially consumed livestock where the flesh seemed to have been almost surgically removed, well beyond the capabilities of known animals like dingoes and razor-backs. In 1991, scat was discovered at Wensleydale near *Otway Forest Park*. A wildlife officer named David Cass with the *Victorian Department of Conservation and Environment* was contacted by a local farmer reporting "really unusual stock kills." The farmer presented Cass with a particularly large faecal sample, which was an unusual colour and had a strong acrid smell, not unlike a cat. Cass sent the sample to a scatologist, who extracted four black hairs which he compared to those from a black leopard at *Melbourne Zoo*, and found they had "very similar features".

In 2012, a government study was conducted, which revealed that an expert from the Zoology Department at *La Trobe University* had identified the hairs from a sample provided by a farmer as those of a leopard. However, the results were not made public due to concerns of contamination with Melbourne Zoo leopard hairs in the laboratory. Nevertheless, this significant finding remains one of the best pieces of evidence for wild big cats in Australia to date. In early June, Apollo Bay real estate photographer, Amber Noseda, encountered a strange animal while on her way home from photographing birds at Mount Sabine in the Otway Ranges. In another encounter, Sophie Hammill was hiking with her father along a trail near the Cape Otway light-house when she heard a sound. Upon looking towards the source of the noise, approximately eight metres away, Sophie observed an animal with "a big thick long black tail swooped toward the path and two black legs". She was adamant that its size was comparable to that of a tiger and not a feral cat.

Unlike the situation in the United States, where native mountain lions and jaguars are found, no big cat has been officially recorded in Australia using trail camera photographs or wildlife surveys. The government of Victoria commissioned a report which concluded that the existing evidence was, "inadequate to establish that a wild population of 'big cats' exists in Victoria." But a 2001 study by *Deakin University* concluded that the existence of big cats in the Grampian Mountains area has been demonstrated and there is "sufficient evidence ... to affirm beyond reasonable doubt the presence of a big cat population in western Victoria." For more than a century, people have reported sightings of the Blue Mountains "panther" or the Lithgow "lion" from the Blue Mountains region west of Sydney. There is speculation that these animals may have descended from circus or zoo escapees, or they could be descendants of U.S. military mascots. In 2003, the New South Wales State Government announced that there is a high probability of several exotic large cats living in the wild close to Sydney without them being detected. Video footage revealing a big black cat close to Lithgow was studied by seven personnel from zoos, museums, parks, and agriculture departments, who decided, based on morphological characteristics, that it was almost certainly an oversized domestic cat, two to three times the normal size.

In 2018, Grant Denyer and his wife Cheryl Rogers, reported their observation of a large cat on their property. Cheryl said, "I was doing the dishes, looking down the paddock and I saw it and I said, 'The panther's back'". Grant Denyer filmed the "panther" from the safety of his home, but the footage is, shall we say, less than convincing. Photographs have also been taken near the Hawkesbury River. In 2002, Kenthurst teenager Luke Walker was attacked by what he claimed was a big cat, suffering deep lacerations during the assault. In addition to pilots, credible sightings have been reported by an officer from the Department of Agriculture, a detective from the New South Wales Police Force, and personnel from the Rural Fire Service. In 2020, encounters continued to be documented in national newspapers with video footage supposedly recorded on the grounds of Sydney Adventist Hospital, Wahroonga. In April 2020, the Go Pro-associated Instagram collective bluemtns_ explored shared pictures of tracks discovered during an excursion in the mountains. The *Grose*

Vale Group, which has been collecting reports of sightings since the late 1990s, claims that it receives roughly 20-30 sightings annually. In 1999, Kevin Sheridan, head of the *Department of Agriculture*, wrote to the director-general of *New South Wales Primary Industries* (NSWP) requesting a report given the considerable number of alleged attacks on livestock. Consequently, the NSWP authorised four reports in 1999, 2003, 2009, and 2013. The first report by Dr. Johannes Bauer of *NSW Agriculture* concluded that it was likely genuine.

As a consequence of this finding, *NSW Agriculture* was ordered to dispatch professional trackers to identify the animal; however, they only sent an agricultural officer and a German shepherd dog. In 2001, Freedom of Information (FOI) requests revealed that the New South Wales State government had opened a file on reports of rumoured big cats. Subsequent biological studies conducted between 2001 and 2003, led the district veterinarian of the Moss Vale Rural Lands Protection Board to surmise that such a cat likely did inhabit the area. In response to concerns raised by the Mayor of Hawkesbury Council and the Moss Vale Rural Lands Protection Board, a report was authorised in 2003 which concluded that while there was no irrefutable evidence, it seemed more likely than not that a big cat population existed. William Atkinson, technical manager of NSW Agriculture, reported being asked to remain quiet on the subject.

While representatives from Hawkesbury publicly expressed their "genuine concern", another study commissioned in 2008 found that it was "more likely than not" that a big cat population existed; this conclusion was later edited before public release, resulting in allegations of a government cover-up. In 2011, a pet alpaca was savagely attacked and killed in Bilpin, with an autopsy revealing seven-centimetre puncture marks to the skull. Following the incident, a report by the Hawkesbury area ranger concluded that it may have been killed by a large felid. Subsequently, a 2013 report written by New Zealand invasive species expert John Parkes asserted that there is no evidence of big cats in the Blue Mountains. However, despite this conclusion, the author has privately stated that they personally believe it is possible for a small population to exist. In response to this report, Ray Williams, member of parliament for Hawkesbury, denounced it as dismissive and potentially dangerous.

Even for a trained observer, accurately assessing the size of an animal during a brief encounter is not a simple task. Feral domestic cats (*Felis catus*) can reach considerable sizes and are almost certainly behind some reports of big cats in Australia.

CHINA

The Indochinese leopard (*Panthera pardus delacouri*) is a rare subspecies found in Mainland Southeast Asia and Southern China. From 2002 to 2009, camera trap surveys were conducted in eleven nature reserves in southern China, with successful detection of leopards only reported at *Changging National Nature Reserve* located within the Qinling Mountains. Despite this, there are some adjacent regions where leopards have a better chance of long-term survival. It is difficult to verify whether unverified reports signal dwindling populations in native countries or merely escaped or illegally released animals from private collections, circuses, or inadequate zoos. Reports of dwindling populations may be due to a decrease in native species or from escaped/illegally released animals. Despite the domestic trade ban on large quantities of leopard bones in China for medicinal use, it is still allowed by the Chinese government.

In October 1976, reports of an unidentified feline predator began to circulate throughout the Hang Hau area of Sai Kung, Hong Kong, thought to have been responsible for the deaths of over twenty canines, some of which were quite large. Despite various attempts to capture it, however, the creature was never found and its true identity remains a mystery. Witnesses described it as a black leopard measuring approximately four feet long with a long tail. By November, however, reports changed from detailing a leopard to that of a dark tiger three feet high and four feet long. Subsequent investigations revealed that one of the earlier accounts was a German Shepherd/Chow crossbreed. Another big cat was purportedly killed in Hong Kong in 1989; since then additional sightings have occurred sporadically across the region.

DENMARK

In 1982, Niels L. Thomsen, a forest supervisor in Denmark, believed that a big cat was inhabiting the woods west of Toftlund in southern Jutland. His suspicions were sparked by the discovery of headless roe deer carcasses found at Lindet Wood and Henning (Hønning) Plantation. Additionally, a leg belonging to another roe deer was found at the latter location, stored in an oak tree with deep scratches assumed to have been made by a large felid. In 1995, a lion was reported in the village of Kertinge in eastern Funen, with the Danish media soon dubbing it the "Beast of Funen."

On May 13th, police received calls from multiple individuals who had seen the "lion" outside their homes. One witness, Peter Tyllesen, noticed a large cougar-like animal walking alongside a motorway while driving his wife to work in Nyborg just after eight o'clock. Tyllesen said, "I'm not one hundred percent certain of what I saw. But I do believe it was a lion. The tail had that distinctive sway to it," he explained, "and it was rather big." It leaped across Storebælt Road and disappeared from sight. When questioned, the *Lion Park of Givskud* reported that none of their lions had escaped. Klaus Dræby, Manager of Vissenbjerg Vivarium in Funen, speculated that the animal may have been a jungle cat, stating: "In Holland and Belgium among other places a number of jungle cats are privately owned, and I know there are some in Denmark too..."

On May 18th, a six-year-old boy by the name of Jacob reportedly witnessed a big cat in Frørup. The youngster watched the animal traverse the road and vanish into a yard. According to one informant, a hunter staying at Ørbæk had come across an enormous lion-like cat near his chicken coop. He asked permission to shoot it, which was granted but by the time he had loaded his hunting rifle, the animal had disappeared. Per Havlit, an ornithologist from Odense, was in Hvirringe wood searching for birds when he: "noticed a yellow-brownish heap of something which at a distance looked like newly felled wood. I looked in my glasses and decided it must be a roe deer. Suddenly I spotted a long thigh, and then the female lion turned around." Per Havlit told the press: "I ran all the way up to my car and at once contacted the manager at Hvirringe estate. When I rang at the door I was drenched with sweat," Accompanied by the manager, he sought out the animal but did not encounter it again. It was not until he was back home Per Havlit called the police: "But the officer only asked how much I'd had to drink. They would not take me seriously even though I was as sober as a judge." The police did confirm that a prior report came from Glorup Estate and that the animal had been observed multiple times in the southern region of Nyborg Police District. Additionally, two boys reported witnessing a large cat crossing a road near their residence before disappearing into an adjacent field. "On Saturday afternoon the animal was seen by two 14-year-old boys at Glorup estate in Ørbæk municipality. And in the days before that, it was seen several times in the southern part of our district. I don't believe it could have moved to a spot north of Kerteminde in twelve hours. Going around the bay it would have to walk more than 60 kilometres. And moving in a straight line it would have to walk straight through the city and across a bridge."

Apparently no one considered the possibility of two or more predators on the loose! A farmer spotted the animal on May 25th at around 9:30 a.m. near Otterup village. Børge Jørgensen of Gundstrup recounts: "I am a sportsman and normally carry my field glasses with me. They came to use when the pale yellow animal was prowling along a hedgerow in a field of spring barley 200 metres away from me. It was almost twice as big as a Labrador dog and had a long tail. The head was round and shaggy, the ears pointed with a small tuft. I was able to follow it in my glasses for about 150 metres until it disappeared into the field. I am almost quite certain it was a lynx. It was a well-nourished lynx and quite beautiful to look at. But all the same, I think it should be shot."

On May 26th, a municipal employee of Otterup was taken by surprise when the Funen beast sneaked up behind him. He recounts: "I heard a spitting sound. Turn my head. And there it is, flashing its fangs. The canine teeth are this long," Ove Rasmussen says, indicating a length of five to seven centimetres between forefinger and thumb. Ove Rasmussen described the animal: "I looked right into its eyes, they were yellowish-brown. It was about the size of a German shepherd dog, with a pale yellow body and the fur a bit thicker on the head, and it had brownish spots on the chest and the foremost part of the belly. The part of it that I could see. And the tail was a bit more dark and tufty. Well, I'm still shocked. And I think of what may happen to little children and domestic animals around here if the animal is allowed to prowl about." On the same date, May 26th, another mysterious beast was afoot in Bårdesø in northern Funen. That evening, Lisbeth and Solveig Kallesøe were sitting at their kitchen table when they heard a sound coming from outside. Simultaneously, the dogs in the neighbourhood began barking. Upon inspection the following day, the Kallesøe family discovered tracks in a newly harrowed field. The prints were seven centimetres long and six centimetres wide, with a gap of approximately 40 centimetres between each one.

FINLAND

In June 1992, reports surfaced that a lion had been prowling near the Finnish-Russian border in Ruokolahti. Subsequent investigations by a government biologist revealed tracks from what was identified as a big cat. In response to this, the Ministry of the Interior granted the biologist permission to capture or kill the animal if necessary. Additionally, border guards were enlisted to aid in the hunt for the alleged lion. Despite all these efforts, no lion was ever captured and the events remain unresolved to this day. A plausible explanation might be that some exotic animals escaped during a railway accident involving a circus train in Russia, crossing over into Finland in the process.

FRANCE

France boasts a complex and violent history involving dangerous cat-like creatures. The most renowned, or rather infamous, of these, is the Beast of Gévaudan. This creature, or creatures as some believe, roamed the now-department of Lozère in southern-central France from 1764 to 1767, leaving destruction in its path across an area that spanned approximately fifty miles (80 km). Witnesses reported the animal had sharp teeth and a long tail, with varying descriptions, such as wolves, dogs, wolf-dog hybrids, and even tigers. In 2002, John D. C. Linnell *et al.* reviewed wolf attacks on humans between the 18th and 20th centuries. Interestingly, the age profile of those killed by wolves during this period showed a significant shift towards older victims. In the case of the Beast of Gévaudan; adults were six times more likely to be attacked than wolf attacks, while children under ten years of age made up only a third of all cases. This indicates that witnesses may not have exaggerated their accounts and that they encountered a large animal unfamiliar to them, which is corroborated as predators usually take on bigger prey depending on their body size.

According to the findings of Linnell *et al.*, approximately 95% of the attacks on humans in Gévaudan from 1764 to 1767 can be attributed to one animal, referred to as La bête or "the Beast," while the remaining assaults were likely committed by wolves. So what was the Beast of Gévaudan? Despite the widely held belief that the beast was a wolf or another wild canid, alternative hypotheses have been proposed; one of which is an African lion. Since the animal was not described with a thick mane, it may have been a subadult male or a lioness. All those who encountered the creature first-hand generally portrayed it as a carnivore quite different from a wolf. It is thus plausible that the Beast of Gévaudan was actually a lion (*Panthera leo*). Its purported size, appearance, behaviour, and strength are consistent with such an assumption; for example, its size is compared to that of a bovine. Furthermore, its characteristics, including a flat muzzle, reddish fur, a dark area along the spine, and spots on the sides of the body are prominent in younger lions, and a body shape that becomes more robust from the rear towards the front, along with its oddly thin tail that was short-haired with a tuft at its tip further supports this hypothesis.

The "Beast of Cézallier" refers to a series of carnivores responsible for livestock attacks from the Auvergne region of central France between 1946 and 1951. During this period, a variety of animals were reported to be involved, yet the singular expression remains standard terminology for these incidents, similar to how multiple creatures that caused havoc in Gévaudan two centuries prior became known as the singular "Beast of Gévaudan". The killing of a wolf in Grandrieu in 1951 appears to have brought the Beast of Cézallier case to an end. However, it is notable that there were similar occurrences prior to this; for example, a lioness managed to escape from a menagerie located in Saint-Germain-du-Teil (Lozère), and another incident was reported in the Vosges area of France in 1978 involving two black leopards. Most notably, February 1983 saw reports regarding the notorious "Beast of Valescure" (also known as "the Beast of Estérel"), variously classified as either a lioness, wolf, puma or another unknown carnivore. Despite attempts to capture the creature, it ultimately evaded such efforts and news reports gradually ceased.

France is now on the list of countries where large non-native felids have been captured. In September 2019, emergency services were dispatched to Armentieres in Northern France upon receiving reports of a juvenile black leopard prowling the roofs of the town. As reported by *La Voix du Nord*, baffled spectators near the Belgian border were shocked to see a black panther wandering on the windowsills and rafters of a three-story building in the city centre. At times it would stop to observe trains passing through or domestic cats walking across the pavement below without any knowledge of its much larger, potentially lethal relative lurking above. In response, police set up a perimeter around the building before the animal made its way inside an apartment owned by its keeper. Thereafter, a team was able to successfully capture it with assistance from a veterinarian who administered sedatives via a dart gun. After being placed in a cage, the panther was handed over to France's Animal Protection League, who noted that it displayed no aggression. As it approached the conclusion of its liberty, the panther came across a flat nearby where a 15-year-old girl encountered it on the stairs.

The six-month-old female leopard weighed approximately twenty kilograms and was of a similar size to that of a Labrador dog. Subsequently, it was moved to an animal sanctuary before being relocated to Maubeuge Zoo. At that time, two investigations were in progress: one by the police against the individual owner, which focused on the danger posed to the public; and a second by hunting and wildlife authorities, which focused on how the animal was obtained and the conditions in which it was kept. Over the coming days, the tale of the Lille Panther took an unforeseen turn when the recaptured animal was stolen from Maubeuge Zoo. Staff at the zoo discovered upon their arrival for work the next day that the door to her enclosure had been broken open and the Lille Panther was missing. This case is significant as it illustrates how exotic felids can escape and given enough time could live in the wild in unfamiliar countries. Unfortunately, however, this individual did not have time to find a natural habitat and gain survival skills in nature and was captured within 24 hours.

GERMANY

In July 1982, Uwe Sander of Oldersbek reported an animal resembling a cougar while driving near Husum in northern Germany. "I followed the animal, and at one point I had to back into a branch road. When I had come close to the animal I got out to fetch a pitchfork in the trunk. I got out of the car, but before I could get hold of the pitchfork the animal jumped on me, going for my head and throat.

We both fell down, but fortunately, I quickly got a grip on the animal's neck with both arms. I also tried to get my legs around the body of the animal, but it scratched its way out of my grip and ran away." Sander felt certain that the animal was a cougar, due to its four large canine teeth, long whiskers, and silvery brown pelage. After a confrontation, Sander was revealed to have sustained injuries; the right side of his face had been lacerated and he had various deep cuts. Subsequently, 50 sportsmen and 20 constables joined the hunt for the cougar and while some tracks were spotted, the cat itself eluded capture. To amplify their search efforts, a helicopter was employed on the following day, yet again without success.

HAWAII

Hawaii does not have any large species of cats, however, in 2003, an anonymous employee at a local hotel told *Big Island Now* that two guests from California had spotted what seemed to be a big cat around 7:45 p.m. when they were entering the premises. They were certain it was a cougar, the employee said. "She saw it going by," said the employee, who was working in the kitchen. "She like, freaked out. She wanted to jump back into the truck." Another employee at the hotel front desk had a conversation with the California couple, who mentioned that they had seen cougars in the past. Shortly after, the security camera footage was reviewed and a grainy image of a cougar-like animal leaving the highway and heading towards the baseball fields was discovered.

In August 2022, a resident of Hawaii reported that he had observed a big cat in his backyard. He was only able to take a few blurry photographs from afar, but the *Department of Land and Natural Resources* deemed it adequate evidence to initiate an official inquiry. A *Honolulu Star-Bulletin* reporter wrote: "A 'mystery cat' in upcountry Maui is apparently still in the area around Olinda, based on a number of sightings over the past two weeks, the Department of Land and Natural Resources reported yesterday in an e-mailed news release. On Wednesday, three residents saw a cat-like animal walking down a pasture fence at around 4 p.m. The next day at about 5:30 a.m., the animal was seen just a quarter of a mile downslope from the previous day's sighting. Two women passing through the area saw the cat from about 7 feet away at about 8:50 p.m. Thursday night. They described the animal as about 7 feet long, with a long tail, black coat, yellow-green eyes, and a flat face. DLNR wildlife officials responded to the sighting and searched the area with infrared equipment. Earlier that week and the week before, homeowners who live in the area heard an animal calling and dogs barking in response."

Approximately one month later, local media reported that an animal similar to the one seen in Kealakekua Bay had been captured on video surveillance footage at the Manago Hotel in a nearby town. Unfortunately, the images are too unclear to make out any distinguishing details, and the witness who saw the creature has chosen to remain anonymous.

ISLE OF WIGHT

The Isle of Wight has had its fair share of big cat sightings. In March 1984, Devon-based naturalist and big cat author, Di Francis visited the Isle of Wight with hopes of securing sponsorship for a three-month expedition to investigate reports of big cats on the island. During her visit, Francis went to the sites of recent sightings to photograph paw prints possibly left by the animal, as well as to speak with an eyewitness who reported witnessing an animal approximately the size of an Alsatian dog while dumping rubbish at a local landfill site. In May 1984, two big cats were seen in Newport. Gavin Parker, a student at Carisbrooke High School, observed one of the mysterious creatures near Wellington Road during the day. Karen Lambert also saw it while walking up Petticoat Lane – she described it as having a dark head and tail with a sandy-coloured body similar to that of a Siamese cat, but much bigger. Additionally, farmer Ken Frogbrook from Stagwell near Parkhurst Forest lost two lambs from his flock of Shetland sheep in April and May 1985; he believes the presence of a big cat in the area as he had witnessed it himself.

According to the County Press reports, approximately 110 reported sightings were registered from the Isle of Wight over a two-and-a-half-year period prior to June 1985. Additionally, that same month, Roy Kingswell of Rowborough Farm close to Shorwell found a dead lamb and brought its 27 kg remains to Jack Corney, owner of the Isle of Wight Zoo in Sandown for examination. Corney concluded that the carcass was the work of a large animal but could not ascertain which species with certainty. In January 1994, Martin Trippett, the founder of the Island Naturalist Group, led members on an evening vigil for big cats using infrared equipment. Unfortunately, no sightings were made. Additionally, Karl Shuker identified an animal killed on the Isle of Wight seven years before as an Asian leopard cat (*Prionailurus bengalensis*).

In April 2002, two sisters captured footage of a purported big cat on the Isle of Wight. This was the first time such an animal had been recorded on video on the Island. The footage was captured in the vicinity of Chequers Inn, Rookley, by sisters Rachael Dethridge of Kingston-Upon-Thames and Beverly Futers of Chale. Beverly said: "There is absolutely no way it was a domestic cat — you could tell by its size and the way it moved with a swagger." After viewing the video, Jack Corney, owner of the Isle of Wight Zoo, suggested that it was probably a small black leopard. In January 2003, personnel at B-N Group airfield in Bembridge observed an animal with feline characteristics for several minutes through binoculars. It was about the size of a Labrador and had dark brown or brindle markings, similar to a leopard. However, upon further investigation by law enforcement, there were no traces left of either the animal or its presence.

In May 2010, Trudy Boulton of Whitepit Lane in Newport and her father, David Boulton, observed a big cat in a field situated behind David's home on Garden Way in Pan. Trudy said: "When I had a look through his binoculars, I could see it walking along the hedgerow.

Normally you can just make out a fox or a badger, but this was huge. "It was a beige colour with a long tail and it moved very gracefully, like a lion." In June 2012, Ventnor mum Michelle Angell experienced a night-time fright after a mysterious big cat allegedly climbed through her bedroom window, smashing a bedside lamp as it entered the room. She said it was too big to be a domestic cat and "was very frantic and behaved like a wild animal." The County Press reported a sighting in February 2021, indicating that big cats remain active on the island.

THE NETHERLANDS

In 2005, reports of a "black cougar" began to surface in a wildlife preserve, which later was positively identified as an interspecific hybrid between the European wildcat and the domestic cat. Despite this identification, reports of anomalous big cats in the Netherlands have become more frequent in recent years.

NEW ZEALAND

Since the late 1990s, alleged sightings of big cats have been documented in New Zealand, both from the North Island to the South Island. Unconfirmed reports have been circulating in Mid-Canterbury near Ashburton and its adjacent Southern Alps for many years. However, searches on behalf of the *Ministry of Agriculture and Forestry* conducted in 2003 proved fruitless with no physical evidence being found. In 1977, a Kaiapoi resident named Frances Clark claimed to have had an encounter with a "tiger". Later, large paw prints and faecal matter were found at Pines Beach, corroborating the report. Around 1996, a woman mountain biking near Twizel reported seeing a large black cat the size of a Labrador dog. Two years later, near Cromwell, an animal resembling a mountain lion was sighted, and residents of Mataura described what they believed to be a bobcat. In 1999, reports of a big black cat surfaced in Mackenzie Country. Following this, alleged sightings of the Moeraki Mountain lion,

Lindis lion, and Ashford black cat were recorded. In 2006, hunting and fishing guide, Al Kircher happened upon what he believed to be a melanistic leopard during a four-day hunting trip.

In 2006, *Biosecurity New Zealand* conducted a search but experts again could not find any physical evidence of a big cat. In 2013, the *Ministry for Primary Industries* declared that there are no big cats in the region. When asked, Nathan Hawke, Spokesperson for *Orana Wildlife Park* in Christchurch mentioned that they have been contacted about wild big cats for many years and would be glad to finally get definitive proof of their existence. Hawke said: "We're not aware of any history of cats escaping New Zealand zoos and establishing a wild population [though] that doesn't mean it hasn't happened [...] Also, we're not aware of any species that have been held in New Zealand zoos that fit the description of this animal." The situation of big cats in New Zealand, much like that in the United Kingdom and Australia, can be partly explained by an unusually large domestic or feral cat. In 2020, I attempted (unsuccessfully) to procure a specimen that was shot by a possum hunter near the Ashley Forest, Canterbury said to have measured an impressive 1.05 meters in length when stretched out. The hunter claimed the animal weighed 11 kg with a 45 cm tail and a 14 mm long canine.

Additionally, he estimated another large black cat seen the previous weekend was approximately twice that size. Domestic adult cats typically weigh between three and six kilograms; however, some Maine Coon breeds may exceed eight kilograms for males as adults. But a breed weighing 11 kilograms? Sadly, once it became clear that the specimen did not fit the definition of a "panther," the possum hunter lost interest in further testing. As of 2023, no credible evidence has been presented to validate claims that large cats are present in New Zealand. It's possible that the creatures described as "big cats" seen on South Island were escaped pets. Feral cats are rampant throughout parts of New Zealand, and they are known to cause destruction to NZ's native birds and lizards. But can they weigh 11 kg, with a 45 cm tail and 14 mm canines? In March 2020, a large feral cat was found with 17 native skinks (and the parts of several others) in its stomach. A "shadow panther" was observed among trees on a New Zealander's property. It appeared to be solid black and did not seem to possess a three-dimensional form. Due to poor weather conditions, no vocalisations of the panther were heard.

Reports suggest that shadow panthers are stealthy and can vanish whenever they detect they have been noticed. They are believed to measure approximately three meters long, including the tail. No documented big cats exist in New Zealand, excluding any that may have been brought into the country illegally by possible owners. It has been surmised that shadow panthers probably eat birds as they are said to never sing in forests occupied by the creature. The shadow panther may belong in the realm of zoo form phenomena, although it could also be a real panther poorly described. There are also sporadic reports of big cats resembling cougars in the mountains of New Zealand's South Island. These could represent an introduced or escaped population of cougar.

POLAND

The Polish mountain lion, otherwise known as Polska Puma, refers to three mountain lions identified by authorities who likely caused attacks on farm animals in the Silesia region of Poland. As reported in 2009, there were five mountain lions reported to have escaped from illicit breeders in the Czech Republic. Three individuals made their way across the border into Poland where they proceeded to feed on livestock and carcasses along train tracks. It is likely, however, that the majority of their diet was comprised of small to medium-sized wildlife. Authorities kept quiet so as to prevent public alarm, instead simply recommending that people avoid going into the nearby wood-lands without offering any additional information. The authorities then opted to shoot the pumas, asserting that tranquillisers were somehow not a viable option in the given circumstances. Unfortu-nately, their decision to withhold information from the public meant that the extent of the events was not revealed for some time. However, once media outlets uncovered and reported on the full story, a clearer picture began to emerge.

RUSSIA

The Russian Panther, or the Russian Mystery Beast, has been largely forgotten in modern times. In 1893, a large carnivore was connected to numerous deaths and maulings of human beings. It was described to have a wolf-like stature, a yellowish colouration, a broad snout, rounded ears, and a long and sleek tail. A released or escaped lioness is a possibility, as it likely wouldn't be afraid of humans. A lynx was described by one observer, as was a tiger, suggesting that more than one species of felid was at large. Tigers are known to have wandered into towns in far eastern parts of the former Soviet Union and in 1987, two rare Amur tigers were shot dead in Vladivostok. Rumours that a melanistic leopard had escaped from a private collection added to the widespread public concern. The panther reportedly killed several people all the while avoiding hunters and their snares. Reports of sightings and attacks ceased by the end of the year corresponding with rumours that it had died somewhere near Vetebet River after eating two poisoned sheep. Some reports describing apparently different species might also suggest the presence of a female leopard, possibly melanistic, accompanied by a normally pigmented cub, which could have been mistaken for a lynx. Alternatively, it could be that more than one animal had escaped or been released from captivity; if so, these would likely have come from the same collection, which may have included African lions.

UNITED KINGDOM

For many years, fleeting glimpses of mysterious dark animals described as "big cats", and discoveries of large cat-like tracks have fuelled the theory that Great Britain is home to one or more species of large felid. They are also known as ABCs (Alien or Anomalous Big

Cats), BBCs (British Big Cats), Phantom Cats, and Mystery Cats, usually described as "panthers", "pumas", or simply "big black cats". Many cryptozoologists do not look upon these apparently out-of-place Felidae as cryptids. According to Heuvelmans' definition, ABCs don't qualify as cryptids because the popular consensus is that they are probably known species existing outside their natural habitats.

However, as with the true cryptid "cats", the existence of a British population remains unproven and their precise identities are unknown, as we are almost certainly dealing with multiple species. This is why I have no significant issues accommodating for ABCs in my own classification system and overall approach to cryptozoology. Many suggestions exist to explain how these animals might have come to inhabit Britain, including that they are animals released following the 1976 *Dangerous Wild Animals Act*, or that they are surviving Ice Age fauna. The latter hypothesis, while in vogue, is highly unlikely, mainly due to the fact that Britain is just too small, overpopulated, and thoroughly explored, and its flora and fauna were classified long ago. Thus, it is highly unlikely that any Ice Age felids remain in Britain undetected by the scientific community to the present day. Most likely, they are escapees or illegally released pets, or (less likely nowadays) escaped zoo animals or their descendants. While the prospect of Ice Age relics surviving undetected in Britain without leaving biological evidence of their existence is an intriguing and romantic notion, it is all but impossible to be true. The only potential exception would be the Eurasian lynx, but even this is highly unlikely.

To my knowledge, the earliest documented reference to the British Big Cat phenomenon is found in a mid-13th century Welsh poem called 'Pa Gwr', from the *Black Book of Carmarthen*. The poem speaks of a creature called 'Cath Palug', or "Palug's Cat", which reportedly roamed Anglesey until it was slain by Cei from Arthurian legend. Another early allusion can be found in the works of the 16th-century chronicler Ralph Holinshead, who asserted, "Lions we have had very many in the north parts of Scotland and those with manes of no less force than those of Mauretania; but how and when they were destroyed as yet I do not read." According to modern records, *Panthera spelaea,* otherwise known as the cave lion, lived in the southern part of Great Britain during the Pleistocene era before going extinct approximately 40,000 years ago.

The first recorded case of a big cat escaping into the British countryside took place in the early 16th century. John Giffard (b. 1534 – d. 1613) was a Staffordshire landowner and member of the English Parliament, notable as a leader of Roman Catholic Recusancy during the reigns of Elizabeth I and James I. In the garden of the lodge at the entrance gates to the oak avenue which leads to the house stands a cross. This is a replica of the original cross that stood on the spot that is now under the archway in the courtyard. The cross reputedly marks the spot where, during the reign of Henry VIII, Sir John Giffard (pronounced 'Jiffard') killed a black leopard dead with a bow and arrow as it was about to attack a woman and child. The leopard, actually part of Sir John's collection of rare animals, had broken out of its enclosure and made its way to nearby Brewood forest. According to the legend, Sir John and his son Thomas went in pursuit of the big cat. As he shot, Thomas whispered to his father "Take [a] breath, pull strong." From this incident, the first of the Gifford family's two crests were designed.

First recorded in the marginalia of an 18th century Bible, the New Forest folktale of the *Stratford Lyon* tells the strange story of how in the year 1400 John de Stratford baited a giant red antlered (tufted-eared?) "lion" from the ground at South Baddesley in the New Forest. During the late 20th century, reports of similar creatures were documented in the area near the Red Lion public house in Boldre. In 1810, the livestock-killing Girt Dog of Ennerdale was claimed by some to have been a lion-like animal, although a large aggressive dog was subsequently shot dead. In 1825, a spaniel-sized cat with lynx-like characteristics was seen in Surrey. Researcher David Walker unearthed another article in *The Times* from 1827 that recorded the sighting of a lynx. A century later a lynx was supposedly killed in

Inverness, Scotland. This has led some to speculate that a relict population of lynx exists in remote parts of Britain.

On March 19th, 1938, Mrs. Irene Roberts of Lightwater in Surrey, claimed in a letter published in *The Field* that she had frequently heard a strange animal calling "of peculiar intensity, expressing, it seems, mortal fear and physical pain" for ten minutes or so, and was "... punctuated by a queer half snorting, half purring sound, produced by something probably considerably larger than a [domestic] cat." She claimed "...they seemed to be something between a bark and a scream, and did not appear to be produced from anything of the shape of a beak. They seemed to begin with a B. "B'yow! 'B'yow!" long drawn out, and penetrating." Not unlike a puma then. In 1959, the phenomenon gained major media attention when sightings near the Surrey-Hampshire border were reported to both law enforcement and newspapers in a case that would come to be known as the "Surrey Puma".

In 1962, two more sightings were reported by personnel from the Hampshire water board. By the winter of 1962 – 63, a big cat-like animal was seen at Bushylease Farm near Crondall in Hampshire. The following year, a bullock was discovered at Bushylease with severe lacerations. At Godalming Police Station, 362 reports were documented over a two-year period, equating to an average of one sighting every other day. In addition, the station held a cast of a large paw print that was identified by London Zoo staff as that of a mountain lion; however, numerous reports highlighted that its size indicated it belonged to an animal much larger than a mountain lion and there were multiple discrepancies with the prints of mountain lions. The investigation remained open until the summer of 1967, when the following year, a former police photographer published a grainy photograph that he claimed to depict the Surrey Puma in Worplesdon.

Moreover, in 1968 a farmer claimed to have shot a puma but was unable to provide any tangible evidence. Subsequently, reports gradually lessened; however, pug marks discovered in the snow in 1970 caused another wave of reports. In 1984, hair samples taken at Peaslake in the Surrey Hills were identified as belonging to a mountain lion. In 1963, a report surfaced of a large tawny-coloured cat with a long tail that was seen beside a road. This sparked headlines regarding the search for the so-called Shooters Hill Cheetah. Subsequently, the animal was spotted fleeing into nearby woods. Despite attempts to locate it, no verifiable evidence of the animal's existence has ever been discovered. The *Dangerous Wild Animals Act was* passed into law in 1976, and for a while, some reports may have been observations of leopards or pumas released from captivity after their owners felt unable to meet the licensing requirements introduced by the new legislation.

In 1998 a large cat was blamed for the slaughter of sheep around Inverness. Sightings of such animals in Scotland grew during the first six years of the 21st century, including places from Ardersier in the north to Inverurie and Fraserburgh, sometimes as far south as the English border, but mostly occurring in rural areas of Aberdeenshire. From May 2000 through January 2002, twenty-two reports of sightings were made to Grampian Police. It was believed, however, that roughly 80% of sightings went unreported. On June 16th, 2001, Ralph Barnett was driving from Dundee to Cupar and when he rounded a sharp bend in the road, his headlights illuminated a dark-coloured cat in the road. After being startled by Barnett's car, the animal quickly ran away out of sight. As it did so, Barnett realised that it had been feeding on the carcass of a roe deer (*Capreolus capreolus*), the remains of which were still lying in the middle of the road. Barnett contacted the local police who promptly arrived at the scene. Unfortunately, they did not retain the carcass and simply dumped it by the roadside. Barnett was able to take several excellent photographs which showed signs of asphyxiation: bulging eyes, an open mouth with protruding tongue, clotted blood pooled on either side of its face, and ruptured eyeballs that were still relatively moist. There was also a series of lacerations on the side of the neck closely resembling the claw marks of a big cat.

The 2001 *Cupar Roe Deer Carcass* provides compelling evidence for the presence of big cats in Scotland at that time. In 1997, Scottish politician Alex Salmond raised issues in the House of Commons regarding livestock attacks attributed to a big cat. This matter was addressed again in 2002 when Ross Finnie, then Minister for Environment and Rural Development, was questioned by Richard Lochhead, an SNP MP representing north-east Scotland, about starting a formal inquiry into the reports. Additionally, there were wounds on the side of the neck that strongly resembled claw marks. In 2006 a Cruden Bay farmer found the carcass of one of his sheep spread across a field; he said he was certain it had not been attacked by a dog and stated that workers had recently seen a "huge, slinky cat skulking around". Big cats are silent, stealthy, and clinical, typically killing with a bite to the prey's neck or if the prey is large, they will bite the nose suffocating the animal that way. They are clean and efficient unlike the messy attack described above, which sounds more like a dog worrying incident. In 2007 a black animal bearing similarities to a cat but measuring around three feet in length crossed a Cruden Bay road in front of a couple. A *Big Cats in Britain* member suggested it was a leopard. In October 2008, a leopard-like animal was seen by a woman in the same area.

The Formartine and Buchan Way follows the 53-mile (85 km) route of the former railway lines in Buchan converted into a pathway and cycling lane in the early 1990s. This area is attractive to wildlife, where in August 2011, a resident of Old Deer reported how they had seen a big cat on two separate occasions. The animal was described as being timid but not scared, larger than the witness's Labrador dog, and jet black in colour with a bushy head and tail. According to a *Scotland on Sunday* newspaper reporter writing in 2006, accounts of the animal varied from greyhound sized up to that of an Alsatian dog. Attacks on humans have allegedly occurred. In 2002, a woman was leaving a stable near Insch when the animal bit and clawed her leg before being chased away. She sustained bruising and painful puncture marks on her upper thigh. Her friend who witnessed the attack described a cat-like, Labrador-sized "sleek black beastie". The legendary *Cat Sith* may have been inspired by early observations of Kellas cats – a hybrid of domestic and wildcat – of which specimens of both have been found in Buchan. The *Zoology Museum* at the *University of Aberdeen* holds a taxidermy specimen of a Kellas cat.

In April 2002, the headless carcass of a cat was discovered on a Boddam roadside by a local farmer who described it as the size of a medium dog or fox, some three feet (0.91 m) in length. A member of the *Scottish Big Cat Society* felt it was too large to be a Kellas, whereas an expert from the University Zoology Department considered it likely to be a large domestic cat or a hybrid. A Kellas cat would unlikely be large enough to kill fully grown sheep and the farmer considered it doubtful that the animal whose carcass he found would be able to either. In 2002, a woman who was familiar with Kellas cats was attacked near Insch and she was certain that the animal that attacked her was not a Kellas.

In 2009, PC Chris Swallows, an off-duty *Ministry of Defence* police dog handler, captured a video after witnessing a "panther-sized big cat" walking along a railway line in Helensburgh, Argyll. This video (the full version can be found on YouTube) shows what is almost certainly a large domestic cat filmed from a convenient camera angle, giving the impression that the tracks it is walking along were closer together and making the subject seem larger than it actually was. When the view of the observer is slightly raised, however, the tracks look much farther apart. This can be clearly seen towards the end of the complete video (https://www.youtube.com/watch?v=vQYrszfSbUE) when the tracks better align with the viewpoint of the camera. At this point in the video (0:48) the cat suddenly looks very small walking along the right-side line, in fact, about the size of a large domestic cat!

PC Swallows told the *BBC* he was helping a friend with their garden when he spotted the black animal on a nearby railway line. The officer, who was stationed at the Faslane naval base on the Clyde, claimed the cat was as big as a Labrador dog. Big cats had been reported in the area in the past, with several sightings of the so-called *Coulport Cougar*. I have examined the footage and presume it is a visual illusion caused by the positioning of the camera in relation to the tracks. Nevertheless, there have been previous reports of both black and tan big cats in this area. I plan to visit this location in the near future to attempt to recreate the video; establishing a sound hypothesis through precise measurements of various felids taken using various camera angles. The falsification principle is whether a dome-shaped camera lens has any bearing on creating the same effect.

More sightings were reported in August 2018 of what was claimed to be a large black cat seen stalking around *Bonnyrigg* in *Midlothian*. There clearly have been (and probably still are) large exotic felids, probably pumas and leopards, living wild in some of the more remote parts of Scotland, particularly in the highlands. The evidence for big cats is relatively good and I expect there will be further cases verified and documented in future. It has been alleged that sightings of ABCs in Scotland may be the descendants of felids owned by USAAF personnel as mascots when based in Scotland during WWII that were supposedly liberated when the pilots did not return. Yet it seems contemporary researchers have been unable to find any records of mascots on American Air Force bases being large felids.

By 1983, an *alien big cat* featured in the popular BBC radio drama *The Archers*, and the *Beast of Exmoor* entered the news, somewhat eclipsing the saga of the Surrey Puma, although reports of the latter continued. Sightings of the *Exmoor Beast* were first reported in the 1970s, although the animal or animals became notorious in 1983 when a South Molton farmer named Eric Ley claimed to have lost over a hundred sheep in the space of just three months, all of them apparently killed by violent throat injuries. The animal was observed "fishing" with its paw in the River Barle at Simonsbath, whilst locals suggested its lair might be in one of the disused mines on the moor.

Deaths of farm animals in the area have been occasionally blamed on the *Beast of Exmoor* ever since. It has been suggested that it may be a mountain lion or melanistic leopard which had been released from a private collection sometime during the 1960s or 70s. Writing in 1992 in *The Folklore Society* journal *Folklore,* the folklorist Michael Goss suggested that while some reports are probably authentic, the majority are a type of contemporary legend. Despite the *Department for Environment, Food and Rural Affairs* (DEFRA) stating that "Based on the evidence, DEFRA does not believe that there are big cats living in the wild in England", the *British Big Cat Society* reported that a skull discovered by a Devon farmer in 2006 was that of a cougar. In 1988, in response to a rise in livestock deaths and farmer grievances resulting from their losses of earnings, the *Ministry of Agriculture* initiated a comprehensive search for the Beast of Exmoor by deploying Royal Marine sharp-shooters onto the moor. A few marines reported briefly seeing a large cat, yet according to the official report, nothing besides a fox was found. DEFRA has published a list of predatory cats that they know to have escaped in the UK, although most of these were recaptured. That same year a jungle cat was found dead on a roadside in Shropshire that had been struck by a motor vehicle. Lynxes and pumas have also been reported from Exmoor. Some investigators maintain that the Exmoor big cats are a mutant race of enormous house cats. Other eyewitnesses claim to have had face-to-face encounters with a black leopard. In the summer of 2021, while working on a pilot episode about ABCs, Jay Opit and I had the chance to interview farmer Eric Ley. Through this conversation, we discovered the probable identities of the Exmoor Beasts. A puma and a black leopard that were kept in a butcher's shop in Barnstaple as security had frequently been seen roaming the moors prior to their disappearance shortly before the reports began. In 1995, the British government conducted an official investigation into the Beast of Bodmin Moor concluding there was no definitive evidence of big cats living in the area; however, it could not be completely ruled out either.

Since the saga of the *Surrey Puma* more than sixty years ago, there has been a major increase in reported sightings. Current estimates suggest that there are between 1000 and 3000 reported sightings across the country each year, as well as many more reports shared on social media but largely forgotten. As we have seen, thousands of people report seeing big cats every year, and from all regions, from the West Country to the East of England, and from the Scottish Highlands to Southampton. A 2006 survey declared there were six thousand sightings of exotic cats since the turn of the century, so roughly a thousand a year, while an article in *The Guardian* speculated that there could be up to seven thousand sightings annually. Regional legends, whether they stem from genuine observations of big cats, mistaken observations of known species, or simply modern folklore and hoaxes, can travel farther than the animals themselves, thus encouraging honest mistakes and potential hoaxes that make it difficult to determine how many of these animals are potentially inhabiting Britain. So far, we are basically limited to testimonial and circumstantial evidence, (e.g., Mr. or Mrs. so and so, observed a female panther with two smaller cubs while walking the dogs the other week – that sort of thing.), which unfortunately, no matter how credible the observer might be, cannot be used as definitive proof of these animals living in a wild state in Britain, let alone accurately predicting important ecological data such as potential breeding and birthing sites.

The famous Fen tiger was first reported In 1982 in Inham, Cambridgeshire, but it wasn't until 1994 when William Rooker managed to capture on film what appears to be a big cat in a field near the Oakington Road in Cottenham, that interest peaked. A year later two police traffic officers claimed they saw a very large black cat in the area of Westwick Hall, a few miles from the location of the Rooker video. The so-called Fen tiger, which if it *was* a big cat is certainly not a tiger, has been recorded on and off since the mid-1990s, during which time sightings began being reported from other areas of East Anglia, perhaps indicating it has a large territory or that there is more than animal at work. In May 2004 the *Cambridge Evening News* printed a story featuring Vernon Whiterod, a Cambridge University janitor, who claimed he had observed a cat similar to an ocelot in between Histon and Waterbeach.

In 2000, Josh Hopkins, an eleven-year-old boy in Monmouthshire, was allegedly attacked by a big black cat, leaving five long scratches on his left cheek. To investigate the incident, police called upon a big cat specialist named Quentin Rose. Five years later in 2005, a man living in Sydenham Park of South East London was attacked by an animal he described as a "big black cat" that knocked him to the ground leaving scratches all over his body. Police were alerted and one officer observed a black cat approximately the size of a Labrador dog nearby. In 2007, an animal described as a panther was spotted in Derbyshire walking along a three-foot-high dry-stone wall. Upon calculating the size of the stones, it was estimated that it had a height of at least 18 inches and a length of three feet not including the tail. It was believed to be a young black leopard, while experts stated that it was too big to be a domestic cat but could potentially be a hybrid.

A large cat dubbed the *Beast of Burnham Thorpe* in Norfolk was spotted near the Queen's Sandringham home in 2009. Experts suggested it was a Scottish wildcat or a lynx, while others claimed it looked more like a large domestic tabby. In December 2009, video footage emerged of what was claimed to be a big black cat prowling fields in rural Herefordshire. Steve Hall contacted the *Hereford Times* when he managed to capture video footage of what he believed was a large black cat resembling a panther crossing farmland near Newtown Crossroads. The observation and video of the alleged animal coincided with a spree of sheep killings in the same area. Mr. Hall was out walking his dog when they spotted the creature... "It was just walking across the hedge and then it saw us and sat in the hedge a bit watching [...] I thought I saw one a few years ago but I wasn't too sure as it was dark, but this footage proves they are local. It was far too big to be a domestic cat." The following year a video claimed to be of a black leopard was recorded in neighbouring Gloucestershire.

Experts have estimated that the animal recorded in the footage was at least five feet in length from nose to tail. Gloucestershire has always been something of a hot spot for alleged big cat activity.

Species reported only occasionally include the leopard cat (*Prionail-urus bengalensis*), which is the size of a large domestic cat but has leopard-like spots; the clouded leopard (*Neofelis nebulosa*), a specialised species from the tropics which was captured after living wild in Kent in 1975, and there are even extraordinary cases of lions (*Panthera leo*) reported in both Devon and Somerset. There have been reports of a big cat known as *The Beast of Bevendean* for several years across Sussex, including Brighton and Hove. In the early months of 2011, a large number of sightings of a "panther" in Shotts, North Lanarkshire, stirred locals and began to be reported by the local media; after a couple of months, these reports suddenly stopped with the general assumption that the animal had moved onto new hunting grounds.

In 2011, Peter Jackson, a semi-retired businessman, informed the *Manchester Evening News* that on January 16th he was awakened by his dog barking and witnessed a "large black cat" in the back garden of his Longnor Road home. Police later issued a warning saying that anyone seeing it should not approach the animal. Jean Bruckshaw of Grendale Avenue, contacted the paper to say she had seen the same animal the day before Mr. Jackson's encounter, corroborating his sighting. Mrs. Bruckshaw said, "At the time I was washing the dishes and looked out of the back window and saw a large black cat prowling in a neighbour's garden [...] It had a big tail similar to a fox but not a bushy one, and I can say I have never seen such a huge cat before." She also stated that she believed the animal lived in an embankment behind her residence.

That summer, a "lion" was seen wandering around Essex. Residents and holidaymakers had reported seeing the mysterious beast in a field and had captured grainy video footage of what they claimed was the big cat on their mobile phones. Police advised residents to stay indoors, and a search was made of the local area, but unsurprisingly nothing was found. Local zoos and visiting circuses were contacted, but none reported an escaped lion. A resident named Murphy later claimed the photograph was that of her pet Maine Coon. In 2013, two sisters witnessed a large black cat with a three-foot stride leap over a fence and enter an adjacent field. Upon returning to the site later that day, they discovered a den and paw prints too large for a typical house cat. Tom Larkham, a former zookeeper at Chester Zoo and Dudley Zoo, opined that the paw prints in question were too small to belong to a panther, yet too big for an ordinary domestic cat. He concluded that it may have been a descendant of the Shropshire jungle cat from the 1980s or an exceptionally large domestic cat.

A brief list of notable British examples:

The Beast of Bucks

In 1983, Bob O'Neill, of Greenwood Avenue in Chinnor, claimed to have encountered a big cat while walking along a footpath with his granddaughter near Chinnor cement works. Mr. O'Neill attempted to scare it away from his granddaughter, but the animal wasn't intimidated. Instead, it flattened its ears back, dropped down into a low position, and continued advancing in their direction. Sensing the impending danger as the cat tensed up ready to attack, O'Neill struck it twice on the nose with his walking stick before it ran away. In 2001, a "puma" attacked a dog in High Wycombe. Experts confirmed prints found at *Wycombe Heights Golf Centre* were probably those of a puma. Since then, locals have reported several sightings of a big black cat in the area, leading it to be nicknamed the "Beast of Bucks". Allegedly, in 2015, a black leopard was seen by a witness in an oncoming car, as it crossed the road adjacent to the golf course at Ashridge. Black leopards have been seen in this part of Buckinghamshire before, including a witness on horseback claiming to see a large black cat kill a dog in 2005.

The Beast of Cumbria

A panther has been reported from the English Lake District, specifically Thirlmere. Numerous sightings have been reported, as well as other non-native big cats.

The Bedfordshire Big Cat

Residents of Silsoe, Bedfordshire have reported sightings of a big black cat larger than a Labrador. According to reports by a dog walker, the animal was observed prowling around a barley field in the nearby area. In 2016, Silsoe Parish Council posted a warning on its Facebook page, describing a cat-like animal, "black and larger than a Labrador" that was apparently "moving from one of the barley fields behind West End Lane towards Thrift Woods, in the Wardhedges direction".

The Bury Beast

In 2018, reports surfaced of a large black animal resembling a panther in the suburbs of Manchester. Leonora Fleming, who regularly rode horseback along the Roch Valley Greenway, stated that she observed the big cat in Pilsworth during October. This was the second such sighting reported in that area; previously, a man claimed he saw a puma near his house in Radcliffe back in July of that year.

The Creature of Cornwall

Duncan, a truck driver, claimed that an African lion appeared in front of his waggon in July near Nanpean and Whitemoor in St Austell. He initially thought it was an unknown species of big cat but later concluded it was likely a puma. Police found very large paw prints at the side of the road and a decapitated deer was discovered close by.

The Dartmoor Devil

The Dartmoor Devil is a leopard-like animal believed responsible for attacks on cattle. In 2017 stunned walkers discovered a mysterious, muscular, cat-like animal on a moorland track. Falconer Martin Whitley, who photographed the animal, said, "It was black and grey and comparable in size to a miniature pony", and that "It had very thick shoulders, a long, thick tail with a blunt end and small round ears", and "Its movements appeared feline, then bearlike". Mr. Whitley was surprised to find a climbing party approaching, but it ignored them. Veteran British Big Cat researcher Mark Fraser said the animal is baffling, adding, "It looks like a wolverine or a bear in some shots and a big wild dog in others. It is a very strange animal." Mr. Whitley also remarked: "I have worked with dogs all my life and it was definitely not that. I have seen a collie-sized black cat in the area about 10 years ago and this was a lot bigger."

The Dartmoor Lynx

In 2016, a Carpathian lynx named Flaviu escaped from Dartmoor Zoo in Devon and was on the loose for over three weeks. Several sightings were reported on the moors, prompting police warnings that it could be dangerous if cornered. Fortunately, Flaviu was recaptured after walking into a humane trap and returned safely to the zoo.

The Hull Hell Cat

A large puma-like animal was observed near Hull. A photo taken in September 2016 by Lee Clifford, of North Cave in Yorkshire, claimed to show a "mystery puma [...] spotted hiding in a field near Hull" is clearly a Photoshopped forgery.

The Pershore Panther

A big black, cat-like animal was observed beside a road in Worcestershire. Robert Ingram and his wife Nicola were astonished to see a "big cat" beside a road in Pershore at 1 am on March 29th, 2016. As they drove along the countryside roads near Pershore in the company of a friend, the four-foot animal suddenly emerged from the shrubbery, causing them to swerve sharply to avoid hitting it with their vehicle.

The Suffolk Panther

Thought to be a big black cat sighted on the Norfolk/Suffolk border. The latest sightings were in Bruisyard village in 2022, where a witness saw... "a huge pure black 'cat' bigger than a Rottweiler" which crossed in front of her car close to the village's bridge. She added: "I swear it was a panther!" In 2016, student Eliot Evans reported a similar sighting in the area when he came face-to-face with a big cat-like creature while out for an evening run near his home in Wickham Market, around eight miles away. The *Eastern Daily Press* traced big cat sightings in the area back to 1965 when four men spotted a big black cat while shooting near Larling, and in both 1993 and 1994, there was also a cluster of puma sightings.

The Warwickshire Wildcat

The video recorded by Philip White, in Great Alne, near Alcester, almost certainly shows a local (then fourteen-month-old) Bengal cat named Hiro. The Bengal cat is a domesticated cat breed created from hybrids of domestic cats – usually the spotted Egyptian Mau, with the Asian leopard cat (*Prionailurus bengalensis*). My own investigation at the Great Alne site conducted only a few days after the footage was made available revealed that the plants seen looming over the cat as it walks by were common stinging nettles. Measuring the tallest stems nearest to the cat, I determined they were only 55.88 cm tall. It is thus clear that the cat in the footage is no more than 25 cm tall to its shoulders – well within the range of domestic cats. My findings were subsequently corroborated when *The Observer* newspaper identified the cat's owner a few days later. This report, like so many others in Britain, is still publicised as a genuine video of a typical spotted leopard, whereas, in truth, it was nothing of the sort.

The Wildcat of Wakefield

Raven Horsechief, of Freestone Drive, reported observing a panther multiple times from late February to early March 2015 on farmland near Kirkthorpe in Yorkshire. She said "My friend was visiting, and she was shocked when she saw it. She said it was a big cat. It was the size of a Labrador or an Alsatian. I have seen it a few times at night in the field opposite my house. It is definitely bigger than just a normal cat." There have been other unexplained sightings of big cats which date back to the turn of the millennium when the "Beast of Ossett" was first reported. Three years later, a large panther-like animal was seen stalking the village of Wintersett.

UNITED STATES OF AMERICA

Nellie was a mysterious animal, described as an African lioness, that allegedly appeared in the state of Illinois in 1917. On July 13th, reports of a lion began to surface near the city of Decatur. Thomas Gullet, who was collecting flowers in the gardens of Robert Allerton Park and Estate southwest of Monticello, encountered the animal and was reportedly attacked. Gullett was fortunate to sustain only minor injuries, yet the report of the incident resulted in a search party of three hundred strong on July 15th that lasted for two weeks before being abandoned. It seems Nellie had already left the area, as while the hunters were out searching for her in vain, she was observed a quarter of a mile away by Mrs. Shaw who described the animal as an "African lioness".

On July 17th, tracks measuring thirteen centimetres with visible claw marks were found in the vicinity of Decatur, suggesting they may have been laid by a canine. Later that same day, two boys claimed to have seen a lion near the Sangamon River. On the evening of July 29th, around 10:30 pm, Earl Hill and Chester Osborn, accompanied by their respective wives, were taken aback when an animal resembling a lion attacked their car while they were parked on Springfield Road. The two men in the front seats reported that they witnessed a big cat in the tall grass along the roadside. They stated that the animal jumped approximately twenty feet and slammed against the side of their vehicle, before falling to the ground. The alarmed couples hastily proceeded to Decatur and reported the incident to the police. They returned later and Nellie, who had been knocked unconscious from the impact, was now back on her feet. She was later seen disappearing over an embankment into the night. On July 31st a truck driver named James Rutherford observed a "large, yellow, long-haired beast" as he drove past a gravel pit. He watched the animal head towards a creek only to disappear from view. Search parties were organised which found a few ambiguous tracks, but no conclusive sign of a lion. Soon after, the Nellie sightings stopped. We will probably never know for certain what Nellie was. My best guess is that she was probably a large mountain lion that has escaped or been released from captivity, but it has also been suggested that she may have been an African lioness (*Panthera leo*) or even a living specimen of *P. atrox*, the officially extinct American lion. Nellie the lion clearly demonstrates that cryptozoology and ABC research are not mutually exclusive.

Reports of alleged mountain lion sightings in northern Delaware forests have been circulating since the late 1990s. The Delaware *Division of Fish and Wildlife* has determined that there could be more than one mountain lion living in the wild in Delaware, likely stemming from animals that were released from captivity. In 2010, a Pike Creek man had a fright when he and his dog encountered a mountain lion on a late-night walk. There had been no confirmed sightings of mountain lions in Delaware for many years until reports started again in 2021. In December of 2021, Pamela Eppinger and Jim Coldiron observed what they believe was a mountain lion while driving through the Brandywine Valley, on their way to a Tractor Supply store at around 1:30 pm. "We were driving down through Brandywine along the river, coming around a curve, and I look into the woods and I see a cat about the size of a golden retriever, a little larger [...] It looked like it was prowling for food." They described seeing a big fawn-coloured cat with a black tip on its tail, Jim Coldiron said, "I'm an outdoorsman. I take people hunting. I know what I saw [...] It didn't care about traffic." Mr. Coldiron said he thought he heard a mountain lion scream a few months before while walking into his Pennsylvania home but didn't see anything.

MassWildlife, charged with the preservation of freshwater fish and wildlife in the Commonwealth, including endangered plants and animals, affirmed two instances of a mountain lion in Massachusetts. There have been numerous other records, as well as alleged photographs, but these remain unverified by state wildlife officials. Black leopards and other large non-indigenous felids have allegedly been observed for many years in the vicinity of Oriental, North Carolina where reports of big cats from locals and visitors have been documented by the local media. The "Dayton Phantom Panther" was a series of sightings of big black cats reported in the area around Dayton, Ohio, during the early 2010s, yet sightings of big cats of several types have been reported from the Ohio area since at least the 1900s.

Contemporary reports describing a big black cat first occurred in April 2011, and by July animal control officials released a statement confirming that three unverified sightings of "panthers" had been reported to them. Things would take a tragic turn on October 18th, 2011 when Terry Thompson, a Zanesville ranch owner, released fifty exotic animals into the wild before taking his own life via a self-inflicted gunshot wound. He appears to have "baited" himself by spreading chicken pieces nearby as he was then bitten by one of the animals he freed, probably a Bengal tiger, shortly before dying from blood loss. The situation would be contained during the following few days, but tragically 48 exotic animals, many of them large predators, were confirmed to have been killed by police. Two were suspected to have been eaten by the other animals, and the rest, three of which were leopards, were recaptured and sent to *Columbus Zoo*. Throughout the rest of October, the Clark County Sheriff's Department publicly announced they were investigating reports of a "black panther" in the area, asserting that the sightings actually predated the Thompson incident. Sightings would continue to be reported until at least April 28th, 2012, when a black leopard was allegedly observed multiple times during the intervening fourteen-fifteen months. As is often the case, most sightings were discredited as either misidentifications or cases of mass hysteria.

CENTRAL AMERICA

According to the informative website messybeast.com, in 1972, El Salvadorian men were alleged to be entering Honduras to hunt Bengal tigers which were rumoured to have descended from tigers that had escaped from a circus decades before. If Bengal tigers were once present in the dense jungles of Honduras, it is highly unlikely that any remnants of the population exist today, especially due to their reported use as game animals by the Salvadorans. That is, however, not to say there are no tigers in the region today. Being a transit point, Honduras has a serious problem with drug trafficking, and with a number of gangs, crime is rampant and criminals operate with a high degree of impunity. Crime and corruption reached the highest levels of government when it was reported in July 2022, that for years, the Honduran government had been aiding and abetting drug traffickers. And for a time, both the corrupt government officials and the criminals enjoyed significant financial gain from the situation, enabling drug lords to display their wealth and power by possessing extravagant items, such as big cats.

The controversial *Joya Grande Zoo* in Santa Cruz de Yojoa was born of this opulence, but from the outset, this zoo was not geared toward ordinary visitors. Its founder, Devis Leonel Rivera Maradiaga, a notorious drug lord and leader of the Cachiros cartel, used to arrive in a helicopter before his confession to seventy-eight homicides and subsequent decision to cooperate with authorities. Today, both Rivera and the former Honduran President Juan Orlando Hernández, the man he assisted in dethroning, are currently being held by U.S. authorities; meanwhile, the animals in the zoo (at least those present at the time of the takeover) are now owned by the Honduran state. Joya Grande, Spanish for "Big Jewel", once held an astonishing collection of animals: thirty jaguars, nineteen tigers, eighteen lions, five hippopotamuses, one giraffe, plus zebras, camels, and more.

While not explicitly designed for the general public, Rivera and his brother nonetheless made their zoo available to them, at least nominally. It made it easier, apparently, to convince foreign countries to sell their exotic animals to drug traffickers. But visiting this zoo isn't exactly an educational experience. There are no tour guides, nor signs detailing the animal's origins, ages, or natural environments. Most of the animals haven't left their cages in years, since the government took over in 2013. Like the rest of Honduras, they are captive to the whims of millionaire drug lords long imprisoned, and a weak government that can't afford to maintain them. Under the government's stewardship, a third of the employees were let go. An electric fence that allowed the big cats to roam the fields fell into disrepair, as did a paintball course. The hippopotamuses stopped breeding due to the limited space in their enclosure, and any of the zoo's animals that could escape did so. It is conceivable, that big cats have escaped from this "narco" run zoo in the past, which may have been selling big cats to gangs and drug lords for years, of which the tiger, being one of the most widely recognised symbols of cunning, strength, and ferocity would make a valuable and prodigious commodity, inspiring the required fear and awe necessary to run a dangerous drug trafficking operation.

———————

5

WHEN FOLKLORE AND FABLE MEET TERATOLOGICAL REALITY?

'Animals like crows, owls, or black cats are not ominous at all; it is the men's superstitious mind which is the inauspicious one.'

— MEHMET MURAT ILDAN

For hundreds of thousands of years, humans – typically hunters and farmers – have coexisted with animals, leading to the emergence of numerous myths and legends involving them. Animals ranging from formidable tigers to tiny spiders have established their place in mythology. The fact that tigers are venerated across multiple cultures illustrates their widespread significance to human society. Animals may serve as stand-ins for humans or human characteristics, as in the African and Native American trickster tales or the fables of the Greek storyteller *Aesop*. In some legends, animals perform heroic deeds or act as mediators or arbitrators for gods and humans. Folkloric animals have always been a popular subject in art and literature, perhaps because they are often unlike any other creatures seen in the real world. Sometimes they are exaggerated versions of known animals, such as the giant "Yule Cat" of Icelandic folklore, but exist only as a kind of cultural warning. Occasionally, however, folklore and fable can have roots in biology, such as unusual domestic breeds, teratological abnormalities, and even stories based on sick or injured animals.

The False Sumxu

The Chinese lop-eared cat, also known as the drop-eared cat, droop-eared cat, hanging-ear cat, and (erroneously) *sumxu*, is a long-haired breed of cat whose existence is now only known through stories. If it was real, it is now probably extinct. Chinese lop-eared cats were kept as pets but were also seen as a delicacy to be eaten with rice. This is not overly surprising when considering that some Chinese people eat dogs, in addition to braised camel hump, monkey brains, and the abhorrently popular shark fin soup. Descriptions of the alleged breed are based mainly on travellers' tales. The Italian Jesuit Martino Martini (b. 1614 – d. 1661) visited China in the 1650s and published the first western atlas of the country, his *Novus Atlas Sinensis* in 1655. In the Peking section, Martini describes a variety of white, long-furred, long-eared, and highly prized cats found in the region. Martini's description of white droop-eared cats was reused in 1673, by John Ogilby and subsequently copied by later authors. Martini's work was supplanted in 1736 by that of French Jesuit Jean-Baptiste du Halde's detailed works on the Chinese Empire, including a description of the white droop-eared cat of Peking Province from Martini's work, and for many years this remained the authoritative reference book on the subject.

Another Jesuit, this time a Polish missionary named Michael Boym (b. 1612 – d. 1659) was the first Westerner to document the "sumxu" in his 1656 book *Flora Sinensis*. "*Sum xu*" is the Portuguese rendering of the name *song-shu*, meaning "pine rat", which probably refers to the yellow-throated marten (*Martes flavigula*). The white lop-eared cat is thought to be distinct and was found only in the far north of the country. Later authors, copying and translating from earlier sources, combined the two unfamiliar creatures which may have also had some similar habits. An illustration from Athanasius Kircher's 1666 book *China Monumentis, Qua Sacris qua Profanis* ("China's Monuments, Which Are Sacred and Which Are Profane") describes the *sumxu* as a cat-like creature, yet the accompanying engraving more closely resembles a small bear with a bushy tail, somewhat like a wolverine. The word has become *songshu* in modern Hanyu Pinyin and *sum xu* in Latin.

Kircher's description, if not a complete invention, may have been based on earlier writers who referred to the animal as the "droop-eared cat". In Vol. 4 of his *Histoire Naturelle,* (c. 1767) (translated into English in 1781 by the brilliant, if unfortunately named William Smellie), the French naturalist, mathematician, cosmologist, and encyclopedist, Georges Louis Leclerc, Comte de Buffon (b. 1707 – d. 1788) describes the pendulous-eared cats of China's Pe-chili Province, but he was uncertain whether the black or yellow *sumxu* was a felid or some other domesticated animal used to control rats, a small dog perhaps.

"Our domestic cats, though they differ in colour, form no distinct races. The climates of Spain and Syria have alone produced permanent varieties: To these may be added the climate of Pe-chi-ly in China, where the cats have long hair and pendulous ears, and are the favourites of the ladies. These domestic cats with pendulous ears, of which we have full descriptions, are still farther removed from the wild and primitive race, than those whose ears are erect... I formerly remarked, that, in China, there were cats with pendulous ears. This variety is not found anywhere else, and perhaps it is an animal of a different species; for travellers, when mentioning an animal called Sumxu, which is entirely domestic, say, that they can compare it to nothing but the cat, with which it has a great resemblance. Its colour is black or yellow, and its hair is very bright and glittering. The Chinese put silver collars about the necks of these animals and render them extremely familiar. As they are not common, they give a high price, both on account of their beauty, and because they destroy rats."

Their fur was said to be soft, with the most common colour being pale yellow; however, some had the standard colouring of a typical tabby cat. The Chinese cat was larger than the average house cat and said to be considerably stronger. Its ears hang down and are bigger than those of regular cats; similar to those of lop-eared rabbits. Although this breed was said to be abundant in its native region, it rarely made its way to European animal markets, thus very little is known about it in the West. Cats with drooping or folded ears have been around for many years, such as the Scottish Fold, which may have actually descended from the original Chinese lop-eared cat. Apparently, in 1796, an English sailor brought a specimen back from China, where the genetic mutation seems to have first been discovered.

By 1777, Buffon concluded that the lop-eared cat was a distinct species and that it might therefore be the cat-like marten known as *sumxu*. Hence the name "*sumxu*" (the yellow-throated marten found in South China) became erroneously attached to an alleged breed of domestic cat found in the northern region. Buffon reached this conclusion because du Halde had failed to mention in his translation that the lop-eared cats were white. Boym's illustration of the *sumxu* didn't draw attention to its ears, whereas Martini described long pendulous ears as the defining characteristic of the white cats of Pe-chili. In *The Cat, by Lady Cust* (1870) there is this brief description: "Bosman relates that in the province of Pe-chili, in China, there are cats with long hair and drooping ears, which are in great favour with the Chinese ladies; others say this is not a cat, but an animal called 'Samxces'." This early booklet on cat care by Mary Anne Boode Cust was much referenced by Victorian and Edwardian cat enthusiasts. The writer and artist Gaston Percheron suggested in 1885, that the lop-eared cat might be hybrids between domestic cats and martens, even though interfamilial hybrids such as this would be impossible.

In 1926, Lillian Jane Gould (b. 1861 – d. 1936) wrote in the magazine *Cat Gossip* that the Siamese cat (described in early breed standards as "sable and dun" coloured) was linked to the marten (described as "sable and yellow" coloured). Percheron's description transformed the 'lop-eared cat' from a pampered pussycat fed on delicacies to an animal that was itself a delicacy, and this, along with the incorrect usage of the name *sumxu*, was continued by later authors further confusing the matter. The German animal artist, author, and book illustrator, Jean Bungartz (b. 1854 – d. 1934) also described the Chinese lop-eared cat as livestock in his *Die Hauskatze, ihre Rassen und Varietäten* ("Housecats, Their Races and Varieties") from *Illustriertes Katzenbuch* ("An Illustrated Book of Cats") in Berlin in 1896:

"The Chinese or Lop-Eared cat is most interesting because it provides proof that by continual disuse of an organ, the organ withers. With the Chinese cat, the hearing and ears have deteriorated. Michel says the Chinese, not only admire the cat in porcelain but also value it for culinary reasons. The cats are regarded as special morsels and are enjoyed particularly with noodles or rice. This cat is bred particularly for the purpose of meat production and is a preferred Chinese morsel; this is not unusual if one considers that the Chinese consume much the sight of which revolts the stomachs of Europeans. The poor creature is confined in small bamboo cages and fattened like a goose on plentiful portions. There is extensive trade with other parts of Asia and the canny Chinese allow no tomcats to be exported so there is no interference in this lucrative source of income.

"Due to the restrictive conditions that have deprived the cat of its actual use, its hearing has decreased because it is no longer needed for hunting its own food. With no need for watchfulness, it had no need of sharp hearing to listen for hidden things, so its hearing became blunted and as a natural consequence its ears lost their upright nature, gradually becoming lower and becoming the hanging ear that is now the characteristic feature of the Chinese cat. At first impression, this is a surprising and amusing look, but this impression is lost with closer examination. If one ignores the characteristic of the ears, one sees a beauty like the Angora cat: a long, close coat of hair, albeit less rich, covers the body. The hair is silky-soft and shining and the colour is usually isabelline or a dirty white-yellow, although some have the usual colouring of the common housecat. In size, it is considerably larger and stronger than a house cat. The ears hang completely, as with our hunting dogs, and are large in relation to the cat. Although the Chinese cat is found in considerable numbers in its homeland, it is rarely found in European animal markets. Only one such cat has reached us in the flesh; we acquired this years ago when a sailor returning from China brought it into Hamburg. The accompanying illustration is based on this cat. In character, it is like the Angora cat and somewhat languid. It prefers to live by a warm fire, is rather sensitive to flattery, hears badly, and is at its most animated when given milk or food. Apart from its unusual ears, it has no attractive characteristics and is a curious specimen of a house cat."

In Frances Simpson's 1903 classic 'The Book of the Cat', contributing author H.C. Brooke (b. 1867 – d. 1930), wrote: "There is said to be a variety of Chinese cat which is remarkable for its pendent ears. We have never been able to ascertain anything definite with regard to this variety. Some years back a class was provided for them at a certain Continental cat show, and we went across in the hope of seeing, and if possible, acquiring some specimens; but alas the class was empty! We have seen a stuffed specimen in a Continental Museum, which was a half-long-haired cat, the ears being pendent down the sides of the head instead of erect; but do not attach much value to this."

Elsewhere, Brooke said that the taxidermy specimen, which he saw in 1882, was "half-coated with yellowish fur", and that it might have been a fake or a cat with its ears deformed by otodectic mange, also known as ear canker – a condition where mites consume the wax and oils by piercing the skin in the ear. As a result, scar tissue may form, contributing to a swollen and deformed look.

In 1926, Brooke wrote in Cat Gossip that for many years continental cat shows had offered substantial prizes for the drop-eared Chinese cat. However, on each occasion, the cat failed to be presented. Other writers suggested that the folded or crumpled ears were the result of damage or haematomas. Brooke wrote that although no one ever saw the cat itself, one always met "someone who knows someone whose friend has seen one." Brooke and several other cat enthusiasts contacted the Chinese Embassy in the UK, and Carl Hagenbeck's animal exchange in Hamburg but his inquiries failed to reveal any further details. The search for this strange cat became so heated during the 1920s that the *American Express Company* instructed their representatives in Shanghai and Beijing to make inquiries with the wild animal dealers who supplied zoos. Sadly, they also had no success finding a specimen of the lop-eared cat. With all avenues of inquiry failing, Brooke went on to declare the Chinese lop-eared cat extinct. The last reported sighting of the Chinese lop-eared cat occurred in 1938 when a specimen was allegedly imported from China.

Winged Cats

My first exposure to the "winged cats" was as a child, during the early 1990s reading the Rupert Bear annuals. In the issue *Rupert and the Blunderpuss*, Rupert and his friends embark on an adventure that leads them in search of a Blunderpuss, a small, black, flying cat, mistakenly conjured up by Tiger Lily's sorcerer father. Rupert must capture and tame the winged creature, then send it back to the land of mystery. The Blunderpuss flutters perfectly into the classic Rupert story-telling format, so much so, that one could be forgiven for thinking that this airborne feline is an original creation of Alfred Bestall, but in truth, cats depicted with wings go back much further than the early 20th century. The winged cat is a recurring theme in palaeoart, and belief in these creatures persists to the present day as an urban legend (much like the American Jackalope or Horned Hare), whereas many recorded sightings of cats with "wings" can be explained by genuine observations of cats with wing-like appendages, that can flap about in an elementary manner as the cat runs.

In fact, as Karl Shuker pointed out, when they jump up into the air or onto a sufficiently high surface, these flaps become more noticeable as they momentarily hang behind and then subsequently catch up with the momentum of the body of the cat. With a little imagination, this might create the illusion of them flying short distances. The concept of big cats with wings, particularly winged lions, was a popular motif among the Sumerians, Mesopotamians, Persians, Akkadians, and Scythians, and these ideas were shared with other cultures in Europe, the Middle East, and the Near East through their contacts. *Aq Bars* is a folkloric winged, snow-white leopard; an ancient symbol of Bulgar and Turkic invention dating back to an uncertain period in prehistory, and emblems of snow leopards with wings can be seen on the coats of arms of Tatarstan, Russian Federation; Uzbekistan; and Nur-Sultan, Kazakhstan. It is unclear when winged cats first appeared in artwork, however, art featuring these improbable felines dates back to at least the Upper Palaeolithic period, circa 40,000 BC.

There are three causes of "winged cats". The most common of these is long-haired cats developing thick matted fur, that can form into long uncomfortable clumps. As the cat runs, these clumps of fur flap about creating the illusion of functional wings. They often cause discomfort and stress for the cat and can harbour unwanted dirt, faeces, and biting parasites. However, as pointed out by Karl Shuker, this does not fully explain the phenomenon of winged cats, as not all examples feature long-haired specimens. Also, anybody who is familiar with cats would be unlikely to mistake clumps of matted fur for true wings, although they might be less apparent to novices. Despite the fact that these unsightly clumps aren't restricted to any specific part of the cat's coat and can develop anywhere on a long-haired cat's body, to those unfamiliar with the condition, they're most noticeable on the flanks, especially when the cat is moving rapidly. A second explanation is a rare hereditary skin disorder called feline cutaneous asthenia (FCA).

Cats suffering from FCA have abnormal elasticity, leading to their skin stretching as they groom themselves. Over time, this results in pendulous wing-like folds on the back, shoulders and haunches. Occasionally, these protrusions appear to have neuromuscular tissues, allowing the cats to move them in a rudimentary fashion. The third explanation for winged cats is polymelia, a rare congenital defect that results in one or more additional limbs. These deformed appendages are typically fur covered and might resemble wings. Though there have been more than one hundred reported cases, many are attributed to clumps of matted fur, cutaneous asthenia or supernumerary limbs, as well as taxidermy fakes and sensationalist tabloid journalism. There are more than thirty reported cases of cats with what appear to be wings, with twenty photographs and one video as evidence. Bats and birds have true wings in place of arms while gliding mammals such as flying squirrels possess skin membranes between their front and rear limbs that are similar to a wingsuit. Classical and contemporary artwork depicting winged cats, as well as their corresponding reports, typically have the wings located on the cat's back in a manner reminiscent of the quadrupedal dragons of European myth and legend.

The earliest documented record of a winged cat presently known is attributed to Henry David Thoreau, which reads as follows:

"A few years before I lived in the woods there was what was called a 'winged cat' in one of the farmhouses in Lincoln nearest the pond, Mr. Gillian Baker's. When I called to see her in June, 1842, she was gone a-hunting in the woods, as was her wont... but her mistress told me that she came into the neighbourhood a little more than a year before, in April, and was finally taken into their house; that she was of a dark brownish-grey colour, with a white spot on her throat, and white feet, and had a large bushy tail like a fox; that in the winter the fur grew thick and flattened out along her sides, forming strips ten or twelve inches long by two and a half wide, and under her chin like a muff, the upper side loose, the under matted like felt, and in the spring these appendages dropped off. They gave me a pair of her 'wings,' which I keep still. There is no appearance of a membrane about them. Some thought it was part flying squirrel or some other wild animal, which is not impossible, for, according to naturalists, prolific hybrids have been produced by the union of the marten and the domestic cat."

In Stanley Peter Dance's 1976 work, "Animal Fakes and Frauds" Dance describes a 19th-century taxidermy winged cat that was offered for sale in the early 1960s. According to the account, its "wings" had apparently developed when it was a kitten. In the 19th century, the cat had been put on display by a circus owner; however, when the original owner requested its return it passed away mysteriously. Its body was then delivered to a taxidermist but by all accounts has not been examined scientifically. In 1868, a "flying cat" was reported in India, with Alexander Gibson allegedly shooting the animal. For a period of time, its skin was exhibited at a meeting of the *Mumbai Asiatic Society* an assembly of the Mumbai Asiatic Society. Although Gibson said it was feline, others argued it was a bat. In August 1894 David Badcock from Reach in England was exhibiting a cat with "wings" that were described as being similar to a duckling's, i.e. short and fuzzy. It was later stolen but showed up in Liverpool but had shed its wings. A cat with "pheasant-like wings" extending from its fourth ribs was reported to have been shot and killed in Matlock, Derbyshire. It was first reported in the *High Peak News* on Saturday, June 26th 1897, with witnesses saying that the cat used its outstretched wings to aid it when running at fast speeds. Sound familiar?

In 1899, London's *Strand Magazine* reported on a winged cat or kitten owned by a woman living in Wiveliscombe, England which had also drawn the attention of H. C. Brooke (b. 1867 – d 1930), an eminent naturalist and expert on cats who wrote about it in the weekly magazine *Cat Gossip* in 1927:

"This cat had growing from its back two appendages which reminded the observer irresistibly of the wings of a chicken before the adult feathers appear. These appendages were not flabby, but apparently gristly, about six or eight inches long, and place in exactly the position assumed by the wings of a bird in the act of taking flight. They did not make their appearance until the kitten was several weeks old."

At some point, somebody attempted to cut off the cat's "wings", with fatal consequences.

In 1936, a peculiar white cat with long fur was found on a farm near Portpatrick, located on the western shore of the Rhins of Galloway in Scotland. The cat reportedly sported rudimentary wings measuring approximately 15 cm in length and 7 cm across, that would flap up and down as it ran. This is consistent with badly matted fur. During World War II, a heavy black-and-white cat in Ashford, Middlesex garnered significant attention due to the abnormally large "wings" that appeared to be extending from its shoulders. This appears to be the result of matted fur. In June 1949, a twenty-pound cat with a 58cm "wingspan" was reportedly shot in northern Sweden. Prof. Rendahl of the *State Museum of Natural History* indicated that the wings were likely caused by skin deformity. In May 1959, Douglas Shelton caught a Persian cat with dense fur wings near Pinesville, West Virginia and named it Thomas. When the capture made headlines, however, Mrs Charles Hicks identified the cat as her missing pet Mitzi. A court case ensued by which time the cat's "wings" had actually fallen off, confirming folklore that such cats shed their wings.

In 1966, a purported wing-bearing cat from Alfred, Ontario in Canada was killed and examined by scientists at Kemptville Agricultural School. Upon inspection of the remains, it was discovered that the wings were merely matted fur. Additionally, upon closer observation, it was noted that the cat had been suffering from fatal symptoms of rabies. In 1975, the *Manchester Evening News* released a photograph of a winged cat that had been living at Banister Walton & Co's builder's yard in Trafford Park, Manchester, England, during the 1960s. The cat had wings extending twenty-eight centimetres from its back as well as flaps of skin on its tail. Witnesses reported that it was able to move its wings, indicating that there was adequate muscular and skin tissue present. In 1986, reports emerged of a winged cat being seen in Anglesey. Subsequently, the wings were shown to be matted fur. Then in April 1995, Martin Millner purportedly witnessed a fluffy winged tabby cat at Backbarrow in Cumbria, England.

In 1998, a black cat was reported from Northwood in Middlesex with wings measuring 5-7.6 centimetres on the shoulder blades; they were twenty centimetres long, ten centimetres wide, two-and-a-half centimetres thick and flapped as the cat moved about. In 2007, a bizarre story began circulating in Xianyang, Shaanxi province, China regarding a one-year-old tomcat named Feng which had grown ten-centimetre "wings with bones" within a month, initially starting out as small lumps. Feng's owner believed that the phenomenon was due to the cat being sexually harassed by other cats. This spurious claim was reported in the Huashang tabloid newspaper. In May 2009, MSNBC, an American news-based cable channel, reported the sighting of another winged cat in China. In 2011, a viral YouTube video brought attention to a winged cat in Tatarstan, Russia, which was informally referred to as Aq Bars after the white leopard with wings on the Tatarstan coat of arms.

A *tressym* is a mystical creature featured in *Dungeons & Dragons* that closely resembles a small cat with wings. Found predominantly in the warm and temperate regions of Faerûn, they were highly esteemed in the village of Eveningstar, where they brought good luck and helped keep rodents away. Additionally, they were often chosen as familiars by benevolent wizards. The term 'tressym' is loosely linked to trejgun, an appellation once used for one of Freyja's cats in Norse legend; however, this association is fairly tenuous. Winged cats are a common fixture of fiction and fantasy, with notable examples such as Whiskers, a recurring winged cat from Michael Moorcock's Multiverse series published between 1967 and 1974, and Catwings, Ursula K. Le Guin's 11-part children's picture book series featuring winged cats. The "Winged Panther" is #40 in the *Monster in My Pocket* series (1989) and a winged cat also appears as a recurring enemy in the *Final Fantasy V* video game (1992). The *Cardcaptor Sakura* manga series (1996 – 2000) and its sequel (2016 – present) feature Spinel Sun, a character capable of transforming into a small, butterfly-winged black cat or a large butterfly-winged black leopard. The *Beyblade* manga series (1999 – 2004) includes Venus, a winged cat referred to as a Bit-Beast. Laura Von Stetina's children's book, *Mewingham Manor: Observations on a Curious New Species* (Greenwich Workshop Press, 2002), also features winged kittens called "flittens" and a line of widely popular flitten figurines has been produced by the publisher. Lastly, *Ni no Kuni: Wrath of the White Witch* video game (2011) contains an Auroralynx familiar which is also a winged cat.

6

FEARSOME CRITTERS, LUMBERJACK TALES AND BOGEYCATS

'The hardest thing of all is to find a black cat in a dark room, especially if there is no cat.'

— CONFUCIUS, PHILOSOPHER

In North American folklore, "Fearsome Critters" is a term used to refer to fictitious creatures that are humorously said to exist, though, in reality, they are nothing more than inventive fabrications. They are typically rumoured to live in and around logging camps, most notably in the region of the Laurentian Great Lakes. Today, this label is also applied to other similar mythical creatures. Lumberjacks who frequently travelled between camps would tell stories about these creatures, resulting in their proliferation across the continent. Several fearsome critters were exaggerated versions designed as explanations for various phenomena, both natural and unnatural. The more outlandish or biologically implausible the "critter" was simply showed how far its story could be pushed beyond what is understood of natural history and biomechanics. Although a lot of literature exists on fearsome critters, many stories did not become widespread and different regions have various interpretations of the same Critter. For example, the Wampus Cat looks entirely different depending on where it is reported from.

The Ball Tailed Cat

The Ball-Tailed Cat (*Felis caudaglobosa*) is very similar to the mountain lion, with the notable exception of a long tail attached to a bulbous mass reminiscent of the defensive appendage of the extinct Cretaceous dinosaur *Ankylosaurus*. The similarities between this alleged cat and the mountain lion go beyond physical features. Tales of ball-tailed cats were once commonplace among woodsmen – giving rise to many variations including the *Digmaul* and Silver Cat. The Ball-Tailed Cat is found in local legends and steeped in folklore, primarily in Pennsylvania's Harney County as well as Oregon's Sullivan County. It is believed that its clawed feet make it a proficient climber enabling the Ball-Tailed Cat to cling to tree limbs over trails where it awaits potential prey. Upon encountering prey, the Ball-Tailed Cat will drop down and strike the unsuspecting victim with its armoured tail. According to tradition the male Ball-Tailed Cats also use their tails to drum on hollow logs in an attempt to lure females. This characteristic could be related to "wood knocks" or "tree knocks" attributed to the North American Bigfoot or Sasquatch.

Cactus Cat

The Cactus Cat of the American Southwest is a lynx-like critter, covered with hairs resembling thorns, featuring particularly long spines protruding from its legs as well as its branching spiked tail. It is speculated that the Cactus Cat uses these spikes to slash cacti at night, causing the juice to seep out of the plant. Allegedly, following this process, the Cactus Cat will return over the next few weeks to drink the fermented juice from the plant. It is said that during this time, the inebriated creature will howl throughout the evening hours. Furthermore, it is believed to be a hostile desert predator that can inflict large puncture wounds or sometimes even fatal injuries on animals that cross into its territory (a similar defence mechanism is seen in porcupines). It is said they avoid extreme heat by hollowing out a cactus for daytime slumber and feasting on insects that gather around it – an ideal source of sustenance and hydration for them. Additionally, they are said to have resilience towards scorpion venom and hunt them at night.

According to traditional lumberjack folklore, these critters are social with a monogamous mating system. It's believed that they can live up to thirty years. During the mating season, the males would break open a saguaro cactus (*Carnegiea gigantea*) and let its scent attract females to the area. Tales claim that two competing females would engage in a fierce fight, usually ending in one of them being pierced or killed by spikes. The victorious female would then drink the juice of the cactus with the male and become intoxicated; subsequently, they would have a litter of kittens within weeks. As with all kittens, they were born blind (and without spikes).

Cat Annis

Black Annis is a phantom witch from English folklore conceptualised as a tall, bony, blue-skinned hag with glowing eyes, long, sharp teeth and claw-like fingers, which she uses to butcher small children and lambs before eating them. She is also known as Black Anna, Black Anny, Black Agnes, and Cat Anna or Cat Annis. In the latter versions of her name, she appears more as a malevolent cat-like spectre, but still dangerous to misbehaved children. The British folklorist Katharine Briggs (b. 1898 – d.1980) described in her books, *The Anatomy of Puck: An Examination of Fairy Beliefs among Shakespeare's Contemporaries and Successors,* and her four-volume, *A Dictionary of British Folk-Tales in the English Language*, how the legend gave rise to a peculiar local tradition called "Black Monday" which was celebrated each Easter Monday where a dead cat soaked in aniseed would be dragged before a pack of hounds in front of Annie's cave to celebrate the end of winter. This macabre ritual ended at the close of the 18th century, replaced in later years by the Dane Hills Fair where annually on midsummer's eve female Morris dancers meet near the site to perform their dances.

Another legend says that Annis (in the form of Cat Anna) lived beneath Leicester Castle and that there was an underground passageway leading to the Dane Hills, through which she passed in her search for children. Other than the obvious similarity of names, it is uncertain why "Cat Annis" was directly associated with aniseed; however, substances like salt and aniseed were used historically to repel evil spirits. Although the origins of the legend are uncertain, there were two fifteenth-century women who it has been suggested might be the origins of Annis. It is likely that the tale existed as early as the 15th century and the women's lives became entangled in the folklore. The first is Agnes Scott, hence why the witch is sometimes known as "Black Agnes". Agnes Scott was a Dominican nun who looked after a community of lepers in Leicestershire and lived in solitude within the Dane Hills caves.

It is believed that, over time, the memory of the nun was distorted, and her legend became that of "Black Annis". The second woman is more tenuous in her association with Black Annis for she is the witch or wise woman who foretold the death of Richard III. Some of the behaviours associated with Annis are remarkably cat-like. Firstly, she was thought to ambush prey from overhead trees; to hang the carcases of her prey outside her cave, and that she would often be heard before she was seen, and her haunting wails would echo throughout the area. Locals believed that Black Annis would reach into their windows at night and snatch children to bring back to her lair. Indeed, parents would often use the tale of the witch to scare misbehaving children into obedience. It is also said that some houses in Leicestershire have small windows in order to deter Black Annis. Perhaps the legend of Black Annis the witch was originally inspired by the predations of a real nocturnal carnivore with an appetite for children and lambs that has become lost to history.

Central American Whintosser

The Central American Whintosser (*Cephalovertens semperambulatus*) is a fearsome critter found in folklore along the coastal regions of California. Originating from the Isthmus of Panama, this small cat-like creature is known for its ferocious behaviour which inspires fear among those who have encountered it. It has a lean muscular body with three sets of legs that allow it to remain upright no matter whatever direction it falls in, making it highly adapted for regions prone to earthquakes. Furthermore, it is said to have rough fur that grows forward instead of back and a head and short tail with swivel joints capable of spinning up to 100x per minute. Additionally, the durability of a *Whintosser* is remarkable as it can survive attacks and injuries that would certainly kill other animals. The only known way to kill a *Whintosser* is by trapping it inside a large-bore pipe; once this happens, its three sets of legs will grip the inside causing it to tear itself apart as it runs through the pipe.

Celofay

According to lumberjack folklore, 'Celofay' is a term that refers to a single creature, or a particular type of fantasy feline which are generally considered female. Celofay is said to have a supernatural ability to throw her voice, whose piercing, scream-like howls can be heard from all directions. She uses this uncanny ability to startle her prey, causing it to travel in a desired direction, often in large circles. Only when the prey is completely disoriented, exhausted, and afraid will she kill it. Celofay seems to enjoy playing with her prey. Some even claim that she feeds as much on fear as the animals and people she captures. She will often stalk her prey for several hours, therefore the best way to escape her, according to folklore, is simply to try and ignore her hellish screams – gather one's wits and head straight back for the safety of your home or vehicle, or if neither are close by, then some other readily defensible structure.

The Celofay was originally described by a French-Canadian lumber-jack from Maine, and her name appears to be a corruption of the French phrase "c'est la feé", which means "of the fairy". Henry Harrington Tryon (b. 1888 – d. 1953), director of Black Rock Forest in upstate New York and author of *Fearsome Critters* (1939), describes how Celofay "can easily project her fearsome squall across a section, right up beside you. Or she can reverse the situation and toss her yowl into some distant cedar swamp while she stealthily stalks you with malicious and atrocious intent." According to folklore, because of her size, Celofay's prey consists primarily of large animals such as elk and deer, as well as bears, coyotes, wolves, dogs, cats, and, according to lore, fear. Celofay is sometimes called Lucifee.

In a report by T. H. Gray in *Downeast Maine*, it is said that "while Lucifee never attacked humans [untrue], her nocturnal screams scared the daylights out of people in the area." The word lucifee is, however, simply an English spelling of the French-Canadian word for the Canada lynx, which is loup cervier, quite similar to "lucifee". But literally and perhaps somewhat confusingly the Italian Lupo Cervino, or Loup Cervier, also known as Lucifee, is the French name for the imaginary Deer Wolf, a monstrous and deceptive creature and a completely different fearsome critter that looks like a normal deer but is a bloodthirsty monster with the jaws and carnivorous habits of a wolf. This is thought to be how the long-legged Canada lynx looked to the early French settlers. The Canada lynx (*Lynx canadensis*) is a flesh-and-blood wild cat found in northern Maine and Canada, particularly in regions where the snow is too deep to support regular bobcat populations. And while it does have an eerie call, the lynx makes that sound only during the mating season and during territorial disputes. The Canada lynx almost exclusively hunts snowshoe hares and is not considered particularly dangerous to humans unless provoked or threatened. The Canadian lynx is the best possible biological basis for Celofay in real life.

Dingmaul or *Plunkus*

In the White Mountains of New Hampshire, between Mount Adams and Mount Jefferson of the Presidential Range, there is a large, visible flat-topped boulder that has been known for generations as "Dingmaul Rock". Local folklore says there are two varieties of Dingmaul; both are feline in appearance with long bodies, slender frames, and short, powerful legs, covered in wolf-like fur. As the American author and humorist Irvin Shrewsbury Cobb (b. 1876 – d. 1944) described:

"He's built low to the ground like a carpet sweeper. The head is round, sessile, feline, with tufted ears and glowing eyes. Neither variety is harmful, but both possess a curious, inquiring nature. They are fond of lying out in open, sunny spots, (the top of Dingmaul Rock for example), and carefully watching what goes on in the valley below. The tall is very long, frequently twice the length of the body; but the California variety caries a medium-sized bony ball at its end. This is used to deter flies, to pound on dead trees to produce a supply of soft pulp for lining their dens, and, in the mating season, for the male to beat on its chest to call a mate. The female also has a ball tail but she only uses it to beat the male when he becomes too unruly. Ranger Bill Gott once watched one of the California variety, galloping along the crest of the Siskiyou mountains, with the ball lashing from side to side and striking the trees with tremendous force "That," commented Ranger Bill, "is the biggest kindlin' cat I ever saw."

Their vocalisations are said to resemble a fearful wailing cry or the sharp whistle of a logging Steam Donkey, a steam-powered winch typically used in logging operations.

Gallywampus

A four-legged variant of the *Wampus cat*, the *Gallywampus* behaves much the same, being extremely fierce and dangerous to woodsmen, but this version has sharp and dangerous tail hooks. It is described as a half-dog, half-cat creature, that can run both bipedally and quadrupedally, rumoured to be seen during twilight hours throughout the Appalachian Mountains. The *Gallywampus's* bite was considered dangerous, perhaps even venomous, and fishermen wouldn't fish in deep, still waters because those were where the *Gallywampus* allegedly lurked. It is said to swim like an enormous mink and to occasionally attack terrestrial livestock. In non-Native American cultures it is described as an evil howling creature, with yellow eyes that supposedly pierce the hearts and souls of those unlucky enough to cross its path; often driving its poor victims into a profound state of insanity. Cherokee folklore, which is filled with legends of evil spirits lurking in the deep, dark forests that surrounded their villages, offers a different view of the *Wampas cat* as an evil demon called *Ew'ah*, the "Spirit of Madness". *Ew'ah* had been terrorising the village of Etowah (or Chota) in what is today North Carolina. The village shamans called for a meeting with the chiefs of war and in their wisdom told the chiefs that sending their braves to hunt and kill the *Ew'ah* would fail, for it had the terrible power to drive men insane with only a single glance.

The chiefs concluded that *Ew'ah* was preying on the dreams of the Cherokee children, and they needed to put a stop to it. Thus, their strongest brave would be tasked with defeating *Ew'ah* in battle and bringing honour to his people. Standing Bear (or Great Fellow in some versions) was renowned for being the strongest, fastest, smartest, and most respected amongst the Cherokee nation, making him the perfect choice for the job. Before setting off on his dangerous journey, Standing Bear was blessed by the village shamans and given an array of weapons to fight the demon. Finally, at the edge of town, his wife Running Deer tearfully bid him farewell. Weeks went by and there was no word from Standing Bear.

Suddenly, late one night, the stricken brave came running back to camp, screaming, and clawing at his eyes in a state of apparent madness. One glance was enough for Running Deer to realise that her husband was no longer the same man she married. Although he could eventually go back to picking berries and labour in the fields,

Standing Bear would never be a capable partner again, making him as good as dead according to Cherokee law. Standing Bear's name was never spoken of again, yet Running Deer cherished her husband and sought her revenge. She consulted the shamans who gave her a ceremonial mask with the face of a bobcat. They informed her that the spirit of the mountain cat could oppose *Ew'ah*, but she would have to take him by surprise. The chiefs also presented her with a magical paste, which when applied to her skin would mask both her scent and physical form. Running Dear kissed her husband goodbye, his blank eyes staring into the beyond, and headed off to seek vengeance. Running Deer knew the woods as well as any brave, and she ate sweet berries to keep her strength up over the many days, but still, she came across no sign of *Ew'ah*.

Then, late one night, she heard a creature moving about near the stream. As she crept towards the water, a snap echoed from behind her. She quickly spun around only to realise how close to danger she had been as a fox dashed across the path before her. "If that had been Ew'ah, I would be mad now" Running Deer told herself, as she continued towards the creek. At the edge of the creek, she found footprints that did not belong there, and her husband's breastplate lay bloody at the edge of a stream. As she followed the prints, Running Deer saw the demon. Its hulking, hideous form lurched over the water, drinking, and polluting the pristine mountain spring with its foul presence. Fortunately, *Ew'ah* had not noticed her. Running Deer stealthily approached, and when she felt as if she could get no closer, she attacked. *Ew'ah* tumbled backwards into the pool, and Running Deer immediately turned on her heels and ran as fast as she could back to the village, never once looking back. When she arrived home, she sang a quiet song to herself – of grief for her husband, but also of joy for the demon's banishment. Some say that the spirit of Running Deer inhabits the *Wampas cat* and that she continues her eternal mission of watching her tribal lands to protect them and their people from the demons that hide in the forests.

Glawackus

The *Glawackus*, also known as the 'Northern Devil Cat', is another legendary creature from the folklore and traditions of the lumberjacks during the 19th and early 20th centuries. It is almost certainly a tall-tale animal. The *Glawackus* is generally described as looking something like a mixture of a bear, a lion, and a leopard. It is well known for its vocalisations that compare to the cackle of a hyena. The creature is blind and uses its keen sense of smell as well as its exceptional hearing to hunt its prey. This is yet another "fearsome critter" purported to possess hypnotic powers, as it was said that one's memory could be erased simply by meeting its gaze. A popular radio network commentator named Lowell Jackson Thomas (b. 1892 – d. 1981) reported that the *Glawackus* had been described and named by a "Connecticut scientist." A hunt for the beast was organised with two Ozark-trained hounds, which of course came back empty-handed. The event, however, was memorialised in verse:

"Say did the fearless hunters, pick up the beastly spoor, while trekking through the jungle, with steps alert and sure?"

The Glawackus is typically reported from Glastonbury, Hartford County, Connecticut. An eyewitness stated: "I was working as a young reporter on the Hartford Courant that year when World War II was in the wings, but we were preoccupied with the developing story about this Glastonbury creature that howled at night, slipped in and out of view and caused dogs, cats, and small farm animals to disappear. As the sightings grew in number, so did the variety of descriptions. First, it was a huge cat. Then some people reported what looked like a dog from the back and a cat in front. Others saw it vice-versa. One man called to say he had seen a big animal in the pitch dark with eyes that glowed like embers. It was clear to us that this weird, unknown animal needed a name. One editor coined the word, Glawackus. "Gla" for Glastonbury; "wack" for wacky; and "us" as a proper Latin ending. It caught on like magic."

Huan

The *Huan*, a cat-like creature of Chinese mythology, is featured in the classic Chinese text *Shan Hai Jing* ("Classic of Mountains and Seas"). It is believed that versions of this ancient text have been around since the 4th century BC, while its present form was not reached until 206 BC with the start of the Han dynasty. The *Huan* resembles a cat but with three tails and a cyclopean single eye. It is said to imitate the sounds of other wildlife and to sometimes sound like "a hundred sounds". It can ward off evil spirits and people would keep them as pets for this reason. Eating its meat or wearing its skin was also said to cure jaundice. The *Huan* can be compared to the *Nekomata*, a somewhat similar creature found in Japanese folklore – a sort of feline *yōkai*.

Mishipeshu

Mishipeshu or *Mishibijiw* (in Ojibwe) is a significant creature for many of the indigenous people from the northeastern woodlands and Great Lakes region, who commonly believe it is an underwater panther. *Mishipeshu* translates as "the Great Lynx". It has the head and paws of a giant cat but is covered with scales and has long thorn-like spikes running along the length of its back to its tail. *Mishipeshu* is believed to inhabit Michipicoten Island on Lake Superior and is thought to be a powerful creature in the traditions of the Anishi-naabe and Ojibwe tribes, but also the Odawa and Potawatomi of the Great Lakes region of Canada and the United States. To the Algonquin people, *Mishipeshu* is the most powerful of all underworld denizens. For centuries the Ojibwe people believed the creatures to be supreme rulers of the water. Some versions of the Nanabozho creation story refer to entire communities of "water lynxes". The Ojibwe have many names and spellings for this mythical being, such as *Mishibizhiw*, *Mishipizhiw*, *Mishipizheu*, *Mishupishu*, *Mishepishu*, *Michipeshu*, or *Mishibijiw*, all subtle variants of *Mishipeshu*, or *Gichi-anami'e-bizhiw*, which translates as "the incredible night panther". It is also referred to as the "great underground wildcat" or "great under-water wildcat".

In the folklore of the indigenous peoples of the Great Lakes, they are said to be water monsters with extraordinarily long tails and the nemesis of the giant thunderbirds. *Mishipeshu* is a composite of parts from many different animals: it has the body of a cat, usually resembling a lynx or mountain lion; horns similar to those of a bison; spines along its back and tail like that of an ancient reptile; and in some cases, even feathers. It is claimed that it roars during thunderstorms or hisses in rushing rapids, i.e. is misheard. Some traditions held the underwater panthers to be beneficent, even helpful, protective creatures, but more often they were viewed as malevolent monsters that only brought death and destruction. According to legend, they often need to be appeased for safe passage across a lake. As late as the 1950s, the *Prairie Band of Potawatomi Indians* performed a traditional ceremony to appease the creature and maintain equilibrium with the thunderbird.

During the 1850s, when German traveller, historian and ethnographer Johann Georg Kohl (1808-1878) visited the United States, he was spoken to by a Fond du Lac chief who showed him an item of copper from his traditional medicine bag. The chief stated that this artefact had been taken from *Mishipeshu*, making it magical, very powerful, and sacred to his people. This assertion is more comprehensible when we take into account the belief that *Mishipeshu* guards the copper near Lake Superior and the Great Lakes Region. Before the arrival of Europeans, the indigenous people had been mining copper in the region for a long time. In the 17th century, missionaries from the Society of Jesus came to the Great Lakes Region. By that time, stealing copper was considered a major transgression by the Ojibwa tribe and was strictly prohibited. It was particularly disrespectful to take it from Michipicoten Island, the home of the "Great Lynx," which was seen by many as stealing from *Mishipeshu* himself. Claude Dablon, a Jesuit missionary, recounted a tale of four Ojibwa Indians embarking on a quest to the home of *Mishipeshu* to procure copper for use in heating water upon their return home. As soon as they pushed off with their canoe, the eerie voice of *Mishipeshu* startled them. The water panther came growling after them, angrily accusing them of stealing from his children. According to the legend, four of the Indians died while attempting to return to their village, the last one surviving (the story wouldn't have been told without at least one survivor) just long enough to tell the tale of what had happened in his final moments before he also died.

Silver Cat

The Silver Cat or *"Felis glabraspiculata"* is a folkloric lynx-like cat with red eyes but with horizontal slits (something like those of a grazing herbivore) instead of the vertical slits standard in small cats. It was also said to have a long powerful tail ending with a spiked club-like appendage. The Silver Cat is said to be an arboreal ambush predator that hangs upside down from tree branches, using its spiked tail to skewer its hapless prey, which it then drags up into the tree to consume. During the mating season, as a courtship ritual, the male Silver Cat is said to use the smooth side of its tail and bang it on its chest like a drum to attract a mate. Adults were believed to weigh approximately 136 kg (about 300 lbs) and had tufted ears. The Silver Cat's tail reaches eleven feet in length and is "as powerful as a boa constrictor", ending with a bony club-like appendage, which is spiked on one side similar to the thagomisers evolved by dinosaurs like Stegosaurus, yet smooth and hard on the other.

Splinter Cat

The Splinter Cat exists in the folklore of the lumberjacks as a ferocious, nocturnal, and somewhat aeronautical cat. It flies swiftly through the air and when it hits a large tree, it knocks the branches off, withers the trunk, and leaves the dead snag standing in place. Trees like these can be found in many parts of the Pacific Northwest perpetuating the legend. The Splinter Cat is said to attack raccoons and bees for their meat and honey respectively. Unfortunately, this act of breaking open trees with its head leads to ongoing headaches, making the Splinter Cat perpetually ill-tempered. The wonderfully named *Splintercat Creek*, in Oregon's northern Cascade Range, is named after this legendary creature. The Splinter Cat also appears in the 1974 children's book *The Last of the Really Great Whangdoodles* by Julie Edwards (the married name of singer and actress Dame Julie Andrews). The Splinter Cat of the story answers to the prime minister of Whangdoodland and also enjoys playing Cat's Cradle with string.

Wampus Cats, aka the Cherokee Death Cat

The *Wampus* or Cherokee Death Cat is a folkloric entity with a variety of appearances, ranging from comical to intimidating; however, its form is always cat-like. It is typically portrayed as a mountain lion with pale tan or yellow fur, intense yellow or green eyes, and to possess supernatural abilities. However, unlike the mountain lion, the *Wampus* has as many as six legs. According to locals in Conway, Arkansas, four of its legs are for running, and two are for fighting. In Clark Fork, Idaho, the creature is said to have a "ball-like formation" at the tip of its tail, supposedly covered with spikes or sharp quills. Some commentators compare the *Wampus Cat* to a similar imaginary being from Cherokee mythology, which is seen as the feline embodiment of a tribeswoman who was punished by her elders for observing a sacred ritual that the women of the tribe were not allowed to see. In the beliefs of several southeastern tribes, the *Wampus Cat* is a shapeshifter. Since the 1920s, there have been numerous reports of the mythical *Wampus Cat* across various towns in the United States. By the 1930s, newspapers were reporting that the creature was preying on livestock from North Carolina to Georgia, and sightings persisted into the 1960s. In response, townspeople took up arms and imposed strict curfews in order to protect themselves from the imaginary creature.

Later references noted the *Wampus Cat* as "an undefined imaginary animal" that was sometimes "heard whining about camps at night" and the Folklorist Vance Randolph (b. 1892 – d. 1980) describes the Wampus as "a kind of amphibious panther which leaps into the water and swims like a colossal mink." Below the Mason-Dixon line: the boundary between Maryland and Pennsylvania, regarded as the northern limit of the slave-owning states before the 13th Amendment abolished slavery in 1865, the legendary creature was known as "*Santer*". Here it was described as rarely dangerous to humans but a frequent predator of livestock. The origins of this creature likely date back to lumberjack tales of the 19th and early 20th centuries where it was described as having a long, slender body covered in reddish, occasionally grey fur. Its head is large and bald with small eyes, it has long legs, and a tail featuring eight hard knots, giving it the appearance of a string of beads. The *Wampus* can skilfully swing its powerful tail with enough force to bring down a cow or a hog with one mighty blow.

The Wampus is associated with wooded wetlands near communities where cattle and pigs are raised. It is remarkably fast and seldom seen but is heard emitting a loud, piercing cry resembling that of a baby's wail, which has been known to frighten even the most courageous of canines. It was first reported in the September 4th, 1890 issue of the *Statesville Landmark* that a police officer named Fettle allegedly shot a *Wampus Cat* while it was hunting a dog. Tracks were found the following morning. It is also said to have eaten seven pigs and fifteen cows. A hunting posse was organised to kill the gluttonous creature, but it was neither seen nor heard. However, tracks claimed to belong to it were found to have been 20 cm long and 10 cm wide. Its hind tracks were strangest of all, said to be similar to those of a bear, i.e. plantigrade.

On October 4th, 1890 news outlets reported that possum hunter Abe Harbin encountered the *Santer*, causing his dogs to run back to him in fright. Another man named Adam Lentz claimed to see "only a glimpse" of the creature. This sighting was enough, however, for

Lentz to say it wasn't quite as big as a cow. On a Monday night, the creature supposedly visited the house of two widows, rearing up against the door and growling menacingly at them. On March 17th, 1897, reports surfaced of a creature allegedly spotted at Roaring River, that was said to have been preying on domestic cats in the area. In an article published on May 5th, 1897, it was proposed that the *Wampus Cat* of the region may have been a lynx that had escaped from a travelling circus that had been exhibited in the area the year before. Reports of the *Santer* surfaced in the June 9th 1897 issue of the *Elkin Times*. It was purported to resemble a large German shepherd dog and had been feasting on local cats and dogs. On May 31st, 1899, it was held responsible for killing and eating twelve chickens. A witness described it as a greyish creature between the size of a cat and a dog. Reports persisted until the 1920s, and given that it was common practice for nineteenth-century newspapers to fabricate stories to boost sales, it is probable that the *Wampus* or *Santer* is nothing more than fabrications and yarns.

Wowzer

The Oklahoma *Wowzer* is a large cougar-like creature described in Ozark folklore. It is said to be five or six times the size of a typical cougar, and capable of easily biting off the heads of oxen.

7

"I TAWT I TAW A PUDDY TAT!"

'There is nothing like the thrill of walking through the jungle looking for a tiger and knowing they could be watching you already.'

— ASHLAN GORSE COUSTEAU

People can be poor eyewitnesses and psychologists have been demonstrating this uncomfortable fact in experiments for many years. It is not possible to put a percentage on how unreliable eyewitnesses can be, but it's reasonable to assume that some mistakes are made. Despite this, die-hard sceptics will often gleefully point out the unreliability of eyewitnesses as if this alone is enough to dismiss all testimonies without attempting to provide a solution to the issue. Rarely do they give the same consideration to the plain and evident fact that this cannot be applied to all reports of a cryptozoological nature. Some lie, others make genuine mistakes, and some just see what they want to see. However, some (perhaps the minority) have probably seen what they say.

The answer is elementary, gather more corresponding evidence that either confirms or denies the report. Don't ignore it, just accumulate as much evidence as possible and follow that evidence (without cherry-picking) to its logical and natural conclusion. It is poor science to ignore or disregard eyewitness testimony simply because it relates to something unusual and seemingly improbable by nature. The same applies to blurry photographs. Below are a few unknown animal forms that were at one time considered possible felids, but were eventually identified conclusively, or at least beyond reasonable doubt, as belonging to other unrelated taxonomic groups. Again, this isn't necessarily a failure for cryptozoology, just miscalculations on the part of the cryptozoologists involved who continue to assert a particular erroneous theory.

Cat-Fox

The "Cat-Fox" was postulated by numerous researchers as a potential new species of carnivoran photographed in the Indonesian portion of Borneo in Southeast Asia. It was initially discovered by the Swiss-based environmental organisation the *World Wide Fund for Nature* (WWF) in 2003 making use of a night vision camera trap in *Kayan Mentarang National Par*k in North Kalimantan Province. The mammal recorded is slightly larger than a domestic cat, with red fur, a long tail, and hind limbs that are visibly longer than the fore pair. Its general appearance is something between a cat and a fox (hence its name), albeit with some similarities to the fossa (*Cryptoprocta ferox*) from Madagascar. The *WWF* planned to employ traps to capture and study the Cat-Fox. New mammals are discovered in Borneo with some regularity. For example, the monotypic rodent *Pithecheirops otion* related to the tree rats in 1993, and the bat *Myotis gomantongensis* endemic to the Sabah district of Malaysia in 1998. Many people have surmised that the creature in the photographs is a recognised, albeit rare species, Hose's palm civet (*Diplogale hosei*). It was thought the Cat-Fox might be "the first new large carnivore discovered on Borneo" since *Melogale everett* – the Borneo ferret badger (actually an omnivore) in 1895. However, a report published in 2007 by Erik Meijaard, Andrew C. Kitchener, and Chris Smeenk suggests that the animal in the photograph may not be a carnivoran after all, but one of the area's large flying squirrels of the genus *Aeromys*, possibly Thomas's flying squirrel (*A. thomasi*). Others have suggested that it may be a red giant flying squirrel (*Petaurista petaurista*).

Chongonga

A Flippered Feline?

According to British palaeontologist and cryptozoological enthusiast Darren Naish in an email sent to Dr. Karl Shuker: 'One of my colleagues here at the [palaeontology] department, Stig Walsh, is working on a Chilean bonebed, and consequently has spent a fair deal of time out there. Today he told me that he heard stories while there of an aquatic (river-dwelling) cat, apparently with flippers, called the Chongonga. We have a sketch and an authoritative source regarding this beast...Ever heard of it? I may have mentioned previously the phocid [seal lacking external ears] that was recently seen in Chile – it turned out to be an otariid [eared seal].'

It is feasible, if unlikely, that an ancestral felid could have adapted to an aquatic lifestyle through convergent evolution with seals by gaining robust flippers for both aquatic and terrestrial locomotion. The most likely hypothesis, however, is that the *Chongonga* might be a large unidentified pinniped (seals, sea lions, and their kin).

(Author's Verdict: 1/5)

Columbus' Ape-Faced Cat

The renowned Italian explorer and navigator, Cristoforo Colombo – better known as Christopher Columbus (b. 1451 – d. 1506) – embarked on four transatlantic voyages from Spain in 1492, 1493, 1498, and 1502 with the ambition of finding a direct sea route westward from Europe to Asia; however, he never succeeded in this endeavour. Unexpectedly, he encountered the Americas instead. Although he did not truly "discover" the "New World", as millions of people already lived there, nor was he even the first to sail there, as 500 years before Columbus, a daring band of Vikings led by Norse explorer Leif Eriksson, appropriately known as Leif the Lucky (b. 960 / 970 – d. 1018 / 1025) had set foot in North America and established a settlement. It was Columbus' journeys, however, that marked the beginning of centuries of exploration and colonisation of North and South America. On his fourth and final expedition, Columbus encountered an unusual animal which he deduced was a type of felid. It eventually became known as Columbus' Ape-Faced Cat and was described as a large aggressive cat with an ape-like face and a prehensile tail. One allegedly killed a peccary with only its foreleg and tail. Columbus sent an armed contingent into the interior of Costa Rica in 1502, and this odd-looking animal was supposedly captured.

"A crossbowman had wounded an animal, which appeared to be an ape, except that it was much larger and had the face of a man. The arrow had pierced it from the neck to the tail, and as a result, it was so fierce that it was necessary to cut off an arm and a leg. When the hog saw it, it bristled up and fled. When I saw this, I ordered the begare, as it is called there, to be thrown where the hog was; coming within reach, although it was on the point of death, and although the arrow was still in its body, it twisted its tail round the hog's snout and holding it very firmly, seized it by the nape of the neck and with its remaining hand struck it on the head, as if it were an enemy. This action was so novel and such a delightful sight that I have described it".

It has been suggested that "begare" was the native word for the peccary and not for the animal that Columbus was describing. The Central American spider monkey (*Ateles geoffroyi*) has a lengthy prehensile tail and is somewhat cat-like in form. It ranges from one to two feet in length and may be the biological basis for this feliform cryptid. The Costa Rican species is brown to silvery on its upper parts and lighter on its underside. When disturbed, it growls and acts threateningly; however, it is doubtful that this mainly frugivorous primate could kill a pig. The kinkajou (*Potos flavus*) is even more cat-like, possessing a prehensile tail, commonly found in Central American forests. It should also be noted that this relative of the raccoon is not aggressive. Herbert Wendt (b. 1914 – d. 1979), the German author of *From Ape to Adam: The Search for the Ancestry of Man*, proposed the notion of an extinct species of carnivorous cat. Columbus' original description of the creature did not allude to any characteristics associated with cats; rather he referred to it as a primate with an opposable tail and a face resembling that of a human, as opposed to a cat having simian characteristics.

Cooncat

Approximately five feet in length, the "Cooncat" is a mysterious creature that is purported to inhabit the northwestern part of the U.S. state of Georgia. This alleged feline displays characteristics of both raccoons and cats. A teenager claimed to have observed the creature while driving in a Dodge caravan on December 19th, 2003. He warned some of his friends, and one of them grabbed a camera phone. Unfortunately, just as they were about to take a photo, the Cooncat took off, up into some trees. However, the following day, the young man returned to the place of his observation and discovered four indistinct footprints that looked like they could have belonged to a cat or a raccoon. "It looked sorta like both", the young man later informed his family. "Sort of like a cat, the body, but the head was definitely not a cat. It was raccoon striped and broader than a normal cat's face."

The witness freely admitted that he might have been too far away to clearly see the "Cat-Coon", but that did not stop him from concluding that it was a new species. The Cooncat was observed once again by a different teenager only a few days later. "It was early morning, so I couldn't get a good look at it," she said. "But it's pretty hard to miss something that big, even in the fog. Looks like it had a coon's face and a cat's tail and body." The girl reported that she saw the animal sprint up the side of an old oak tree and disappear into the woods. She described it as having a brown body with black paws, a bushy brown tail adorned with white rings, and a broad, flat head resembling that of a raccoon, complete with its signature mask.

Sat Kalauk

The *sat-kalauk*, also referred to as Nabashing or the "Burmese Bloodsucker", is a feliform cryptid said to exist in the Mandalay Division and Kachin State of Myanmar (formerly Burma). It is reported to leap onto the necks of Sambar Deer (*Cervus unicolour*) and to suck their blood like a feline vampire. In 1954, a yellow-throated marten (*Martes flavigula*), an agile member of the Mustelidae family with a remarkable yellow throat patch, was reportedly captured near Myatkyin and identified by locals as a *sat-kalauk*.

Sunda Horned Cat

Native accounts collected by journalist and tiger conservationist Deborah Martyr (best known in cryptozoological circles for her personal sightings of the Sumatran cryptid, the alleged bipedal primate, the orang pendek) described the Sundanese Horned Cat as a small cat-like creature, about the size of a large domestic cat breed, from the islands of Alor and Solor, by the island of Flores in Southeast Asia. It is usually depicted as grey in colour, with a black and white banded tail, something like those of racoons or ring-tailed lemurs, with two strange stumpy projections on its head resembling small horns, each located just above the eyes. Also known as the Lesser Sunda Cat, it is often associated with legends of demonic cats and as such is not taken seriously by scientists or by most cryptozoologists. If this feliform cryptid does exist as a living flesh and blood species, it may not be a true cat at all, but perhaps evolved convergently with cats, sharing a similar ecological niche and evolving into a feline doppelganger – perhaps a civet or a cat-like marsupial.

Harimau jalor

Another Horizontally Striped Cat?

The *harimau jalor* (Malaysian: "striped tiger") is another feliform cryptid that is likely to be based on an optical illusion. They are said to be larger than the average tiger, with stripes reported to run horizontally across their body instead of the typical pattern of tigers.

(Author's Verdict: 2/5)

8

REPORTED SOCIAL BEHAVIOUR IN OTHERWISE HABITUALLY SOLITARY SPECIES

'Cats have it all — admiration, an endless sleep, and company only when they want it.'

— BY POET ROD MCKUEN (STANYAN STREET & OTHER SORROWS)

Named by Karl Shuker from specimens discovered near the hamlet of Kellas, located in Morayshire in the Scottish Highlands (not to be confused with Kellas in Angus, more than a hundred miles away on the other side of the Cairngorms), the **Kellas cat**, also known as the Black Beast of Moray, *Cat-Sìth*, and "Wangie Cat," gained media attention during the 1980s due to speculation that it might have been a new species or a species on the verge of speciation. By analysing their genetic makeup, it has been established that the true Kellas type is an introgressive hybrid between Scottish wildcats (*Felis silvestris silvestris,* syn. *Felis silvestris grampia*) and domestic cats (*Felis catus*). Whether or not the melanism comes from the native wildcat or the introduced domestic lineage is uncertain, as one specimen on record does appear to be a genuine melanistic wildcat. It was even suggested by some researchers that they might be the young of the black panthers reported by the Scottish media. Some of these ideas are still floating around the internet, as are many pictures of black domestic cats, labelled as "black panthers", which is a great shame because they muddy some genuinely intriguing evidence. What has rarely been remarked upon to any great extent, however, is the reported social hunting behaviour of the Kellas cats that has been documented over the years. For the most part, wildcats are solitary, living alone, except during mating or when females are raising their young. Kellas cats exhibit a dispersed social system, in which male territories are interconnected with one or more female territories. In areas where resources are abundant, these territories overlap to a greater extent than in areas where resources are less so.

It is extremely difficult to distinguish between solitary living and group living as the distinctions between the two are relatively artificial. This is because many species of animals who spend the majority of their life alone, at some point in their life, will join a group or engage in social behaviour. Examples of this occur when animals of the same species come together to mate, raise offspring, or exploit resources. There have been multiple different hypotheses proposed to explain how group living evolved in animals. Research shows that grouping habits may differ between individuals, and this tendency to group can be inherited. Research also shows that grouping tendency depends heavily on the interaction of certain genes, as well as experiences gained by an individual and the environmental conditions surrounding it. Other studies argue that the main driving force of the evolution of social grouping is phylogenetic inertia combined with ecological pressures. Has something occurred in Scotland over the last few thousand years to trigger this evolutionary adaptation? Evolution is a dynamic process, and Kellas cats may represent an emerging species triggered by hybridisation and environmental changes. They have been consistently reported to be social hunters, generally working together in pairs during daylight and they are good swimmers, which is unusual (but not unheard of) as most cats of the genus *Felis* have a natural aversion to water. Wildcats are not 'pack' animals but will sometimes form small social groups. When social groups are present, they tend to function optimally when the members have an existing familiarity and when there is minimal competition regarding food or other resources. Melanistic wildcats hunting in groups or pairs might have a particular advantage over the standard forms' preference for solitary hunting. Species that form groups through social interaction result in increased protection against predators, access to potential mates, and social information. Perhaps since Scotland's forests were depleted over a millennia ago, environmental changes and hybridisation with domestic cats have triggered the emergence of a new ecotype to develop, one in the very early stages of biological speciation, but nonetheless morphologically and behaviourally distinct. One might say it's evolution in action.

The **waracabra "tiger"**, also known as *warracaba*, is said to be similar in form to a regular jaguar; however, its size and colour vary greatly. Reports indicate that this feliform cryptid inhabits the mountains of Central-West Guyana, where one eyewitness described it as "slim and mouse-coloured" while another said it was "grey-coloured except for a small mark over the eyes." It is noteworthy for its pack-hunting behaviour, which, according to reports, can involve up to one hundred individuals dominating a territory. According to one eyewitness, packs consist of two large alpha and beta animals, whilst the rest are smaller subordinates. Another who found its spoor said it appeared the pack was "composed of animals of all sizes." Unlike the behaviour attributed to the Kellas cats, the waracabra tiger is said to be afraid of water, yet apparently shows no fear around fire. They live in the mountains during the rainy season, but during the dry season are said to descend to the lowlands driven by hunger. Włodzimierz Jędrzejewski *et.al* has presented data showing that, under certain conditions, male coalitions do occur in jaguar populations.

Factors that drive male coalitions in lions and cheetahs, but not in other species of large cats, have long remained unclear. The data shows that in jaguars, lions, and cheetahs, the concentration of females likely plays the most important role. In jaguars, the probability of male coalition occurrence is highest in populations with the smallest mean female home range size, while in lions, male group size is strongly correlated with female group size. Collaborative behaviours were likely not recorded before due to methodological limitations, such as the short duration of most camera trapping projects (Jędrzejewski *et al.* 2018). Although prior research (e.g. Cavalcanti and Gese 2009) and the recent study by Jędrzejewski *et.al* show that most male jaguars are solitary, and although collaborative or tolerant behaviours are relatively rare in jaguar populations, they can occur, but claims of packs of a hundred or more are probably greatly exaggerated.

The **Peruvian jungle wildcat** is reported from montane forests in Peru's Lower Rio Urubamba region. It is described as the size of a domestic cat, with a blotched pattern and noticeably long canines. Whereas the jaguar is typically a solitary hunter, the jungle wildcat is said to hunt small animals in packs of ten or more individuals; sometimes in the company of jaguars and ocelots. They are also said to vary considerably in size but are typically described as small cats with a blotched pattern and noticeably long fangs.

According to reports, the **social jungle cat**, or *tsere-yawá* (Shuar: "marmoset tiger") is a small, amphibious, cat-like creature with brown fur, measuring less than one meter in length, known to hunt in packs of eight to ten individuals. This feliform cryptid was first brought to cryptozoological attention by Angel Morant Fores. A man by the name of Christian Chumbi claimed to have observed eight *tsere-yawá* at a distance of approximately fifteen metres away near the Yukipa River. Confusing matters further, the social jungle cat, whatever it is, has also been described as *"a kind of tiger."* Karl Shuker has suggested the *tsere-yawá* reported from Ecuador may be the small-eared dog or *zorro* (*Atelocynus microtis*), which does vaguely resemble a cat but is also like a cross between a grey fox and a fossa. Its paws are partly webbed owing to its semi-aquatic habitat. It has also been noted by several cryptozoologists that descriptions of the social jungle cat resemble that of a bush dog in both appearance and alleged behaviour. Exaggerated accounts of larger than average jaguarundis have also been suggested, or an unknown social hunting species, perhaps closely related to the jaguarundi.

The social jungle cat might be a species of otter. Stories of packs of up to a hundred individuals are probably apocryphal and purely folkloric. Feliform cryptids of this type reported from Peru, may in fact be a smaller variety of the larger type reported from Guyana, or they may represent an extension of the Guyanese waracabra legend. Although they have been described as "a kind of tiger" the *tsere yawa* could be a new species of giant otter. Or a true felid convergently evolved with the otter as a top aquatic predator, potentially contributing to controlling prey species population sizes that help keep the river ecosystem in balance.

The *ndalawo* of East Africa, sometimes spelled *"ondurlarwo"* is said to be the size and shape of a leopard but with black fur on its back and grey on its flanks. It is very dangerous to humans and hunts together in packs of three or four, uttering a strange hyena-like laugh as they stalk the forests. The Accawoio Indians know and fear a creature they call **y'agamisheri**, which they claim varies greatly in both size and colour and that as many as a hundred individuals can make up a single pack. Is it possible that a pseudo-melanistic morph, having a disadvantage over the normal spotted variety, might behave differently as a response? Group living is sometimes confused with *collective animal behaviour.*

Collective animal behaviour is the interactions between individuals of a group that gives rise to social patterns. Group living, however, focuses on the long-term social interactions between individuals of a group and how animals have evolved from solitary living. There have been multiple different hypotheses proposed to explain how group living evolved in animals. Research shows that grouping habits may differ between individuals, and this tendency to group can be inherited. Research also shows that grouping tendency depends heavily on the interactions of genes, as well as experiences gained by an individual and the environmental conditions surrounding that individual. A key advantage to group living is the ability for individuals in a group to access information gained by other group members. This ability to share information can benefit many aspects of a group's success, such as increased foraging efficiency and increased defences against predators. Animals that are more closely related are more likely to share resources. Why are relatives more likely to be the recipients of altruistic acts than non-relatives? Individuals are far more likely to perform altruistic acts for siblings than for nephews, and even less likely for third cousins. The mechanism behind the effect of relatedness on altruism is kin selection.

Natural selection reflects how an individual passes on copies of their own genes through survival and reproduction, but kin selection reflects how copies of an individual's genes are passed down through the survival and reproduction of their relatives. Just as the principle of natural selection predicts that an individual will act to maximize their own fitness, the principle of kin selection predicts that an individual will act altruistically to maximize the fitness of their relatives. But there are limits to altruism. An individual's direct fitness is measured by copies of her own genes passed on to children, grandchildren, and so on, whereas indirect fitness is the measure of copies of genes passed on through non-descendant relatives such as cousins, nieces, nephews, and siblings. Selection will favour an altruistic act if the benefit of the act (in terms of indirect fitness) exceeds the cost of the act (in terms of direct fitness). When individuals are more closely related, they have a greater relatedness and altruism is more likely to occur. By conducting research into how organisms interact with their environment and how the environment is predictive of their survival and reproductive success, researchers are able to explain how social behaviour has evolved via the mechanism of natural selection.

CONCLUSIONS

'If the kind of creature being described in fact actually existed, it would be akin to when the astronauts first set foot on the moon!'

— PROF FRANK EUGENE POIRIER

What Are The Chances?

The point Professor Poirier was making when he voiced the above statement for a television special in 1990, that discovering the *yeren* or "Chinese wildman" would have a comparable impact on humanity to that of the first Apollo moon landing, is a valid one. What we can infer from the professor's statement is that prior to the historic Apollo 11 mission, it would have seemed considerably less likely for humans to take steps on the Moon (a heavenly body that has been in wonderment of humankind for over 200,000 years) than there is a reality to tales of the wildman. Neil Armstrong, the first astronaut to take a physical step onto the fine, dark grey, "talcum powder-like" dust on the surface of the Moon, estimated that their mission had a 50% chance of succeeding and roughly a 90% chance of all crew members safely returning to Earth. Despite this, many people around the world who followed its launch on television or radio would have likely found this to be an incredibly unbelievable prospect prior to the event.

If one were to travel back to the early years of the 1950s, before the start of the "space race", and ask a typical person on the street which was more likely: that prehistoric humans could be living unnoticed in some isolated corner of the world or that humans would eventually send a powerful rocket into outer space and effortlessly walk on the moon; it is likely they would view the former as the more realistic and less like science fiction. It is also safe to say that if a yeren were to be discovered living in an isolated, mountainous region of China, it would be the most remarkable zoological discovery of the 21st century – and perhaps of all time. The revelation that we are not alone and that we might have wild "cousins" living in some of the planet's last untouched wildernesses would have immense humanitarian, environmental, religious, political, and ecological implications. Such an event would undoubtedly bring about impacts so profound that they can only be imagined at this time. At the very least, such a discovery would compel us as a species to reevaluate what is important with respect to wide-scale habitat destruction, human (*Homo sapiens*) overpopulation, and biodiversity loss.

Professor Poirier was, however, overlooking one very simple fact – that despite the immense challenges and risks involved with successful interplanetary spaceflight, two Apollo 11 astronauts did indeed make history by walking on the moon. It required tremendous amounts of money and resources, which ultimately led to significant technological advancements; furthermore, the astronauts undertook tremendous risks with remarkable dedication and courage. Remarkably, despite all these obstacles, it eventually came to fruition. On July 1969, Neil Armstrong and Buzz Aldrin made history by taking "one small step for man, one giant leap for mankind" on the Moon, and to this day, ten more American astronauts have followed in their footsteps, experiencing the weaker – approx. 1.62 m/s^2 surface gravity on the gravely desolate, but undeniably beautiful surface of the Moon. Unfortunately, the two things cryptozoology doesn't have is unlimited amounts of money and resources. Cryptozoologists are not provided with any officially-approved government funding, and with the alarming rate of climate change as well as the damaging environmental consequences of deforestation and desertification, there is likely little time remaining to locate them and take action. In fact, it could be argued that the time to act is now before it's too late.

The Cenozoic Era saw the emergence of cat-like mammals as opposed to the big cats that we are familiar with today. The Island Continents had cat-like, or cat, analogue species that were more similar to marsupials than actual big cats and, according to cryptozoological evidence, this group may survive in parts of Australia and New Guinea, as the Queensland marsupial tiger and moolah respectively. The Prehistoric big cats or true big cats, such as the sabretooth were next in line but according to conventional wisdom were rendered extinct at least 10,000 years ago. Or were they? The "water tigers" reported from South American rivers, particularly in Guyana, Suriname, French Guiana, and north-west Brazil, distinguished by their prominent canines, are usually speculated to be a species of amphibious sabre-toothed cat, although other theories posit that they may be otters or thylacosmilid sparassodonts. The water "lions", water "leopards", or jungle "walruses" reported from rivers and wetlands across tropical Africa, particularly in the Central African Republic, are also regarded to be living sabretooths. The May 1994 report from the Shennongjia region of China's northwestern Hubei Province might have been similar, and now there is fossil evidence to support the claim. In 2021, for the first time, archaeologists discovered part of a fossil of a sabre-tooth in China. This important finding helps to explain the big cat's migration worldwide. Details were published in the international palaeontology journal *Historical Biology*. The discovery concerned a section of the jaw, described as the "mandibular horizontal branch with buccal teeth." There were many types of sabre-toothed cats, but scientists believe the jawbone found in China most likely evolved from the European sabre-toothed "tiger".

Reports detailing unusual variants, e.g. melanistic lions or adult lions with spots, and alleged little-known varieties of cheetah, like the woolly and Qattara cheetahs are relatively common, as are striped or otherwise unusually marked leopards. These are all staples of the feliform cryptozoology of Africa; of them, the least likely to exist as living biological species are, at least in my opinion, the alleged surviving sabre-toothed types. When the original sources are scrutinised and the accounts that relate to them, it becomes clear they are not reliable and are in fact rather poor in terms of data quality. They are certainly not strong enough to be realistically considered descriptions of unknown animals. It is possible that Africa's anomalous lions, particularly the spotted variety such as the *marozi*, could be a newly-emerging subspecies that fill an unoccupied ecological niche. Cryptids do not require verification as new species to be of merit to scientific research; they merely need to be unique and officially undocumented by science, which can occur at any level, not just that of species. The potential discovery of unconfirmed colour morphs is sufficiently valid as cryptozoological, as are undocumented cheetah forms. They inspire the same level of awe regardless of their taxonomy. Does it really matter whether the Maltese tigers of China's Fujian Province are shown to be a strange new species of blue tiger, or if they are a hitherto undocumented colour morph? Of course, it doesn't, what truly matters is they are real animals and they are blue (or rather smokey-grey).

Hybridisation between lions and cheetahs is extremely unlikely, however, lion x leopard hybrids are known in captivity. Male leopard and female lion hybrids are generally referred to as leopons and are very rare indeed. Whereas a lipard or liard is the proper term for a hybrid of a male lion with a leopardess. These are even rarer and are sometimes known as reverse leopons. But could these bizarre-looking hybrid cats occur in nature without human involvement? Firstly, the problem is structural, namely, the size difference between a male lion and a leopardess usually makes their mating difficult. Aggression is also likely to occur, usually resulting in the smaller animal being injured or even killed. But no matter how unlikely it may be, such an occurrence is not impossible in nature. If it does happen though, the possibility of rearing hybrid offspring into adulthood is slim. Given the aggressive coupling often carried out by large cats under normal circumstances, the possibility of this happening occasionally in nature is still a viable hypothesis. Even if these specimens are likely sterile, they would only need to have been encountered once and observed by someone for the stories to have originated. However, alleged crosses between lions and leopards may be suppositional on the part of the local people and simply a way of describing something.

Reports of African tigers are probably either misidentified leopards whose spots have merged into stripes or they could be the living descendants of tigers that were introduced to Africa in the past. It is also possible that reports are based on introduced tigers that have since disappeared and are now only present in folklore. The common usage of the word for tiger in Africa does point to the possibility that if this occurred it did so a very long time ago. There is no fossil evidence to suggest there have ever been tigers in Africa. This is surprising to many as part of the Felidae family of cats' ancestors of tigers originated in Africa. Even though both tigers and lions did at one time co-exist in Asia, the chances that a variety of tigers have evolved independently in Africa along with lions and yet somehow remained undetected by science is, shall we say, dubious. Finally, the palaeo felids were recognised as a ghost species that developed parallel to cats, but they too, are now officially extinct.

As the Earth changed and landmasses emerged, it also caused water levels to rise and fall resulting in cats moving with the changes and evolving into new and better-adapted species. The *Panthera* were the first to appear while *Felis silvestris lybica*, the ancestor of the domestic cat appeared last. The Bering land bridge was crucial for cats to migrate from Asia to North America and later, it was seen that cats of

American ancestry returned to Asia. The Alaskan "tiger" may be a previously unidentified species or subspecies of tiger that potentially made this migration. It was claimed in 2016 that an Amur tiger had been sighted in Alaska and that it had walked from Russia to the United States using the Bering Strait pass during winter. Unsurprisingly this was revealed as an April Fool's joke. A common misconception is that the Bering Strait freezes in the wintertime and it is easy to walk across the ice. In reality, there is a strong current flowing north through the strait which usually creates large channels of open water. On occasion, these open channels become clogged with moving chunks of pan ice, so it is theoretically possible to jump from chunk to chunk, along with some swimming across the open. There is, however, no tangible evidence of true tigers in America, yet if there are unknown tigers in Alaska, they have been there for a very long time.

Their innate territorial tendencies and instinct to track and ambush prey allowed cats to spread across vast distances, giving rise to a range of sizes, colours, and coat patterns that better enabled their ambush-hunting strategies. The cheetah is regarded as one of the earliest divergences in felid evolution, occurring around 8.5 million years ago. The officially extinct *Acinonyx pardinensis*, a larger species than today's cheetah, moved from North America to Asia, Europe, and Africa, but is it possible that the species did not entirely die out in North America and lives on as the Tennessee Red Cheetah? The large feliform cryptids reported from North America are typically thought to be remnant populations of jaguars; lithe, cougar-like cats; cougars still inhabiting the eastern states; an alleged native tiger species, and "maned lions."

Of these, the latter is perhaps the most perplexing. It is highly unlikely that any breeding populations of authentic African lions are living anywhere in the United States. Lions (*P. leo*) inhabit grasslands, savannas, and shrublands – all open areas perfect for their hunting strategies and social behaviour. Lions are the most social of all felid species, living in groups or 'prides' of related members with their offspring. The average pride consists of around fifteen lions, including four males and several adult females and their cubs of both sexes. Large prides, consisting of up to thirty individuals, have been recorded. The sole exception to this pattern is the *Tsavo lions* which appear to have just one or two adult males per pride. Usually, lions are more diurnal than other wild cats, but when persecuted, will quickly adapt to being active at night and during twilight hours. They also have the loudest roar of all big cats, so loud it can reach 114 decibels and can be heard from as far away as five miles due in part to the shape of the larynx, but also because of their open habitat. Lions spend much of their time resting and are inactive for about twenty hours a day.

Although they can be active at any time, their movements generally peak after dusk with a period of socialising, grooming, and defecating. Intermittent bursts of activity continue until dawn when hunting most often takes place. They spend an average of two hours a day walking and about an hour eating. Lions are easily detectable and would be unlikely to occur in significant numbers in the United States. There is no confirmed evidence of true lions in America, but there is ample circumstantial and testimonial evidence that suggests otherwise. Individual escapees or illegal releases seem to be the most likely scenarios. Whatever they are, a suitable solution needs to be determined because many honest people are certainly seeing something. The most surprising element of the American Maned Lions is their vast ranges throughout much of North America, especially in the eastern states.

Reports come from Dierks and Dover in Arkansas. El Toro, Fremont, and Lake County, California. Loxahatchee, Florida. Alapaha, and Berrien County, Georgia. Centralia, Decatur, Joliet, Peoria County, Piatt County, Rockford, Roscoe, Will County, and Winnebago County, Illinois. Abington, Elkhorn Falls, and Warrick County, Indiana. Muscatine, and Wapello, Iowa. Penobscot County, Maine. Cross Timbers, Missouri. Ceresco, Surprise, and Waterloo, Nebraska. Gagetown, and McAdam, New Brunswick, Canada. North Brunswick, New

Jersey. Rutherfordton, North Carolina. Clinton County, Dodson Township, Geauga County, Groesbeck, Hillsboro, Lorain County, Mentor, Miami Township, Morning Sun, North Avondale, North Olmsted, and Springboro, Ohio. Craig County, Rogers County, and Vinta, Oklahoma. Kapuskasing, Ontario, Canada. Bald Eagle Mountain, Clinton County, Jackson, Lackawanna County, Newton Township, Nicholson, Pike County, Susquehanna County, and Wyoming County, Pennsylvania. Fort Worth, Texas. Spokane, Tacoma, Washington. And West Marlinton, West Virginia.

As I said before, with reports coming from such a wide geographic area, I think it's safe to say that people are seeing something, but whether these reports are of bona fide African lions living undetected in North America remains to be seen. Despite the eastern cougar being thought to have gone extinct from the north-eastern United States over a century ago, reports of sightings have continued; however, none of these has been verified as belonging to the eastern cougar subspecies. Therefore, their current conservation status remains as extinct. It is debated among cryptozoologists whether or not the eastern cougar still exists, especially since their western cousins may be expanding their range eastward. Some are of the opinion that the puma-like *onza* might be a surviving species of the American cheetah (*Miracinonyx*), which was more closely related to pumas than modern cheetahs. Officially *Miracinonyx* went extinct with other Pleistocene megafauna around 12,000 years ago. Many locals hold the belief that *onzas* are jaguar x puma hybrids, though specimens collected and purported to be *onzas* demonstrate very few, if any, characteristics of a jaguar. Some claim that the *onza* is a new species closely related to the puma. It is, however, more likely that *onzas* are simply large-statured, and emaciated, but otherwise are normal pumas adapted to their particular environment.

The Tinicum cat, reported from the rocky and wooded hills of Bucks and Fayette Counties in Pennsylvania, as well as in southern Illinois, has been suggested by some to be a hybrid between bobcats (*Lynx rufus*) and feral domestic cats (*Felis silvestris catus*). There are reports of bobcats breeding with domestic cats, but evidence of offspring remains unconfirmed. A long-established regional phenotype of a feral cat population is perhaps a more likely explanation.

Reports from South and Central America describe "water tigers", unusually large melanistic jaguars, unconfirmed colour variants of the jaguar, oversized otter-like "cats", huge puma-like creatures, two supposedly novel jaguar species, unidentified pack-hunting "big cats" reported from Ecuador, and what are probably striped jaguars displaying a mutation.

The genus *Felis* split from the rest of the Felidae family around 3.4 million years ago. The domestic cat came about by artificial selection, whereas the *Felis* species evolved through sympatric or incipient parapatric speciation alongside humans as pest-controlling companions. As I mentioned at the beginning of this book's introduction, cats are incredibly elusive and naturally mysterious, making them perhaps the perfect cryptids. They are nocturnal predators that will, at times, actively hunt our species and this alone makes them rather "monstrous".

While a living hominid would be immensely significant with regard to our evolution, it must be said that discovering new species of cats would be considerably less astonishing. It would, however, be invaluable data for mammal conservation. Asia is a promising continent for possible new felid species, subspecies, and feline enigmas. Asian reports of large feliform cryptids describe surviving tiger populations of formally extinct types, such as the Bali tiger (*Panthera tigris balica*), Javan tiger (*Felis tigris sondaicus+*), and the Caspian tiger (*P. tigris virgata*); as well as unconfirmed colour variants of tiger, cheetah and leopard. Supposedly surviving Javan leopards; unconfirmed tigers reported from Borneo; a large, slope-backed, hyena-like animal with a ruffed neck; alleged tiger x leopard hybrids; and tigers with anomalous markings or even with no markings at all.

The zoo-folklore of Asia (at least that told to visiting foreigners) is less concerned with prehistoric species and has more to do with recognisable animals. Species that went extinct in the last one hundred years (Type 2b) offer a much greater opportunity for rediscovery than species that are documented only through fossils. Of the three extinct tigers discussed, the Javan variety is the least likely to be rediscovered. This is mainly due to Java's status as the world's most populous island – making up 55% of Indonesia's population and devastating deforesting projects. Originally Java supported rich biodiversity, where numbers of endemic species flourished, such as the Javan rhinoceros, banteng, warty pig, hawk-eagle, silvery gibbon, mousedeer; and of course, the leopard, and tiger.

Today, several national parks exist in Java that protect the remnants of its fragile wildlife, such as Ujung Kulon, Mount Halimun-Salak, Gede Pangrango, Baluran, Meru Betiri, Bromo Tengger Semeru, and Alas Purwo. The Javan leopard probably has a better chance of survival than the tiger. The Bali tiger might fare a little better, as forest reserves still cover some 125,000 hectares on the island, or about 21% of its total surface area, whereas the island of Java is 131,412 km², but only 18,755 km² (14%) remains forested. The Caspian tiger might have the best chance. Not isolated to islands, its range extended from eastern Turkey, northern Iran, Mesopotamia, the Caucasus around the Caspian Sea, and from central Asia to northern Afghanistan and the Xinjiang region of western China. Until the Middle Ages, it was also found in Ukraine and southern Russia. There are a few places left that remain isolated enough to have remnant tiger populations. With a colossal area of 427,500 km² (165,100 square miles), Borneo is the third-largest island in the world and the largest in Asia; and with rainforest estimated to be around 140,000,000 years old, it is one of the oldest rainforests in the world. Borneo is the centre of the evolution and distribution of many endemic species of plants and animals, and its rainforest are some of the few remaining natural habitats for the endangered Bornean orangutan. Borneo is an important refuge for many endemic forest species, including the Borneo elephant, the Asian two-horned rhinoceros, the Bornean clouded leopard, and Hose's palm civet. Having mounted an expedition to the island in

2013, there is little doubt in my mind that some parts of Borneo are large, wild, and underpopulated enough to have a native tiger remain hidden.

The Sumatrans claim to see *cigaus* near the market town of Bangko in Jambi Province and Mount Kerinci in West Sumatra. These provinces, where new and exciting species are still discovered, give the *cigau* a significantly higher probability of being a real animal than many other feliform cryptids reported from Asia. Based on my teams' 2022 investigation, the little-known *harimau tingkiah* seems to represent a hitherto undocumented range extension by the Sumatran tiger. By examining anecdotal evidence of a profoundly folkloric nature, we eventually uncovered an unrecorded population of Sumatran tigers, perfectly illustrating the advantages of an analytical cryptozoological approach.

The British Situation With Regard To 'ABCs'

Sightings describing unknown medium-size cats are often compared to the lynx, particularly those reported from the United Kingdom. The most famous historical case is that of William Cobbett. While unlikely, the possibility of late surviving British lynx is a still viable theory, however, the cat observed by Cobbett is more likely to have escaped from a private collection.

The asymmetry of Monty Bell Jr.'s discovery in the Forest of Dean, along with the lack of claw marks and what appears to be a faint three-lobed plantar pad, all hint that an average-sized felid species is responsible. We can see signs of the skeletal structure of the animal's foot, which is consistent with that of a felid. Moreover, there is an obvious canine track positioned slightly to the right of the mystery track. A number of significant interested parties feel this track is more likely feline than canine in origin, even though the different enthusiasts, experts, academics, and professionals questioned had some contrasting observations.

In my original paper, I suggested that an individual, or possibly one or more members of an illegally run "rewilding" organisation, have released lynxes (or at least lynx-sized felids of unknown species) into the Forest of Dean perhaps in an attempt to control deer or fox numbers. Once resident in Scotland, the lynx is thought to have gone extinct in the UK during the medieval period around 1,300 years ago. But could they have survived somewhere in the British Isles? Well, it's possible, but I doubt it. What's more plausible is they are escaped or illegally released animals and/or the descendants of those animals. A feral population of lynx, with their minimal range requirements, smaller size, elusive nature, and crepuscular hunting habits, would be one of the more suitable felid species, or even groups of closely related species, to survive undetected in British forests. Given that felids are by nature highly secretive animals that generally operate during hours when we are forced by physiology to be largely inactive, the likelihood of uncovering new species is actually reasonably high, particularly if they inhabit remote wildernesses and/or distinct geographic regions.

As we have already touched upon, the widely-accepted theory is that the British big cats are the progeny of felids that were released from private collections when the *Dangerous Wild Animals Act* was enforced in 1976, requiring costly licensing for big cats. In the 1970s, purchasing a big cat was relatively inexpensive. For example, a zoo-bred puma or lion cub could cost as little as £20. However, black panthers have always been highly sought after and thus more costly. In 1976, when the *DWAA* began (it was later updated in 2010), anyone who owned a melanistic leopard could have sold it for at least £500, which at the time was roughly the cost of a decent car and is the equivalent of approximately £8000 today. It is reasonable to assume that if the owner of a menagerie had for whatever reason decided to release some of their big cats, they would likely have released the cheaper common pumas, or ordinary spotted leopards into the wild while keeping the valuable and highly sort after "black panther" to sell on. And yet, if the present sightings statistics are anything to go by, it appears the opposite occurred. Of course, it is possible that some might have escaped, but what is certain is that the *DWAA* had a significant impact on the situation, as there was a major increase in the number of reports around that time. It is difficult to judge how much of this increase was due to newly released animals, and how much to increased publicity encouraging people to come forward with their sightings of big cats already living wild in Britain. Big cats were being reported long before 1976, though the records are, by comparison to today, relatively few and far between.

Approximately 25% of sightings logged in the UK each year are of animals broadly resembling brown or fawn-coloured cougars, and lynx about 5%, but a staggering 70% of sightings describe black panther-like animals, and yet, among the thousands of big cats reported over the past sixty years or so, reports of normal spotted leopards are suspiciously rare, some might even say absent. Perhaps the answer is simple. Isolated populations with very low genetic diversity can produce spontaneous melanistic individuals. Melanism is recessive in leopards, meaning that two spotted leopards carrying the gene may produce black cubs, but will breed true when paired together. Genetic drift is more prevalent in small isolated populations with otherwise hidden mutant gene alleles expressing themselves. Spontaneous mutation will be more apparent in these populations, whereas, in larger populations, it will largely be masked. In other words, the presence of black leopards in Britain, as opposed to reports of the normal spotted variety, is perhaps evidence of low genetic diversity among isolated populations.

Another popular theory regarding the origin of these big cats is they may have escaped from zoos, circuses, or menageries in the past and bred in the wild. Travelling menageries were popular attractions in the 19th and 20th centuries. The *Exeter Flying Post* of 1806 described one which visited Weymouth as displaying an adult Bengal tiger that *"devoured a whole bullock's head, horns and all"*, a lion and lioness, leopards (both "panthers" and the normal spotted variety), a hyena, a lynx, an ostrich, and a kangaroo.

In 1868, five leopards escaped from their enclosures while being transported between Lockerbie and Moffat in Scotland. These were later recaptured. *Felicity the puma* is often cited as evidence that large non-native felids are living in the UK. Others, however, claim that her capture was a hoax. What is almost certain is that she was a pet who had either escaped or had been recently released as she was quite tame. Additional support came from Dr. Hans Kruuk of the *Institute of Terrestrial Ecology* at Banchory, who analysed faeces from Felicity collected during her first hours in captivity which showed that she had recently fed on deer, rabbit, and sheep, suggesting that in spite of her advanced age and docility, she had actually been hunting and surviving in the wild for some time, perhaps two or three months. After her capture, Felicity was kept for some time at the *Highland Wildlife Park* where she became something of a celebrity. When she eventually died in 1985, she was preserved by a taxidermist who was given specific instructions not to taxiderm her in an aggressive posture, as she was not at all ill-tempered while held in captivity. This request would have no doubt pleased the taxidermist as it is far more difficult to sculpt the folds and creases of a snarl out of clay.

Felicity can be viewed in the *Inverness Museum and Art Gallery*. Dismissing this case as potential evidence completely misses the point, as in my view; most, if not all, of these big cats, like Felicity, are either escapees from captivity or they have been illegally released. I am not suggesting that breeding has never occurred, quite the contrary in fact, but I doubt whether the British population is predominantly sustained that way, i.e. one wild-born big cat breeding with another big cat also born in the wild, and producing viable offspring; so on and so forth. It was rumoured that in 1993, yet another puma was captured in Scotland, this time in the Aviemore area in the Cairngorms National Park. The 2019 case of a panther filmed prowling the rooftops of a northern French town is a good example of how these big cats can potentially end up wild if they are not recaptured quickly. Most are illegal pets, purchased by irrespon-sible owners, which then get dumped or escape from inadequate enclosures and occasionally survive in the wild. There are conflicting reports of DNA evidence confirming the existence of big cats in Britain. In 2011, it was announced by the *Centre for Fortean Zoology* that DNA testing, carried out by *Durham University* on hairs discovered in rural north Devon showed that a leopard of sub-Saharan origin was living in the area. In 2012, DNA testing of two deer carcasses found in Gloucestershire revealed only fox DNA, despite local reports of sightings and assertions that the deer had been preyed upon by a large cat. In 2022, myself and the team from *Dragon Fly Films* found leopard hairs snagged on a barbed wire fence in Gloucestershire. These were then studied by geneticists and DNA sequencing confirmed the findings in May 2023.

For centuries, the legend of the Black Dog has been part of British folklore. They are described as large black hell-hounds seen in remote areas but with no tangible evidence of their existence beyond rumours and folklore. Some have argued that stories about big black cats in Britain are simply updated versions of these earlier myths, retaining similar elements but now rooted in theories such as escaped or released animals instead of supernatural forces. In addition, stories of big cats are popular in the tabloid press, leading to their wide exposure and rapid dissemination. This almost certainly accounts for a percentage of reports, but I believe, or rather, I presume, based on the available evidence, there is biological truth hidden beneath the folklore, mistaken observations and hoaxes. Sighting of big cats on farmland and quiet country lanes is one thing, but sightings in and around large towns and cities are a different matter altogether. Escaped leopards, pumas, and lynx, once fully wild, will instinctively avoid these built-up places unless they have no other choice. In India, where leopards are becoming more audacious and entering towns and cities to hunt domestic animals during the night, it should be remembered that these locations generally sit on territories previously used by these species for many thousands of years. Human populations are at an all-time high and leopard numbers have never been so low. The cause of this is clear and the unusual behaviour we're observing in areas where these animals naturally occur speaks to how far human intrusion is pushing these typically elusive animals to adjust their behaviours in order to cope with the unnatural situation. It would not be impossible for a big cat to find itself in a built-up area. But that animal, if it fails to learn to avoid all human activities, will be quickly recaptured or terminated. As we have seen, this has happened a few times and is actually one of the better lines of evidence for big cats in Britain.

I speculate that some breeding has taken place in Britain, and there is some evidence to support this, but it is highly unlikely that the population is maintained solely through encounters with wild-born individuals. So where do they come from? One cannot keep pointing fingers at zoos (although I still believe that some privately-run facilities pose a genuine issue) since they are now obliged to abide by exceptionally strict regulations just to stay operational; they would never risk their standing with the relevant authorities by failing to report an escapee, particularly when it is a dangerous apex predator. The pet trade, both legal and illegal, is the only other serious explanation. There are various pieces of film footage and photographs that show animals resembling big cats, but so far there is very little detailed enough to conclusively establish what species they might be. One of the best photos was taken by Tara-Leigh Eggiman and two of her colleagues who witnessed a big cat at Burton Bradstock in November 2006. They were about two hundred yards away and estimated it was approximately three feet long, excluding the tail.

It Is feasible that large non-native felids exist in Britain, supplemented by continuous illegal releases and escapees from private collections which could potentially add to the gene pool. There is some evidence of breeding, resulting in what are likely genuine observations of cubs alongside an adult. Nevertheless, the British population is likely primarily the result of escapes and illegal releases. And the actual number will be significantly lower than some researchers and the media claim. Eyewitnesses generally describe these animals as being about the size of a Labrador dog, with low, slender bodies and long, curved tails. The biggest issue I have regarding the British situation is the sheer volume of reports and the unfortunate, undeniable lack of solid corresponding evidence for them.

The media and some so-called experts would have us believe there are literally thousands of these big cats and that they are thriving in every county; not just in England, but all over the United Kingdom and Northern Ireland. The most reported species, as we have already noted, is the melanistic colour variant of the leopard commonly known as the "black panther", yet it is difficult to ignore that this species actually has the least tangible evidence in its favour, except, of course, when it comes to eyewitness reports, which are evidently plentiful. With regard to leopards, two genotypes ("AA" and "Aa") express the dominant phenotype of normal colouring while the "aa" genotype expresses the recessive phenotype of black colouring.

This means that two spotted leopards carrying the gene may produce black cubs, but will breed true when paired together. Jaguars, on the other hand, express melanism due to the dominant allele of a gene but this dominance does not increase the frequency of black jaguars observed in their natural habitat. It's accepted that melanism in both jaguars and leopards is expressed in about 10% of each population. Environmental conditions do not directly impact the expression of melanism as it is a purely genetic-driven trait. It does, however, impact the success of melanistic individuals via natural selection, which impacts the frequency of those genes in any given population.

This non-random distribution of the melanistic trait suggests there is likely some sort of adaptive selection occurring. In some environments, having black colouring can be either helpful or harmful to that species' survival and reproduction. For instance, melanistic cats are more common in humid forests, for example in Malaysia, which suggests an adaptive advantage in these environments, perhaps related to thermoregulation or some other physiological characteristic. In contrast, more open habitats, such as regions of Africa and

China, show almost no presence of melanism, which we might theorise is due to natural selection where melanistic individuals are less adapted to those habitats and so do not pass on their genes as frequently as normally patterned individuals do.

Melanistic forms for both jaguars and leopards are more likely to be found in moist forests. For example, black leopards have been documented in Southeast Asia, but not in Central Asia or China. Similar data has been recorded for jaguars, with more melanistic forms observed in dense forest habitats, but not in the more open or temperate forests of the Americas. I think, given that the jaguar is less suited to the British climate, it is best to focus on the leopard as the primary explanation for sightings of "big black cats". Leopards inhabit a variety of terrain. They are most populous in mesic woodlands, grassland savannas, and forests. They also occupy mountain, shrub, and desert habitats, but prefer trees throughout their range and have been recorded from Tanzania's 5,638-meter dormant volcano Mount Kilimanjaro. They can therefore live quite happily in both warm and cold climates.

The climate in the United Kingdom is defined as a humid temperate oceanic climate, which it shares with most of northwest Europe. Regional climates are influenced by the Atlantic Ocean and latitude. Northern Ireland, Wales, and western parts of England and Scotland, being closest to the Atlantic Ocean are generally the mildest, wettest, and windiest regions of the UK, where temperatures are seldom extreme. Eastern areas are drier, cooler, and less windy, and also experience the greatest daily and seasonal temperature variations. Northern areas are generally cooler and wetter and have slightly greater temperature ranges than southern areas, which are generally warmer and drier. The UK is mostly under the influence of the maritime polar air mass from the northwest.

Carl Marshall meets Felicity the Puma 1.

Carl Marshall meets Felicity the Puma 2.

Felicity 1.

Felicity 2.

Northern Ireland and the west of Scotland are the most exposed to the maritime polar air mass which brings cool moist air; the east of Scotland and north-east England are more exposed to the continental polar air mass which brings cold dry air. The south and south-east of England are the least exposed to polar air masses from the north-west, and on occasion see continental tropical air masses from the south, which bring warm dry air in the summer. On average, the temperature ranges from 18 to 25 °C (64 to 77 °F) which at the low end is a little on the cool side, but nonetheless is quite suitable for both leopard and cougar. It is even possible that there is an adaptive advantage to the melanistic trait in Britain's cool and humid environment, perhaps when it comes to thermoregulation and camouflage in a damp forested habitat. Dark colours absorb more radiated heat from the sunlight while lighter colours reflect it. That's why wearing a black shirt on a sunny day makes you feel warmer than when you're wearing a white shirt. Therefore, not only are black animals harder to see, especially at night, but being black might actually give them a slight thermoregulatory advantage.

Population Sizes

Can it really be true that there are thousands of big cats living wild in Britain, yet without leaving strong evidence of their presence in such numbers? To put it plainly, the answer is no. In the National Parks of Kenya there is approximately one leopard in every ten square kilometres of territory, whereas in the UK, I would expect it to be somewhere closer to one in every five hundred square kilometres. This isn't many, somewhere between 50 and 150: both pumas and leopards, occurring largely unnoticed in the British countryside. This, along with their extensive territories and highly elusive lifestyles means the chance of finding a big cat in Britain is very slim indeed and substantiates their existence remaining unproven. It is also safe to assume that many of the reports are triggered by honest misidentifications on the part of the witnesses. A fleeting glimpse of a dark-coloured animal in a lay-by, or slinking along a dark woodland path, does not constitute viable evidence, at least not in the eyes of scientists. And then, of course, we cannot ignore the inevitable hoaxes that also come in, often unnoticed, and fairly frequently. If we simply accept all reports at face value, then it might seem like there are thousands or at least many hundreds of these animals. This cannot be the case, or we would already have better evidence of their long-term presence. After all, this is Britain, not Canada!

The problem is there is no filter to the reports made each year, throughout the country. Once the media announces the presence of a big cat, especially one with a cool-sounding regional name, that's it... in the eyes of the public, it becomes set in stone, no matter how strong the original report[s] may have been. When the problem is then explored analytically and we ask important questions like, what are their primary prey types? Or why don't they behave as they do in their countries of origin? Such as arboreal caching behaviour (in fact, this has occurred, though it is rarely reported, yet when it is, it provides better quality evidence). At best, we are uncertain and, at worst, totally lost due to inadequate data.

Their existence remains unproven due to:

- *Low population densities.*
- *Surveillance of very large, sometimes overlapping territories.*
- *Insufficient data to form testable theories.*
- *The preconceptions of observers in the case of misidentifications.*
- *Lack of acknowledgement by relevant academics.*
- *Credulity and lack of knowledge by some so-called experts.*
- *Lack of a peer-reviewed system, clearing unreliable non-testimonial data.*
- *The confusion caused by false or unreliable information published by the media.*
- *Insufficient time and funds for practical fieldwork.*
- *Lack of unanimity among professional researchers.*
- *Human error.*

Indeed, as already mentioned, evidence for the existence of big cats in Britain is rather limited, that is, other than eyewitness accounts. The strongest evidence thus far is the few biological samples that have been collected, analysed, and confirmed.

The cougar arguably has the best evidence for its presence in Britain, at least at one time. *Felicity the Puma* and the more recent case in France, are both good examples of big cats that hadn't fully "rewilded". The juvenile panther captured alive in France and then stolen a few days later had only been free for a day and as such hadn't had an opportunity to adjust to, or even come close to finding a natural habitat; unfortunately, being situated in the worst possible place, in the centre of a bustling city during daylight hours.

The decomposing remains of another cougar were discovered by hikers in 1985 in a remote area, and another was reported to have been shot and killed by police near Greenwich Observatory in 1987. The species with the best physical evidence of its presence in Britain is the lynx (*Lynx sp.*). In 1926, three large, fierce, yellowish animals of unknown species were shot or trapped following a spate of attacks on sheep. Subsequently, they were identified as lynx. After being stored for a short time in the farmer's freezer, one was then sold to a local game dealer, who had it preserved by a taxidermist and then sold it on to a local collector, who now apparently has it on display at their home.

On February 18th, 1996, a second lynx was shot dead by an RUC marksman near the village of Fintona in Northern Ireland. The shooting followed reports over several days of a "young lion" roaming the area. The lynx was believed to have escaped from a private collection. Another lynx was discovered in London in 2001 following a witness report of a leopard resting on a garden wall. Thankfully, this lynx, a female, was captured alive this time after being sedated by a vet with a dart and blowpipe and was later taken to *London Zoo* where she was treated for a minor paw injury. She was later affectionately given the name *Lara the Lynx*. A lynx, this time a museum specimen (probably a Canadian lynx, *Lynx canadensis* despite its tiny feet) was discovered in 2013 by Dr. Max Blake, then a PhD student at the *Institute of Biological, Environmental, and Rural Sciences* (IBERS) at Aberystwyth University, incorrectly labelled in the bowels of the *Bristol Museum and Art Gallery*. This discovery provides further evidence for dismissing the popular view that species such as the lynx, only entered the UK countryside following the introduction of the *Dangerous Wild Animals Act* of 1976. Whereas feral lynx, along with cougars and leopards, may have been living in the wilds of Britain much earlier, again due to escapees and deliberate releases. In 2006, a lynx was captured on CCTV prowling an industrial estate in Evesham, Worcestershire. A security guard at Unipart in Shinehill Lane reported seeing the animal and stated that this was the third sighting he had observed on the property. Sadly *Lilith the Lynx*, who escaped from *Borth Wild Animal Kingdom* in 2017, and was subsequently shot dead, was linked to the killing of eight sheep on farmland neighbouring the zoo.

There are other confirmed cases of escapes, kills, and captures involving non-native felids in the UK. Compared with the large territories of both leopards and pumas (especially the latter) which are known to be highly adaptive and can be found in a very large variety of habitats, including forests, tropical rainforests, grasslands, and even arid desert regions, whereas the ranges required by wild lynx can be as little as twenty square kilometres.

Final Thoughts

We must discover if we are to project. Bernard Heuvelmans famously stated in his classic *On the Track of Unknown Animals*, that *"the great days of zoology are not done"* and this is certainly true. We have already seen, despite popular belief, that the inventory of the world's species is far from complete. Recent mathematical modelling estimates that a minimum of 160 terrestrial mammal species and an astronomical 3,050 amphibian species have yet to be identified and described by science. Unfortunately, there is also the possibility that many of these undiscovered species will perish before they can be documented – a phenomenon known as "crypto-extinction". If all wild cat species went extinct tomorrow, it would be like losing the top 10% of their ecological pyramid of numbers, biomass, and energy. Also, many other species of animals that were the prey of these cats would over-populate, and in turn, the species they hunt would be in danger of extinction. So, in the context of worldwide biodiversity loss, wildlife biologists and conservationists focus their efforts on protecting the numerous endangered species that we know to exist. Why waste time and resources contemplating and searching for unknown or hidden animals?

It should be noted that cryptozoology evolved alongside and even partly inspired conservation biology. While there are strong grounds in terms of ecological and empirical data to be cautious when crediting the existence of certain "unknown animals", conservationists should not dismiss the subject totally out of hand, as the study of cryptozoology can and has contributed to conservation biology. Conservationists work hard to protect and maintain known flora and fauna – but it is not always acknowledged just how many species remain undescribed. In 2016 alone, scientists discovered over 130 new plant and animal species, many in areas undergoing rapid habitat destruction. The study of cryptozoology involves a considerable amount of conjecture in areas often regarded as data-deficient, yet groundbreaking discoveries can breathe new life into calcified beliefs, enabling us to gain greater insight into and catalogue the natural world. It appears that we are on the cusp of a new period of biological discovery, with scientific descriptions of new species reaching levels akin to the golden era of zoological exploration from the 16th to the 18th centuries. It is time for cryptozoology to emerge from obscurity and be incorporated into zoology. Wonder and speculation must play a role in energising conservation efforts. It is imprudent of scientists to ignore the powerful ecological insight that might be gained from cryptozoology. Just possibly, some of these unknown animals do exist,

ready to provide dejected zoologists with the ultimate "inspiration"-
an insight not considered since Cuvier's indiscriminate dismissal in
1812.

> *'How tragic it is that such wonderful creatures have no concept, no aware-*
> *ness, of just how beautiful and magical they are. Then again, perhaps they*
> *do – after all, they are cats...'*

> — *KARL SHUKER*

APPENDICES

ON THE ORIGINS OF THE 'DANGEROUS WILD ANIMALS ACT' OF 1976

BY TIMOTHY WHITTARD

For those of us who are intrigued by the frequent reports of big cat sightings in the wilderness and countryside of Britain, the 'Dangerous Wild Animals Act' of 1976 is likely to be familiar. It is an essential component of the tale, which is referred to by all enthusiasts and experts, but is actually understood in depth by very few. Everyone knows that the UK government introduced this legislation as a means of restoring order and control to the unregulated exotic pet trade of the British Empire which had continued as an extravagant fashion trend right into the mid-late 20th century. Many commentators will even be able to quote significant parts of the act word-for-word verbatim, and whilst some may agree that this demonstrates an in-depth understanding, it fails to capture the chronology of events which brought about its introduction; particularly the one key incident which resulted in the media spotlight being blindingly cast onto the exotic pet trade and the subsequent furore of debates in parliament which aimed to rectify any enduring legacy of irresponsible ownership of dangerous animals and the unregulated trade that ensured a steady stream of such creatures into our little island.

The incident in question took place on Monday 26th October 1970 and judging by the few remaining written records which are easily available in the public domain, it must have been absolutely terrifying; on this day, eight-year-old 'James Tyler' was with his mother at the 'Oldfields Trading Estate' on Oldfields Road in Sutton, Surrey. As James ran towards his mother, he was suddenly and unexpectedly attacked by a large mountain lion which leapt out of the back of a parked van. James and his mother were assisted in the struggle by a man who came to their rescue; according to (Brown, 2020) this unnamed man tried to defend James using an iron bar to beat the mountain lion into retreat, but not before young James had already sustained serious injuries to his head and neck.

Thankfully James was able to make a full recovery, and as far as can be told from researching this incident, he remains alive and well to this day; as does another interesting key figure connected to this incident... The mountain lion (otherwise known as a cougar or a puma) was a large female called 'Tara', who was owned by a gentleman named 'Maurice Wheeler', a local builder; and in my research role behind the camera for the documentary 'Britain's Big Cat Mystery' part of my duties entailed revisiting historic cases, trying to contact those involved and also to ascertain whether there are any details to add, which may not have been captured by journalists and written reports from the time.

To my amazement, I was actually able to make contact with Maurice, but perhaps unsurprisingly he declined to comment once I had explained the purpose of my contacting him. Maurice was known to keep several large cats at the time of this incident, and such was the concern about his ownership of dangerous animals in the immediacy of the following days, that factory workers on the 'Oldfields Trading Estate' went on strike, threatening not to return until Maurice's collection of big cats had been removed; eventually his exotic cats were re-homed by a zoo, but this was not the end of the debate. This incident caught the attention of the UK government, and only three days after the attack on James Tyler, a debate began in the 'House of

Lords' to implement measures which would prevent such an incident from occurring again in the future (Hansard, 2020). It took nearly six years for the UK government to complete this, but the end result was the passing of the 'Dangerous Wild Animals Act' of 1976 into British law, and the introduction of measures designed entirely to make domestic ownership of exotic or dangerous animals beyond the means of the average Joe. Logically then, it is fair to assume that this culminated in a wave of multiple releases of big cats across Britain by private owners who could not afford the licences required to legally keep their 'pets'. The rest, as they say, is history.

On the Origins of the Naturalised Big Cats of Britain

In my previous piece, "On the Origins of the 'Dangerous Wild Animals Act' of 1976", I discussed and outlined the events which brought about the introduction of the aforementioned legislation (Whittard, 2020). However, this is not the true origin of the British big cat phenomenon, and there is an additional story to be told, which goes some considerable way to shedding further light on the mystery of how the big cats of Britain came to be living and breeding in the wilderness of the United Kingdom. Imagine if you will; the year is 1944 and the rumbles and screams of enormous engines can be heard, as fighter planes litter the skies over RAF Ibsley in Hampshire. This sight is not an unusual occurrence; the 'Battle of Britain' is well underway and the collective efforts of the over-stretched allies are thrown into repelling the aerial invaders of the Luftwaffe. However, the fighter planes in question are not being flown by British pilots, but by American ones; specifically, the 494th Fighter Squadron of the US Air Force, affectionately nick-named 'The Panthers' (The Wartime Memories Project, 2020). So why is this relevant to the British big cat story, especially given that these "panthers" were not literal ones? The answer is simple; their mascots... The insignia of the 494th Fighter Squadron featured a big black cat, a ferocious and menacing depiction of a panther, designed to instil a sense of confidence in the servicemen and women, whilst promoting fear in their enemies.

This artful exercise in pinning a unique identity to the squadron did not remain the exclusive realm of the tailors and seamstresses tasked with embroidering the iconic emblems onto the uniforms of the servicemen and women; nor was it restricted to the painters and sign-writers who emblazoned the aircraft with colourful logos and designs. For in amongst the chaos of war and the mass movement of people heading east across the Atlantic Ocean to the battlefront in Europe, there were a (potentially large) number of soldiers and military personnel with unusual travelling companions. Essentially, the point I am getting to is that a number of American soldiers are thought to have arrived in Britain, with pumas and panthers in tow. These majestic apex predators were essentially mascots, animal icons that served to inspire and motivate the soldiers who travelled alongside them; and yet, one important question remains.

Upon arrival on the shores of Britain during the height of rationing, and further beyond to the aftermath of the war, what became of these mascots?! The truth is that records are at best sketchy, and at worst riddled with omissions and missing details; so the remnants of the story must be pieced together if any accuracy is to be garnered and helpful conclusions are to be drawn. Essentially much of the story of the big cats of Britain remains 'out there' to be told, but the details are scattered haphazardly in the old handwritten journals which were kept by homesick soldiers, many of which now serve as heirlooms in the private collections of families long bereft of their fallen war heroes. However, that is not the end of the story and there are further layers of the metaphorical onion which can be peeled back in hopeful examination for more clues. One such notion which rears its head from time to time, focuses on the enforced rationing which was commonplace across and throughout Britain during WW2.

Feeney-Hart (2013) reports on this very issue, describing how the British government advised its citizens to enact a cull of their animals in order to preserve food rations for the human population; this later became known as the 'British Pet Massacre of 1939', and in the space of one week, it is estimated that 750,000 pets were killed. Newquay

Zoo (2020) also point out that zoo animals were not always much luckier... Reading between the lines it is clear that some owners of exotic big cats would have had very difficult decisions to make with the outbreak of war and the onset of rationing; the choice between feeding their family, or feeding their cats, the latter of which being obligate carnivores would have been unable to obtain the necessary nutrition to survive from any source other than a diet consisting purely of meat. So there it is; the outbreak of WW2 may have itself directly contributed to the first wave of deliberately released big cats in the British Isles. Such animals may have been initially released from the pre-existing collections and menageries of exotic animals accrued during the previous decades and centuries of British colonialism. This may have seeded the initial nucleus of a new pseudo-population of big cats in Britain, which it seems were possibly further stocked by the arrival of military mascots from across the pond.

On the Origins of the 'Dangerous Wild Animals Act' of 1976 – PART II (Those Who Forget History are Destined to Relive it)

To recap, this piece of legislation is of particular interest to the folk who research and study the subject of big cats in Britain; for it is considered by many to be the very bedrock of the phenomenon – a notion I personally dispute, yet have already partially explored and written about other hypotheses (Whittard, 2020b), but that said, I cannot deny its significance. In order to understand this better, earlier this year I set about researching the reasons why the Dangerous Wild Animals Act (1976) was brought into law, and I was able to piece together an account of a harrowing attack on an 8-year-old boy called 'James Tyler' on Oldfields Road in Sutton, Surrey.

This incident took place in October of 1970, and later that same week, it was directly cited in a debate in the 'House of Lords' as the reason as to why the then government felt it should intervene in the extremely popular, yet unregulated exotic pet trade in the United Kingdom of the time – in the interest of safety. The source I referenced at the time of my first article stated the involved puma was a large female called 'Tara' (Brown, 2020; Whittard, 2020a). However, I now stand corrected and have found other reference material which originates more reliably from sources published a lot nearer to the time of the incident. James was indeed attacked by a large puma, but it was a male named 'Dax' (Glenton, 1971).

In the lead-up to the terrifying incident, James (known as 'Jimmy'), was being dropped off by his father (a serving police officer) with his sister in the nearby industrial estate. Jimmy's father then left him and his sister to walk the short distance to meet their mother nearby, who was scheduled to finish work. Jimmy was unaware of the large male puma named 'Dax', hiding under a nearby van (to which it was secured by a long chain, but with more than enough slack for it to be able to ambush, pounce on and maul an unsuspecting passerby); had he known of the puma's presence it is likely that Jimmy would have suppressed his instinct to run to his mother as he saw her exiting her workplace... Alas, Jimmy did not know of the mountain lion that was waiting for him to approach, and nor was he able to defend himself from what happened next.

Fortunately, he was rescued by a brave, fast-acting and quick-thinking man, who previously was stated to be 'unnamed'; however, I am now able to name the man as George McKnight (Sussex History Forum, 2014). He was working nearby, witnessed the attack unfold, and without any hesitation stepped forward to the defence of Jimmy; using an iron bar to beat Dax into retreat, he was able to wrestle Jimmy free from the claws of the mountain lion, "before throwing James clear" out of the reach of the cat and thus ending the attack. Without the bravery and quick reactions of George McKnight, it seems incredibly likely that Jimmy would have needed a lot more emergency care than the short spell in the hospital and the 38 sutures to his face, neck and throat that he did. Jimmy Tyler indeed owes his life to George McKnight, as is made absolutely clear by this following computer-rendered sketch constructed from a long-lost photograph taken in the hospital at the time, which shows the scale and severity of the injuries. The owner of the puma (or mountain lion) involved here is known by the name of 'Maurice Wheeler', (his full name is 'William Henry Maurice Wheeler'); interestingly this was not the first incident where a child was attacked and injured by one of his animals.

Incredibly, just two months earlier, in August 1970, a 9-year-old boy named 'Peter Cliff' was also attacked by another of Maurice Wheeler's 'pet' pumas; in this incident, Peter was passing the animal "when it jumped at him, gripped his shoulder and knocked him to the ground" near to a fishing lake in Dorking, Surrey (Glenton, 1971).

What is even more unfathomable is that neither of these two incidents was the first and that in fact, both were preceded by another traumatising event which occurred only 3 months before the attack on Peter Cliff, and 5 months before the attack on Jimmy Tyler. Unbelievably, on Friday 29th May 1970, the first recorded serious untoward incident occurred, when another 9-year-old, this time a girl named 'Lorraine Wheeler', (Maurice's own niece) was bitten by one of his apes whilst she played in her own back garden! Now most of us can be forgiven for thinking that 2020 has been a year of unrivalled chaos, but for the three children, the two pumas and the one ape (or two apes if we include Mr. Wheeler) that were involved in the events I have just described, the year 1970 totally trumps anything 2020 has served up for the majority of us.

In my previous article, I mentioned that I had been able to make contact with Maurice Wheeler, but that any detailed discussions were halted as soon as I mentioned my interest in the history of Britain's big cats. Indeed from perusing the social media accounts attached to this evidently eccentric individual, it does not take long before the image of a wannabe hybrid between 'Peter Stringfellow' and 'Lenny McLean' emerges, with numerous photos depicting a life immersed in extravagance, wild nightclub culture, and unsavoury gang-minded machismo; a view reinforced all the more by descriptions of his "dominant personality" and reports from investigations at the time of the attack on Jimmy Tyler, that "several people on the estate had witnessed various unreported incidents" associated with Maurice's mismanaged menagerie of man-eaters, but also that there was a well-established "reluctance on the part of witnesses to these events to commit their observations to writing" due to "fear of some form of retaliation" (Sussex History Forum, 2014).

With this in mind, I personally suspect that action would have been a lot slower, if at all forthcoming, were it not for the fact that Jimmy's father was a respected and serving police officer at the time. It is often said by the learned and wise that 'those who forget history are destined to relive it' (Santayana, 1906), and clearly, this sentiment rings true; despite the Dangerous Wild Animals Act (1976) being decreed into law nearly half a century ago, problems persist with horrifying incidents of similar magnitude recurring. For example, in 2003, nearly three decades after the law was passed, an investigative journalism exposé revealed that the closed Basildon Zoo had been selling lion cubs and leopard cubs illegally for as little as £700 through a 'black market' pet shop in Enfield, London which was run by 'Steve Haswell' in conjunction with the zoo's then owner, 'Yolanda Surcouf' (BBC News, 2003; BBC Press Office, 2003).

As recently as August of this year, a video surfaced which showed a 16-year-old girl being attacked by a captive puma, kept under license by 'Reece Oliver' at his farm in Strelley, Nottinghamshire (Gray, 2020); the girl (whose identity has been protected) was employed as a stable-hand, with no experience or training in caring for large carnivores, and yet on the day of the incident, she was instructed to work alone and unsupervised with the dangerous big cats, including the African lions, as well as the pumas - with terrifying results.

The following article from Pattinson (2020) contains a video which shows, some efforts to ensure security at the site were clearly made (indicated by the presence of the CCTV camera itself), and yet this alone was clearly not sufficient, as the footage demonstrates how easily the puma was able to over-power its human keeper and escape

the enclosure; which could have had even more disastrous consequences should the animal have made it beyond the perimeter fence.
It must be stated and emphasised that in all of the incidents outlined
above, the animals involved were captive ones. This is of vital impor-
tance to remember, as whilst wild big cats do pose a threat to human
life, it is markedly and drastically less significant than any risk posed
by a similar captive animal; where the creature's entire existence is
constrained to range-limiting enclosures and forced dependency
upon human caregivers, who themselves, by the very nature of the
responsibilities associated with owning a "Category 1" dangerous
animal (such as a big cat) as defined by DEFRA (2012), are required to
come into close contact with the animal on routine occasions, for
provision of the numerous essential care and maintenance duties.
This results in every moment of contact between human and any
such captive big cat, being ripe with potential for catastrophé, given
the slightest momentary lapse in concentration or common sense.

Wild big cats would not naturally choose to socialise with humans
and would exhibit an entirely different behavioural profile, which
means that they would seldom, if ever, approach people and would
prefer to avoid contact with humans in almost all circumstances.
Interestingly, it does seem that despite the vast majority of licence
holders for the ownership of dangerous animals in the United
Kingdom being extremely responsible individuals, there does seem to
be an ongoing degree of confusion surrounding the legislation, which
persists. One could be forgiven for thinking that the Zoo Licensing
Act (1981) does not apply to private animal owners, and yet upon
closer inspection it is somewhat more ambiguous, stating that "the
Secretary of State may from time to time specify standards of modern
zoo practice" which must be adhered to; and upon reading the
current revision of these standards, as outlined by DEFRA (2012), I
was amazed to learn that the definition of a "zoo" can include private
collections, "to which members of the public have access, with or
without charge for admission, on seven days or more in any period of
12 consecutive months".

By this definition, it is possible that any owner of dangerous animals who keeps them at their residency could find their 'private collection' classified as a 'zoo', should they have visitors to their home on more than 7 occasions in one year. This may seem pedantic, but it is in fact a serious distinction to make, because in inadvertently crossing into the classification of a 'zoo', the licensed animal owner suddenly becomes liable and responsible for a whole plethora of other contingency plans and safety precautions which are otherwise not mandated by law, which can include; comprehensive plans for a "response to an escape in all situations", such as plans for "recapturing the animal", "the provision of firearms and darting equipment to tranquillise or kill escaped animals ", which in turn, requires "regular training with firearms and darting equipment", as well as an appropriately protected vehicle to aid the "recapture party", and the preparedness to euthanise any escaped animal. It stands to reason then, that some private big cat owners will fall into a grey legal area, where neither the owners, nor the authorities are entirely clear of their responsibilities, requirements, and of the laws, standards and guidelines which may apply. To summarise, here we have seen a small selection of the many incidents which highlight the failings of the Dangerous Wild Animals Act (1976) in firstly, restricting and controlling the sale of big cats (and other exotic animals) without a license, and secondly, in ensuring that avoidable attacks on humans from captive dangerous wild animals do not occur.

We have also seen how easily the distinction between 'zoo' and 'private collection' can be blurred within the current legal frameworks. This is before even beginning to try to tackle the known (and rumoured) deliberate releases of big cats into the British countryside, and the domino effect of issues that could arise from having a range of apex predators secretly living and breeding alongside humans on this little island. Significantly, Shepherd et al (2014) state that whilst "large felid carnivore attacks cause exponentially fewer injuries than human conflicts, falls, or other environmental exposures, they have become a not infrequent and potentially preventable cause of significant human morbidity and mortality in the last several decades", before adding that communities of people "who live, work, and pursue travel and recreation at the urban-wildlands interface", as well as individuals "who may be exposed to the increasing numbers" of "felid carnivores" in both "captive" and "wild" settings, should be educated carefully with regard to the "risks inherent to these activities". So clearly, this is not going to be the end of the story; there will no doubt be further avoidable and untoward injuries resulting from human-animal conflict in both captive and non-captive settings, and there remains much work to be done if we are to even to begin to attempt to address the failings and pitfalls of the Dangerous Wild Animals Act (1976), as well as the unintended consequences of enacting this law. Quite how to achieve this, whilst mitigating any risks to both the public and any cats that may be out there, is another matter altogether.

PROOF OF BIG CAT CONSPIRACY REVEALED IN NEW 'FREEDOM OF INFORMATION' TREASURE TROVE! An exclusive 86-page dossier of controversial top secret evidence for the big cats of Britain has been obtained following a 'Freedom of Information' request.

An exclusive 86-page dossier of controversial top secret evidence for the big cats of Britain has been obtained following a 'Freedom of Information' request. The leaked documents include several previously unreleased photographs, and a detailed email chain between various government agencies (including the police), which proves they KNOW big cats are living wild in the British countryside, and actively investigate big cat reports, whilst also simultaneously SUPPRESSING THE EVIDENCE.

The government department concerned stated on its website that they are "committed to publishing all information released in response to Freedom of Information requests", but only published part of the information released, suspiciously omitting this 86-page document from their publication. Within the pages are a multitude of shocking revelations, including; UNRELEASED PHOTOS OF THE BEAST taken in 2011; testimony from a former police officer that there are at least four big cats living in one area known to him; a government wildlife expert who firmly believes in British big cats; reference to various recent deliberate animal releases in the British wilderness; and the analysis of the carcases of various prey animals (including photos) suspected to have been killed by big cats (where all known native wild animals were categorically eliminated as suspects).

The email chain shows a detailed discussion of a spate of recent "savage" livestock killings, with photographs of a young calf which had had its TAIL TORN OFF by an unknown predator that only left a number of claw marks as clues to its identity – clues which could not have been left behind by a fox or a dog. In another case from November 2018, experts found the carcass of a dead ewe which had been dragged 20 yards "up a rock face". The ewe had "two puncture marks on the front of her right shoulder and two at the back", and "the wounds were over three inches apart". A police official agrees with a wildlife expert that they are "inclined to think" this was the work of a cat.

Elsewhere, a sheep farm repeatedly targeted by an unknown predator lost over 36 sheep at the rate of approximately 2 killed per week. In the document, one expert says WILD BIG CATS ARE REAL, but "very rare" and that in some cases "there is a risk to livestock and people". Later, a government wildlife management officer tells a government advisor on non-native species that they "will need to be prepared" for the possibility of "disappearing sheep" being "raised with the Cabinet Secretary". In a more sinister turn, the experts and officials openly and frankly discuss their options for responding to any 'problem' big cats, with one expert stating they "would prefer tranquillizer dart" over live rounds, being met with the firm response from another official of "if it's non-native there's no protection by law", adding "they can shoot it".

Any "concerns for public safety" linked to big cats on the loose were glossed over with the reassuring sentiment from one detective inspector who said he was "happy that there's not an imminent risk to public safety if it's well fed" – but without reliable and accurate data on the number of big cats at large and precisely how well fed they are, I fail to see how this can be much of a reassurance – especially since all efforts to collate decent scientific data on the British big cat populations are entirely stalled by the persistent refusal of nearly every establishment and institute of officialdom with a stake in the debate, to outwardly and publicly admit the reality of the situation.

One of the leaked emails reveals that a review of the financial expenditure and resources used by the Norwegian government in compensating their farmers for livestock killed by their native 'Northern Lynx' was described as "sobering"; with the additional suggestion that parties in Britain promoting lynx re-introduction programmes should "take this very well documented information into account before making a decision on the re-introduction of these predators" – but also within the 86 pages of emails is evidence that THE LYNX IS ALREADY HERE and has been for "some 30 years"!

In stark contrast to the details contained within the leaked 86-page document, the 'Department for Environment, Food & Rural Affairs' (DEFRA) responded to a separate Freedom of Information request by declaring that they "do not hold any records of big cat sightings or encounters in the UK". LEOPARD AT LARGE? All this comes after a former sub-contractor to South Somerset District Council (who wishes to remain anonymous) made big cat researchers aware of the case of an alleged escaped leopard from a now-closed zoo exhibit in Cricket St. Thomas between the years 2004 and 2005. She said: "There were modifications and upgrades done on the leopard enclosure around that time. Nobody noticed that the new fence boundary was too close to a tree inside the enclosure and we think the leopard got out by jumping over the fence from the lower tree branches. "I know it was reported at the time, and I think they tried to recapture the animal but I don't think they ever saw it again. I don't think it was even mentioned in the local news at the time, probably because it would panic locals and damage the park's reputation."

In response to a Freedom of Information request about this alleged incident, South Somerset District Council said: "We have no records of escaped animals from zoo/tourist attractions in the Cricket St. Thomas area for the period requested (or any time)." BIG CAT DNA LABORATORY CENSORSHIP!? In southern England, two biological samples collected by wildlife researchers which have been analysed for DNA by a laboratory at a top British university (which cannot be named for legal reasons) have only added to the confusion in the big cat debate.

"The samples, collected from two separate locations in the British wilderness, have BOTH been identified as originating from HYBRID animals from the cat family, but in a SHOCKING twist, the laboratory in question is refusing to disclose the parent species for both samples! Jon McGowan, a wildlife expert who recently scooped a 'Gold Award' in the category of 'Best Performance' at the Fortean Film Festival last month for his role in 'Cat Hunters: The Search for the Beast of Exmoor' said: "Positive DNA results for both puma and leopard have been found in the British wilderness in recent years, and there is also a history of laboratories suppressing these kinds of results." Seemingly there is a desire to maintain an official stance that big cats are not living in our countryside, despite a growing stack of evidence to support claims to the contrary, including; photographs, video footage, thousands of eye-witness reports, dead sheep and deer frequently found over 30ft up trees, forensically verified big cat teeth impressions found on the bones of dead prey animals, forensically verified big cat paw tracks, positive DNA results, bodies of big cats being killed in collisions with vehicles on UK roads, as well as live big cats being captured.

Cat Hunters presenters, Carl Marshall and Jay Opie by nightvision in a wildlife hide in The Search for the Beast of Exmoor.

BTS - Filming for Cat Hunters (from left to right, Carl Marshall, Rhoda Watkins, Tim Whittard, Matt Everett).

BODIES OF EVIDENCE... One recent case of an escaped exotic cat which made the headlines was that of a Savannah hybrid which was found in an upmarket residential area of London in May of last year, nicknamed the 'Beast of Billionaire's Row'. This came after a lynx escaped from 'Dartmoor Zoological Park', Devon back in July 2016, and another lynx escaped from the 'Borth Wild Animal Kingdom', Ceredigion in October 2017. Let's not forget the famous case of 'Lara' the lynx either! Back in May 2001, staff from London Zoo and the police worked together to humanely capture a lynx that had been seen roaming a residential part of north London. Initially dubbed the 'Beast of Barnet', the lynx was eventually taken to London Zoo where she was renamed 'Lara'. Lara lived at London Zoo for three years before being transferred to the 'Parc Zoologique du Bois de Coulange' in France, where she sadly passed away in 2009.

THE CONSEQUENCE OF UNEQUIVOCAL PROOF... The majority of British big cat researchers are incredibly worried that any change in the status quo may result in a formal governmental response which will threaten the safety and well-being of the big cats of Britain, with a well-documented track record of them ordering localised eradication programmes in recent history. First in 1983, when the Royal Marines were dispatched to Devon for several weeks to hunt and kill a creature which became known as the 'Exmoor Beast'; and then two decades later in 2003, armed police were sent into the Welsh mountains for a stake-out which lasted days, after an officer witnessed a farm dog being eaten by a big black cat and a survey carried out by expert animal trackers revealed that up to seven different individual big cats could have been at large in the region at the time. Former Royal Marine, John Holden was present in Exmoor in 1983 and witnessed his rifle instructor open fire on "a big black cat". He believes the animal was either fatally wounded or scared out of the area following the encounter. Efforts have been made to contact officers involved in the 2003 eradication programme in the Welsh mountains (some of whom have now retired from the force), but no response has been forthcoming.

However, it is clear from this new 86-page leaked document that some government agencies are more than prepared to load their rifles and train their crosshairs on any big cats which may be living in the forests and green rolling hills of the British countryside – a move which would be sure to upset lovers of our British big cat legends and those who have some sympathy for these animals, which were essentially brought to our shores to serve the extravagances of our eccentric ancestors, and which have either escaped, or been released and abandoned to survive off-grid in the remaining fragments of wilderness on our islands, in small but sufficient numbers to persist decades later – a feat worthy of a medal if you ask me, particularly as if true, one can make the argument that these cats are now naturalising, and as such I would be keen to see a review of the classification and the legal protections afforded to any such animals which may be out there.

I certainly do not want to see any harm come to our British big cats, and am sure that many other Brits (and tourists alike) have a fondness for the big cat legends of our islands, so a more pragmatic solution is needed than the simple and flawed mantra of 'kill the beast'. Seemingly, the biggest hurdle in all this is the awkward absence of open-minded representatives from the institutes and establishments of officialdom in the worlds of British wildlife and nature science who decline to budge from their long-held positions of denial. Sadly, until a dialogue of common sense can begin which involves all concerned parties, the scientific study of this phenomenon will be stifled, compensation for livestock farmers will not be forthcoming, public education and safety initiatives will be met with ridicule, proper legal protections for the naturalised British panthers and our 'Lazarus' population of native European Lynx will not be in place, and the authorities will no doubt continue to play hot-potato and be perplexed (in hushed whispers, behind closed doors) by the occasional 'problem' cat.

LARGE-SIZED FELIFORM CRYPTIDS BY CONTINENT

BY C. P. MARSHALL

NORTH AMERICA: Alaskan Tiger, American Maned Lions, Arizona Jaguar, Beast of Bladenboro, Biped Panthers, Black Cougar, *Carraguar*, *Cuitlamitztli*, Dorsal Jaguar, Eastern Cougar, Georgia Mystery Cat, *How-how*, Long-Tailed Wildcats, *Lunkasoose*, Mex Ruffed Cat, Ozark Howler, Pennsylvanian Mountain Lion, Tennessee Red Cheetah.

SOUTH AMERICA: *Aypa*, *Chongonga*, *Entzaeia-yawa*, Giant Black Panther, *Iemisch*, *Jaguarete*, *Juikam yawa*, *Kintanari*, H.Vs Rock Jaguar, *Maipolina*, *Mitla*, *Onca*, *Onca-cangucu*, *Pama yawa*, Peru Jungle Lion, Peru Stripped Tiger, Rainbow Jaguar, *Shaishai-yawa*, Siemel's Mystery Cat, Speckled Tiger, Striped Jaguar, *Tigre dantero*, Warracaba Jaguar, Water Tigers, *Yaguaru*, *Yana puma*.

AFRICA: *Abasambo*, *Abu sotan*, *Bakanga*, Beast of Bungoma, Black Cheetah, Black Lion, *Bung-bung*, *Chakpuar*, *Coje ya menia*, *Damasia*, Dark Leopards (anomalous), *Dilali*, *Dingonek*, Ennidi Tiger, *Gassin-gram*, Grahamstown Mystery Cats, Green Leopard, Green Lion, *Hadjel*, *Ikimizi*, *Kimbanbangwe*, *Kitanga*, Malagasy Lion, *Marozi*, Mayanja Monster, *Mngwa*, *Mourou n'gou*, *Mpisimbi*, *Ndalawo*, *Ngoroli*, *Ntarargo*, *Ntambo wa luy*, *Nzemendim*, Qattara Cheetah, Sahara Lions,

Tigre de montagne, *Uruturangwe*, *Yassou*, *Vassoko*, Water Leopards, Water Lions, *Wanjilanko*, *Wobo*, Zanzibar Leopard.

ASIA: *Bai hu*, Bali Tiger, Bornean Tiger, Brown Tigers, Caspian Tiger, China's White Sabretooth, *Cigau*, *Doglas*, Green Tiger, *Guoshanhuang*, *Harimau jalor*, Javan Tiger, King Cheetah (Asian), Maltese Tiger, Mint Leaf Leopard, *Nellimpatti Leopard*, *Pogeyan*, Sai Kung Mystery Cat, *Seah malang poo*, *Shanbiao*, Shing Mun Tiger, Stripe-less Tigers, *Tanuak*, *Tubao*, Xinjiang Tiger, *Yamamaya*, *Zouyu*.

OCEANA: New Guinea Lion, Queensland Tiger, *Warrigal*.

POSSIBLE PREHISTORIC SURVIVORS
BY C. P. MARSHALL

South American Water Tigers:

- *Aypa*: Head and neck of a tiger, extremely large canine teeth, sometimes said to be covered in scales. Brazil.
- *Maïpolina*: Large-bodied, very short fawn-coloured fur, whitish chest, stripe along its back, and the back of its head. Sometimes said to have drooping ears. Maroni River, French Guiana.
- *Onça-tigre*: Described conflictingly, ruffed and tailless, oddly patterned. Japurá River, Brazil.

Disputed:

- *Entzaeia-yawá*: Not described as having sabre teeth, a wide range of colour morphs (black, white, brown and reddish). Ecuador.
- *Iemisch*: Ferocious and aggressive. Speculated to be a giant otter; its connection with true, long-fanged water tigers is unclear. Argentina.

- *Yaquaru*: Giant otter-like animal with "large canines". Paraná River, Argentina; Tebicuary River, Paraguay.

Terrestrial:

- *Tigres dantero*: Long-fanged. Approximately jaguar size. Venezuela.

AFRICAN "WATER LIONS", "WATER LEOPARDS" OR "JUNGLE WALRUS"

BY C. P. MARSHALL

- *Bingolo*: Data deficient. Gabon.
- *Coje ya menia*: Size of a small hippopotamus. Tracks similar to those of an elephant. Cuango and Cuanza Rivers, Angola.
- *Dilali*: Horse-like body, claws of a lion, and large tusks like those of a walrus. Ouham River, Chad.
- *Ghéboghabogha*: Data Deficient. Gabon.
- *Mamaïmé*: Dark with blackish skin, shaggy fur on the neck, red eyes. Central African Republic/South Sudan.
- *Mourou-ngou*: Leopard-shaped, 8' to 12' in length, brownish fur either striped or dappled with blue and white spots. Chari River, Chad; Bamingui, Bangoran, Gribingui, Iomba, Kotto, Koukourou, Mbari, and Ouaka Rivers, Central African Republic.
- *Ndzin médzim*: Originally speculated to be a kind of giant otter. Cameroon; Gabon.
- *N'gooli*: Resembles a massive leopard, sometimes said to have a mane like a lion. Very large canine teeth, which protrude from its upper jaw. Boumba and Lokomo Rivers, Cameroon.
- *Ngoroli*: Vovodo River, Central African Republic.

- *Ntambo wa luy*: Capsizes canoes eating the occupants. Luembé River, Central African Republic.
- *Ntambue ya maï*: Shares similarities with water lions such as the *ntambo wa luy* and *simba ya mail*. Democratic Republic of the Congo.
- *Nzèghwa nini*: Data deficient. Bouenguidi River, Gabon.
- *Simba ya mail*: Synonymous with *ntambue ya maï* and the *ntambo wa luy*. Lupudi River, Democratic Republic of the Congo.
- *Ze-ti-ngu*: Synonymous with *mourou-ngou*. Central African Republic.
- "Water leopard": Lake Bangweulu and Lukanga Swamp, Zambia.
- "Water lion": Upper Congo River, Democratic Republic of the Congo.
- "Water lion": Falémé River, Mali/Senegal/Guinea.
- "Water lion": Central African Republic.
- "Jungle walrus": Ituri Rainforest, Democratic Republic of the Congo.

Disputed:

- *Chipekwe*: Either reported inconsistently or there are three different cryptids of Lake Bangweulu and the Bangweulu Wetlands termed "chipekwe": one similar to the *emela-ntouka*, one similar to the *mokele-mbembe* (both dinosaur-like), and one appears to be a water lion. Lake Bangweulu, Kafue River, and Kafue Flats, Zambia.
- *Dingonek*: Originally regarded as a neodinosaur. Bernard Heuvelmans suggested that the armour was an optical illusion and classified it as a water lion. Migori and Mara Rivers, Kenya.
- *Mamba mutu*: Forelimbs similar to those of the lobster, fish-like tail, humanoid head. Lake Tangayika,

Burundi/Democratic Republic of the
Congo/Tanzania/Zambia.

- *Ndamathia*: Description was reptilian and the English bible translation is "Dragon". Tana River, Kenya.
- *Ndgoko na maiji*: Usually regarded as a proboscidean. Congo and Kasai Rivers, Democratic Republic of the Congo.
- *Nsanga*: Usually regarded as saurian. Easily mistaken for a crocodile, were it not for its smooth, scaleless skin and clawed feet. Lake Bangweulu, Zambia.
- *Nyokodoing*: Ferocious and agile, hippo-sized, covered in red hair. Sudd, South Sudan.
- *N'yamala*: Usually regarded as a dinosaur-like animal, and has been equated with the *mokele-mbembe*, although it is alternatively described as a huge cat-like predator. Ogowe and Ngounie Rivers, Gabon.
- *Nzéfu-loï*: Very large tusks, has been associated with neodinosaurs, water elephants, pseudodeinotheria, and water lions. Kamolondo Depression, Democratic Republic of the Congo.
- *Ol-umaina*: Similar to the *dingonek*, possibly reptilian. Amala River, Kenya.

Terrestrial: ("Tigres de Montagne")

- *Coq-djingé*: Possibly synonyms with *biscoro*, *gassingrâm*, wanjilanko and *hadjel*. Massif des Bongos, Central African Republic.
- *Gassingrâm*: Larger than a lion, brown base colour, bright shining eyes. Central African Republic.
- *Hadjel*: Larger than a lion, short, hyena-like tail, large mane, very long canine teeth. Guera Massif, Chad.
- *Nisi*: Data Deficient. Tibesti Mountains, Chad.
- *Tigre de montagne*: Synonymous with *biscoro*, *gassingrâm*, *hadjel,* and *wanjilanko*. Ennedi Plateau, Chad.

- *Vassoko*: Synonymous with the *gassingrâm*. Central African Republic.
- *Yassou*: Very aggressive, resembles a bear, walks on the soles of its feet. Ouaddaï Highlands, Chad.
- "Imatong tiger": Akin with the Ennedi mountain tiger. Imatong Mountains, South Sudan.
- "Cave lion": Data Deficient. Mali.

Disputed:

- *Abu sotan*: Large tiger-like cat, possibly a regional name for the *wobo*. Sudan.
- *Ikimizi*: Resembles a cross between a lion and a leopard, with large canine teeth. Virunga Mountains, Rwanda.
- *Siruku*: Hyena-like. Liberia.
- *Wanjilanko*: Large and long-fanged, similar to the *tigres de montagne*. Casamance Forest, Senegal.

PREVIOUSLY OF CRYPTOZOOLOGICAL SIGNIFICANCE

BY C. P. MARSHALL

- *Onza*: Large slender-bodied mountain lions. North America. Mexico.
- Buffalo Lions: Large mane-less male lions. Africa. Kenya.
- King Cheetah: Rare mutation. Southern Africa.
- Shuker's Cheetaline: Rare mutation. Africa. Tanzania, Kenya.
- Woolly Cheetah: Rare mutation. South Africa. Beaufort West.
- *Harimau tingkiah:* Hitherto unknown Sumatran tiger population, embellished with folklore. SE Asia. Sumatra.

SOLID EVIDENCE: ESCAPEES, ILLEGAL RELEASES, AND SPECIMENS CAPTURED OR KILLED IN BRITAIN AND NORTHERN IRELAND

BY C. P. MARSHALL

- A lynx was shot in Devon in 1903. Rediscovered by Max Blake, the preserved remains are held in the collection of the Bristol Museum.
- Three lynxes were shot and trapped in Inverness-shire in 1926 after a spate of sheep killings.
- A small black leopard was shot by authorities sometime during the 1930s after it was sighted by a group of teenagers in the Medway area of Kent.
- Three servals were allegedly released in Wales in 1974.
- A cougar escaped from a private menagerie in Hereford in 1974. Authorities were unable to recapture or kill the animal.
- A black jaguar was released near Nottingham in 1974.
- Circus owner Mary Chipperfield allegedly released three cougars in Dartmoor in 1974.
- In 1974 a black leopard and cougar were supposedly released onto the Pennines by Leslie Maiden, a former lion-tamer from Chipperfield's Circus.
- In 1975 two jungle cats escaped their enclosure in Wiltshire.
- A cougar was released near Snowdonia in 1976.

- A clouded leopard is alleged to have been at large in Canterbury after escaping in 1977.
- A lynx was shot in Kintyre in 1980. The body was allegedly buried on a private estate.
- 'Felicity', this puma was captured alive by farmer Ted Noble near Inverness in 1983.
- A butcher from Barnstaple is alleged to have released a black leopard and a cougar in 1983, which may be the origin of the legendry 'Beast of Exmoor'.
- In 1988 a leopard cat was shot after killing pheasants on an estate near Jedburgh.
- A jungle cat was hit and killed by a vehicle near Ludlow in 1989.
- In 1991 a Eurasian Lynx was shot dead in Norfolk.
- It is rumoured a cougar was captured in 1993 near Aviemore.
- In 1994 a tiger is alleged to have escaped from Belfast Zoo. It was later found dead, apparently drowned in a moat.
- An ocelot was shot on the Isle of Wight in 1994.
- A large caracal was shot by police marksmen near Fintona in 1996.
- A leopard is reported to have escaped its enclosure in Peterhead, Aberdeenshire in 2001.
- In 2002 a caracal escaped from a wildlife park in Dumfries and Galloway.
- A black leopard was allegedly released near Ulster in 2003.
- A private owner reported releasing a black leopard and a cougar in Antrim in 2003.
- A lynx escaped from 'Dartmoor Zoological Park', Devonshire in July 2016.
- A lynx escaped from the 'Borth Wild Animal Kingdom', Ceredigion in October 2017.
- A Savannah hybrid was found in London in May 2020, nicknamed the 'Beast of Billionaire's Row'.

COMPLETE LIST OF WILD CATS INCLUDING SUB-SPECIES

BY C. P. MARSHALL

Kodkod

(Leopardus guigna)

Weight: 2 - 2.5 kg (4.4 - 5.5 lb).

L. g. guigna (Molina, 1782) – occurs in southern Chile and Argentina.

L. g. tigrillo (Schinz, 1844) – occurs in central and northern Chile.

Oncilla

(Leopardus tigrinus)

Weight: 1.5 - 3 kg (3.3 - 6.6 lbs).

Results of a morphological analysis of 250 samples of skins and skulls indicate that there are three distinct oncilla groups: namely one in South America's northern, north-western and western range countries, one in eastern and one in southern range countries. Based on these results, the eastern group was proposed to be a distinct species *Leopardus emiliae (Thomas, 1914)*.

Southern Tiger Cat

(Leopardus guttulus)

Weight: 1.8 - 3.5 kg (3.9 - 7.7 lbs)

Long considered to be a subspecies of the oncilla (*Leopardus tigrinus*). It was recognized as a distinct species in 2013.

(monotypic species)

Margay

(Leopardus wiedii)

Weight: 2.3 - 4.9 kg (5 - 11 lbs).

L. w. wiedii (Schinz, 1821) – occurs south of the Amazonas.

L. w. vigens (Thomas, 1904) – occurs north of the Amazonas.

L. w. glauculus (Nelson and Goldman, 1931) – occurs in Central America.

Geoffroy's Cat

(Leopardus geoffroyi)

Weight: 2 - 7.8 kg (5 - 17 lbs).

Near Threatened. Exploited heavily during the boom of the cat skin trade in the late 1960s to the 1980s.

(monotypic species)

Andean Mountain Cat

(Leopardus jacobita)

Weight: 4 - 6 kg (8 - 13 lbs).

First described by Emilio Cornalia, named in honour of Jacobita Mantegazza.

(monotypic species)

Pampas Cat

(Leopardus colocola)

Weight 3 - 7 kg (6 - 15 lbs).

L. c. colocola (Molina, 1782) – Chile; restricted to the "province of Valparaiso."

L. c. pajeros (Desmarest, 1816) – C, NC and S Argentina.

L. c. braccatus (Cope, 1889) – SW and C Brazil, Paraguay.

L. c. garleppi (Matschie, 1912) – S Colombia, Ecuador, Peru E of Andes.

L. c. budini (Pocock, 1941) – NW Argentina and Bolivia E of Andes.

L. c. munoai (Ximénez, 1961) – Uruguay.

L. c. wolffsohni (Garcia-Perea, 1994) – Tarapacá province, N Chile W of Andes.

Ocelot

(Leopardus pardalis)

Weight: 6.5 - 15.4 kg (14.5 - 34 lbs).

L. p. pardalis (Linnaeus, 1758) – range extends from Texas and Arizona to Costa Rica.

L. p. mitis (Cuvier, 1820) – occurs in South America as far south as northern Argentina.

Serval

(Leptailurus serval)

Weighs 8 - 18 kg (18 - 40 lbs).

L. s. serval (Schreber, 1776), the nominate subspecies, in Southern Africa.

L. s. constantina (Forster, 1780) – occurs in Central and West Africa.

L. s. lipostictus (Pocock, 1907) – occurs in East Africa.

Bornean Bay Cat

(Catopuma badia)

Weight: 3 - 4 kg (6 - 9 lbs).

Estimated that fewer than 2,500 mature individuals exist.

(monotypic species (no subspecies))

Asiatic Golden Cat

(Catopuma temminckii)

Weight: 9 - 16 kg (20 - 35 lbs).

C. t. temminckii (Vigors and Horsfield, 1827) – occurs in Sumatra and the Malay Peninsula.

C. t. moormensis (Hogson, 1831) – occurs from Nepal eastwards to Southeast Asia.

Black-footed Cat

(Felis nigripes)

Weight: 1 - 2.5 kg (2.2 - 5.5 lbs).

The smallest wild cat in Africa with a hunting success rate of 60%, the highest of all cats.

(monotypic species)

Sand Cat

(Felis margarita)

Weight: 1 - 3.5 kg (3 - 7.5 lbs).

F. m. margarita (Loche, 1858) – occurs in North Africa.

F. m. thinobia (Ognev, 1927) – occurs in West and Central Asia.

Afro-Asiatic Wildcat

(Felis lybica)

Weight: 2.4 - 5.5 kg (5.3 - 12.1 lb).

F. l. lybica (Forster, 1780) – occurs in North Africa and Sinai to Sudan.

F. l. cafra (Desmarest, 1822) – occurs in southern and eastern Africa.

F. l. ornata (Gray, 1830) – occurs from the eastern Caspian Sea north to Kazakhstan, into western India, western China and southern Mongolia.

European Wildcat

(Felis silvestris)

Weight: 3 - 8 kg (6 - 18 lbs).

F. s. silvestris (Schreber, 1777) – occurs in continental Europe, Scotland and Sicily.

F. s. caucasica (Satunin, 1905) – occurs in Turkey and the Caucasus.

Jungle Cat

(Felis chaus)

Weight: 5 - 9 kg (11 - 20 lbs).

F. c. chaus (Schreber, 1777) – occurs in Caucasus, Turkestan, Iran, Baluchistan and Yarkand, East Turkestan, Palestine, Israel, southern Syria, Iraq, Egypt; northern Afghanistan and south of the Amu Darya River; along the right tributaries of the Amu Darya River, in the lower courses of the Vakhsh River ranging eastwards to the Gissar Valley and slightly beyond Dushanbe.

F. c. affinis (Gray, 1830) – occurs in South Asia: Himalayan region ranging from Kashmir and Nepal to Sikkim, Bengal westwards to Kutch and Yunnan, southern India and Sri Lanka.

F. c. fulvidina (Thomas, 1929) – occurs in Southeast Asia: ranging from Myanmar and Thailand to Laos, Cambodia and Vietnam.

Chinese Mountain Cat

(Felis bieti)

Weigh from 6.5 - 9 kg (14 - 20 lbs).

Some authorities consider the *chutuchta* (Mongolian) and *vellerosa* (Chinese) subspecies of the wildcat as Chinese mountain cat subspecies.

Pallas's Cat

(Otocolobus manul)

Weight: 1.8 - 4.9 kg (4 - 11 lbs).

O. m. manul (Pallas, 1776) syn. O. m. ferrugineus (Ognev, 1928) – western and northern Central Asia from Iran to Mongolia.

O. m. nigripectus (Hodgson, 1842) – Himalayas from Kashmir to Bhutan.

Jaguarundi

(Herpailurus yagouaroundi)

Weight: 3 - 7 kg (6.6 - 15 lbs).

Secretive and alert, the jaguarundi is typically solitary or forms pairs in the wild.

(monotypic species)

Marbled Cat

(Pardofelis marmorata)

Weight: 4 - 8.1 kg (9 - 18 lbs).

P. m. marmorata (Martin, 1836) – from the Malay Peninsula to Sumatra and Borneo.

P. m. longicaudata (Blainville, 1843) – from Nepal to north of the Isthmus of Kra.

Rusty-spotted Cat

(Prionailurus rubiginosus. Geoffroy Saint-Hilaire, 1834)

Weight: 0.9 - 1.6 kg (2.0 - 3.5 lbs).

One of the cat family's smallest members.

Flat-headed Cat

(*Prionailurus planiceps*)

Weight 1.5 - 2.5 kg (3.3 - 5.5 lbs).

Native to the Thai-Malay Peninsula, Borneo, and Sumatra.

(monotypic species)

Sunda Leopard Cat

(*Prionailurus javanensis*)

Weight. 0.5 - 3.8 kg (1.1 - 8.3 lbs).

Phylogeographical evidence has recognised two subspecies of the Sunda leopard cat:

Prionailurus javanensis javanensis on Java and Bali.

Prionailurus javanensis sumatranus on Sumatra, Borneo and the Philippines.

Mainland Leopard Cat

(*Prionailurus bengalensis*)

Weight: 1.7 - 7 kg (4 - 15 lbs).

P. b. bengalensis (Kerr, 1792) – South and East Asia, from Pakistan to China, and probably the Malay Peninsula.

P. b. euptilura (Elliott, 1871) – native to the Russian Far East, Manchuria, Korea, Taiwan, Iriomote and Tsushima Islands.

Fishing Cat

(Prionailurus viverrinus)

Weight: 5 - 14 kg (11 - 31 lbs).

Thought to be primarily nocturnal, very much at home near the water. Can swim long distances, even underwater.

(monotypic species)

African Golden Cat

(Caracal aurata)

Weight: 6.9 - 15.9 kg (15.4 - 35.2 lbs).

C. a. aurata (Temminck, 1827) – east of the Congo River.

C. a. celidogaster (Temminck, 1827) – west of the Cross River.

Caracal

(Caracal caracal)

Weight: 6 - 20 kg (13 - 44 lbs).

Southern caracal *(C. c. caracal. Schreber, 1776)* – occurs in Southern and East Africa.

Northern caracal *(C. c. nubicus. Fischer, 1829)* – occurs in North and West Africa.

Asiatic caracal (C. c. schmitzi. Matschie, 1912) – occurs in Asia.

Iberian Lynx

(Lynx pardinus)

Weight: 7 - 10 kg (15 - 22 lbs).

Endangered.

(monotypic species, formerly included in *Lynx lynx* (Johnson et al. 2004))

Canada Lynx

(Lynx canadensis)

Weight: 8 - 12 kg (17 - 26 lbs).

(monotypic species, shows little morphological or genetic differences)

Bobcat

(Lynx rufus)

Weight: 6.4 - 18.3 kg (14 - 40 lbs).

L. r. rufus (Schreber, 1777) – east of the Great Plains.

L. r. fasciatus (Rafinesque, 1817) – west of the Great Plains.

Eurasian Lynx

(Lynx lynx)

Weight: 15 - 29 kg (33 - 64 lbs).

Northern lynx (L. l. lynx, Linnaeus, 1758) – ranges from Fennoscandia, Baltic states, Poland, Belarus, European Russia, Ural Mountains, Western Siberia east to the Yenisei River.

Turkestan lynx (L. l. isabellinus, Blyth, 1847) – widespread from the west in Central Asia, from South Asia to China and Mongolia.

Caucasian lynx (L. l. dinniki, Satunin, 1915) – ranges from Caucasus, Iran, Turkey, and European Russia.

Siberian lynx (L. l. wrangeli, Ognew, 1928) – Russian Far East, in the Stanovoy Range and east of the Yenisei River. Balkan lynx *(L. l. balcanicus, Bures, 1941)* – Eastern Serbia and western North Macedonia, with smaller populations in Montenegro and Albania.

Carpathian lynx (L. l. carpathicus, Kratochvil & Stollmann, 1963) – Carpathian Basin of Romania, Slovakia, Hungary, Ukraine and Bulgaria.

Mainland Clouded Leopard

(Neofelis nebulosa)

Between 11.5 and 23 kg (25 and 51 lb).

(monotypic species, lack of evidence for sub-speciation)

Sunda Clouded Leopard

(Neofelis diardi)

Weight: 10 - 25 kg (22 - 55 lbs).

Molecular, craniomandibular, and dental analysis indicates the Sunda clouded leopard has two distinct subspecies with distinct evolutionary histories:

Bornean clouded leopard (N. d. borneensis. Wilting et al, 2007).

Sumatran clouded leopard (N. d. diardi. Cuvier, 1823).

Cheetah

(Acinonyx jubatus)

Weight: 35 - 60 kg (77 - 132 lbs), though *Cheetah Conservation Botswana* reported on July 8, 2014, the capture of a 71kg (157 lb) specimen.

Southeast African cheetah *(A. j. jubatus. Schreber, 1775).*

Asiatic cheetah *(A. j. venaticus. Griffith, 1821)*.

Northeast African cheetah *(A. j. soemmeringii. Fitzinger, 1855)*.

Northwest African cheetah *(A. j. hecki. Hilzheimer, 1913)*.

Mountain Lion

(Puma concolour)

Weight: 52 to 100 kg (115 to 220 lbs), though the largest on record weighed 125 kg (276 lbs), but a specimen of this size is extremely rare.

P. c. concolour (Linnaeus, 1771) – South America, possibly excluding the region northwest of the Andes.

P. c. cougar (Kerr, 1792) – North and Central America and possibly northwestern South America.

Snow Leopard

(Panthera uncia)

Weight: 27.2 - 50 kg (60 - 110 lbs), though the largest on record, a male nicknamed "Duke" (ID. M15) weighed 52 kg (114 lbs), which is almost 8 kg more than the previous record male.

Results of a phylogeographic analysis indicate that three subspecies should be recognised:

P. u. uncia (Schreber, 1775) – in the range countries of the Pamir Mountains.

P. u. irbis (Ehrenberg, 1830) – in Mongolia.

P. u. uncioides (Horsfield, 1855) – in the Himalayas and Qinghai.

This view has been both contested and supported by different researchers.

Leopard

(Panthera pardus)

Between 20.8 - 74.8 kg (46 - 165 lbs), though the largest wild leopard in Southern Africa was reportedly 96 kg (212 lbs).

African leopard *(P. p. pardus. Linnaeus, 1758)* – the most widespread leopard subspecies and is native to most of Sub-Saharan Africa.

Indian leopard *(P. p. fusca. Meyer, 1794)* – native to the Indian subcontinent, Myanmar and southern Tibet.

Javan leopard *(P. p. melas. Cuvier, 1809)* – native to Java in Indonesia, Critically Endangered.

Arabian leopard *(P. p. nimr. Hemprich and Ehrenberg, 1830)* – native to the Arabian Peninsula, but considered locally extinct in the Sinai Peninsula. Smallest leopard subspecies.

P. p. tulliana (Valenciennes, 1856) – native to eastern Turkey, the Caucasus, southern Russia, the Iranian Plateau and the Hindu Kush. Considered Endangered. The Balochistan leopard population possibly evolved in the south of Iran, Afghanistan and Pakistan, being separated from the northern population by the Dasht-e Kavir and Dasht-e Lut deserts

Amur leopard *(P. p. orientalis. Schlegel, 1857)* – native to the Russian Far East and northern China, but is locally extinct in the Korean peninsula.

Indochinese leopard *(P. p. delacouri. Pocock, 1930)* – native to mainland Southeast Asia and southern China.

Sri Lankan leopard *(P. p. kotiya. Deraniyagala, 1956)* – native to Sri Lanka.

Jaguar

(Panthera onca)

Weight: 68 - 113 kg (149 - 250 lbs), though the largest ever recorded in the wild was a male that reportedly weighed 149 kg (328 lbs).

Largest known cat in the Americas.

(considered a monotypic taxon since 2017)

Lion

(Panthera leo)

Weight: 120 - 250 kg (265 - 550 lbs), though the largest ever recorded in the wild reportedly weighed 312 kg (690 lbs), shot in South Africa's Transvaal region in 1936.

P. l. leo (Linnaeus, 1758) – the nominate lion subspecies include the Asiatic lion, the regionally extinct Barbary lion, and lion populations in West and northern parts of Central Africa.

P. l. melanochaita (Smith, 1842) – includes the extinct Cape lion and lion populations in East and Southern African regions.

Tiger

(Panthera tigris)

Weight: 65 - 310 kg (143 - 683 lbs), though the largest captive individual weighed 423 kg (932 lb).

Bengal tiger *(P. t. tigris. Linnaeus, 1758)* – based on descriptions by earlier naturalists.

Siberian tiger (formerly *P. t. altaica. Temminck, 1844)* – based on an unspecified number of tiger skins traded between Korea and Japan.

South China tiger (formerly *P. t. amoyensis. Hilzheimer, 1905*) – based on five tiger skulls purchased in Hankou, southern China.

Indochinese tiger (formerly *P. t. corbetti. Mazák, 1968*) – based on 25 specimens in museum collections that were smaller than tigers from India and had smaller skulls.

Malayan tiger (formerly *P. t. jacksoni. Luo et al., 2004*) – proposed as a distinct subspecies on the basis of *mtDNA* and micro-satellite sequencing.

Sumatran tiger (formerly *P. t. sumatrae. Pocock, 1929*) – Pocock described a dark skin of a tiger from Sumatra as the type specimen that had numerous and densely-set broad stripes.

SELECTED TEXTS CITED/FURTHER READING

Heuvelmans, Bernard; Rivera, Jean-Luc; Barloy, Jean-Jacques. *Les Felins Encore Inconnus d'Afrique (Still Unknown Cats in Africa),* (Heuvelmansian Library, 2007).

Eberhart, George M. *Mysterious Creatures: A Guide to Cryptozoology* (CFZ Press, 2013).

Shuker, Karl P. N. *The Beasts that Hide from Man: Seeking the World's Last Undiscovered Species* (Paraview Press, 2003).

Shuker, Karl P. N. ShukerNature: NELSON MANDELA AND THE AFRICAN TIGER (karlshuker.blogspot.com Nov 21, 2012).

Heuglin, Theodor von. *Reise nach Abessinien, den Gala-Landerm, Ost-Sudan und Chartum* (1868).

Heuglin, Theodor von. *Reise in Nordost-Afrika* (1877).

Ricatte, Rene. *De Ile du Diable aux Tumuc-Humac* (La Pensee Universelle, 1978).

Shuker, Karl P. N. *In Search of Prehistoric Survivors: Do Giant 'Extinct' Creatures Still Exists?* (Blandford, 1995).

Shuker, Karl P.N. *Still In Search of Prehistoric Survivors: The Creatures That Time Forgot?* (Coachwhip Publications, 2016).

Xu, David C. *Mystery Creatures of China, The Complete Cryptozoological Guide* (Coachwhip Publications, 2018).

Coudray, Philippe. *Guide des Animaux Caches* (Editions du Mont, 2009).

Fayetteville (N.C.) Observer (January 5-9, 1954).

Gallehugh Jr., Joseph F. "*The Vampire Beast of Bladenboro,*" (North Carolina Folklore 24, 1976).

Futch, Micheal. "*Beast of Bladenboro Put Town on Map,*" (Fayetteville Observer, 2000.)

Hall, Mark A."*The Vampire Beast of Bladenboro,*" (Wonders 7, 2002).

Coleman, Loren. "*Cryptid Long-Tailed Wildcats,*"(http://cryptomundo.com/cryptozoo-news/more-lingtails), (June 19, 2009).

Coleman, Loren. "*Long-Tailed Bobcats*" (http//cryptomundo.com/cryptozoo-news/long-tails-bc) (June 9, 2008).

Shuker, Karl P.N. *Mystery Cats of the World Revisited: Blue Tigers, King Cheetahs, Black Cougars, Spotted Lions, and More* (Anomalist Books, 2020).

Roberts, Alexandra (translated); Bereridge, Henry (edited), *Memoirs of Jahangir* (Tuzuk-i-Jahangiri) (Ulan Press, 31 Aug 2012).

Morris, Steven *et al. Spotless Cheetah Snapped in the Wild* https://www.theguardian.com/environment/2012/apr/25/spotless-cheetah-pictures-wild (April 25, 2012)

'GuateGojira'. *"Tiguar" and "white" cheetah???* (https://www.tapatalk.com/groups/animalsversesanimals/tiguar-and-white-cheetah-t3186.html)

Bottriell, Lena Godsall. *King Cheetah: The Story of the Quest* (Brill Academic Pub Sep 1, 1987).

Clark, Jerome; Coleman, Loren. *Cryptozoology A-Z* (New York: Simon & Schuster, 1999).

Divyabhanusinh. *The End of a Trail: The Cheetah in India* (Oxford University Press, Jan 3, 2002).

Newton, Michael. *Encyclopedia of Cryptozoology: A Guide to Hidden Animals and Their Pursuers* (Jefferson, North Carolina: McFarland & Company, 2005).

Hitchens, Captain W., *"African Mystery Beasts"*, (Discovery, 1937).

Pocock, R. I., *"Description of a New Species of Cheetah (Acinonyx)"* (Proceedings of the Zoological Society of London", April 1927).

Sclater, Philip. *"Zoological Society of London"*, (1877).

Stoneham H. F., Letters, *"Nature in East Africa"*, (1925).

Martyr, Debbie. *"An Investigation of the Orang Pendek, the 'Short Man' of Sumatra,"* (Cryptozoology 9, 1990).

Shuker, Karl P.N. *"A Supplement to Dr Bernard Heuvelmans' Checklist of Cryptozoological Animals,"* (Fortean Studies 5, 1998).

Freeman, Richard. *"Sumatra Expedition Report."* (Animals & Men 31, 2003).

Freeman, Richard. *"Return to Sumatra; Into the Lost Valley,"* (Animals & Men 34, 2004).

Volmer, Rebekka *et. al.* *"Niche Overlap and Competition Potential Among Tigers (Panthera tigris), Sabretoothed Cats (Homotherium ultimum, Hemimachairodus zwierzyckii) and Merriam's Dog (Megacyon merriami) in the Pleistocene of Java. (Palaeontology, Palaeoclimatology, Palaeoecology* Vol. 441, October 2015).

Fontinha, Mario. *Ngombo (Adivinhacao): Tradicoes no Nordeste de Angola,* (1999).

Martins, Joao Vicente. *Crencas, Adivinhacao e Tradicionais dos Tutchokew do Nordeste de Angola,* (1993).

Heuvelmans, Bernard. *On the Track of Unknown Animals* (Rupert Hart-Davis, 1958).

Heuvelmans, Bernard. *Les derniers dragons d'Afrique* (Paris: Plon, 1978).

Fores, Angel Morant. *"An Investigation into Some Unidentified Ecuadorian Mammals"* (Virtual Institute of Cryptozoology, cryptozoo.pagesperso-orange.fr, 1999).

Shuker, Karl P. N. *Karl Shuker's Alien Zoo: From the Pages of Fortean Times* (CFZ Press, Oct 5 2010).

Bottasso, Juan. *Los Shuar y los Animales* (1986).

Tirira Diego, *Nombres de los Mamiferos del Ecuador* (2009).

Heuvelmans, Bernard. *Les derniers dragons d'Afrique* (Paris: Plon, 1978).

Annabell, Maxine. *Red, Pale, Brown, and Unstriped Tigers* (http://;airweb.org.nz/tiger/orange.html)

Jacoby, Charlie. *"A Century on and the Adventure Continues in Hunt for the Giant Sloth"* (The Express, Nov 20, 2000).

Gilmore, David D. *Monsters: Evil Beings, Mythical Beasts, and All Manner of Imaginary Terrors.* p. 112. (University of Pennsylvania Press, May 26, 2012).

Hatcher, J. B. *"Review".* (Science. American Association for the Advancement of Science. 10 (257): 815, Dec 1, 1899).

Simpson, George Gaylord. *"Mammals and Cryptozoology".* Proceedings of the American Philosophical Society. (American Philosophical Society. 128 (1): 13, March 30, 1984).

Wilhelm, Prince of Sweden, *Among Pygmies and Gorillas* (London: Gyldendal, 1923).

Shuker, Karl P.N. *In Search of Prehistoric Survivors: Do Giant 'Extinct' Creatures Still Exist?* (Blandford, 1995).

Shuker, Karl P.N. *Still in Search of Prehistoric Survivors: The Creatures That Time Forgot* (Coachwhip Publications, 2016).

Coleman, Loren; Clarke, Jerome. *Cryptozoology A to Z: The Encyclopaedia of Loch Monsters, Sasquatch, Chupacabras, and Other Authentic Mysteries of Nature* (Simon & Schuster, 1999).

Heuvelmans, Bernard. *"Annotated Checklist of Apparently Unknown Animals With Which Cryptozoology is Concerned"* (Cryptozoology 5, 1986).

Mackal, Roy P. *Searching for Hidden Animals: An Inquiry into Zoological Mysteries* (Cadogan Books, 1980).

Raynal, Michel. *"Le "tigre a dents en sabre" sud-americain"* (Institut Virtuel de Cryptozoologie, cryptozoo.pageperso-orange.fr).

Shuker, Karl P. N. *The Beasts that Hide from Man: Seeking the World's Last Undiscovered Animals* (Paraview Press, 2003).

'Ark Lady.' *North American Jaguar (Panther onca) Collared in Arizona* (Ark Animals, Feb 2009).

Davis, Tony. *Guide describes roaring, powerful jaguar* (Arizona Daily Star, Nov 2011).

Milberg, Monica. *El Jefe, Arizona's mighty jaguar, is missing in action* (AZCentral).

Davis, Tony. *Jaguar Roves near Rosemont site* (Arizona Daily Star, June 2013).

Main, Douglas. *Rare Jaguar Sighting in Arizona, 60 Miles North of Mexican Border* (Newsweek, Feb 2022).

Williams-Grand Canyon News. *Jaguar seen on Fort Huachuca trail camera* (December 27, 2016).

Kenoun, Sabrina. *Potential jaguar habitat at U. S.- Mexico border identified by UArizona researchers* (Cronkite News, April 16, 2021).

Montoya Bryan, Susan. *"Feds set aside habitat in Southwest for jaguar"* (Yahoo! News, March 2014).

Hocking, Peter J. *"Large Peruvian Mammals Unknown to Zoology"* (Cryptozoology, 1992).

Naish, Darren. *"Mystery big cat skulls from the Peruvian Amazon not so mysterious anymore"* (Tetrapod Zoology, 2014).

Shuker, Karl P. N. *Mystery Cats of the World: From Blue Tigers to Exmoor Beasts.* (London: Hale, 1989).

Fores, Angel Morant, *Virtual Institute of Cryptozoology* *"An Investigation into Some Unidentified Ecuadorian Mammals"* (cryptozoo.pagesperso-orange.fr. October 12, 1999).

Shuker, Karl P. N. *ShukerNature: THE WARRACABA TIGER AND OTHER SOUTH AMERICAN PACK HUNTING MYSTERY CATS*, (karlshuker.blogspot.com. April 12, 2017).

Shuker, Karl P. N. *Mystery Cats of the World* (London: Robert Hale, 1989).

Kenneth C. Gandar Dower, *The Spotted Lion* (Boston: Little, Brown, 1937).

Gunther, Albert. *Note on a Supposed Melanotic Variety of the Leopard, from South America* (Proceedings of the Zoological Society of London, March 3, 1885).

Collins, Holdridge Ozro. *Bulletin of the Southern California Academy of Sciences* (1915).

Hamilton-Snowball, G. *"Spotted Lions," The Field* 192 (Oct 1948).

Prater, S. H. *The Book of Indian Animals* (Mumbai, India: Bombay Natural History Society, 1971).

Wood, Gerald L. *The Guinness Book of Animal Facts and Feats*, 3d ed. (Enfield, England: Guinness Superlatives, 1982).

Rebsamen, Bill. *"A Mounted Cat Mystery,"* (North American BioFortean Review 1, no. 1, April 1999).

Prater, S. H., *JBNHS*, Vol. 39, 381-2 (1937).

Walsh, Martin T; Goldman, Helle V. *Cryptids and Credulity: The Zanzibar leopard and other imaginary beings* (1st ed. Routledge: 2016).

Goldman, H. V.; Walsh, M. T. *A Leopard in Jeopardy: An Anthropological Survey of Practices and Beliefs which Threaten the Survival of the Zanzibar Leopard (Panthera pardus adersi)* (Report). (Zanzibar Forestry Technical Paper No. 3, Jozani-Chwaka Bay Conservation Project, 1997).

Goldman, H. V.; Walsh, M. T. *"Killing the King: The Demonization and Extermination of the Zanzibar Leopard"*. (Paris: Editions de l'LRD. pp. 1133 – 1182).

Goldman, H. V.; Walsh, M. T. *Human-Wildlife Conflict, Unequal Knowledge and the Failure to Conserve the Zanzibar Leopard (Panthera pardus adersi)*. Field Biology and Conservation Conference, Wildlife Conservation Research Unit. (University of Oxford, 17-21, Sept 2007).

Rossi, L.; Scuzzarella, C. M.; Angelici, F. M. *"Extinct or Perhaps Surviving Relict Populations of Big Cats: Their Controversial Stories and Implications for Conservation"* (Problematic Wildlife II: New Conservation and Management Challenges in the Human-Wildlife Interactions. (Cham: Springer International Publishing, 2020).

Swai, I. S. *Wildlife Conservation Status in Zanzibar* (M.Sc. dissertation). (Dar es Salaam: University of Dar es Salaam, 1983).

Walsh, M. T.; Goldman, H. V. *Killing the King: The Demonization and Extermination of the Zanzibar Leopard.* (Scribd, 2007).

Li, Johanna. *"Zanzibar Leopard Captured on Camera, Despite Being Declared Extinct"*. (Inside Edition, June 7, 2018).

Hepter, V. G.; Sludskij, A. A. *"Lion"*. Mammals of the Soviet Union. Vol. 2, Part 2. Carnivora (Hyaenas and cats): (Washington DC: Smithsonian Institute and the National Science Foundation. pp. 83 – 95, 1992).

Black, S. A.; Fellous, A.; Yamaguchi, N.; Roberts, D. L. *"Examining the Extinction of the Barbary Lion and its Implications for Felid Conservation"*. (PLOS ONE. 8 (4), 2013).

Bauer, H.; Packer, C.; Funston, P. F.; Henschel, P. & Nowell, K. *"Panthera leo"* (IUCN Red List of Threatened Species, 2017).

Nowell, K & Jackson, P. *"African lion, Panthera leo (Linnaeus, 1758) (PDF) Wild Cats: Status and Conservation Action Plan"*. (Gland, Switzerland: IUCN/SSC Cat Specialist Group. pp. 17 – 21, 1996).

Wozencraft, W. C. *"Panthera leo"*. In Wilson, D. E.; Reeder, D. M. (eds.). Mammal Species of the World: A Taxonomic and Geographic Reference (3rd ed.). (John Hopkins University Press. p. 546, 2005).

Kitchener, A. C. et.al. *"A Revised Taxonomy of the Felidae: The final report of the Cat Classification Task Force of the IUCN Cat Specialist Group"* (PDF). (Cat News (Special Issue 11): 71 – 73, 2017).

Antunes, A.; Troyer, J. L.; Roelke, M. E.; Pecon-Slattery, J.; Packer. C.; Winterbach, C.;

Winterbach, H. & Johnson, W. E. *"The Evolutionary Dynamics of the Lion Panthera leo revealed by Host and Viral Population Genomics".* (*PLOS Genetics*. 4 (11), 2008).

Bertola, L. D. et al. *"Phylogeographic patterns in Africa and High-Resolution Delineation of genetic clades in the Lion (Panthera leo)"* (*Science Reports*. 6, 2016).

Manuel, M. D. et al. *"The evolutionary history of extinct and living lions"* (*Proceedings of the National Academy of Sciences of the United States of America*. 117 (20), 2020).

Mazak, V. *"The Barbary lion, Panthera le oleo (Linnaeus, 1758): some systematic notes, and an interim list of the specimens preserved in European museums",* (*Zeitschrift fur Saugetierkunde*. 35: 34 – 45, 1970).

Mazak, J. H. *"Geographical variation and phylogenetics of modern lions based on craniometric data".* (*Journal of Zoology*. 281 (3): 194 – 209, 2010).

Yamaguchi, N.; Haddane, B. *"The North African Barbary Lion and the Atlas Lion Project"* (*International Zoo News*. 49 (8): 465 – 481, 2002).

Barnett, R.; Yamaguchi, N.; Barnes, I.; Cooper, A. *"Lost populations and preserving genetic diversity in the lion Panthera leo: Implications for its ex-situ conservation"* (PDF). (*Conservation Genetics*. 7 (4): 507 – 514, 2006).

O'Brien, S. J.; Joslin, P.; Smith, G. L.; Wolfe, R.; Schaffer, N.; Heath, E; Ott-Joslin, J.; Rawal, P. P.; Bhattacharjee, K. K.; Martenson, J. S. *"Evidence for African Origins of Founders of the Asiatic Lion Species Survival Plan".* (*Zoo Biology*. 6 (2): 99 – 116, 1987).

Barnett, R.; Yamaguchi, N; Barnes, I. & Cooper, A. *"The origin, current diversity, and future conservation of the modern lion (Panthera leo)"* (PDF). (*Proceedings of the Royal Society B: Biological Sciences*. 273 (1598): 2119 – 2125, 2006).

Linnaeus, C. *"Felis Leo". Systema naturae per regna naturae: secundum classes, ordines, genera, species, cum characteribus, differentis, synonymis, locis,* (in Latin). Vol. 1 (10th ed.). (*Holmiae (Laurentii Salvii)*. p. 41, 1758).

Meyer, J. N. *Dissertatio inauguralis anatomico-medica de genere felium*. Doctoral thesis. (*Vienna: University of Vienna*, 1826).

Blainville, H. M. D. de. *"F. leo nubicus". Osteographie ou description iconographique compare du squelette et du systeme dentaire des mammiferes recents et fossils pour server de base a la zoologie et la geologie*. Vol. 2 (*Paris: J. B. Bailliere et Fils*. p. 186, 1843).

Pocock, R. I. *"The lions of Asia".* (*Journal of the Bombay Natural Historical Society*. 34: 638 – 665, 1930).

Johnston, H. H. *"The lion in Tunisia". In Bryden, H. A. (ed.). Great and small game of Africa.* (*London: Rowland Ward Ltd.* pp. 562 – 564, 1899).

Pease, A. E. *"The lion in Algeria". In Bryden, H. A. (ed.). Great and small game of Africa.* (*London: Rowland Ward Ltd.* pp. 564 – 568, 1899).

Tefera, M. *"Phenotypic and reproductive characteristics of lions (Panthera leo) at Addis Ababa Zoo".* (*Biodiversity and Conservation*. 12 (8): 1629 – 1639).

Shuker, Karl P. N. *ShukerNature: FROM BLACK LIONS TO LIVING SABRE-TOOTHS – MY TOP TEN MYSTERY CATS.*

Shuker, Karl P. N. *ShukerNature: MADAGASCAN MYSTERY CATS – WITH FELINE FELICITATIONS FROM THE FITOATY AND THE FOSSA* (Karlshuker.blogspot.com, 11 March 2020).

Drinnon, Dale A. *Frontiers of Zoology: Persisting Giant Lemurs of Madagascar* (Frontiersof-zoology.blogspot.com, 16 July 2013).

Coleman, Loren. *Mysterious America: The Revised Edition* (Paraview Press, 2001).

Peters, Hammerson. *Legends of the Nahanni Valley* (PublishDrive, 2018).

Weatherly, David. *Monsters of the Last Frontier: Cryptids & Legends of Alaska* (Leprechaun Press, 2020).

Shuker, Karl P. N. *"A Supplement to Dr Bernard Heuvelmans' Checklist of Cryptozoological Animals"* (Fortean Studies, Vol. 5, 1998).

Hocking, Peter J. *"Further Investigation into Unknown Peruvian Mammals"*(Cryptozoology, No. 12, 1998).

Platt, John R. *"When Did the Barbary Lion Really Go Extinct?"* (*Scientific American*, April 22, 2013).

Heuvelmans, Bernard; Hopkins, Peter Gwynvay. *The Natural History of Hidden Animals* (Routledge, 2007).

Krumbiegal, Ingo. *"Was ist der 'Lowe des Wassers'?"* (Kosmos, no, 42, 1947).

Krumbiegal, Ingo. *Von Neuen und Unentdeckten Tierarten* (1950).

Heuvelmans, Bernard. *Les Derniers Dragons d'Afrique* (1978).

Ballot, Michel. *Mokele – Mbembe Expeditions: L'Expedition de Juin – Juillet* (mokelembembeexpeditions.blogspot.com, 9 July 2010).

Macrae, Farquhar Baliol. *"More African Mysteries,"* (The National Review, No. III, Dec 1938).

Shuker, Karl P. N. *Still In Search of Prehistoric Survivors: The Creatures That Time Forgot?* (Coachwhip Publications, 2016).

Ricatte, Rene. *De Ile du Diable aux Tumuc-Humac, La Pensee Universelle* (1978).

Vaudrey, Glen. *CRYPTOZOOLOGY ONLINE: Still on the Track: GLEN VAUDREY: Whole Wide World (the missing bits)* (forteanzoology,blog-spot.com, March 10 2011).

Voillemont, Christian. *Le Popoke, le Maipolina, la Mamadilo – Adventure en Guyane* (aventuresenguyane.com, June 29, 2016, modified October 27, 2021).

Raynal, Michel. *"Le "tigre a dents an sabre" sud-americain" Institut Virtuel de Cryptozoologie* (cryptozoo.pagesperso-orange.fr, August 9 1999).

Mackal, Roy P. *Searching for Hidden Animals: An Inquiry into Zoological Mysteries* (Cadogan Books, 1980).

Dower, Gandar. *The Spotted Lion* 1st, Ed. (London: William Heinemann Ltd, 1937).

Coleman, Loren. *Mysterious America: The Revised Edition* (New York: Paraview Press, 2001).

Newton, Michael. *Encyclopedia of Cryptozoology: A Global Guide to Hidden Animals and Their Pursuers* (North Carolina: McFarland & Company, 2005).

Fawcett, Brian; Fawcett, Percy. *Exploration Fawcett* (Hutchinson, 1953).

Fawcett, P. H. *Bolivian Exploration, 1913 – 1914* (The Geographical Journal, Vol. 45, no. 3, March 1915).

Shuker, Karl P. N. *Cats of Magic, Mythology, and Mystery* (CFZ Press, 2012)

Shuker, Karl P. N. *Extraordinary Animals Revisited* (CFZ Press, 2007).

Shuker, Karl P. N. *ShukerNature: TRAILING THE MITLA – A DOG-LIKE CAT, OR A CAT-LIKE DOG?* (karlshuker.blogspot.com Feb 21, 2013).

Mallinson, Jeremy. *Travels in Search of Endangered Species* (David & Charles UK, 1989).

Mackal, Roy P. *Searching for Hidden Animals: An Inquiry into Zoological Mysteries* (Cadogan Books, 1980).

Hichens, William. *"On The Trail of the Brontosaurus: Encounters with Africa's Mystery Animals"* (Chamber's Journal, 1927).

Hichens, William. *"African Mystery Beasts"* (Discovery 18, 1937).

Shuker, Karl P. N. *ShukerNature*: NUNDA – IN SEARCH OF THE STRANGE ONE (karlshuker.blogspot.com, April 17, 2010).

Sunquist, Mel; Sunquist, Fiona. *Wild Cats of the World,* (University of Chicago Press, 2002).

Nark, Jason. *"Spotting mountain lions is becoming a Pennsylvanian pastime. But they're probably bobcats* (The Philadelphia Inquirer, Feb 16, 2022).

Schneck, Marcus. *"Eastern mountain lion officially declared extinct"* (PENN LIVE Patriot News, Jan 29, 2018; Updated: Jan 30, 2019).

Folkard, C. *The Guinness Book of World Records* (Hachette, 2004).

Nielsen, C.; Thompson, D.; Kelly, M.; Lopez-Gonzalez, C. A. "Puma concolour". IUCN Red List of Threatened Species (ISSN 2307-8235, online, 2015).

Heuvelmans, Bernard. *Les derniers dragons d'Afrique* (Paris: Plon, 1978).

Newton, Michael. *Hidden Animals: A Field Guide to Batsquatch, Chupacabra, and Other Elusive Creatures* (Greenwood, 2009).

Le Noël, Christian. *LE TIGRES DES MONTAGNES: DES FELINS A DENTS EN SABRE AU COEUR DE L'AFRIQUE?* (Institut Virtuel de Cryptozoologie, https://cryptozoo-pagesperso--orange-fr.translate.goog/dossiers/tigrmont.htm?_x_tr_sl=fr&_x_tr_tl=en&_x_tr_hl=en&_x_tr_pto=sc)

Pitman, Charles. *A Game Warden Among His Charges* (Nisbet & Company, 1931).

Hichens, William. *"African Mystery Beasts,"* Discovery: The Popular Journal of Knowledge, Vol. 18, No. 216 (December 1937).

Kirk, John. *CRYPTOMUNDO* (http://cryptomundo.com/public-forum/the-onca-mystery-cat)

Naish, Darren. *Science Blogs,* "Multiple new species of large living mammal (part 5)", (https://scienceblogs.com/tetrapodzoology/2007/06/01/multiple-new-species-of-large-3)

Carmony, Neil B. *Onza! The Hunt for a Legendary Cat* (High Lonesome Books, 1995).

Marshall, Robert E. *The Onza: The Story of the Search for the Mysterious Cat of the Mexican Highlands* (Exposition, 1961).

Reyes, Ernesto Alverado. *"The Legend of the Mexican "onza"* pp. 147-148 (Mastozoologia Neotropical 15, 2008).

Arment, Chad. *Cryptozoology: Science & Speculation* (Coachwhip Publications, 2004).

Ashton, Saul; Hawthorne, Cornus. *Tales of the Ozark Howler* (Independently published May 9, 2009).

Fields, Jan; Brundage, Scott. *Hunt the Ozark Howler* (Calico Chapter Books: Illustrated Ed., Aug 15, 2016).

Malone, Ross. *Billy Bob's Howler* (Bluebird – St. Louis Jan 1, 2014).

Ashton, Saul; Hawthorne, Cornus. *Tales of the Ozark Howler* (Independently published May 9, 2009).

Fields, Jan; Brundage, Scott. *Hunt the Ozark Howler* (Calico Chapter Books: Illustrated Ed., Aug 15, 2016).

Malone, Ross. *Billy Bob's Howler* (Bluebird – St. Louis Jan 1, 2014).

Sandesh, Kandur. Natural World, 2008-2009, The Mountains of the Monsoon (BBC Documentary).

Moiser, C. "*The melanistic leopards of Eastern Cape, South Africa", pp. 43-50* (CFZ Yearbook, 1997).

McCollough, Mark. "*Eastern puma (cougar) (Puma concolour cougar) 5-year review: Summary and Evaluation*" (PDF) (Maine Field Office Orono, Maine: U. S. Fish and Wildlife Service, March 2011).

Culver, M.; Johnson, W. E.; Pecon-Slattery, J.; O'Brien, S. J. "*Genomic ancestry of the American puma (Puma concolour)* (Journal of Heredity. 91 (3): 186 – 187, 2000).

Boswell, Randy. "*Montreal Gazette: U. S. officials declare eastern cougar extinct, despite sightings in Canada*" (Montreal Gazette, Postmedia News, March 2, 2011).

Young, S. P.; Goldman, E. A. *The puma: Mysterious American cat* (American Wildlife Institute, 1946).

Hall, E. R. *The Mammals of North America.* Second edition (John Wiley & Sons, New York, 1981).

Kitchener, A. C. et al. "*A revised taxonomy of the Felidae: The final report of the Cat Classification Task Force of the IUCN Cat Specialist Group* (PDF) (Cat News, Issue 11: 33 – 34).

Barringer, Felicity. "*U.S. Declares Eastern Cougar Extinct, With an Asterisk*" (The New York Times, March 11, 2011).

Bolgiano, C. *Mountain lion: An unnatural history of pumas and people* (Stackpole Books, Harrisburg, Pennsylvania, 1995).

Suhr, Jim. "*Study: Cougars again spreading across Midwest*" (Associated Press, June 14, 2012).

Baron, David. "*The Cougar Behind Your Trash Can*" (New York Times, July 28, 2011).

West, Valerie. "*Cougar sightings prompt dispute among wildlife organizations*" (Daily Tribune, Nov 30, 2008).

Van Arsdale, Scott. "*Big Cat Tales: Investigating Cougar Sightings in New York*" (New York State Department of Environmental Conservation, Feb 2008).

McNeil, Kelvin. "*Some Little-Known Cougar Sightings in New Hampshire*" (PDF) (North American BioFortean Review. 3 (7): 20 – 23, Oct 2001)

Prevo, Robert "*Arkansas "Black Panthers""* (PDF). (North American BioFortean Review. 3 (7): 51 – 52, Oct 2001).

Author Unknown. Tennessee Officials Confirm First Cougar Sighting in 100 Years (Field & Stream).

Scott, F. W. *Update of COSEWIC status report on cougar (Felis concolour couguar), eastern population.* (Committee on the Status of Endangered Wildlife in Canada, 1998).

Zuckerman, Laura. "*Eastern U.S. cougar declared extinct 80 years after last sighting.*" (Routers, Jan 23, 2018).

Shuker, Karl P. N. *Still In Search of Prehistoric Survivors: The Creatures That Time Forgot?* (Coachwhip Publications, 2016).

He Xin Huang and Wang Zheng, Liu. *Shennongjia in China*; ("'Why were 'leopard hunt heroes' sentenced?"), (Minzudajiating, no. 3, 1997).

Shen Shixi. "Shanbiao," (Toutiao, no. 12, 2015).

Hocking, Peter J. *"Large Peruvian Mammals Unknown to Zoology"*. (Cryptozoology 11. 1992).

Jackson, J. K., *"Animal Life in the Imatong Mountains"* (Sudan Wildlife and Sport, Vol. 1, no, 4, Dec 1959).

Werdelin, Lars; Sanders, William Joseph. (Cenozoic Mammals of Africa, 2010).

Kitchener, A. C. Et al. *"A revised taxonomy of the Felidae: The final report of the Cat Classification Task Force of the IUCN Cat Specialist Group"* (PDF) (Cat News (Special Issue 11): 66-68, 2017).

Goodrich, J. Et al. *"Panthera tigris"* (IUCN Red List of Threatened Species, 2015).

Seidensticker, J. *"Large carnivores and the consequences of habitat insularization: ecology and conservation of tigers in Indonesia and Bangladesh"*. Cats of the World: biology, conservation, and management. (Washington DC: National Wildlife Federation. pp. 1-41, 1986).

Annabell, Maxine. *The C. T. Buckland Black Tiger Story*.

Annabell, Maxine. *Early Evidence of Black Tigers*.

Clark, Jerome; Coleman, Loren. *Cryptozoology A-Z*. (New York: Simon & Schuster, 1999).

Coleman, Loren. *Mysterious America: The Revised Edition*. (New York: Paraview Press, 2001).

Douchan, Gersi. *Dans la jungle de Borneo* (Paris: Editions, G.B., 1975).

Kitchener, A. C. *"Tiger distribution, phenotypic variation and conservation issues"*. 19 – 39. *Riding the Tiger: Tiger Conservation in Human-Dominated Landscapes*. (Cambridge University Press, 1999).

Meijaard, Erik. *"The Bornean Tiger: speculation on its existence,"* 12-15. (Cat News no. 30, Spring 1999).

Piper, P. J.; Rabett, Earl of Cranbrook. *"Confirmation of the presence of the tiger Panthera tigris (L.) in Late Pleistocene and Holocene Borneo"*. 259 – 267. (Malayan Nature Journal. 59 (3), 2007).

Freeman, Richard. *"If You Were the Only Gul in the World and I the Only Boy,"* (Animals & Men 66/7, Nov 2018).

Matthiessen, Peter. *The Cloud Forest* (Pyramid Books, 1966).

Raynal, Michel. *"Sabre-Toothed Cat in Paraguay?"* (Virtual Institute of Cryptozoology, cryptozoo.pagesperso-orange.fr).

Shuker, Karl P. N. *"Venezuelan Mystery Cats"* (Fortean Times, no. 383, Sept 2019).

Shuker, Karl P. N. *From Flying Toads to Snakes with Wings* (Bounty Books, 1997)

Hance, Jeremy. *"Javan Officials Employ Camera Traps to Find Extinct Tiger"* (Mongabay, March 13, 2012).

Mazak, J. H.; Groves, C. P. *"A Taxonomic Revision of the Tigers (Panthera tigris)"* (PDF) pp. 268 – 287 (Mammalian Biology. 71 (5), 2006).

Partington, C. F. *"Felis, the cat tribe"*. (Orr & Smith: The British Encyclopaedia of Natural History, 1986).

Seidensticker, J. *"Large Carnivores and the Consequences of Habitat Insularization: Ecology and Conservation of Tigers in Indonesia and Bangladesh"* pp. 1 – 41 (PDF) *In Miller, S. D; Everett, D. D. (eds) Cats of the World: biology, conservation, and management.* (Washington DC: National Wildlife Federation, 1986).

DetikNews: Pendaki Wanita Tewas di Gunung Merbabu, Diduga Diterkam Harimau. (JawaPos Jan 24, 2009: Harimau Teror Warga Ringin Agung. Archived 2009: Wayback Machine).

Mazak, V. *"Panthera tigris"* (PDF) pp. 1 – 8 (Mammalian Species. 152 (152), 1981).

ProFauna, "HOT NEWS: Sight of Javan Tiger in Mt. Arjuno Went Viral" (Protecting Forest and Wildlife, profauna.net, June 27, 2016).

Bambang, M. *"In Search of 'Extinct Javan Tiger,"* (The Jakarta Post, Oct 30, 2002)

The Sydney Morning Herald. *Tiger rumors swirl below Indon Volcano.* (The Sydney Morning Herald, Nov 2, 2010).

The New York Times. "Tiger Species Thought Extinct is Possibly Spotted in Indonesia". (NY Times. 1017. Retrieved Nov 2017).

Souef, A. S; Burrell, Harry. *The Wild Animals of Australasia* (London: George G. Harrap & Company Ltd, 1926).

Raynal, Michel. *"Queensland's "Tiger-Cat"* Virtual Institute of Cryptozoology. (cryptozoo.pagesperso-orange.fr, Aug 13, 2011).

Scott, Walter J. "Letter from W. J. Scott, addressed to the Secretary, Respecting the Supposed 'Native Tiger' of Queensland". (*Proceedings of the Zoological Society of London*, 1872).

Scott, Walter J. "Notice of the Existence in Queensland of an Undescribed Species of Mammal" (*Proceedings of the Zoological Society of London*, 1871).

Clacher, Paul. "Big Cats: Others Who Have Had Experiences and Eyewitness Reports." (Big Cat Witnesses, 2010).

Gilroy, Rex. *Rex & Heather Gilroy Research of the Australian Panther* (Queensland Research: mysteriousaustralia.com, 2003)

Harrison, Dean. Thylacoleo sighting, Gilderoy, Victoria, 2002. (Australian Yowie Research, December 6, 2005).

Troughton, Ellis. *Furred Animals of Australia.* (Scribner's, 1931).

Naish, Darren. *Hunting Monsters: Cryptozoology and the Reality Behind the Myths.* (Arcturus, 2016).

Kane, Joe. *"The Rebels of the Rain Forest".* (Conde Nast's Traveller Vol. 33, Dec 1998).

Morant Fores, Angel. Virtual Institute of Cryptozoology "An Investigation into Some Unidentified Ecuadorian Mammals". (cryptozoo.pagesperso-orange.fr, Oct 12, 1999).

Morant Fores, Angel. "Investigation en Torno a Algunos Mamiferos no Identificados del Ecuador". (criptozoologia.org, July 2003).

Rueda, Marco Vinicio. *Setenta Mitos Shuar* (Quito, Ecuador: Mundo Shuar, 1983).

Hong Kong MA. (Fortean Times no. 25, Spring 1978).

Anders, Forsman. *Is colour polymorphism advantageous to populations and species?"* Molecular Ecology. (Wiley Online Library, (https://onlinelibrary.wiley.com/doi/full/10.1111/mec.13629) (May 14, 2016).

Hocking, Peter J. *"Large Peruvian Mammals Unknown to Zoology"*, (Cryptozoology, 11, 1992)

Fores, Angel Morant. Virtual Institute of Cryptozoology "An Investigation into Some Unidentified Ecuadorian Mammals". (cryptozoo.pagesperso-orange.fr, Oct 12, 1999).

Salazar, Mariano Gutierrez. *Gramatica Didactica de la Lengua Pemon.* (Universidad Catolica Andres, 2001).

Beebe, William. *Tropical Wildlife in British Guiana: Zoological Contributions from the Tropical Research Station of the New York Zoological Society.* (New York City: The New York Zoological Society, 1917).

Heuglin, Theodor von. *Reise in Nordost-Afrika.* (Braunschweig, G. Westermann, 1877).

Coleman, Loren. *The Wobo.* (cryptonews.com, Oct 9, 2008).

Brown, Charles Barrington. *Canoe and Camp Life in British Guiana* (1876).

Everard Ferdinand. Among the Indians of Guiana (1883)/

Freeman, Richard. *"Yamamaya the great cat of Iriomote"*. (http://forteanzoology.blogspot.com, May 8, 2009).

Duyvendak, J.J.L. *"The True Dates of the Chinese Maritime Expeditions in the Early Fifteenth Century"*. (T'oung Pao, Second Series, 34 (5), 1939).

Bagrow, Leo R.; Skelton, A. *History of Cartography.* (Transaction Publishers. p. 204, 2009).

Lust, John. *Chinese Popular Prints.* (Brill Publishers. p. 301, 1996).

Breakdown of the 'Fantastic Beasts: The Crimes of Grindelwald' Comic-Con Official Trailer! – The-Leaky-Cauldron. Org". (The-Leaky-Cauldron.org, 2018-07-21).

Shuowen Jiezi, radical (tiger). (https://ctext.org/shuo-wen-jie-zi/hu-bu?searchu=%E9%A8%B6%E8%99%9E&searchmode=showall#result)

W. Shoemaker, Henry. *"Felis Catus in Pennsylvania? Being Reports of the Taking of a Genuine European Wild Cat in Tinicum Township, Bucks County"* (Altoona, Pa.: Times Tribune Co., January 16, 1922).

R. Lyman Sr, Robert. Amazing Indeed! Strange Events in the Black Forest (Coudersport, Pa.: Potter Enterprise, 1973).

Arment, Chad. "More Odd 'Wildcat' Reports," (North American BioFortean Review 2, no. 2 (2000): 41, http:// www.strangeark.com/nabr/NABR4.pdf).

Coleman, Loren; Clark, Jerome. *Cryptozoology A to Z: The Encyclopedia of Lack Monsters, Sasquatch, Chupacabras, and Other Authentic Mysteries of Nature* (Simon & Schuster, 1999).

Tryon, Henry Harrington. Fearsome Critters. (Cornwall, NY: Idlewild Press, 1939).

Cohen, Daniel. Monsters, Giants, and Little Men from Mars: An Unnatural History of the Americas. (New York: Doubleday, 1975).

Cox, William T. with Latin Classifications by George B. Sudworth. *Fearsome Creatures of the Lumberwoods.* (Washington, D.C.: Judd & Detweiler Inc., 1910)

H. Tryon, Henry. "The Come-at-a-Body" from Fearsome Critters (1939).

Engl, New; Legends. "Podcast 100 – Hunting Glastonbury's Glawackus – New Eng-land Legends".

Matthews, John. *The Element Encyclopedia of Magical Creatures* (Barnes and No-ble Inc. NY, 2005).

Belanger, Jeff. *Hunting Glastonbury's Glawackus* (2019).

Republican Newsroom, et al. "Son of 'Caveman,' Springfield Bookstore President Charlie Johnson Marks 90th Birthday." (www.masslive.com/news/index.ssf/2018/02/son_of_caveman_springfield_boo.html, 2 Feb. 2018).

H. Tryon, Henry. "The Silver Cat" from Fearsome Critters (1939).

H. Tryon, Henry. "The Santer" from Fearsome Critters (1939).

Statesville Landmark Newspaper Article (1890).

Vigne, J. D. "Zooarchaeology and the biogeographical history of the mammals of Corsica and Sardinia since the last ice age". (Mammal Review. 22 (2): 87–96. 1992).

Kitchener, A. C, *et al* "A revised taxonomy of the Felidae: The final report of the Cat Classification Task Force of the IUCN Cat Specialist Group" (PDF), (Cat News. Special Issue 11: 17–20, 2017).

Christopher Columbus' *Letter to the Sovereigns* (1503).

Fawcett, P. H. *Bolivian Exploration, 1913 – 1914* (The Geographical Journal, Vol. 45, no. 3, March 1915).

Shuker, Karl P. N. *ShukerNature*: TRAILING THE MITLA – A DOG-LIKE CAT, OR A CAT-LIKE DOG? (karlshuker.blogspot.com Feb 21, 2013).

Mallinson, Jeremy. *Travels in Search of Endangered Species* (David & Charles UK, 1989).

Mackal, Roy P. *Searching for Hidden Animals: An Inquiry into Zoological Mysteries* (Cadogan Books, 1980).

Hocking, Peter J. "Large Peruvian Mammals Unknown to Zoology" (Cryptozoology 11, 1992).

Shuker, Karl P. N. *ShukerNature*: THE WARRACABA TIGER AND OTHER SOUTH AMERICAN PACK-HUNTING MYSTERY CATS karlshuker.blogspot.com, April 12, 2017).

Mythical Creatures in Classics of Mountains and Seas (https://www.viewofchina.com/mythical-creatures/)

Francis, Dianne. My Highland Kellas Cats. Cape, 1993).

Kitchener, A. "Investigating the identity of the Kellas Cats". Francis, D. (ed.). My Highland Kellas Cats. Cape, 1993).

Nowak, R. M. *Walker's Carnivores of the World*. Johns Hopkins University Press. p. 237, 2005).

"Elgin Museum, collection", Museums Galleries Scotland, archived from the original on 5 March 2016.

Bowers, Aron, "Kellas Cats, Scotching the Myth", Scottish Big Cat Trust, archived from the original on 14 September 2015.

Forés, Angel Morant. "An Investigation into Some Unidentified Ecuadorian Mammals" (Virtual Institute of Cryptozoology, cryptozoo.pagesperso-orange.fr, 12 October 1999).

Bottasso, Juan. Los Shuar y los Animales (1986).

McCollough, Mark. "Eastern puma (cougar) (Puma concolour cougar) 5-year review:

Summary and Evaluation" (PDF). Maine Field Office Orono, Maine: U.S. Fish and Wildlife Service. p. 35, March 2011).

Culver, M.; Johnson, W.E.; Pecon-Slattery, J.; O'Brien, S.J. "Genomic ancestry of the American puma (Puma concolour)". Journal of Heredity. 91 (3): 186–197, 2000).

Kerr, R. The animal kingdom, or zoological system of the celebrated Linnaeus (London, England, 1792).

Young, S.P. and Goldman, E.A. The puma: Mysterious American cat. (American Wildlife Institute, Washington, D.C, 1946).

Cardoza, J.E.; Langlois, S.A. "The eastern cougar: A management failure?". Wildlife Society Bulletin. 30 (1): 265–273, 2002).

Jackson, H.H.T. "The Wisconsin puma". (Proceedings of the Biological Society of Washington. 68: 149–150, 1955).

Hall, E.R. The Mammals of North America, Second edition (John Wiley and Sons, New York, 1981).

"U.S. Fish and Wildlife Service concludes eastern cougar extinct". fws.org. March 2, 2011.

Barringer, Felicity. "U.S. Declares Eastern Cougar Extinct, With an Asterisk". (The New York Times, March 2, 2011).

Bolgiano, C. Mountain lion: An unnatural history of pumas and people (Stack-pole Books, Harrisburg, Pennsylvania, 1995).

Suhr, Jim. "Study: Cougars again spreading across Midwest" (Associated Press, June 14, 2012).

Baron, David. "The Cougar Behind Your Trash Can" (New York Times. Boulder, Colorado, July 28, 2011).

Eastern cougar declared extinct, confirming decades of suspicion, a March 2, 2011, CNN News blog post.

Johnson, Kirk "The Mountain Lions of Michigan". Endangered Species Update. Ann Arbor, MI. 19 (2): 27–31, March–April 2002).

West, Valerie "Cougar sightings prompt dispute among wildlife organizations" (Daily Tribune. Journal Register News Service, November 30, 2008).

Bolgiano, Chris; Roberts, Jerry. The Eastern Cougar: Historic Accounts, Scientific Investigations, And New Evidence. Mechanicsburg: Stackpole Books. pp. 67–78, August 10, 2005).

"Wisconsin DNR Wants Hearings on Killing Cougars". Eastern Cougar. January 26, 2011.

Lester, Todd "Search for Cougars in the East North America" (PDF), (North American BioFortean Review. 3 (7): 15–17, October 2001).

"Mountain lion killed in Northeast Missouri". Hannibal Courier-Post. January 24, 2011.

On June 10, 2011, a cougar was observed roaming near Greenwich, Connecticut. State officials at the time said they believed it was a released pet "Mountain lion reportedly spotted roaming Connecticut town"(Fox News, June 10, 2011).

On June 11, 2011, a cougar, believed to be the same, was killed by a car on the Wilbur Cross Parkway in Milford, Connecticut. "Mountain Lion killed by car on Connecticut highway". CNN. June 11, 2011. When wildlife officials examined the cougar's DNA, they concluded that it was a wild cougar from the Black Hills of

South Dakota, which had wandered at least 1,500 miles east over an indeterminate time.

Van Arsdale, Scott "Big Cat Tales: Investigating Cougar Sightings in New York". New York State Conservationist (New York State Department of Environ-mental Conservation, February 2008).

Miller, Kevin "Despite Hundreds of Sightings, Cougar's Status Re-mains in Doubt". Bangor Daily News, December 3, 2010).

McNeil, Kelvin "Some Little-Known Cougar Sightings in New Hampshire" (PDF). North American BioFortean Review. 3 (7): 20–23, October 2001).

Prevo, Robert "Arkansas "Black Panthers"" (PDF). North American Bio-Fortean Review. 3 (7): 51–53, October 2001).

Tennessee Officials Confirm First Cougar Sighting in 100 Years, (Field & Stream).

"Mountain Lions Headed for Atlantic City?". Insight on the News. 19 (#17): 16–17. August 5, 2003.

Gilbert, S. L., Slivy, K. J., Pozzanghera, C. B., DuBour, A., Overduijn, K., Smith, M. M., Prugh, L. R. Socioeconomic Benefits of Large Carnivore Recolonization Through Reduced Wildlife-Vehicle Collisions, 2016, June 28, 2016.

Scott, F.W. Update of COSEWIC status report on cougar (Felis concolour couguar), eastern population. Committee on the Status of Endangered Wildlife in Canada (Environment Canada, Ottawa, Ontario, Canada, 1998).

Thurston, Harry. "Can the eastern cougar debate be laid to rest?". (Canadian Geographic. 119 (#6): 18, September–October 1999).

Government of Canada, COSEWIC, Committee on the Status of Endangered Wildlife in Canada. "COSEWIC Species Database: Results 1–10". Cosewic.gc.ca.

McNeil, Scott (March 5, 2011). "Eastern cougars still exist, Ontario ministry insists U.S. claim of species' extinction disputed". (Ottawa Citizen, March 5, 2011).

MacDonell, Kevin. "Cougars in the Maritimes: Fact or Fiction?". (Outdoor Nova Scotia, December 29, 2001).

Scullion, Ronnie "Review: The Eastern Panther – Mystery Cat of the Appalachians". (Outdoor Nova Scotia, December 2, 2003).

"Newfoundland west coasters set up motion-activated camera near Deer Lake in hopes of spotting cougar | CBC News".

"Ontario Puma Foundation, Ontario, Canada". Ontariopuma.ca.

Klandagi/Cougar Rewilding Foundation: Correspondence with Manito-ba/Saskatchewan biologists, March/2017.

Zuckerman, Laura. "Eastern U.S. cougar declared extinct 80 years after last sighting". Reuters, January 23, 2018).

"Eastern Puma Declared Extinct, Removed from Endangered Species List". (Center for Biological Diversity. June 17, 2015).

Miriam, Jordan. "Does Your Mascot Have a DNA Sequence? School Boosters Now Use Science to Compete". (The Wall Street Journal, 4 March 2016).

Evanitsky, Maya N.; George, Richard J.; Johnson, Stephen; Dowell, Stephanie; Perry, George H. "Mitochondrial genomes of the regionally extinct Nittany Lion (Puma concolour from Pennsylvania)". (bioRxiv, 10 November 2017).

Forth, Gregory. *Images of the Wildman in Southeast Asia: An anthropological perspective.* (Routledge, 10 Dec 2008).

Satunin, C. *The Black Wild Cat of Transcaucasia.* (Proceedings of the Zoological Society of London, October 1904).

Zielinski, Sarah. *The Daemon Cat that Never Was.* (ScienceNews, October 31, 2013).

Shoemaker, Henry W., *Felis catus* in Pennsylvania? (Biodiversity Heritage Library, January 16, 1922).

Stonestreet, O.C. *O.C. Stonestreet IV, Curse of the Wampus, and other Short Spooky Stories of Piedmont North Carolina* (1st ed.). (Duke Libraries: Createspace. p. 74, 2016).

Tribune, Dale Gowing Mooresville. "*Wampus and other spooky tales...*". (Mooresville Tribune. Retrieved January 28, 2019.

Owens, Judy "*Reporters Looking for Stories, Finding Wampus Cats* | Daily Yonder | Keep It Rural". (Daily Yonder, June 20, 2008).

Randolph, Vance. *We Always Lie to Strangers: Tall Tales from the Ozarks.* (New York: Columbia University Press, 1951.)

Whittall, Austin. Yaguarú, *Patagonian Monsters* patagoniamonsters.blogspot.com [Accessed 2 July 2019]

Falkner, Thomas. *A Description of Patagonia and the adjoining parts of South America, with a grammar and a short vocabulary, and some particulars relating to Falkland's Islands, 1774).*

Musters, George Chaworth. *At Home with the Patagonians, 1871).*

Chatwin, Bruce. *In Patagonia* (Jonathan Cape, 1977).

"*Amid sightings and claims of a cover-up, could the Lithgow panther actually exist?*". www.abc.net.au. 12 June 2018.

Bucklow, Andrew. "Grant Denyer claims to have spotted the Blue Mountains panther". NewsComAu. (News.com.au., 12 November 2018).

Loomes, Phoebe. "Aussies share more sightings of big cats in backyards". (NewsComAu. 10 December 2019).

Schmitt, Natalie. "*Hunt for the black panther*". (The Sydney Morning Herald. 27 February 2005).

Loomes, Phoebe. *Big cat sightings: Black panther caught on video in Sydney's North Shore.* (NewsComAu. News Corporation. 23 July 2020).

Loomes, Phoebe. "Influencers find evidence of big cats". news.com.au — Australia's leading news site. (News Corp, 26 April 2021).

Hambrett, Micaela. "Amid sightings and claims of a cover-up, could the Lithgow panther actually exist?". (ABC News. 12 June 2018).

"Hawkesbury Panther or big cat alpaca attack?". Hawkesbury Gazette. 9 November 2011.

Isrin, Kietley. *Hawkesbury Panther or big cat alpaca attack?* (09 Nov 2011).

Duff, Eamonn. "Hawkesbury panther spotted in River-stone". Hawkesbury Gazette, 16 December 2013).

Decatur Herald, Nellie the Lion July 14-20, 30, and August 1, 1917.

Clark Jerome; Coleman Loren, "On the Trail of Pumas, Panthers and ULAs: Part 2," (Fate 25: 92-99, July 1972).

Coleman, Loren. Mysterious America, rev. ed. Pp.105-107 (New York: Paraview, 2001).

Kirch, Robert. "Animaux inconnus en Afrique?", (Connaissance de la Chasse 60, April 1981).

Stow, George William. Rock-Paintings in South Africa (London: Methuen, 1930), pl. 39.

Leo Frobenius; Douglas C. Fox. "The Water Lions," in Africa. (New York: Stackpole, 1937)

Wilfarth, Martin. "*Leben heute noch Saurier?*" (Prisma, October 1949).

Hunter, John A. *Hunter by Hunter* (London: Hamish Hamilton, 1952)

Conan Doyle, Adrian. *Heaven Has Claws* (London: John Murray, 1952).

"Strange Animals in the Blue Mountains" (The Sydney Morning Herald, 20 October 1953).

Shuker, Karl P. N. *ShukerNature*: MARSUPIAL SABRE-TOOTHS, QUEENSLAND TIGERS, BLUE MOUNTAINS LIONS, AND A MOST ELUSIVE CRYPTO-CUTTING

Huygen, Meg Van. *14-legends-about-cats-around-world* (Mental Floss, Oct 3, 2017).

Andrews, Ted. *Black Panther* (Animal-Speak, 1914).

Kozma, Leila. *Are Snow Leopards Endangered? Poaching Has Led to The Species' Decline* (GREENMATTERS) April. 2022).

Caitlin. *Cat Sìth: including 5 Legendary Tales* (HIGHLAND TITLES, September 7, 2021).

Black, Riley. *Have the hunting habits of leopards shaped primate evolution?* (NATIONAL GEOGRAPHIC, April 6, 2010).

Smith, Malcolm. *Bunyips and Bigfoots: Up-Dated Second Edition* (Malcom Smith, Feb 4, 2021).

Shuker, Karl P. N. "Venezuelan Mystery Cats," (Fortean Times, No. 383, September 2019).

Dark Leopard: Unusual big Cat of Africa and Asia.

Holyoke, John. *Reader seeks help identifying mystery cat.* (Bangor Daily News April 9, 2021).

Povey, K.; Sunarto, H. J. G.; Priatna, D.; Ngoprasert, D.; Reed, D.; Wilting, A.; Lynam, A.; Haidai, I.; Long, B.; Johnson, A.; Cheyne, S.; Breitenmoser, C.; Holzer, K. & Byers, O. Clouded Leopard, and Small Felid Conservation Summit Final Report (2009).

McLaughlin, D. "*Russia's big cats claw back territory under Kremlin protection*". (The Irish Times, 2021).

Werdelin, L.; Yamaguchi, N.; Johnson, W. E.; O'Brien, S. J. (2010). "Phylogeny and evolu-tion of cats (Felidae"". In Macdonald, D. W.; Loveridge, A. J. (eds.). Biology and Conservation of Wild Felids. Oxford, UK: Oxford University Press, 2010).

Sjögren, Bengt.*Famous Wonders*. (Laholm: The setter, 1980).

Flannery, Michael A. "*The Medicine and Medicinal Plants of C. S. Rafinesque*". (Economic Botany. 52 (1), 1998).

Rafinesque, Constantine Samuel *Atlantic Journal and Friend of Knowledge* (1883).

Groves, Colin P.; Lay, Douglas M. *A new species of the genus Gazella* (Mammalia: Artio-dactyla: Bovidae) from the Arabian Peninsula. (Mammalia 49(1), 1985).

Mallon, D.P.; Al-Safadi, M. Yemen. In: D.P. Mallon and S.C. Kingswood (com-pilers). (Antelopes. Part 4: North Africa, the Middle East, and Asia. Global Survey and Regional Action Plans, 2001).

Research in Arabia, 1987 and 1992: visits to King Khalid and National Wildlife Research Centres (Saudi Arabia), Al Wabra Wildlife Farm (Qatar), Al-Areen Wildlife Park and Reserve (Bahrain) and Al Ain Zoo (United Arab Emirates).

Swaisgood, R.; Wang, D. & Wei, F. [errata version of 2016 assessment]. *"Ailuropoda melanoleuca"*. (IUCN Red List of Threatened Species. 2017).

David, A. "Voyage en Chine". *Bulletin des Nouvelles* (Archives du Muséum. 5, 1869).

Scheff, Duncan. *Giant Pandas. Animals of the rain forest* (illustrated ed.). (Heine-mann-Raintree Library, 2002).

Pinnock, Don. *New hope for the elusive okapi, Congo's mini giraffe new hope for the elusive okapi, Congo's mini giraffe.* (Earth Touch News, February 23, 2016).

Timmins, R.J.; Belden, G.; Brodie, J.; Ross, J.; Wilting, A.; Duckworth, J.W. "Muntiacus atherodes". (IUCN Red List of Threatened Species. 2016).

Meijaard, E. *"The Bornean Tiger; Speculation on its Existence"*. Cat News. No. 30, 1999).

Timmins, R. J.; Hedges, S. & Robichaud, W. [amended version of 2016 assessment]. *"Pseudoryx nghetinhensis"*. (IUCN Red List of Threatened Species. 2016).

Dung, V. V.; Giao, P. M.; Chinh, N. N.; Tuoc, D.; Arctander, P. & MacKinnon, J. "A new species of living bovid from Vietnam". Nature. 363, 1993).

Grubb, P. "Species *Pseudoryx nghetinhensis*". In Wilson, D.E.; Reeder, D.M (eds.). Mammal Species of the World: A Taxonomic and Geographic Reference (3rd ed.). (Johns Hopkins University Press, 2005).

Stone, R. *"The Saola's Last Stand"*. (Science. 314, 2006).

Stone, R. "Mystery in Vietnam". (Smithsonian, August 2008).

"Saola Rediscovered: Rare Photos of Elusive Species from Vietnam". World Wildlife Federation. 2013.

Van Strien, N.J.; Manullang, B.; Sectionov, Isnan W.; Khan, M.K.M.; Sumardja, E.; Ellis, S.; Han, K.H.; Boeadi, Payne J. & Bradley Martin, E. *"Dicerorhinus sumatren-sis (Sumatran Rhinoceros'"*. (IUCN Red List of Threatened Species. 2008).

Hance, Jeremy. *Vietnamese Rhino Goes Extinct* (Mongabay, 25 October 2011).

Vigne, J.-D. "Zooarchaeology and the biogeographical history of the mammals of Corsica and Sardinia since the last ice age". (Mammal Review. 22 (2), 1992).

Kitchener, A. C.; Breitenmoser-Würsten, C.; Eizirik, E.; Gentry, A.; Werdelin, L.; Wilting, A.; Yamaguchi, N.; Abramov, A. V.; Christiansen, P.; Driscoll, C.; Duckworth, J. W.; Johnson, W.; Luo, S.-J.; Meijaard, E.; O'Donoghue, P.; Sanderson, J.; Seymour, K.; Bru-ford, M.; Groves, C.; Hoffmann, M.; Nowell, K.; Timmons, Z. & Tobe, S. "A re-vised taxonomy of the Felidae: The final report of the Cat Classification Task Force of the IUCN Cat Specialist Group" (PDF). Cat News. Special Issue II, 2017).

Saplakoglu, Y. *"Meet the Cat-Fox, an Oddball Feline Roaming Around a French Island"*. (Live Science, 2019).

Willingham, A.J. *"A new species of 'cat fox' may be prowling French island of Corsica"*. CNN, 2019).

Chambers, Suzanna. *Bid to have legendary Corsican 'fox-cat' listed as a new species.* (The Connexion, Dec 5, 2021).

Kitchener, A. C.; Beaumont, M. A. & Richardson, D. *"Geographical Variation in the*

Clouded Leopard, Neofelis nebulosa, Reveals Two Species". (Current Biology. 16 (23), 2006).

Kitchener, A. C.; Breitenmoser-Würsten, C.; Eizirik, E.; Gentry, A.; Werdelin, L.; Wilting, A.; Yamagu-chi, N.; Abramov, A. V.; Christiansen, P.; Driscoll, C.; Duckworth, J. W.; Johnson, W.; Luo, S.-J.; Mei-jaard, E.; O'Donoghue, P.; Sanderson, J.; Seymour, K.; Bruford, M.; Groves, C.; Hoffmann, M.; Nowell, K.; Timmons, Z. & Tobe, S. "A revised taxonomy of the Felidae: The final report of the Cat Classification Task Force of the IUCN Cat Specialist Group" (PDF). (Cat News (Special Issue 11), 2017).

Villazon, Luis. *How many species have yet to be discovered?* (Science Focus Magazine).

Kirch, Robert. "Animaux inconnus en Afrique?", (Connaissance de la Chasse 60, April 1981).

Newton, Michael. *Hidden Animals: A Field Guide to Batsquatch, Chupacabra, and Other Elusive Creatures.* (2009).

Shuker, Karl P. N. Dr Shuker's Casebook: In Pursuit of Marvels and Mysteries. (CFZ Press, 2008).

Shuker, Karl P. N. *"The Secret Animals of Senegambia,"* (FATE, No. 51, November 1998).

Anon. *The Wanjilanko: The Mysterious Giant Lion of West Africa* (africadreaming.co.uk, January 2006).

Kane, Mouhamadou. *The Silent Destruction of Senegal's Last Forests* (enactafrica.org, 10 January 2019).

Holland, Jennifer S. *The True Origin Story of Madagascar's 'Forest Cat' Turns out this big, striped lemur-eater didn't come from mainland Africa.* (Atlas Obscura, March 23, 2020).

Holyoke, John. *"You have varied opinions on the identity of this mystery cat"* (Bangor Daily News, April 13, 2021).

Naish, Darren. *Meeting the Hayling Island Jungle cat.* (TetZoo, Mar 23, 2022).

Saunders, Kate. *The Beast of Hayling Island?* (The Spring, March 21, 2016).

Povey, Jennifer R. *A Cryptid That Turned Out to be Real — Scotland's Kellas Cats.* (jennifer-rpovey.medium, Mar 9, 2021).

Crew, Bec. *A Cat That Can Bever be Tamed.* (Scientific American, June 27, 2012).

Shuker, Karl P, N. *ShukerNature: KELLAS CATS, RABBIT-HEADED CATS, FAIRY CATS, AND DAEMON CATS – A CLOWDER OF FORMER FELINE CURIOSITIES. (July 16, 2021).*

Nikolay, Spassov. *Evidence for the Lynx recovery in Bulgaria: the Lynx discovered in Western Rhodopes.* (Research Gate, March 2015).

Redfern, Nick. *Nick Redfern's Britain's (Historical) Alien Big Cats* (Mysterious Universe, Feb 24, 2014).

Hurn, Samantha. *Anthropology and Cryptozoology: Exploring Encounters with Mysterious Creatures.* (Routledge, 3 Nov 2016).

Yamaguchi, N.; Kitchener, A.; Driscoll, C.; Nussberger, B. *"Felis silvestri".* (IUCN Red List of Threatened Species. 2015).

Yamaguchi, N.; Kitchener, A.; Driscoll, C. & Nussberger, B. "Craniological differentiation between European wildcats (*Felis silvestris silvestris*), African wildcats (*F. s. lybica*) and Asian wildcats (*F. s. ornata*): implications for their evolution and conservation" (PDF). Biological Journal of the Linnean Society. 83, 2004).

Kurtén, B. "On the evolution of the European Wild Cat, *Felis silvestris Schreber*" (PDF). (Acta Zoologica Fennica. III, 1965).

Clutton-Brock, J. "Cats". A Natural History of Domesticated Mammals (Second ed.). (Cambridge: Cambridge University Press, 1999).

Pocock, R. I. "*Felis silvestris*, Schreber". Catalogue of the Genus Felis. (London: Trustees of the British Museum, 1951).

Sunquist, M.; Sunquist, F. "European wildcat *Felis silvestris silvestris*". Wild Cats of the World. (Chicago: The University of Chicago Press, 2002).

Bourne, Hope. L. *Living on Exmoor*. (Halsgrove, 31 May 2022).

Rev. Wood, J.G. *The Illustrated Natural History*. (Arkose Press, 7 Oct. 2015. Reprint).

Wozencraft, W. C. "*Order Carnivora*". In Wilson, D. E.; Reeder, D. M. (eds.). Mammal Species of the World: A Taxonomic and Geographic Reference (3rd ed.). (Johns Hopkins University Press, 2005).

"Success of the Lynx Reintroduction Program". Colorado Division of Wildlife. September 7, 2010. Archived from the original on August 27, 2010.

Moore, Matthew "*Lynx 'should be reintroduced to Britain to cull deer'*". (London: Telegraph.co.uk. Archived from the original on February 16, 2009).

"*Status and conservation of the Eurasian Lynx (Lynx lynx) in Europe in 2001*" (PDF). Coordinated research projects for the conservation and management of carnivores in Switzerland (KORA). Retrieved January 8, 2014.

"Deletion of Bobcat (*Lynx rufus*) from Appendix II" (PDF). Thirteenth Meeting of the Conference of the Parties, Proposal 5. Convention on International Trade in Endangered Species of Wild Fauna and Flora. October 2004. (Archived from the original (PDF) on November 2, 2013).

Hamilton, William J.; Whitaker, John O. Mammals of the Eastern United States. Cornell University Press, 1998).

"Iberian lynx (*Lynx pardinus*)". *Cat Specialist Group Species Accounts*. IUCN – The World Conservation Union. 1996. (Archived from the original on July 24, 2011).

Cobbett, William. Rural Rides, the political register (1830, English publication).

Whittard, Timothy. *Paws for Thought*. (Petlife 2021).

Whittard, Timothy. Star Of 'Tiger King' Says New Discovery Is "Definitely" Evidence of Big Cats in England. (https://www.higgypop.com, April 2022).

Coe, Jon B.; Young, Simon. *The Celtic Sources for the Arthurian Legend*. [Felinfach]: Llanerch, 1995).

Koch, John T. "*Ambrosius Aurelianus*". In Koch, John T. (ed.). (Celtic Culture: A Historical Encyclopedia. Volume 1. Santa Barbara, 2006).

Bromwich, Rachel. Trioedd Ynys Prydein: The Triads of the Island of Britain. (University Of Wales Press, 2006).

MacGillivray, Deborah. "The Cait Sidhe". (Archived from the original on 21 August 2012).

Robin Mudge. "Meet the "King of Cats" From Celtic Folklore". (Catster, 28 January 2015).

Rowan Moffet "The Cat Sìth in Celtic Mythology". (Scotclans, 15 August 2018).

Nicholls, Edward. *Most Haunted New Forest Pubs,* (The Spooky Isles, 17 February 2021).

Waller, Jon. "*Legendary New Forest Stratford Lyon myth evoked after claims of recent 'beast' sighting at the Red Lion pub in Boldre, New Milton Advertiser and Lymington"* (Times, 3 September 2021).

Callander & Dixon. 1864 The Story of the Wild Dog of Ennerdale: Reprinted from the Whitehaven Herald. Whitehaven, England. (Callander & Dixon. 1864).

Callander & Dixon. The Story of the Wild Dog of Ennerdale: Reprinted from the Whitehaven Herald. Whitehaven, England. (Callander & Dixon. 1864).

Watson, Jeremy "The Beast of Buchan", (Scotland on Sunday, 24 December 2006).

Buchan, Jamie *"Fears beast of Buchan is back on the prowl"* (*Press & Journal*, 27 October 2006).

"Traditions, folklore and traditions". *Exmoor National Park.* (Archived from the original on 8 March 2008).

"Exmoor National Park". *BBC Science and Nature: Animals.* (Retrieved January 15, 2008).

"The mystery of Britain's alien big cats", (The Week, January 8, 2015).

"The Beast of Bodmin Moor – The Natural History Museum, London". Nhm.ac.uk. (Archived from the original on 9 June 2007).

"Beast of Dartmoor mystery solved after famous circus owner Mary Chipperfield 'set three Pumas free in 1970s'", (The Daily Telegraph, 21 July 2016).

Boggan, Steve *"Boffins Hunt the Beast Of Bodmin".* The Independent, 13 January 1995).

Ryder, Alistair. *All of the Fen Tiger sightings in and around Cambridgeshire over the past decade* (Cambridgeshire Live, January 1, 2020).

Walker, David. *"Are there any big cats in Scotland and where do they live"*? (Scottish Daily Express, October 18, 2021).

Coussins, Jordan. *Every big cat sighting in Derbyshire reported to police since 2007.* (Derbyshire Live, July 8, 2018).

Roper, Matt. *Is this big cat the Beast of Burnham Thorpe?* (Mirror, Sep 1, 2011).

Elliott, Emily-Ann. *Big cat dubbed Beast of Bevendean.* (The Argus, June 9, 2008).

Vowles, Neil. *Beast of Bevendean is breeding claims Brighton woman.* (The Argus, 16th December 2009).

Sandals, Tim. *The Beasts of Dartmoor.* (Legendary Dartmoor, July 22, 2016).

Salkeld, Luke. *That's not the Beast of Dartmoor... it's my pet dog.* (Daily Mail, August 3, 2007).

Criddle, Cristina; Mendick, Robert. *"Beast of Dartmoor mystery solved...".* (The Telegraph, July 21, 2016).

Mclelland, Euan. *Panther Watch: Seventh sighting as big cat spotted in Shotts.* (April 13, 2011).

Lockett, Jon. *BIG CAT MYSTERY Puma 'spotted hiding in a field near Hull' by man who claims big cats are rife in the UK* (The Sun, September 18, 2016).

George, Thomas. *Second 'big cat' sighting sends horses into a frenzy in Bury* (Bury Times, October 29, 2018).

Muncaster, Mike. *"Big cat' spotted prowling in Wakefield.* (Wakefield Express, March 4, 2015).

Whitehouse, Helen. *FOUR-FOOT MONSTER: Have this couple spotted the 'Pershore Panther'?* (The Daily Star, April 2, 2016).

Christodoulou, Holly. *WILDCAT SPOTTED? New dad stunned after capturing what he believes is the notorious Wildcat of Warwickshire on camera.* (The Sun, Jun 26, 2017).

Woodings, Simon. *VIDEO: Big cat spotted in Great Alne again.* (Stratford Herald, November 10, 2016).

Birchall, Guy. *BEAST OF SILSOE Villagers' fear after 'cat as big as Labrador' seen roaming Bedfordshire parish.* (The Sun, Aug 24, 2016).

Hale, Jennifer. *WAS DOG ATTACKED BY 'BEAST OF BUCKS'? Dog suffered horror wounds after being savaged by a PUMA on country walk, owner claims.* (The Sun, Oct 13, 2016).

Wareham, Stephanie. *Beast of Bucks is back after terrified driver reports spotting mystery feline.* (Bucks Free Press, December 6, 2018).

Sandals, Tim. *Flaviu the Lynx.* (Legendary Dartmoor, July 13, 2016).

Yedroudj, Latifa. *Big cat WARNING: Alert after ANOTHER 'panther-like' creature spotted in Cornwall.* (Express, April 8, 2019).

Briggs, Stacia. *'Beast of Bruisyard' spotted minutes from Ed Sheeran's estate.* (Eastern Daily Express, May 6, 2022).

Lu, Donna. *Tall Tails: why does the myth of exotic big cats prowling the Australian bush persist?* (The Guardian, Dec 28, 2021).

Guerrero, D.L. *"North American Jaguar (Panthera onca) Collared in Arizona".* (Arkanimals.com, February 24, 2009).

Nowell, K.; Jackson, P., eds. *"Panthera Onca" (PDF). Wild Cats. Status Survey and Conservation Action Plan.* (Gland, Switzerland: Cat Specialist Group, 1996).

Larson, S. E. *"Taxonomic re-evaluation of the jaguar".* (Zoo Biology. 16 (2), 1997).

Bonney, Neville. The Tantanoola Tiger, (Lynton Publications, Jan 1, 1976).

Bonney Neville. *Tantanoola 1879-1979.* (The South Eastern Times, 1979).

Gallagher, Patrick J. The Tantanoola Tiger: And Other Australian Big Cat Sightings. (CreateSpace Independent Publishing Platform, (Jan 12, 2016).

Topsfield, Jewel. *The hunt for big cats in Australia.* (The Sydney Morning Herald, July 5, 2020).

Prema, Shive. *Is this the 'Otways Panther'? Giant feral cat is photographed roaming Australian mountain range famous for mysterious sightings – and locals say they've NEVER seen anything like it.* (Daily Mail Australia, 8 June 2020).

Schmitt, Natalie. *Hunt for the black panther.* (The Sydney Morning Herald, February 27, 2005).

Williams, Mike. *Hawkesbury Panther or big cat alpaca attack.* (Yowiehunters Forum, November 09, 2011).

Author Unknown. *Canterbury Panther: The search for the mysterious big cat.* (Otago Daily Times, August 22, 2022).

Author Unknown. *'Panthers' spotted taking advantage of NZ travel bubble.* (Stuff 9News Staff. Oct 27, 2020).

Lucas, Ian. *DO PUMAS AND BLACK PANTHERS REALLY ROAM OUR COUNTRYSIDE?* (NZ Cryptozoologist, 2007).

Kenny, Lee. *New South Island big cat sightings, the latest in a 50-year mystery.* (STUFF, September 13, 2020).

Rostro-Garcia, Susana; Kamler, Jan; Reuben Clements, Gopalasamy Reuben; Lynam,

Antony J. *Panthera pardus ssp. Delacouri* (Indochinese Leopard). THE IUCN RED LIST OF THREATENED SPECIES, December 2019).

Hutchins, Cpt. Robert. *"Delaware Cougar Confirmations"*. (cougar-net.org, February 26, 2011).

Kubota, Gary. *"Expert thinks big cat is dangerous"*. (Honolulu Star-Bulletin, October 2003).

Hurley, Timothy. *"State suspends hunt for Maui cat"*. (The Honolulu Advertiser, November 22, 2003).

Schmidt, Robert. "Forget catching ghost cat". (The Honolulu Advertiser, August 2003).

Hurley, Timothy. *"For Maui, it was year of the cat"*. (The Honolulu Advertiser, November 30, 2003).

Bellow, Heather. *"Are the mountain lion sightings in Monterey for real?"*. (New England Newspapers Inc, December 2018).

Graham, George. *"Facebook photo reignites debate about mountain lions in Massachusetts"*. (MassLiv, August 8, 2017).

Aydelette, Jeff. *"Most say panthers exist"*. The County Compass, November 17, 2011).

Dance, Peter. Animal fakes & frauds. (England: Sampson Low, 1975).

Collier, LL; Leathers, CW; Counts, DF. *"A clinical description of dermatosparax-is in a Himalayan cat"*. (Feline Practice, 1980).

Lynda, Cornelison. "Feline cutaneous asthenia (Ehlers-Danlos syn-drome). Seminar SF610.1 2003 C67". (Cornell University, October 9, 2002).

Counts, DF; Byers, PH; Holbrook, KA; Hegreberg, GA. "Dermatosparaxis in a Himalayan cat: I. Biochemical studies of dermal collagen". The Journal of Investigative Dermatology. 74 (2), February 1980).

Freeman, LJ; Hegreberg, GA; Robinette, JD; Kimbrell, JT. *"Biomechanical properties of skin and wounds in Ehlers-Danlos syndrome"*. (Veterinary Surgery. 18 (2), March 1989).

Freeman, LJ; Hegreberg, GA; Robinette, JD. *"Cutaneous wound healing in Ehlers-Danlos syndrome"*. (Veterinary Surgery. 18 (2), March 1989).

Shuker, Karl P. N. *"Blue Tigers, Black Tigers, and Other Asian Mystery Cats,"* (Cat World, No. 214, December 1995).

Tryon, Henry Harrington. *Fearsome Critters*. (Cornwall, NY: Idlewild Press, 1939).

Cohen, Daniel. *Monsters, Giants, and Little Men from Mars: An Unnatural History of the Americas*. (New York: Doubleday, 1975).

Briggs, Katharine. *Encyclopedia of Fairies*. (Pantheon Books, 1976).

Turner, Patricia; Coulter, Charles Russell. *Dictionary of Ancient Deities*. (Oxford University Press, 2001).

Spence, Lewis. *The Minor Traditions of British Mythology*. (Ayer, 1972).

Hutton, Ronald. *The Triumph of the Moon: A History of Modern Pagan Witchcraft*. (Oxford University Press, 2001).

Conway, Thor. *Spirits in Stone*. (Heritage Discoveries, 2010).

Kohl, Johann. *Kitchi-Gami: Life Among the Lake Superior Ojibway*. (Minnesota Historical Society Press; 1st edition 1859).

Barnes, Michael. *"Aboriginal Artifacts"*. Final Report — 1997 Archaeological Excavations La Vase Heritage Project. City of North Bay, Ontario.

Bolgiano, Chris. *"Native Americans and American Lions"*. Mountain Lion: An Unnatural History of Pumas and People. (Stackpole Books, August 1995).

Gidmark, Jill B. *"Mishi-Peshu"*. *Encyclopedia of American literature of the sea and Great Lakes*. (Greenwood Press, November 30, 2000).

Lemaître, Serge. *"Mishipeshu"*. (The Canadian Encyclopedia, April 12, 2007).

Penney, David W. *North American Indian Art*. (London: Thames and Hudson, 2004).

Strom, Karen M. *"Morrisseau's Missipeshu – Cultural Preservation"*. (Native American Indian Resources, August 3, 1996).

Godfrey, Linda S. Weird Michigan: your travel guide to Michigan's local legends and best kept secrets. (New York: Sterling Publishing Co, 2006).

Thwaites, Reuben Gold. *Jesuit Relations*, (Volume LIV. Chapter XI. Section 26, 1889).

Fox, William A. *"Dragon Sideplates from York Factory, A New Twist on an Old Tail"*. (Manitoba Archaeological Journal. 2 (2), 1992).

Butler, Rhett A. *New fox species discovered in jungle of Borneo*. (MONGABAY, May 10, 2005).

Naish, Darren. *The mystery mammal of Kayan Mentarang*. (Scientific American, February 25, 2013).

Wendt, Herbert. *Out of Noah's Ark*. (Weidenfeld & Nicolson, 1956).

Donkin, R. A. *The Peccary: With Observations on the Introduction of Pigs to the New World*. (American Philosophical Society, 1985).

Shuker, Karl P. N. *ShukerNature: TRAILING THE MITLA – A DOG-LIKE CAT, OR A CAT-LIKE DOG?* (karlshuker.blogspot.com, February 2013).

Mallinson, Jeremy. *Travels in Search of Endangered Species*. (David & Charles, 1989).

Karl P. N. Shuker. SHUKERNATURE: *SAT-KALAUK – A BURMESE BLOODSUCKER* (May 20, 2012).

Springer, Brandon. *"Animal Hybrids: Ligers and Tigons and Pizzly Bears, Oh My!"* (Smithsonian Magazine, July 7, 2010).

Marchetti, Donna. *"Borneo's Wild Side"*. (The New York Times, August 2, 1998).

Phillipps, Quentin; Phillipps, Karen. *Phillipps' Field Guide to the Mammals of Borneo and Their Ecology: Sabah, Sarawak, Brunei, and Kalimantan*. (Princeton University Press, May 10, 2016).

McCollough, Mark. *"Eastern puma (cougar) (Puma concolour cougar) 5-year review: Summary and Evaluation"* (PDF). (Maine Field Office Orono, Maine: U.S. Fish and Wildlife Service, March 2011).

Culver, M.; Johnson, W.E.; Pecon-Slattery, J.; O'Brien, S.J. "Genomic ancestry of the American puma (Puma concolour)". (Journal of Heredity. 91 (3), 2000).

Boswell, Randy. "Montreal Gazette: U.S. officials declare eastern cougar extinct, despite sightings in Canada". Montreal Gazette, Postmedia News, March 2, 2011).

Forés, Angel Morant "An Investigation into Some Unidentified Ecuadorian Mammals" cryptozoo.pagesperso-orange.fr (Virtual Institute of Cryptozoology, October 12, 1999).

Peru Expedition Report: September–October 2017 (2017) – Online

RESOURCES

Big Cat Conversations Podcast: https://bigcatconversations.com/

Centre for Fortean Zoology: https://cfz.org.uk/

ShukerNature: https://karlshuker.blogspot.com/

BTS filming Felicity the puma for Panthera Britannia Declassified 1/2:
https://www.youtube.com/watch?v=wCuA-_kTQE8

BTS filming Felicity the puma for Panthera Britannia Declassified 2/2:
https://www.youtube.com/watch?v=er8L-vYFzSc

Cat Hunters. The Search for the Beast of Exmoor: https://www.
youtube.com/watch?v=skYzBxLNUP8

Carl Marshall talks about the suspected lynx tracks he and his apprentice found in the Forest of Dean: https://www.youtube.com/watch?v=EcHbngynHBs

Panthera Britannia Declassified: https://www.amazon.com/Panthera-Britannia-Cliff-Barackman/dp/B0B8TZ9XQ7/

Trail cam video of tiger filmed in Pariangan region of Sumatra: https://youtu.be/dMcjH6Oqb14?si=BrE2fXGp-U2EgJ76

AFTERWORD

Go to hangaripublishing.com to learn more about the Authors and stay up to date with their newest releases.

www.ingramcontent.com/pod-product-compliance
Lightning Source LLC
Chambersburg PA
CBHW061131120626
46546CB00005B/1740